The Complete Book of
Pickling

250 recipes from pickles & relishes to chutneys & salsas

D1092737

Jennifer MacKenzie

Robert
ROSE

For complete cataloguing information, see page 326.

Disclaimer
The recipes in this book have been carefully tested by our kitchen and our tasters. To the best of our knowledge, they are safe and nutritious for ordinary use and users. For those people with food or other allergies, or who have special food requirements or health issues, please read the suggested contents of each recipe carefully and determine whether or not they may create a problem for you. All recipes are used at the risk of the consumer.

We cannot be responsible for any hazards, loss or damage that may occur as a result of any recipe use.

For those with special needs, allergies, requirements or health problems, in the event of any doubt, please contact your medical adviser prior to the use of any recipe.

Design and Production: Kevin Cockburn/PageWave Graphics Inc.
Editor: Sue Sumeraj
Proofreader: Sheila Wawanash
Indexer: Gillian Watts
Photography: Colin Erricson
Food Styling: Kathryn Robertson
Prop Styling: Charlene Erricson

Cover image: Kosher-Style Dill Pickles (page 32)

We acknowledge the financial support of the Government of Canada through the Book Publishing Industry Development Program (BPIDP) for our publishing activities.

Published by Robert Rose Inc.
120 Eglinton Avenue East, Suite 800, Toronto, Ontario, Canada M4P 1E2
Tel: (416) 322-6552 Fax: (416) 322-6936
www.robertrose.ca

Printed and bound in Canada

4 5 6 7 8 9 MP 17 16 15 14 13

Contents

· · ·

Introduction

In the days before enormous supermarkets, where you can now get almost any ingredient any day of the year, preserving the harvest (during the harvest) was the only way to assure you would have fruits and vegetables to nourish your family through those long months between crops. Agricultural technology, transportation and refrigeration have changed our lifestyles dramatically. The need to preserve our own food has been eliminated, yet there is still great satisfaction in taking freshly harvested produce and turning it into delicious pickles, chutneys, salsas, relishes, salsas . . . the list goes on.

I was lucky to grow up with a mom who taught me the joys of canning preserves. Each summer we would trek to farm stands to load up on cucumbers and take over the kitchen with the production of Aunt Thelma's Bread-and-Butter Pickles — a must to accompany grilled cheese sandwiches — carefully slicing, salting and pickling those fresh cucumbers. Later in the summer there were baskets of peppers and tomatoes to create The Family Chili Sauce in preparation for the Christmas Eve tourtière (in our family, you can't have one without the other!). Some years there were pickled beets; one year we got a gorgeous bushel of the most flavorful peaches from a farm on a trip to Niagara, and we made pickled peaches to share with everyone! Once salsa came into fashion, we embarked on many creations to use up those bushels of tomatoes, chile peppers and other zesty ingredients. And to this day, I can't eat a store-bought chutney or tomato sauce without wishing it was one I'd made myself.

I like to buy as much local food as possible, but where I live, in south-central Ontario, that means a bounty between June and October and slim pickings for fresh produce the rest of the year. By buying the produce in season and turning it into savory preserves, not only do I support local agriculture, but I have an array of delicious foods to use all year long and to give to family and friends. Preserving is certainly a wonderful way to support local farmers or use up the produce you've grown in your own garden and, in turn, reduce your carbon footprint by reducing "food miles." And if you've made it yourself, you know exactly what you're eating. As well, in-season food is considerably more economical than foods imported throughout the year, and homemade preserves are much less expensive than commercially prepared ones.

That said, I do take advantage of exotic foods to incorporate international flavors into my repertoire. They may not be local, but you can take advantage of seasonality in other countries when mangos are bountiful and on sale by the case, or fragrant pineapples call to you at the grocery store, or you want to create more exotic savory preserves.

Yes, it can seem like a lot of work, and sometimes, about two-thirds of the way through a bushel of tomatoes, I wonder what I've gotten myself into, but there is nothing more satisfying than popping open a lovely jar of homemade pickles or chutney or chili sauce, knowing that each ingredient was prepared by hand and the freshness of the harvest is captured beneath that lid — it's absolutely worth it.

I hope these recipes will inspire you to embrace the joys of home canning, and I'm sure your friends and family will happily embrace the fruits (and vegetables) of your labors.

Happy canning!

How Does Home Canning Work?

For the purposes of this book, only boiling-water canning, not pressure canning, will be explained and used. Pressure canning is a completely different process, using different equipment.

To understand the process of home canning, it's helpful to understand the need for the process. Food naturally decays when exposed to oxygen. I'm sure you've seen this with a banana left in the fruit basket too long. This decay is caused by the activity of plant enzymes and microorganisms. Bacteria, yeast and mold are microorganisms that feed on foods in the presence of oxygen and, in particular, in the absence of acid (a banana is low in acid and will rot a lot faster than a very acidic lemon when exposed to the same conditions). To preserve a food, we need to make the food and its storage conditions inhospitable to these microorganisms and destroy the enzymes that encourage decay.

Home preserving using the boiling-water canning method is designed exclusively for high-acid foods. This means the pH is 4.6 or lower. A pH of 7 is neutral — neither acidic nor alkaline — pure water, for example. Pickles, chutneys, salsas, relishes, sauces and other condiments can be made from lower-acid foods (cucumbers have a pH of around 5, for example) by adding enough acidic ingredients to lower the pH to 4.6 or below. Any foods that are less acidic are not safe for preserving by the boiling-water canning method and must be canned in a pressure canner. All of the recipes in this book have been formulated and tested to ensure they have a pH of 4.6 or lower.

The first important element of home canning recipes is to make sure foods are acidic enough to resist the growth of microorganisms. This is achieved by adding specific amounts of vinegar and/or citrus juices to recipes. Heating the food adequately and removing oxygen from the jars is the next step. The food to be preserved is heated, or the liquid or brine to be added is heated, and the food is placed in hot canning jars. Filled jars are processed in the boiling-water canner to heat the food to a high enough temperature for a long enough time that enzymes are deactivated and microorganisms are destroyed, contributing to the preservation of the food. This process also removes the oxygen from the jars and, in combination with the specially designed lids, hermetically seals them (gives them an airtight seal). The seal prevents air and microorganisms from entering jars. We now have food that will resist spoilage; therefore, it is preserved.

One bacterium, *Clostridium botulinum*, is of particular concern in home canning. The spores of the bacteria can come from the soil and dust that clings to raw foods, and often can't just be rinsed off. These spores produce a toxin that can cause botulism, a potentially fatal form of food poisoning. The tricky thing is that these spores grow without oxygen (they are anaerobic). Therefore, when we remove the oxygen from jars of preserves, we are actually creating an environment that is beneficial to them. They are, however, destroyed by acid and heat. So, to ensure that your preserves are safe, it is very important to follow the recipe carefully, add the exact amount of ingredients that is called for and process the jars in the boiling-water canner for the right amount of time.

Preserving Techniques: Step-by-Step Home Canning

Preserving is not difficult and is certainly much more efficient if you follow these simple steps to have the ingredients and equipment prepared and ready when you need them.

1. *Read the recipe:* Before you even head out to buy the ingredients, read the recipe all the way through. Be sure you have all of the necessary equipment and ingredients and the amount of time necessary to complete the recipe without delays. And just before you start cooking, read the recipe through again. If the preparation takes more than one day, it is noted at the top of the page. *Key point: Plan your canning.*

2. *Prepare the canner:* Fill the canner with water, making sure the water level will cover jars by at least 1 inch (2.5 cm) once they are submerged. It is better to add more water if you're not sure, since it is easier to remove some if the pot is too full. If the water doesn't cover the jars and you have to add more, it will slow down the processing. Cover the pot and bring the water almost to a boil over medium-high heat; this will take 30 to 60 minutes, depending on your stove and pot. Once the water is almost to a boil, reduce the heat to keep it at a low simmer until you're ready to fill the pot. Keep the lid on to reduce the amount of water that evaporates.

   If you have hard water or use a water softener, minerals from the water in the canner can get deposited onto jars when processing. To prevent this, crumple up a piece of foil and add it to the canner water. The minerals will stick to the foil instead.

   Key point: Make sure the canner is ready so the filled jars don't cool down.

3. *Prepare the jars:* Wash jars thoroughly in hot, soapy water and rinse well, or run through a sanitizing cycle in a dishwasher (start this before preparing the canner if you plan to use the dishwasher). Do not towel dry. Prepare an extra jar or two (even one in a smaller size is helpful), just in case you have more product than the recipe specifies. Jars that are to be used for foods that will be processed for 10 minutes or longer do not need to be sterilized before filling. Inspect all jars to make sure they are free from cracks, chips or other damage. Do not use any that are even slightly damaged, as they can break during filling or processing.

   The jars need to be hot when you fill them. To heat jars, run them under hot tap water so they warm up slightly. Then place them in a pot of hot water, filling the jars with the water. Place the pot over low heat; do not let boil, but keep it steaming. If you have a canner with a rack that can be rested by the handles on the sides of the pot, you can put jars filled with hot water on the rack and keep the water at a low simmer to keep the jars hot. Again, do not let the water boil. If they are in the dishwasher, time it so the hot jars are ready when the preserves are. Never heat jars in the oven. Dry heat can damage the glass. *Key point: Make sure jars are free from damage and are clean and hot.*

4. *Prepare the lids:* Wash and rinse the number of discs and screw bands you'll

need (I always prepare one or two extra, just in case). Fill a small saucepan with about 2 inches (5 cm) of water. Add the metal disc portion of the lid and bring to a simmer over medium heat. Do not let boil. Once the water comes to a simmer, remove the pot from the heat, cover and keep the discs hot. If the water cools, the sealing compound will harden and will not create a proper seal on the jars. Do not prepare the lids any earlier than about 20 minutes before you plan to fill the jars. *Key point: Have the lids ready just before you're ready to fill the jars.*

5. *Prepare the ingredients:* Follow the recipe exactly and measure each ingredient carefully. For details, see Ingredients and Preparation, page 14, and Measuring Primer, page 19. *Key point: Follow the recipe. Don't make substitutions unless specified in the recipe.*

6. *Cook/heat the ingredients and/or pickling liquid:* Once you start cooking or heating the food, it is important to proceed with the entire recipe. Do not let food cool or sit before filling and processing jars. If the cooking time is 30 minutes or more, the jars and lids can be prepared while the food is cooking. If the cooking time is longer than 1 hour, the canner can be prepared while the food is cooking. *Key point: Follow the method in the recipe.*

7. *Fill the jars:* Working quickly, using a jar lifter and/or your hands while wearing silicone oven mitts (it's handy to have the jar lifter in one hand and a silicone oven mitt on the other to brace the jar while moving it), remove jars, one at a time if so directed in the recipe, from the hot water, canner or dishwasher and drain well. Do not towel dry.

If preserving raw-pack pickles, pack the produce into the hot jars as specified. Place the funnel in the mouth of the jar and fill the jar with the pickling liquid or other preserve, leaving the amount of headspace specified in the recipe. The headspace is the space above the food and below the lid in the jar. It has to be carefully measured to allow room for expansion of the food during heat processing and to ensure the proper vacuum seal upon cooling. Lift the funnel above the rim of the jar when filling the top portion of the jar to be sure the food doesn't spill over the edge and to get a good view of the level of the food.

Carefully insert a narrow, non-metallic spatula between the food and the side of the jar, all the way to the bottom of the jar, pressing gently into the center of the jar to remove any air bubbles trapped in the food. Repeat this three or four times around the jar. This is particularly important for raw-pack foods, which tend to have lots of air trapped between the pieces. Measure the headspace with a ruler or the notches on a bubble remover (see page 13) and add more hot pickling liquid or preserves, if needed, to adjust the headspace. If necessary, use a small spoon to remove any excess liquid. Never touch the inside of the jar with a metal utensil, as this can damage the jar. *Key point: Fill jars quickly so the food and jars don't cool down.*

8. *Apply the lids:* Using a paper towel dipped in clean hot water, wipe the rim and threads of the jar, switching to a clean section of the paper towel as it gets food on it to be sure no food will interfere with the lid's seal. Using a magnetic lid lifter or silicone-coated tongs, remove a disc from the hot water and place it on top of the jar, then place the screw band over it. Screw

the band onto the jar firmly, but only until fingertip-tight. If the band is too tight, air can't escape from the jar and the lid may fail to seal. Using the jar lifter or lifting carefully with your hand around the neck of the filled jar (not around the screw band), place the jar, without tilting at all, on the rack in the canner. Repeat with the remaining jars. *Key point: Clean the rims of the jars well to ensure a proper seal.*

9. *Process in the boiling-water canner:* Once all jars are filled and in the canner, use the handles to carefully lower the rack to the bottom of the canner, if necessary. The jars should not touch each other or the sides of the canner. The water should cover the jars by at least 1 inch (2.5 cm). If there is not enough water, add more boiling water, pouring it between the jars, not on top of them. If the water is too deep and there isn't at least 2 inches (5 cm) between the water level and the top of the canner, use a saucepan with a handle to scoop out some of the water, being careful not to touch the jars and making sure the jars are still sufficiently covered.

   Place the lid on the canner and increase the heat to high. Bring the water to a full rolling boil. Start the timer once the water is boiling. Let the water boil, turning the heat down slightly if it starts to boil over, but making sure it maintains a full boil for the time specified in the recipe. Adjust the time as necessary for altitudes above 1,000 feet (305 m); see page 321. When the processing time is complete, turn off the heat, remove the lid from the canner and let the jars stand in the canner for 5 minutes. This time allows the pressure in the jars to stabilize and reduces the chance of liquid leaking from jars. *Key point: Be sure the water is at a full rolling boil for the time specified in the recipe.*

10. *Let the jars cool:* Lift the canner rack to the edge of the canner, if possible. Using the jar lifter or your hand in a silicone oven mitt, grasp the neck of each jar (not the screw band) and transfer the jars, without tilting, to a towel-lined heat-resistant surface. A wooden cutting board or a stable wire cooling rack work well. Let jars cool at room temperature, without moving them, for 24 hours. Do not dry or touch the lids or jars, and do not retighten screw bands. Any movement of the jars and lids can interfere with a proper seal. While the jars and lids cool, the sealing compound in the discs cools and hardens, forming a tight seal around the rim of the jar. You will hear a "pop" or a "snap" sound as a lid forms the seal (this is a good sound!).

    After 24 hours, remove the screw bands and check to make sure all the lids have sealed. Properly sealed lids will be slightly concave. To test that they are sealed, press the middle of the lid with your finger. You shouldn't feel any movement in the lid. A lid without a proper seal will flex down when pressed and then back up as you release your finger.

    Any unsealed jars should be refrigerated immediately and used within a few days. You can reprocess unsealed jars within 24 hours. You must check the jar for any imperfections and change jars if necessary, use a new disc and reheat the food. This can often degrade the quality of the food, so if only one jar is unsealed, it is best to eat the food instead. *Key point: Check that cooled jars have tightly sealed lids.*

11. *Store the jars:* Rinse and wipe jars and lids and let air dry. Do not replace the screw bands, as jars are best stored without them. Label jars with the contents and the date you made them. Store jars in a cool, dry, dark place for up to 1 year

(unless otherwise specified in the recipe). Be sure the jars are not near hot water pipes, in a place where the temperature may drop below freezing, in an area that fluctuates in temperature often, in direct sunlight or in a very humid area. *Key point: Temperature and humidity can affect the quality of stored preserves.*

12. *To use preserves:* Rinse and wipe jars and lids after storing. As long as proper processing methods were followed and the food was stored properly, the risk of spoilage is low. However, it's best to inspect jars for any signs of spoilage before opening. The lid should still be sealed — if it's not, throw out the contents of the jar. Look for signs of a bulging lid, bubbles rising in the food or an unnatural color. Discard any food that you suspect may be spoiled.

To open the lid, place the dull side of a knife horizontally between the narrowest thread on the jar and the metal disc and angle the knife, exerting gentle pressure against the lid to pop it off. You should hear a distinct sound indicating the release of the vacuum. You can also use the rounded end of a church key–style bottle opener to lift the lid. Check the inside of the lid, the inside of the jar and the top of the food for any signs of mold, and smell to make sure there are no off-aromas. After opening, replace the metal lid with a plastic storage lid (cap), if desired, and refrigerate preserves. All preserves are best if used within 1 month of opening. *Key point: Enjoy your efforts!*

Extra Safety Tips

- Use current, tested recipes that include instructions for processing in a boiling-water canner. Older recipes are not necessarily food-safe and can include ingredients that are no longer considered safe for consumption.
- Never use any animal products or oils in preserves that are processed in a boiling-water canner. The food will not be safe for room temperature storage.
- Use only high-quality produce. Any produce that is starting to mold, rot or otherwise deteriorate can ruin your preserved product.
- Be sure all utensils are clean and dry before using them to prepare ingredients for preserves. This includes your hands!
- Only use jars and lids specifically designed for canning. Do not reuse jars from commercially prepared products unless they are mason jars that fit two-piece metal lids.
- If in doubt, throw it out! If you're unsure whether a preserved product has been sealed and stored properly, or you don't know how long it's been stored, it's best not to take a risk by eating it.

Equipment

Essential

Large pot for boiling-water canner: A specifically designed canning pot (usually made of porcelain-covered steel) or any large, heavy pot with a minimum capacity of 21 quarts (20 L) with a snug-fitting lid is suitable for processing filled jars. The pot must be deep enough to allow for at least 1 inch (2.5 cm) of briskly boiling water above the lids of the immersed jars. If you use an electric stovetop, when the canner is centered on the burner the bottom of the canner should not extend more than 2 inches (5 cm) beyond the diameter of the burner to ensure even heat distribution. If you use a glass or ceramic cook top, a flat-bottomed pot is best.

Rack for canner: This can be a commercially made rack that often comes with a canner, or you can use a wire cake rack that fits into your canner. The commercially made racks are handy, as they are usually designed so the handles can be perched on the sides of the canner, ready for the jars to be loaded and lowered in. Alternatively, you can make a rack: using strong twine, tie six screw bands (from two-piece canning lids) together into a ring, then tie one in the center. To prevent rusting, be sure to remove the rack from the canner after removing the jars and let it dry thoroughly.

Canning jars: Mason jars are glass jars specifically designed for home canning and are the only jars considered safe to use. They have a threaded neck that fits the two-piece canning lids. They come with openings in standard ($2\frac{3}{8}$ inches/70 mm) and wide-mouth sizes (3 inches/86 mm) and volumes of 4-ounce, 8-ounce, 12-ounce, pint, $1\frac{1}{2}$-pint, quart and half-gallon sizes in the United States and 125 mL, 250 mL, 500 mL, 700 mL, 1 L and 1.5 L sizes in Canada.

Two-piece canning lids: These are composed of a disc and a screw band. The tin-plated steel disc has a ring of food-safe sealing compound on the underside that softens, allowing the air to escape the jar during processing, and then hardens around the rim of the jar upon cooling to create a tight seal. The disc is designed for one-time use only and should be discarded after use. The screw band is a threaded metal ring that holds the disc in place during processing. Screw bands can be washed and reused; however, they should be discarded if they start to rust.

Plastic storage lids (caps): Once a jar of preserves is opened, it is best to replace the metal two-piece lid with a plastic lid (cap) designed for storage. Acidic ingredients can corrode metal lids during storage, causing premature spoilage of food.

Kitchen scales: Weighing produce before preparation is the most accurate way to know you've got the right amount for certain ingredients. A scale that can weigh at least 5 lbs (2.5 kg) with a large platform that can fit a bowl to hold produce is the most useful.

Large stainless steel pot: A pot made of heavy-gauge stainless steel is best for cooking preserves, particularly chutneys, salsas, sauces and relishes. A thin-bottomed pot tends to have hot spots and may scorch foods. For the recipes in this book, a pot that is about $9\frac{1}{2}$ inches (24 cm) in diameter on the inside, is 6 to 7 inches (15 to 17.5 cm) deep and holds about 8 quarts (7.8 L) is ideal.

A narrower pot can increase the cooking time and make a thinner cooked product, since surface evaporation is decreased. A wider pot can decrease the cooking time and make a thicker cooked product, because surface evaporation is increased. Both of these differences can alter the final acidity level of the cooked preserves.

Small saucepan: To heat the disc portions of two-piece lids, use any small saucepan.

Bowls: You'll need sturdy bowls made of a non-reactive material such as stainless steel, glass or ceramic. If you plan to make pickles or relishes, a very large bowl or container is essential for soaking produce in salt and/or brine. For fermented pickles, such as sauerkraut, you'll need a container large enough not only for the produce, but also for the liquid and bubbling action. A deep, straight-sided bowl or pot that is 9 to 11 inches (23 to 27.5 cm) across and 6 to 7 inches (15 to 17.5 cm) deep will fit the largest recipes in this book. Having several small bowls handy will be helpful when you're weighing and preparing ingredients for all preserves.

Measuring cups and spoons: For liquids, use glass measuring cups in 1-, 2- and 4-cup (250, 500 and 1 L) sizes. The large 8-cup (2 L) measuring bowls are useful as bowls, but tend not to be as accurate for measuring. For dry ingredients, use metal or plastic nesting measuring cups. For quantities under ¼ cup (50 mL), use measuring spoons.

High-heat-resistant plastic composite spoons (such as Exoglass): These spoons look like wooden spoons but are made from a composite plastic material that withstands high temperatures. They are far superior to wooden spoons because they don't absorb flavors from the food, are dishwasher safe and don't harbor bacteria. They are more

expensive than wooden spoons and other plastics, but they are long-lasting and very durable.

Stainless steel slotted spoon: A slotted spoon is an efficient tool for transferring pickled products into jars so you can get the right proportion of pickles and liquid in each jar. Stainless steel is best because it is easiest to keep clean and will not absorb off flavors from the food.

Cheesecloth: Made of 100% cotton, this finely woven cloth has a number of uses in home canning. It can be found at hardware stores, grocery stores and other stores that carry home canning supplies.

Wide-mouth funnel: A plastic or metal funnel specifically designed to fit the mouth of canning jars is the cleanest way to fill jars, particularly with thick mixtures like chutneys, relishes, salsas and sauces.

Silicone or rubber spatulas: Heat-resistant, stain-resistant spatulas are very helpful when working with preserves. It's useful to have spatulas in various sizes, but you'll definitely need a long, flexible, narrow one for removing the bubbles from jars (unless you have a bubble remover; see page 13).

Lint-free towels: Finely woven towels made of natural fibers (cotton or linen) allow for air circulation when covering fermenting produce and for the best absorption when draining produce. Avoid terrycloth towels, which tend to lose fibers.

Y-shaped vegetable peeler: These work better than traditional straight potato peelers, especially for more tender fruits and vegetables. It is best to have one with a very sharp blade so you can peel off just the skin, losing less flesh. They don't last forever, so if you think the blade is getting dull, it's worth investing in a new peeler.

Ruler: A washable plastic or metal ruler is best for measuring headspace in jars. I find it helpful to use a permanent marker to highlight the ½-inch (1 cm) mark on the ruler for easy identification of the correct headspace.

Kitchen timer: An accurate kitchen timer, preferably digital, will help you keep track of timing when cooking preserves and is essential for timing the processing in the boiling-water canner.

Optional, but Helpful

Mandoline: This manual slicing tool is used to cut foods into thin, even slices. Mandolines can be large, stainless steel, commercial-grade contraptions or simple plastic holders with a metal slicing blade — or something in between. A Japanese type, called a Benriner, is my particular favorite for its economical price, effectiveness and compact size for easy storage.

Jar lifter: These specialized tongs are coated with silicone and are designed to fit around the necks of jars. They make lifting jars easier and safer.

Silicone-coated tongs: Long- or short-handled metal tongs with heatproof silicone coating on the ends are ideal for packing hot foods into jars, especially when you're trying to neatly pack foods such as asparagus, beans or slices of cucumbers. Metal tongs without silicone coating are not suitable, as the metal can scratch the jars.

Silicone oven mitts: These are heat- and water-resistant and are very helpful for handling the canning rack and hot, wet jars.

Disposable latex or rubber gloves: Wear these when handling hot chile peppers to prevent stinging and burns and when handling dark-colored produce such as beets, cherries and red cabbage to prevent staining on your hands. They're available at pharmacies and hardware stores.

Bubble remover: This long, thin, plastic tool is inserted into filled canning jars to remove air bubbles before sealing. It often has notches in one end that you can use to measure headspace.

Magnetic lid lifter: This long, plastic, wand-like stick with a magnet stuck to one end makes plucking the disc portion of the lid out of hot water a breeze. With some strong, waterproof glue, a magnet and a chopstick, you can make one yourself.

Food mill or Victorio strainer: For tomato sauces in particular, pass the sauce through a food mill or a Victorio strainer (a hand-cranked or electric grinder) to remove skins and seeds, eliminating the step of peeling and seeding the tomatoes before cooking.

Ingredients and Preparation

Produce

All produce should be rinsed well and lightly rubbed under cool running water before it is prepared (the exception is mushrooms; see page 16). Rinse root vegetables such as carrots, onions and beets again after peeling.

- *Apples:* Different varieties of apples have different uses in cooking, and in preserves in particular. Varieties that hold their shape and have a flavor that withstands cooking, such as Granny Smith, Northern Spy or Crispin (Mutsu), are good for chunky chutneys. Those that break down when cooked but still hold their flavor, such as McIntosh, are good for sauces where you want a smoother texture. A combination of both types of apples is sometimes used. Other cooking apples can be used, but their flavor may get lost.

- *Beans, green and yellow wax:* Use the freshest beans possible, as they tend to wilt quickly after harvest. Look for mature beans that are crispy but not woody or stringy. Trim off the stem end just before using.

- *Beets:* If possible, keep the leaves on beets until just before use so the beets stay fresh. When ready to use, trim off leaves, cutting about 1/4 inch (0.5 cm) off the top of the beet. Trim off root end until almost flush with the bulb of the beet. Unless otherwise specified in the recipe, cook beets before using in preserves. Beets can sometimes have a "muddy" flavor, so it is best to cook and taste one beet before preparing an entire batch.

- *Bell peppers:* Remove the stem, core and seeds before chopping. To chop through the thick skin, it's easiest to place peppers skin side down on the cutting board.

Green bell peppers have their own unique flavor; do not substitute them for other colors unless the recipe specifies that you can do so. Red, orange and yellow bell peppers can be used interchangeably.

- *Berries:* Use tender berries, such as strawberries, as soon as possible after harvest. Blueberries tend to hold a little longer but will deteriorate if stored too long. If necessary, spread berries in a single layer on a towel-lined baking sheet or shallow container and refrigerate for up to 1 day. Rinse berries in a colander in small batches to avoid bruising and spread out on a towel-lined baking sheet to drain thoroughly. Remove strawberry hulls after washing and just before using.

- *Carrots:* Peel and trim ends before chopping, slicing or grating. Small- or medium-size carrots are best, as very large carrots can have very woody cores and a spongy texture that makes for soft pickles.

- *Cherries:* Either sweet cherries or sour (tart) cherries can be used in preserves, but not interchangeably. Rinse cherries in a colander in small batches to avoid bruising. Remove stems and pits just before using. If you don't have a cherry pitter, hold the cherry over a bowl, grip the cherry firmly with one hand and, using a chopstick with the other hand, insert the end of the chopstick into the stem opening of the cherry and push through to the bottom of the cherry. The pit will come out the bottom. If you're chopping the cherries, use a small paring knife to cut around the circumference of the cherry, starting and finishing at the stem opening. Twist the two halves of the cherry in opposite directions around the pit. Use the tip of the paring knife to flick the pit from the half it sticks in. Then chop cherries as desired.

- *Hot chile peppers:* For preserves, it is best to remove the seeds from chile peppers before chopping, as they tend to add a bitter flavor when cooked for a long time. Leaving the ribs of the peppers in does increase the amount of heat slightly. Chile peppers range in heat — even those of the same variety — so if possible, taste them before using (but not Scotch bonnets or habaneros — they're too hot to eat raw) to see if they are on the hotter or milder side. If they are mild, you can add a little more to the recipe. If you're not sure, stick to the amount specified and add hot pepper sauce or minced fresh hot chile peppers to the preserve just before serving to spice it up.

- *Citrus fruits:* Choose citrus fruits with taut, shiny skin that feel heavy for their size. If using the skin, gently scrub it to remove any wax or other coatings. When whole or peeled citrus fruits are chopped, the juices that accumulate on the cutting board are included with the flesh unless otherwise specified in the recipe. Recipes calling for juice were tested with freshly squeezed limes, lemons and oranges. However, bottled lemon juice is sometimes used when an exact acidity is required; this will be specified in those recipes. To grate zest, use a fine-toothed Microplane-style grater or the fine side of a box cheese grater. It is much easier to grate the zest before squeezing out the juice.

- *Corn:* Fresh corn on the cob is used in all recipes unless otherwise specified. To preserve the fresh texture and flavor, wait to remove husks and silks until just before cooking. Cook whole or halved cobs in a large pot of lightly salted boiling water for about 5 minutes, or until kernels are easily pierced with a fork. Plunge cobs into cold water to stop the cooking. Holding each cob in a deep bowl, use a small, serrated knife to slice off the kernels.

- *Cucumbers, field:* For best results in making preserves, look for field cucumbers that haven't been waxed. Choose small or medium cucumbers that feel heavy for their size; avoid very large ones, which tend to be softer and spongy. If you use waxed cucumbers, peel them before chopping; you will end up with a paler preserve. Cut field cucumbers in half lengthwise and scoop out the tough seeds before chopping.

- *Cucumbers, pickling:* These small varieties of cucumbers are grown specifically for pickling. Use cucumbers up to about 6 inches (15 cm) in length. Different sizes are suited to different preserves; the appropriate size is noted in the recipes. Use only firm cucumbers with no blemishes, splits or soft spots. The thinner skin on these cucumbers makes them deteriorate faster, so they are best used within a day or two of harvest. To wash them efficiently, put the weighed amount of cucumbers in a sink of cold water and let them soak for about 10 minutes. Then, using a clean waffle-weave dishcloth, gently rub each cucumber all over to remove any grit. Rinse the cucumber under running water and let drain in a colander. Always trim off about $\frac{1}{8}$ inch (3 mm) from the blossom end before using, as there is an enzyme in the blossom that can cause cucumbers to soften when pickled.

- *Eggplant:* Choose small or medium eggplant that feel heavy for their size and have tight, shiny skin. Very large or wrinkled eggplant will be spongy and can have very tough and bitter seeds.

- *Fruit in general:* For any fruit with inedible skin, pits or seeds, the fruit is peeled and pits are discarded before the fruit is chopped unless otherwise specified in the recipe.

- **Garlic:** Use the freshest garlic possible. The heads should be tightly closed and show no signs of mold or sprouting. Peel and trim the root end of each clove before using. If there are any green sprouts inside the cloves, remove them to prevent a bitter flavor.

- **Gingerroot:** Look for plump gingerroot with shiny skin and no signs of rot or mold. Store gingerroot in a paper bag in the crisper in the refrigerator. Trim ends and peel before chopping, slicing or mincing.

- **Herbs:** Use the freshest herbs possible. To store fresh herbs, wrap in a paper towel or a lint-free towel and store in a plastic bag (not tied tight) in the crisper. Rinse herbs well under cool running water just before using. Pat dry with towels or use a salad spinner to remove excess moisture. Use within a couple of days for the best flavor. Discard any yellowed or dark green, mushy leaves. Chop just before using.

- **Mangos, green:** These are not the same as sweet mangos, which have golden yellow-orange flesh; green mangos are a completely different variety. They are often found in Asian grocery stores and well-stocked supermarkets, displayed with the vegetables. They are firm and tart and will never ripen into sweet, fragrant mangos. They can be peeled and cut in the same way as sweet mangos (see below).

- **Mangos, sweet:** Ripe sweet mangos have a fragrant aroma, and the skin yields slightly to pressure when gently squeezed. Do not use mangos that are wrinkled or have soft spots. There are many varieties of sweet mangos available, and they are interchangeable in recipes. The neatest and most efficient way to prepare a firm, ripe mango is to peel it with a sharp vegetable peeler. After peeling off the skin, hold the mango upright, with the

stem down, on a cutting board. Using a sharp knife, cut close to the flat side of the seed on both sides, creating two "cheeks." Carefully cut all remaining flesh from around the seed. Chop the flesh into pieces of the desired size.

- **Mushrooms:** Mushrooms are the exception to the rule of rinsing all vegetables. It is best to wipe mushrooms individually with a damp paper towel to remove any dirt. Do this just before using them. They are best used for preserves as soon as possible after harvest. If necessary, store mushrooms in brown paper bags in the refrigerator. There are many exotic varieties of mushrooms available, but avoid portobellos, as their dark gills will turn any pickling liquid black.

- **Onions:** The recipes use regular yellow cooking onions unless otherwise specified. Be sure onions are fresh and firm, with no signs of sponginess or mold. Sweet onions have a milder, sweeter flavor than cooking onions and are better suited to some recipes. Look for those labeled "sweet" or with variety names such as Vidalia, Texas Sweet, Walla Walla, Maui or Spanish. Red onions have a purple skin and pink-purple flesh; they are sometimes called purple onions.

- **Peaches:** Freestone peaches are easiest to work with for all preserves and are essential for nice-looking pickled peach halves or slices. Ripe but firm peaches feel heavy for their size, yield slightly to pressure when gently squeezed and have a fragrant aroma. To peel peaches, drop 4 to 6 peaches at a time into a large pot of boiling water for 30 seconds. Using a slotted spoon, transfer peaches to a large bowl or sink of ice-cold water and let cool completely, refreshing water as necessary to keep cool. Drain well. Using a sharp paring knife, lift off the skins from the stem opening; the rest should slip off easily. If the skins seem difficult to remove, increase the blanching time to 1 minute or use a very sharp Y-shaped vegetable peeler to remove the skins.

- **Pears:** Choose pear varieties that hold their shape and flavor when heated, such as Bartlett, Bosc, Packham, Concorde or Seckel. Pears ripen from the inside out, so when the outside is soft, the inside will be overripe. Test a pear for ripeness by gently pressing the neck near the stem. The flesh should yield just slightly, but should not be soft. Peel and chop pears just before using, as they brown when exposed to the air. For chutneys, sauces and relishes, it is best to first measure the vinegar into the pot and then add the pears directly to the vinegar as they are chopped and measured.

- **Tomatoes:** For most preserves, plum (Roma) or other paste-type tomatoes are best, unless otherwise specified in the recipe. They have less liquid that needs to be boiled off to make a thick sauce and tend to have a more consistent amount of liquid than globe tomatoes. Choose tomatoes that have firm, shiny skin, feel heavy for their size and have no signs of blemishes or mold. Ripe tomatoes yield slightly to pressure when gently squeezed and have a slightly fragrant aroma. A pungent aroma is a sign of overripeness and possibly rot inside.

  If you buy a large quantity of tomatoes, it is best to spread them out to provide air circulation and reduce deterioration. Line shallow boxes with clean newspaper and arrange tomatoes in a single layer, or a maximum of two layers. Store out of the sun, in a cool place such as a garage or basement (but not in the refrigerator), and check daily to remove any that start to spoil.

  To peel tomatoes, drop 6 to 10 tomatoes at a time into a large pot of boiling water for 30 seconds. Using a slotted spoon, transfer tomatoes to a large bowl or sink of ice-cold water and let cool completely, refreshing water as necessary to keep cool. Drain well. Using a sharp paring knife, cut out the core and lift off the skins from the opening; the rest should slip off easily. If the skins seem difficult to remove, increase the blanching time to 1 minute.

- **Zucchini:** For best results when pickling, use small or medium zucchini. Larger zucchini can be used for relishes as long as they are not soft and spongy. You may want to remove the seed portion from larger zucchini if it is soft. Fresh zucchini has shiny, smooth skin and no signs of decay or soft spots. To clean zucchini, gently rub it with a clean waffle-weave dishcloth. Always trim off the stem and blossom ends before using.

Other Ingredients

- **Nuts:** Use only very fresh nuts. For more flavor, nuts can be toasted before use. Spread nuts on a baking sheet and bake in a 375°F (190°C) oven, stirring once or twice, for 5 to 8 minutes (depending on the size of the nuts), or until nuts are toasted and fragrant. Watch carefully, as they burn easily. Transfer immediately to a bowl and let cool.

- **Pickling or canning salt:** Salt is an integral ingredient in preserving. It draws juices out of vegetables and fruits, allowing the pickling liquid or brine to enter the cells and preserve the food. It also contributes greatly to the texture of pickles, and is essential for the formation of lactic acid in fermented foods such as sauerkraut. Pure salt without any additives is necessary for good-quality pickles and other preserves; it is labeled "pickling salt" or "canning salt." Table salt and other iodized salts cause cloudiness in brines. Remember, you can't get safe results if you don't use the correct amount of salt.

- *Spices:* Whole spices, such as bay leaves, cinnamon sticks, mustard seeds, celery seeds, cloves and allspice, are often used in preserves. They can be left in the pickling liquid or, when a clear liquid is desired, can be tied in a spice bag made of cheesecloth, then discarded after their flavor has infused the liquid. Ground spices are sometimes used for a more even distribution of flavor. For both whole and ground spices, use good-quality dried products that are fragrant and have no signs of mold or dirt.
- *Sugar:* Use only real sugar for preserves. Sugar substitutes are not suitable unless a recipe has been specifically created for their use. Granulated sugar and brown sugar can be used interchangeably in a recipe; however, the resulting flavor will be slightly different. Use light brown (golden yellow) sugar for a delicate molasses flavor or dark brown sugar for a deeper flavor.
- *Vinegar:* The white vinegar, cider vinegar, white wine vinegar and red wine vinegar used in these recipes are 5% acetic acid. White balsamic and regular balsamic vinegars are 6% acetic acid. The rice vinegar used in these recipes is natural vinegar without added sugar and salt (do not use seasoned rice vinegar) and is 4.3% acid. Do not substitute vinegars with other acidity levels in a recipe, as this can adversely affect the final pH of the product and the flavor balance.
- *Water:* Water is an important ingredient in pickles and preserves, especially those that are fermented. Hard water has a high amount of dissolved minerals in it and can have adverse effects, such as cloudy brine and off-flavors, on pickles and preserves. It is worth having your tap water checked to determine if it is hard. If you have hard water, you can use reverse osmosis water or bottled water that has a regulated mineral level. To soften hard water, in a large stainless steel pot, bring about twice as much water as you'll need to a boil over high heat. Boil for 15 minutes. Remove from heat and let stand undisturbed for 24 hours. Skim any scum off the surface and discard. Carefully ladle or pour the water into another container, without disturbing the sediment that has collected on the bottom of the pot (these are the minerals you want to remove).

About These Recipes

Measuring Primer

- Produce is medium-sized unless otherwise specified.
- Where an exact quantity of vegetables and fruits is important, a weight or volume is given (e.g., $\frac{1}{2}$ cup/125 mL chopped onions). Where it isn't imperative, a number is given (e.g., 3 onions, chopped).
- Dry ingredients, including chopped vegetables and fruit, are measured in dry, nesting-style measuring cups. Ingredients such as granulated sugar are spooned in and leveled off, not tapped or packed. Brown sugar is packed into the cup just enough so that it holds its shape when dumped out of the cup, but not so tightly that it is difficult to remove from the cup.
- Liquid ingredients are measured in a liquid measuring cup with graduated volume markings, and generally with a handle and a spout. The volume is read at eye level.
- Measuring spoons are used for quantities of both dry and liquid ingredients that are less than $\frac{1}{4}$ cup (50 mL).
- Both imperial and metric quantities are provided. They are not, however, interchangeable. If you use imperial measures, measure all ingredients in imperial; if you use metric measures, measure all ingredients in metric.

Definitions

Coarsely chopped: Pieces are random in shape and $\frac{3}{4}$ to 1 inch (2 to 2.5 cm) in size.

Chopped: Pieces are random in shape and $\frac{1}{2}$ to $\frac{3}{4}$ inch (1 to 2 cm) in size.

Finely chopped: Pieces are random in shape and $\frac{1}{8}$ to $\frac{1}{4}$ inch (3 mm to 0.5 cm) in size.

Minced: Pieces are random in shape and very tiny, but are still discernable pieces (not mashed or puréed).

Diced: Pieces are uniform cube shapes and about $\frac{1}{4}$ inch (0.5 cm) in size.

Cubed: Pieces are uniform cube shapes and about $\frac{1}{2}$ inch (1 cm) in size.

Heat until steaming: The liquid or food is very hot; steam rises from the surface and small bubbles form but do not rise and break the surface.

Simmer: Bubbles break the surface of the liquid at a slow but constant pace.

Boil gently: Larger bubbles break the surface at a moderate pace. If stirred, bubbles will subside slightly, then resume as soon as stirring stops.

Boil: Large bubbles break the surface at a rapid pace. If stirred, bubbles will continue to break the surface, but slightly more slowly.

Full rolling boil: Many large bubbles break the surface at a very rapid pace. If stirred, bubbles do not subside at all.

Gift-Giving Ideas

Gifts of preserves are wonderful to give and to receive. Fun combinations of savory preserves wrapped in clever packaging are certain to thrill any recipient, and you'll know you're giving a gift made with love. Be sure to label each jar with the contents, your name (it's nice for people to know who made it) and serving suggestions if it's not necessarily obvious. Enclosing plastic storage lids (caps) is a nice touch as well.

Here are some fun ideas to get you started.

Housewarming present: A mixing bowl lined with a new tea towel and filled with basic condiments such as Dill Cucumber Relish (page 255), Classic Barbecue Sauce (page 174), Black Bean Tomato Salsa (page 157) and Aunt Thelma's Bread-and-Butter Pickles (page 35).

Wedding shower gift: A large stainless steel pasta pot, a colander, a package of fancy dried pasta and a few jars of Classic Tomato Sauce (page 167), Spicy Tomato Sauce (page 168) or Vodka and Rosemary Tomato Sauce (page 173).

Houseguest thank-you gift: A bag of tortilla chips, some pita crisps or crackers and dips, such as Chipotle Tomato Salsa (page 152), Mild Tomato and Sweet Pepper Salsa (page 153) and Eggplant and Tomato Caponata (page 182).

Cottage visit thank-you gift: A set of cloth napkins or a package of decorative paper napkins, along with Coffee-Spiked Barbecue Chili Sauce (page 176), Grilled Corn and Tomato Salsa (page 155) and Homemade Spicy Ketchup (page 180).

Dinner party host gift: A box of crisp flatbreads and a selection of spreads, such as Mushroom and Lemon Tapenade (page 280), Tomato and Olive Antipasto (page 184), Caramelized Onion Relish (page 276) and Blueberry, Tart Apple and Onion Chutney (page 199).

Birthday gift for the adventurous eater: A set of small bowls, along with jars of more exotic preserves, such as Pickled Okra and Hot Peppers (page 83), White Balsamic and Pepper Pickled Strawberries (page 133), Asian Pickled Eggplant (page 289) and Date and Tamarind Chutney (page 314).

Vegetable Pickles

continued on next page

• • •

Vegetable Pickle Basics

Pickling vegetables can be as simple as packing cold vegetables into hot jars and pouring in a vinegar-based liquid, or it can be a more complex fermenting process — or somewhere in between. The basic purpose of pickling is to add or create acid to make the pH low enough to preserve the vegetables (see page 6 for more about pH). In the process, spices, herbs and other seasonings can be added to create wonderful flavors.

For "quick" pickles, the vegetables are trimmed and/or chopped, sliced or left whole. In some cases, they are blanched. Then they are packed into jars in one of two ways: either a heated pickling liquid is poured over the vegetables in the jars, or the vegetables are heated in the liquid before being packed into jars. It's as simple as that.

Some vegetables, such as cucumbers and zucchini, benefit from having some of their natural water removed before you add the pickling liquid. Salt the vegetables, using either just salt or a salt-water brine, and let them stand for the time specified in the recipe (anywhere from a few hours to an entire day). During this time, the salt will draw water out of the vegetables. This pretreatment allows the pickling liquid to penetrate into the cells of the vegetables, giving the pickles more flavor and better texture, and increasing their shelf life.

Brined pickles are a little more complex. This process gradually draws the water out of vegetables in stages of soaking and draining and soaking again, using a salt-water brine and/or a vinegar brine. The cells of the vegetables can then be completely saturated with pickling liquid, providing a special flavor and texture. Sweet gherkins and Diana's 9-Day Pickles are classic examples of brined pickles.

Fermented pickles, such as sauerkraut, rely on a different method completely. The vegetables are covered in a salt-water brine and allowed to stand at a specific temperature to ferment. The salt draws the liquid out of the cells, and naturally occurring microbes digest the sugars and form lactic acid (among other substances). The lactic acid then lowers the pH to a level that preserves the vegetables. Through this process, the food develops aromas and flavors that give fermented pickles their unique character.

Vegetable pickles can be packed into jars using one of two different methods. In the raw-pack method, cold vegetables are packed into hot jars just before a boiling hot pickling liquid is added. (Despite the name, the vegetables aren't necessarily raw; they may have been blanched and chilled.) This technique tends to be used for hard or crunchy vegetables such as cucumbers and carrots. It is best to pack and fill raw-pack jars one at a time so that the cold vegetables don't cool the jars down too much before the liquid is added. Raw-pack pickles sometimes require more time in the canner than hot-pack pickles, to make sure the food is heated to a high enough temperature to destroy any microorganisms.

In the hot-pack method, vegetables are added to the boiling pickling liquid in the pot and either heated just until the liquid returns to a boil or boiled or simmered long enough to cook the vegetables and infuse the liquid into the vegetables. The vegetables are then packed into the jars and the hot liquid is added. These pickles can be packed in an assembly-line fashion. Use tongs or a slotted spoon (depending on the vegetable) to place the vegetables in the jars, dividing them evenly between the jars, then use a ladle or a heatproof measuring cup to scoop liquid out of the pot and pour it over the vegetables. With this method, it is easier to avoid ending up with one jar that is only partially filled. You do, however, need to work quickly enough to prevent the jars and food from cooling down.

Raw-pack pickle recipes can generally be doubled easily, as long as the filled jars will all fit in your canner at once. Hot-pack pickle recipes aren't as easy to double, because the food may take too long to heat if there is too much in the pot (the bottom vegetables will get mushy before the top ones are heated through). If you want to double hot-pack recipes, make two batches simultaneously in two pots, but only if you can fit all the jars in the canner at once. If you will have too many jars to fit in the canner, delay the start of your second batch by about 10 minutes longer than the processing time of the recipe to give you time to handle the first batch.

If you haven't pickled vegetables before, start with one of the easy recipes, such as Classic Quick Dill Pickles (page 26), Dill Pickled Carrot Sticks (page 65) or Classic Pickled Cauliflower (page 67), to get your feet wet and master the basic technique. If you're a seasoned pickle-maker, you may want to try some of the more adventurous recipes to expand your pickling horizons while you're stocking your pantry.

Vegetable Pickle Pointers

- Use the freshest produce possible, discarding any vegetables that show signs of spoilage.
- Don't alter the amounts of vinegar, water, salt and sugar. The balance of these essential ingredients is important for preserving. The recipes in this book have been carefully created for optimal flavor balance as well.
- The type of vinegar used can be adjusted according to taste as long as the strength of the acetic acid is the same. Five percent white vinegar, cider vinegar, white wine vinegar and red wine vinegar are interchangeable.
- Spices and seasonings (except for salt and sugar) can be adjusted according to taste. Feel free to get creative, but keep in mind that the flavors will be stronger after the pickles stand for a while.
- To prevent a salty taste in your finished product, it is important to thoroughly rinse vegetables after salting them.
- When the instructions specify to cover a bowl or container, you can use a lid or plastic wrap. If they specify a lint-free towel, be sure the towel is made of a natural fiber, such as cotton or linen, or use several layers of cheesecloth, so that contaminants are kept out of the bowl but air can still flow in and out.
- Choose the size of jar that best suits your needs, keeping in mind that you'll need to eat the pickles within a month of opening the jar.
- The easiest way to pack cold vegetables into a hot jar is to hold the jar with one hand in a silicone oven mitt, or with a dry towel, and use the other hand to place the vegetables in the jar. Pack them in an organized fashion to maximize the number you fit.
- When packing hot vegetables into jars, place a funnel in the mouth of a jar

and use a slotted spoon to drain the vegetables from the pot and spoon them into the jar through the funnel. Gently tilt and shake the jar (don't bang it) to help the vegetables pack down into the jar. Once you've filled all of the jars, you'll see that the vegetables in the first jars have packed down more, so you may need to add more to top the jars up. If you don't think the vegetables are packed enough, you can use a rubber or plastic spatula to gently nudge them down in the jar, being careful not to mash or break them.

- When packing foods that you want to stay upright in the jars, such as asparagus, carrot sticks or cucumber spears, hold the jar with one hand in a silicone oven mitt, or with a dry towel, and tilt the jar toward you at about a 45-degree angle. Use the other hand or silicone-coated tongs to place the pieces of food upright in the jar, leaning against the bottom inside wall. Gently shake the jar on the angle once it's full to help the pieces settle, adding more if necessary.

- If you're using different-sized jars that require different processing times, fill the larger jars and place them in the canner, keeping the smaller jars and food hot, then fill the smaller jars and add them to the canner later, timing it so that both sizes finish at the same time.

- Most pickles benefit from standing for at least a week after they're made to allow the flavors to meld.

- For the best texture, chill pickles in the refrigerator before serving.

Classic Quick Dill Pickles

My friend Pat Burley won first prize at the Lindsay Agricultural Fair in Ontario for several years running with this quick and easy pickle technique, earning her the title "Queen of the Dills" among her friends and family.

Makes about seven quart (1 L) jars

● ● ●

Tips

On average, you can pack 11 to 14 cucumbers of this size into a quart (1 L) jar. You may need a little more or a little less than 7 lbs (3.5 kg).

This quick method of pickling doesn't tend to keep the pickles as long as other methods. These are best used within 6 months.

7 lbs	3- to 4-inch (7.5 to 10 cm) pickling cucumbers (see tip, at left)	3.5 kg
1 cup	pickling or canning salt	250 mL
⅔ cup	granulated sugar	150 mL
12 cups	water	3 L
5 cups	white vinegar	1.25 L
7	large dill heads, broken in half	7
3½	cloves garlic, cut into quarters	3½

1. Prepare canner, jars and lids (see pages 7 to 8).
2. Scrub cucumbers gently under running water. Trim off ⅛ inch (3 mm) from each end. Set aside.
3. In a pot, combine salt, sugar, water and vinegar. Bring to a boil over medium-high heat, stirring often until salt and sugar are dissolved. Reduce heat to low and keep liquid hot.
4. Working with one jar at a time, place half a dill head and 1 piece of garlic in hot jar. Pack cucumbers into jar, leaving about 1 inch (2.5 cm) headspace, and top with another half dill head and piece of garlic. Pour in hot pickling liquid, leaving ½ inch (1 cm) headspace. Remove air bubbles and adjust headspace as necessary by adding hot pickling liquid. Wipe rim and place hot lid disc on jar. Screw band down until fingertip-tight.
5. Place jars in canner and return to a boil. Process for 15 minutes. Turn off heat, remove canner lid and let jars stand in water for 5 minutes. Transfer jars to a towel-lined surface and let stand for 24 hours. Check lids and refrigerate any jars that are not sealed.

Extra-Garlic Garlic Dills

Crispy garlic-laced pickles with lots of crunch — you can't go wrong with these dills!

Makes about seven quart (1 L) jars

● ● ●

Tip
The garlic may turn blue in the pickling liquid. It's perfectly safe to eat; the color change is just a reaction between the minerals in the garlic and the acid from the vinegar.

Day 1

8 lbs	3- to 4-inch (7.5 to 10 cm) pickling cucumbers (88 to 96)	4 kg
1 cup	pickling or canning salt	250 mL

Day 2

2 tbsp	mustard seeds	25 mL
1 tbsp	pickling or canning salt	15 mL
7 cups	water	1.75 L
6½ cups	white vinegar	1.625 L
21	cloves garlic, each cut into 4 slices	21
14	dill heads	14

Day 1

1. Scrub cucumbers gently under running water. Trim off ⅛ inch (3 mm) from each end and prick all over with a fork.
2. In a large bowl, layer cucumbers and salt, using about one-quarter of each per layer. Add cold water to cover by about 1 inch (2.5 cm). Place a plate on top to weigh down cucumbers. Cover and let stand at a cool room temperature for at least 12 hours or for up to 24 hours.

Day 2

1. Prepare canner, jars and lids (see pages 7 to 8).
2. In a colander, working in batches, drain cucumbers and rinse well. Drain again and set aside.
3. In a pot, combine mustard seeds, salt, water and vinegar. Bring to a boil over medium-high heat, stirring often until salt is dissolved. Boil for 1 minute. Reduce heat to low and keep liquid hot.
4. Working with one jar at a time, place 6 pieces of garlic and 1 dill head in hot jar. Pack cucumbers into jar, leaving about 1 inch (2.5 cm) headspace, and top with 6 pieces of garlic and 1 dill head. Pour in hot pickling liquid, leaving ½ inch (1 cm) headspace. Remove air bubbles and adjust headspace as necessary by adding hot pickling liquid. Wipe rim and place hot lid disc on jar. Screw band down until fingertip-tight.
5. Place jars in canner and return to a boil. Process for 15 minutes. Turn off heat, remove canner lid and let jars stand in water for 5 minutes. Transfer jars to a towel-lined surface and let stand for 24 hours. Check lids and refrigerate any jars that are not sealed.

Baby Dills

Smaller cucumbers take on a light, fresh dill flavor in these classic crunchy pickles.

Makes about seven quart (1 L) jars

● ● ●

Tip

Each quart (1 L) jar will hold about 22 cucumbers of this size when tightly packed, so you'll use a total of about 154 for this recipe.

Variation

Garlic Baby Dills: Increase the garlic to 14 or 21 cloves, adding 4 or 6 pieces at a time to jars.

Day 1		
7 lbs	2½- to 3-inch (6 to 7.5 cm) pickling cucumbers	3.5 kg
¾ cup	pickling or canning salt	175 mL
Day 2		
2 tbsp	mustard seeds	25 mL
1 tbsp	pickling or canning salt	15 mL
8 cups	water	2 L
7½ cups	white vinegar	1.875 L
14	dill heads	14
7	cloves garlic, each cut into 4 slices	7

Day 1

1. Scrub cucumbers gently under running water. Trim off ⅛ inch (3 mm) from each end and prick all over with a fork.
2. In a large bowl, layer cucumbers and salt, using about one-quarter of each per layer. Add cold water to cover by about 1 inch (2.5 cm). Place a plate on top to weigh down cucumbers. Cover and let stand at a cool room temperature for at least 12 hours or for up to 24 hours.

Day 2

1. Prepare canner, jars and lids (see pages 7 to 8).
2. In a colander, working in batches, drain cucumbers and rinse well. Drain again and set aside.
3. In a pot, combine mustard seeds, salt, water and vinegar. Bring to a boil over medium-high heat, stirring often until salt is dissolved. Boil for 1 minute. Reduce heat to low and keep liquid hot.
4. Working with one jar at a time, place 1 dill head and 2 pieces of garlic in hot jar. Pack cucumbers into jar, leaving about 1 inch (2.5 cm) headspace, and top with 1 dill head and 2 pieces of garlic. Pour in hot pickling liquid, leaving ½ inch (1 cm) headspace. Remove air bubbles and adjust headspace as necessary by adding hot pickling liquid. Wipe rim and place hot lid disc on jar. Screw band down until fingertip-tight.
5. Place jars in canner and return to a boil. Process for 15 minutes. Turn off heat, remove canner lid and let jars stand in water for 5 minutes. Transfer jars to a towel-lined surface and let stand for 24 hours. Check lids and refrigerate any jars that are not sealed.

Dilly Pickled Cucumber Chips

This is a good recipe in which to use cucumbers that are a little too big for whole pickles. When you open the jar, they're sliced and ready to add to burgers or sandwiches, or just to munch on.

Makes about six pint (500 mL) jars

● ● ● ●

Tips

Use a mandoline or kitchen slicer to make quick work of slicing the cucumbers.

Feathery dill sprigs (instead of dill heads) are best for these pickles, as they add a lovely dill flavor and fit nicely in the jars with the slices.

Day 1

4 lbs	pickling cucumbers	2 kg
¼ cup	pickling or canning salt	50 mL

Day 2

1 cup	granulated sugar	250 mL
4 tsp	dill seeds	20 mL
6 cups	white vinegar	1.5 L
3 cups	water	750 mL
12	large dill sprigs	12

Day 1

1. Scrub cucumbers gently under running water. Cut crosswise into ⅛-inch (3 mm) slices, trimming off ⅛ inch (3 mm) from each end.
2. In a large bowl, layer cucumbers and salt, using about one-third of each per layer. Add cold water to cover by about 1 inch (2.5 cm). Place a plate on top to weigh down cucumbers. Cover and let stand at a cool room temperature for at least 8 hours or for up to 18 hours.

Day 2

1. Prepare canner, jars and lids (see pages 7 to 8).
2. In a colander, working in batches, drain cucumbers and rinse well. Drain again and set aside.
3. In a large pot, combine sugar, dill seeds, vinegar and water. Bring to a boil over medium-high heat, stirring often until sugar is dissolved. Add cucumbers and return to a boil, pressing occasionally to immerse cucumbers in liquid. Remove from heat.
4. Divide half the dill sprigs among hot jars. Using a slotted spoon, pack cucumbers into jars, leaving 1 inch (2.5 cm) headspace, and top with the remaining dill sprigs. Pour in hot pickling liquid, leaving ½ inch (1 cm) headspace. Remove air bubbles and adjust headspace as necessary by adding hot pickling liquid. Wipe rim and place hot lid disc on jar. Screw band down until fingertip-tight.
5. Place jars in canner and return to a boil. Process for 10 minutes. Turn off heat, remove canner lid and let jars stand in water for 5 minutes. Transfer jars to a towel-lined surface and let stand for 24 hours. Check lids and refrigerate any jars that are not sealed.

Barrel-Fermented Dills

These are the richly flavored dills of deli fame. You may know them as crock-cured dill pickles or deli dills. Regardless of what you call them, they're made to accompany a deli meat sandwich.

Makes about five quart (1 L) jars

● ● ●

Tips

You may need extra brine to cover the cucumbers or to add later in the fermenting process if too much evaporates or is skimmed off. Use ¼ cup (50 mL) pickling or canning salt dissolved in 4 cups (1 L) water and ½ cup (125 mL) white vinegar (or multiply in the same proportions for more). Extra brine can be stored in an airtight container in the refrigerator for up to 2 months. Let warm to room temperature before adding to crock.

Here are the keys to success with these pickles: make sure there is brine covering the cucumbers, be diligent about skimming the brine while they ferment, and make sure they're at the right temperature.

Day 1

1 cup	pickling or canning salt	250 mL
¼ cup	pickling spice	50 mL
16 cups	water	4 L
2 cups	white vinegar	500 mL
6 lbs	3- to 4-inch (7.5 to 10 cm) pickling cucumbers (66 to 72)	3 kg
2 cups	packed dill sprigs	500 mL

Final Day

	Dill seeds

Day 1

1. In a pot, combine salt, pickling spice, water and vinegar. Bring to a boil over high heat, stirring often until salt is dissolved. Let cool to room temperature.
2. Meanwhile, scrub cucumbers gently under running water. Trim off ⅛ inch (3 mm) from each end.
3. In a large crock, glass bowl or other non-reactive container, layer cucumbers and dill sprigs, using about one-third of each per layer. Pour brine over cucumbers and place a plate on top to weigh down cucumbers. Fill a couple of glass jars with water (see tip, at right) and place on plate to keep it weighted. Cover with a lint-free towel or several layers of cheesecloth. Let stand at room temperature (70°F to 75°F/21°C to 23°C) for 3 to 6 weeks.

During Fermentation

1. Skim off scum daily and check to make sure pickles are fermenting. You should see some slight bubbling, and the aroma will change. Add more brine (see tip, at left) if necessary to make sure pickles are covered. If there are any signs of mold or a foul aroma, discard pickles and liquid. Let ferment until bubbles stop and pickles are well flavored.

Final Day

1. Prepare canner, jars and lids (see pages 7 to 8).
2. Place a colander over a large bowl and line colander with several layers of cheesecloth. Drain pickles, in batches as necessary, straining the liquid through the cheesecloth. Set pickles aside. Discard cheesecloth, including spices and dill.

3. Line colander with several layers of clean cheesecloth and set over a pot. Strain pickling liquid once again to filter out any solids. Bring liquid to a boil over high heat. Reduce heat and boil gently for 5 minutes. Reduce heat to low and keep liquid hot.

4. Working with one jar at a time, place 1 tsp (5 mL) dill seeds in hot jar. Pack cucumbers into jar, leaving about 1 inch (2.5 cm) headspace. Pour in hot pickling liquid, leaving $\frac{1}{2}$ inch (1 cm) headspace. Remove air bubbles and adjust headspace as necessary by adding hot pickling liquid. Wipe rim and place hot lid disc on jar. Screw band down until fingertip-tight.

5. Place jars in canner and return to a boil. Process for 15 minutes. Turn off heat, remove canner lid and let jars stand in water for 5 minutes. Transfer jars to a towel-lined surface and let stand for 24 hours. Check lids and refrigerate any jars that are not sealed.

Tips

To weigh down the plate, you can use sterilized glass jars with tight-fitting lids full of water or a large, heavy-duty sealable plastic bag filled with cooled extra brine (don't use water, just in case it leaks, because water would dilute the brine and ruin the fermentation).

Many recipes for fermented dills don't give instructions to process them in the canner, but this step extends the shelf life of the pickles and prevents them from getting over-fermented.

Kosher-Style Dill Pickles

There are many opinions on what makes a perfect kosher dill pickle, but the basic consensus is a tangy, flavorful and crunchy pickle. This version satisfies all of those criteria.

Makes about seven quart (1 L) jars

● ● ●

Tips

To ensure crunchy pickles, use the freshest, crispest cucumbers for this recipe.

This size of cucumber is easy to pack into jars and tends to have the best texture. If you have larger cucumbers, cut them into halves or quarters. They may have a softer texture once pickled.

To make a spice bag, cut a 4-inch (10 cm) square piece of triple-layered cheesecloth. Place the pickling spice in the center of the square and bring the edges together into a bundle. Tie tightly with kitchen string. Alternatively, use a large mesh tea ball.

Day 1

8 lbs	3- to 4-inch (7.5 to 10 cm) pickling cucumbers (88 to 96)	4 kg
1 cup	pickling or canning salt	250 mL

Day 2

3 tbsp	pickling spice, tied in a spice bag	45 mL
9 cups	water	2.25 L
7¾ cups	white vinegar	1.9 L
7	bay leaves	7
7	cloves garlic, halved	7
7	each dill heads and dill sprigs	7

Day 1

1. Scrub cucumbers gently under running water. Trim off ⅛ inch (3 mm) from each end and prick all over with a fork.
2. In a large bowl, layer cucumbers and salt, using about one-quarter of each per layer. Add cold water to cover by about 1 inch (2.5 cm). Place a plate on top to weigh down cucumbers. Cover and let stand at a cool room temperature for at least 12 hours or for up to 24 hours.

Day 2

1. Prepare canner, jars and lids (see pages 7 to 8).
2. In a colander, working in batches, drain cucumbers and rinse well. Drain again and set aside.
3. In a pot, combine pickling spice, water and vinegar. Bring to a boil over medium-high heat. Boil for 1 minute. Reduce heat to low, cover and simmer for 5 minutes or until liquid is flavorful. Discard spice bag and keep liquid hot.
4. Working with one jar at a time, place 1 bay leaf, 1 piece of garlic and 1 dill head in hot jar. Pack cucumbers into jar, leaving 1 inch (2.5 cm) headspace, and top with 1 piece of garlic and 1 dill sprig. Pour in hot pickling liquid, leaving ½ inch (1 cm) headspace. Remove air bubbles and adjust headspace as necessary by adding hot pickling liquid. Wipe rim and place hot lid disc on jar. Screw band down until fingertip-tight.
5. Place jars in canner and return to a boil. Process for 15 minutes. Turn off heat, remove canner lid and let jars stand in water for 5 minutes. Transfer jars to a towel-lined surface and let stand for 24 hours. Check lids and refrigerate any jars that are not sealed.

Fiery Dill Slices

These tangy dill slices with a punch from hot peppers are ready to zest up burgers and sandwiches straight from the jar.

Makes about six pint (500 mL) jars

• • •

Tips

Fresh chile peppers can vary in heat, but the small dried red ones are sure to be fiery, making them better for these pickles. The little flakes of red even make the pickles *look* spicy.

It is best to slice these cucumbers by hand, rather than using a mandoline, as cucumbers tend to slide around when you're slicing lengthwise.

To make a spice bag, cut a 4-inch (10 cm) square piece of triple-layered cheesecloth. Place the pickling spice in the center of the square and bring the edges together into a bundle. Tie tightly with kitchen string. Alternatively, use a large mesh tea ball.

Day 1		
4 lbs	3½- to 4-inch (8.5 to 10 cm) pickling cucumbers (about 45)	2 kg
¼ cup	pickling or canning salt	50 mL
Day 2		
6	dried hot red chile peppers, crumbled	6
1 tbsp	pickling spice, tied in a spice bag	15 mL
4½ cups	water	1.125 L
4 cups	white vinegar	1 L
6	each dill heads and dill sprigs	6

Day 1

1. Scrub cucumbers gently under running water. Cut crosswise into ¼-inch (0.5 cm) slices, trimming off ⅛ inch (3 mm) from each end.

2. In a large bowl, layer cucumbers and salt, using about one-quarter of each per layer. Add cold water to cover by about 1 inch (2.5 cm). Place a plate on top to weigh down cucumbers. Cover and let stand at a cool room temperature for at least 8 hours or for up to 18 hours.

Day 2

1. Prepare canner, jars and lids (see pages 7 to 8).

2. In a colander, working in batches, drain cucumbers and rinse well. Drain again and set aside.

3. In a pot, combine chile peppers, pickling spice, water and vinegar. Bring to a boil over medium-high heat. Reduce heat to low, cover and simmer for 5 minutes or until liquid is flavorful. Discard spice bag and keep liquid hot.

4. Working with one jar at a time, place 1 dill head in hot jar. Pack cucumbers into jar, leaving 1 inch (2.5 cm) headspace, and top with 1 dill sprig. Pour in hot pickling liquid, leaving ½ inch (1 cm) headspace. Remove air bubbles and adjust headspace as necessary by adding hot pickling liquid. Wipe rim and place hot lid disc on jar. Screw band down until fingertip-tight.

5. Place jars in canner and return to a boil. Process for 10 minutes. Turn off heat, remove canner lid and let jars stand in water for 5 minutes. Transfer jars to a towel-lined surface and let stand for 24 hours. Check lids and refrigerate any jars that are not sealed.

Easy Sweet Pickles

These classic pickles are quicker to make than most sweet pickles and have a lightly spiced sweet flavor with a touch of tanginess. They are sure to be a hit with sweet pickle lovers.

Makes four to five pint (500 mL) jars

● ● ●

Tips

For an interesting texture, use a crinkle cutter to slice the cucumbers.

Use cucumbers that are evenly sized and less than 1 inch (2.5 cm) in diameter for the best texture.

Depending on how these pickles get packed, you may get either four or five pint (500 mL) jars. It's best to prepare an 8-ounce (250 mL) jar as well, in case you don't have quite enough for the fifth pint.

Day 1

4 lbs	pickling cucumbers	2 kg
4 cups	ice cubes	1 L
3 tbsp	pickling or canning salt	45 mL

Day 2

3½ cups	packed brown sugar	875 mL
1 tbsp	mustard seeds	15 mL
1 tsp	whole allspice	5 mL
1 tsp	celery seeds	5 mL
¼ tsp	whole cloves	1 mL
3 cups	cider vinegar	750 mL

Day 1

1. Scrub cucumbers gently under running water. Cut crosswise into ¾-inch (2 cm) slices, trimming off ⅛ inch (3 mm) from each end. You should have about 12 cups (3 L).
2. In a large bowl, layer cucumbers, ice cubes and salt, using about one-quarter of each per layer. Add cold water to cover by about 1 inch (2.5 cm). Place a plate on top to weigh down cucumbers. Cover and let stand at a cool room temperature for at least 8 hours or for up to 18 hours.

Day 2

1. Prepare canner, jars and lids (see pages 7 to 8).
2. In a colander, working in batches, drain cucumbers and rinse well. Drain again and set aside.
3. In a large pot, combine brown sugar, mustard seeds, allspice, celery seeds, cloves and vinegar. Bring to a boil over medium heat, stirring often until sugar is dissolved. Boil for 1 minute. Add cucumbers and return to a boil, pressing occasionally to immerse cucumbers in liquid. Remove from heat.
4. Using a slotted spoon, pack cucumbers into hot jars, leaving 1 inch (2.5 cm) headspace. Pour in hot pickling liquid, leaving ½ inch (1 cm) headspace and dividing spices as evenly as possible. Remove air bubbles and adjust headspace as necessary by adding hot pickling liquid. Wipe rim and place hot lid disc on jar. Screw band down until fingertip-tight.
5. Place jars in canner and return to a boil. Process for 10 minutes. Turn off heat, remove canner lid and let jars stand in water for 5 minutes. Transfer jars to a towel-lined surface and let stand for 24 hours. Check lids and refrigerate any jars that are not sealed.

Aunt Thelma's Bread-and-Butter Pickles

This is the pickle that got me hooked on eating and eventually making pickles. It wasn't until I'd been making them for years that I discovered Thelma wasn't really my aunt but a distant relation by marriage. I also discovered that this is a pretty classic recipe, but I'd like to thank the late Aunt Thelma nonetheless for introducing our family to it.

Makes about five quart (1 L) jars

● ● ●

Tips

Feel free to make half a batch if you prefer and use pint (500 mL) jars. But be prepared! You might run out before the next cucumber season once everyone has a taste.

Don't pack these pickles too tightly. Make sure there's enough room for liquid — that's where the flavor comes from.

You may get 4 full quarts (1 L) and one partial one. Prepare a pint (500 mL) jar as well, in case you don't have enough for the fifth full quart.

Serving Suggestions

Serve with old (sharp) Cheddar cheese and grilled cheese sandwiches.

Make a liver pâté and pickle sandwich (trust me — it's delicious!).

Day 1		
8 lbs	pickling cucumbers	4 kg
½ cup	pickling salt	125 mL
Day 2		
3½ cups	granulated sugar	875 mL
3 tbsp	mustard seeds	45 mL
2 tbsp	celery seeds	25 mL
1 tsp	curry powder	5 mL
7 cups	white vinegar	1.75 L

Day 1

1. Scrub cucumbers gently under running water. Cut crosswise into ⅛-inch (3 mm) slices, trimming off ⅛ inch (3 mm) from each end.
2. In a large bowl, layer cucumbers and salt, using about one-quarter of each per layer. Add cold water to cover by about 1 inch (2.5 cm). Place a plate on top to weigh down cucumbers. Cover and let stand at a cool room temperature for at least 8 hours or for up to 18 hours.

Day 2

1. Prepare canner, jars and lids (see pages 7 to 8).
2. In a colander, working in batches, drain cucumbers and rinse well. Drain again and set aside.
3. In a large pot, combine sugar, mustard seeds, celery seeds, curry powder and vinegar. Bring to a boil over medium heat, stirring often until sugar is dissolved. Increase heat to medium-high. Add cucumbers and return to a boil, pressing occasionally to immerse cucumbers in liquid. Remove from heat.
4. Using a slotted spoon, pack cucumbers into hot jars, leaving 1 inch (2.5 cm) headspace. Pour in hot pickling liquid, leaving ½ inch (1 cm) headspace. Remove air bubbles and adjust headspace as necessary by adding hot pickling liquid. Wipe rim and place hot lid disc on jar. Screw band down until fingertip-tight.
5. Place jars in canner and return to a boil. Process for 10 minutes. Turn off heat, remove canner lid and let jars stand in water for 5 minutes. Transfer jars to a towel-lined surface and let stand for 24 hours. Check lids and refrigerate any jars that are not sealed.

Bread-and-Butter Pickles with Onion and Red Pepper

Cucumbers take on a sweet and savory flavor in these traditional pickles. They are beautiful, too, with the addition of red pepper and golden turmeric.

Makes about five quart (1 L) jars

● ● ●

Tips

To make nice thin strips of onion, cut in half lengthwise, then place flat side down and cut crosswise into thin slices.

If you have pickling liquid left over after filling the jars, whisk in a little vegetable oil and Dijon mustard to make a salad dressing or marinade for grilled vegetables.

Day 1

6 lbs	pickling cucumbers	3 kg
1 lb	onions, thinly sliced (about 4 cups/1 L)	500 g
½ cup	pickling salt	125 mL

Day 2

3½ cups	granulated sugar	875 mL
2 tbsp	mustard seeds	25 mL
2 tbsp	celery seeds	25 mL
¼ tsp	ground turmeric	1 mL
⅛ tsp	ground cloves (optional)	0.5 mL
7 cups	cider vinegar	1.75 L
3 cups	finely chopped red bell peppers (about 3 large)	750 mL

Day 1

1. Scrub cucumbers gently under running water. Cut crosswise into ¼-inch (0.5 cm) slices, trimming off ⅛ inch (3 mm) from each end.
2. In a large bowl, layer cucumbers, onions and salt, using about one-quarter of each per layer. Add cold water to cover by about 1 inch (2.5 cm). Place a plate on top to weigh down vegetables. Cover and let stand at a cool room temperature for at least 8 hours or for up to 18 hours.

Day 2

1. Prepare canner, jars and lids (see pages 7 to 8).
2. In a colander, working in batches, drain cucumber mixture and rinse well. Drain again and set aside.
3. In a large pot, combine sugar, mustard seeds, celery seeds, turmeric, cloves (if using) and vinegar. Bring to a boil over medium heat, stirring often until sugar is dissolved. Increase heat to medium-high. Add cucumber mixture and red peppers; return to a boil, pressing occasionally to immerse vegetables in liquid. Remove from heat.

4. Using a slotted spoon, pack vegetables into hot jars, leaving 1 inch (2.5 cm) headspace. Pour in hot pickling liquid, leaving $\frac{1}{2}$ inch (1 cm) headspace. Remove air bubbles and adjust headspace as necessary by adding hot pickling liquid. Wipe rim and place hot lid disc on jar. Screw band down until fingertip-tight.

5. Place jars in canner and return to a boil. Process for 10 minutes. Turn off heat, remove canner lid and let jars stand in water for 5 minutes. Transfer jars to a towel-lined surface and let stand for 24 hours. Check lids and refrigerate any jars that are not sealed.

Tip

Don't pack these pickles too tightly. Make sure there's enough room for liquid — that's where the flavor comes from.

Sweet and Tangy Gherkin Slices

Tiny sweet gherkins were one of my favorite pickles growing up — I couldn't get enough of them. I'm not sure if it was because of their sweetness or because they were made from those cute, tiny cucumbers. The tiny cucumbers can be hard to find, so I created this sliced version with the same fantastic flavor as the originals.

Makes about seven pint (500 mL) jars

● ● ●

Tip

Adding the sugar in stages prevents the cucumbers from wrinkling and having a spongy texture. They may wrinkle just slightly because of the high concentration of sugar and vinegar, but they will still have a crunchy texture.

Day 1

6 lbs	pickling cucumbers	3 kg
1/3 cup	pickling or canning salt	75 mL

Day 2

	Boiling water	
7	sticks cinnamon (each 3 inches/7.5 cm long)	7
3 cups	granulated sugar	750 mL
1 tbsp	mustard seeds	15 mL
2 tsp	whole allspice	10 mL
2 tsp	celery seeds	10 mL
6 cups	cider vinegar	1.5 L

Day 3

1 1/2 cups	packed brown sugar	375 mL

Day 4

1 1/2 cups	packed brown sugar	375 mL

Day 1

1. Scrub cucumbers gently under running water. Cut crosswise on a diagonal into 1/2-inch (1 cm) slices, trimming off 1/8 inch (3 mm) from each end. You should have about 18 cups (4.5 L).
2. In a large heatproof non-reactive bowl, gently combine cucumbers and salt. Add cold water to cover by 1 inch (2.5 cm). Place a plate on top to weigh down cucumbers. Cover and let stand at a cool room temperature for at least 12 hours or for up to 24 hours.

Day 2

1. In a colander, working in batches, drain cucumbers and rinse well. Rinse bowl, drain cucumbers again and return to the bowl. Pour boiling water over cucumbers and drain again. Return to the bowl and set aside.
2. In a pot, combine cinnamon sticks, granulated sugar, mustard seeds, allspice, celery seeds and vinegar. Bring to a boil over medium heat, stirring often until sugar is dissolved. Boil for 1 minute. Pour over cucumbers and let cool. Place a plate on top to weigh down cucumbers. Cover and let stand at a cool room temperature for at least 12 hours or for up to 24 hours.

Day 3

1. In a colander set over a large pot, working in batches if necessary, drain liquid from cucumbers. Rinse plate and bowl. Return cucumbers and cinnamon sticks to bowl and set aside.

2. Stir brown sugar into liquid. Bring liquid to a boil over medium heat, stirring often until sugar is dissolved. Boil for 1 minute. Pour over cucumbers and let cool. Place a plate on top to weigh down cucumbers. Cover and let stand at a cool room temperature for at least 12 hours or for up to 24 hours.

Day 4

1. Prepare canner, jars and lids (see pages 7 to 8).

2. In a colander set over a large pot, working in batches if necessary, drain liquid from cucumbers. Set cucumbers and cinnamon sticks aside. Stir brown sugar into liquid. Bring liquid to a boil over medium heat, stirring often until sugar is dissolved. Boil for about 20 minutes or until reduced by about one-third. Reduce heat to low and keep liquid hot.

3. Pack cucumbers and 1 cinnamon stick into each hot jar, leaving 1 inch (2.5 cm) headspace. Pour in hot pickling liquid, leaving $\frac{1}{2}$ inch (1 cm) headspace. Remove air bubbles and adjust headspace as necessary by adding hot pickling liquid. Wipe rim and place hot lid disc on jar. Screw band down until fingertip-tight.

4. Place jars in canner and return to a boil. Process for 10 minutes. Turn off heat, remove canner lid and let jars stand in water for 5 minutes. Transfer jars to a towel-lined surface and let stand for 24 hours. Check lids and refrigerate any jars that are not sealed.

Variations

Traditional Sweet Gherkin Pickles: Use 6 lbs (3 kg) tiny pickling cucumbers ($1\frac{1}{2}$ to 2 inches/ 4 to 5 cm long) in place of slices. Trim $\frac{1}{8}$ inch (3 mm) from the blossom end of each and leave whole. Pierce all over with a fork after rinsing on Day 2 in Step 1.

Vanilla-Scented Sweet Gherkins: Add $\frac{1}{4}$ vanilla bean, split lengthwise, with the cinnamon sticks. Discard the pod before filling jars.

Classic Icicle Pickles

There's a debate on whether the name of these pickles comes from their icicle shape, the cooling effect of the vinegar on the palate or the fact that the cucumbers are layered with ice to make them crisp. Regardless, these pickles are a classic to be enjoyed.

Makes about seven pint (500 mL) jars

• • •

Tip

To keep cucumber spears upright when packing them into jars, hold the jar with one hand in a silicone oven mitt, or with a dry towel, and tilt the jar toward you at about a 45-degree angle. Use the other hand or silicone-coated tongs to place the spears upright in the jar, leaning against the bottom inside wall. Gently shake the jar on the angle once it's full to help the pieces settle, adding more if necessary.

3 lbs	3½- to 4-inch (8.5 to 10 cm) pickling cucumbers	1.5 kg
4 cups	ice cubes	1 L
1½ cups	granulated sugar	375 mL
¼ cup	pickling or canning salt	50 mL
6 cups	white vinegar	1.5 L
1½ cups	water	375 mL
½ cup	finely chopped onion	125 mL
14	celery sticks (each 3 by ½ inch/7.5 by 1 cm)	14
	Mustard seeds	
	Celery seeds	

1. Scrub cucumbers gently under running water. Trim off ⅛ inch (3 mm) from each end and cut cucumbers lengthwise into quarters.
2. In a large bowl, layer cucumbers and ice cubes, using about one-quarter of each per layer. Add cold water to cover by about 1 inch (2.5 cm). Place a plate on top to weigh down cucumbers. Cover and let stand at a cool room temperature for 3 hours.
3. Meanwhile, prepare canner, jars and lids (see pages 7 to 8).
4. In a colander, working in batches, drain cucumbers. Set aside.
5. In a pot, combine sugar, salt, vinegar and 1½ cups (375 mL) water. Bring to a boil over medium heat, stirring often until sugar and salt are dissolved. Boil for 5 minutes. Reduce heat to low and keep liquid hot.
6. Working with one jar at a time, place a heaping tablespoon (15 mL) of onion in hot jar. Pack cucumbers and 2 celery sticks into jar, leaving 1 inch (2.5 cm) headspace. Add ½ tsp (2 mL) mustard seeds and ¼ tsp (1 mL) celery seeds. Pour in hot pickling liquid, leaving ½ inch (1 cm) headspace. Remove air bubbles and adjust headspace as necessary by adding hot pickling liquid. Wipe rim and place hot lid disc on jar. Screw band down until fingertip-tight.
7. Place jars in canner and return to a boil. Process for 10 minutes. Turn off heat, remove canner lid and let jars stand in water for 5 minutes. Transfer jars to a towel-lined surface and let stand for 24 hours. Check lids and refrigerate any jars that are not sealed.

Fire and Ice Pickles

The cooling tang of classic icicle pickles, a touch of sweetness and a hit of heat add up to exhilaration in these pickle spears.

Makes about seven pint (500 mL) jars

● ● ●

Tip

Fresh chile peppers can vary in heat, so taste a tiny piece (or a bigger piece if you're brave) to make sure your hot peppers are indeed hot.

3 lbs	3½- to 4-inch (8.5 to 10 cm) pickling cucumbers	1.5 kg
4 cups	ice cubes	1 L
1½ cups	granulated sugar	375 mL
¼ cup	pickling or canning salt	50 mL
5 cups	white vinegar	1.25 L
2½ cups	water	625 mL
7	long hot red chile peppers, seeded and cut lengthwise into 6 strips	7
	Mustard seeds	

1. Scrub cucumbers gently under running water. Trim off ⅛ inch (3 mm) from each end and cut cucumbers lengthwise into quarters.
2. In a large bowl, layer cucumbers and ice cubes, using about one-quarter of each per layer. Add cold water to cover by about 1 inch (2.5 cm). Place a plate on top to weigh down cucumbers. Cover and let stand at a cool room temperature for 3 hours.
3. Meanwhile, prepare canner, jars and lids (see pages 7 to 8).
4. In a colander, working in batches, drain cucumbers. Set aside.
5. In a pot, combine sugar, salt, vinegar and 2½ cups (625 mL) water. Bring to a boil over medium heat, stirring often until sugar and salt are dissolved. Boil for 5 minutes. Reduce heat to low and keep liquid hot.
6. Working with one jar at a time, pack cucumbers and 6 hot pepper strips into each hot jar, leaving 1 inch (2.5 cm) headspace. Add ½ tsp (2 mL) mustard seeds. Pour in hot pickling liquid, leaving ½ inch (1 cm) headspace. Remove air bubbles and adjust headspace as necessary by adding hot pickling liquid. Wipe rim and place hot lid disc on jar. Screw band down until fingertip-tight.
7. Place jars in canner and return to a boil. Process for 10 minutes. Turn off heat, remove canner lid and let jars stand in water for 5 minutes. Transfer jars to a towel-lined surface and let stand for 24 hours. Check lids and refrigerate any jars that are not sealed.

Diana's 9-Day Pickles

When I told my friend Laura Szamreta I was writing a book about pickles, she suggested I ask her mom, Diana Szamreta, for her 9-Day Pickle recipe, which is an essential part of all their family gatherings. My thanks to Diana for sharing this delicious sweet pickle recipe with me. Despite the name, these don't require you to attend to them every day, and they will actually be finished on the 10th day.

Makes about seven pint (500 mL) jars

• • •

Tips

Tiny cucumbers have thin skins and get soft and deteriorate quickly after they're picked, so make these pickles as soon after harvesting as possible.

If small cucumbers aren't available, use larger (2- to 4-inch/ 5 to 10 cm) pickling cucumbers and cut crosswise into ¾-inch (2 cm) slices.

Diana makes a "cheat sheet" with the basic step for each day to stick on the fridge door or a cupboard as a reminder while she's making these pickles.

Day 1

2 cups	pickling or canning salt	500 mL
12 cups	water	3 L
6 lbs	1½- to 2-inch (4 to 5 cm) pickling cucumbers (see tip, at left)	3 kg

Day 7

8 cups	water	2 L
2⅔ cups	white vinegar	650 mL
4	sticks cinnamon (each 3 inches/7.5 cm long), broken in half	4
8 cups	granulated sugar	2 L
2 tbsp	celery seeds	25 mL
1 tbsp	whole allspice	15 mL
6 cups	cider vinegar	1.5 L

Day 1

1. In a pot, combine salt and 12 cups (3 L) water. Bring to a boil over medium-high heat, stirring often until salt is dissolved. Let cool to room temperature.
2. Scrub cucumbers gently under running water. Trim off ⅛ inch (3 mm) from each end.
3. In a large non-reactive bowl, pour salt brine over cucumbers (it should cover them by at least 1 inch/2.5 cm). Place a plate on top to weigh down cucumbers. Cover and let stand at a cool room temperature for Day 2 and Day 3.

Day 4

1. Drain cucumbers and rinse bowl. Return cucumbers to the bowl and add fresh cold water to cover by at least 1 inch (2.5 cm). Place a plate on top to weigh down cucumbers. Cover and let stand at a cool room temperature for 1 day.

Day 5

1. Repeat Day 4.

Day 6

1. Repeat Day 4.

Day 7

1. Drain cucumbers. In a large pot, combine 8 cups (2 L) water and white vinegar. Bring to a boil over medium-high heat. Add cucumbers and return to a boil, gently stirring occasionally. Reduce heat and simmer for 1 to $1\frac{1}{2}$ hours or until cucumbers are translucent. Drain well, in batches as necessary, and place cucumbers in a clean large crock, glass or stainless steel bowl. Set aside.

2. In a clean large pot, combine cinnamon sticks, sugar, celery seeds, allspice and cider vinegar. Bring to a boil over medium heat, stirring often until sugar is dissolved. Boil for 5 minutes. Pour over cucumbers and let cool. Place a plate on top to weigh down cucumbers. Cover and let stand at a cool room temperature for 1 day.

Day 8

1. In a colander set over a large pot, working in batches if necessary, drain liquid from cucumbers. Rinse plate and crock. Return cucumbers and cinnamon sticks to crock. Bring liquid to a boil over high heat. Pour over cucumbers and let cool. Place a plate on top to weigh down cucumbers. Cover and let stand at a cool room temperature for 1 day.

Day 9

1. Repeat Day 8.

Day 10

1. Prepare canner, jars and lids (see pages 7 to 8).

2. Transfer cucumbers and liquid to a large pot. Bring to a boil over medium-high heat.

3. Using a slotted spoon, pack cucumbers and half a cinnamon stick into each hot jar, leaving 1 inch (2.5 cm) headspace. Pour in hot pickling liquid, leaving $\frac{1}{2}$ inch (1 cm) headspace. Remove air bubbles and adjust headspace as necessary by adding hot pickling liquid. Wipe rim and place hot lid disc on jar. Screw band down until fingertip-tight.

4. Place jars in canner and return to a boil. Process for 10 minutes. Turn off heat, remove canner lid and let jars stand in water for 5 minutes. Transfer jars to a towel-lined surface and let stand for 24 hours. Check lids and refrigerate any jars that are not sealed.

Serving Suggestions

Serve with extra-sharp Cheddar or other sharp cheese and crackers.

Chop these pickles and add to tuna salad or egg salad for a sweet and tangy touch.

Herb-Pickled Artichokes

Fresh artichokes are around for only a short time each year, so these herbed pickles are a nice way to preserve them.

Makes about six pint (500 mL) jars

● ● ●

Tips

Avoid putting your fingers in your mouth after handling the artichokes. There is an astringent substance in the leaves that will leave a bad taste in your mouth.

These pickles benefit from standing for at least 2 weeks after processing to allow the herb flavors to infuse the artichokes.

Serving Suggestions

For a quick dip, finely chop artichokes and stir into melted cream cheese with a little of the liquid.

To make marinated artichokes, after opening, add ½ cup (125 mL) olive oil per pint (500 mL) of pickled artichokes and refrigerate for at least 1 day or for up to 3 days. Use as directed in recipes or serve on an antipasto platter.

	Juice of 1 lemon	
7 lbs	baby globe artichokes	1.75 kg
6	cloves garlic, halved	6
¼ cup	pickling or canning salt	50 mL
3 cups	white vinegar	750 mL
2 cups	white wine vinegar	500 mL
6	small bay leaves	6
6	sprigs thyme (each 4 inches/ 10 cm long)	6
6	sprigs rosemary (each 4 inches/10 cm long)	6
6	sprigs parsley (each 4 inches/10 cm long)	6

1. Prepare canner, jars and lids (see pages 7 to 8).
2. In a large bowl, combine lemon juice and 8 cups (2 L) water. Working with one artichoke at a time, trim 1 inch (2.5 cm) off the top (see tip, page 45). Using a paring knife, cut off dark green outer leaves until you only have light green or yellow leaves. Using a vegetable peeler, trim off thick skin from stem. Cut each artichoke in half lengthwise and scoop out the fuzzy choke with a melon baller or spoon. Place heart in lemon water. Set aside.
3. In a large pot, combine garlic, salt, white vinegar, white wine vinegar and 2¾ cups (675 mL) water. Bring to a boil over medium-high heat, stirring often until salt is dissolved.
4. Drain artichokes well and add to pot. Return to a boil. Boil for 1 minute. Remove from heat.
5. Place 1 bay leaf and 1 sprig each of thyme, rosemary and parsley in each hot jar. Using a slotted spoon, pack artichokes into jars, leaving 1 inch (2.5 cm) headspace, and top with 2 pieces of garlic. Pour in hot pickling liquid, leaving ½ inch (1 cm) headspace. Remove air bubbles and adjust headspace as necessary by adding hot pickling liquid. Wipe rim and place hot lid disc on jar. Screw band down until fingertip-tight.
6. Place jars in canner and return to a boil. Process for 10 minutes. Turn off heat, remove canner lid and let jars stand in water for 5 minutes. Transfer jars to a towel-lined surface and let stand for 24 hours. Check lids and refrigerate any jars that are not sealed.

Hot Pickled Artichokes

A bit of heat combined with astringent lemon and artichokes provides a burst of flavor in these attractive pickles.

Makes about six pint (500 mL) jars

● ● ●

Tip

When working with artichokes, work quickly to avoid browning, dipping artichokes in lemon water as you work if they do start to brown.

Serving Suggestion

For a quick sauce, cut artichokes into chunks and add with liquid to pasta tossed with olive oil.

³⁄₄ cup	freshly squeezed lemon juice, divided	175 mL
7 lbs	baby globe artichokes	1.75 kg
6	dried small hot red chile peppers, crumbled	6
¹⁄₄ cup	pickling or canning salt	50 mL
4¹⁄₂ cups	white vinegar	1.125 L
	Black peppercorns	

1. Prepare canner, jars and lids (see pages 7 to 8).
2. In a large bowl, combine ¹⁄₄ cup (50 mL) of the lemon juice and 8 cups (2 L) water. Working with one artichoke at a time, trim 1 inch (2.5 cm) off the top (see tip, at left). Using a paring knife, cut off dark green outer leaves until you only have light green or yellow leaves. Using a vegetable peeler, trim off thick skin from stem. Cut each artichoke in half lengthwise and scoop out the fuzzy choke with a melon baller or spoon. Place heart in lemon water. Set aside.
3. In a large pot, combine chile peppers, salt, vinegar, the remaining lemon juice and 2³⁄₄ cups (675 mL) water. Bring to a boil over medium-high heat, stirring often until salt is dissolved.
4. Drain artichokes well and add to pot. Return to a boil. Boil for 1 minute. Remove from heat.
5. Place ¹⁄₄ tsp (1 mL) peppercorns in each hot jar. Using a slotted spoon, pack artichokes into jars, leaving 1 inch (2.5 cm) headspace. Pour in hot pickling liquid, leaving ¹⁄₂ inch (1 cm) headspace. Remove air bubbles and adjust headspace as necessary by adding hot pickling liquid. Wipe rim and place hot lid disc on jar. Screw band down until fingertip-tight.
6. Place jars in canner and return to a boil. Process for 10 minutes. Turn off heat, remove canner lid and let jars stand in water for 5 minutes. Transfer jars to a towel-lined surface and let stand for 24 hours. Check lids and refrigerate any jars that are not sealed.

Classic Pickled Asparagus

The delightful fresh flavor of this cherished spring vegetable is captured in a lightly seasoned pickle. The crispness and tang make them wonderful to add to a salad or to eat on their own.

Makes about four pint (500 mL) jars

● ● ●

Tips

For the best texture when pickling, choose medium-size spears of asparagus, about ½ inch (1 cm) thick.

Silicone-coated tongs work well to handle the hot asparagus when packing the jars. Be gentle with the spears so the tips don't get crushed.

● **Baking sheets or trays, lined with lint-free towels**

4 lbs	asparagus	2 kg
¼ cup	granulated sugar	50 mL
2 tbsp	pickling or canning salt	25 mL
3½ cups	white vinegar	875 mL
2½ cups	water	625 mL
4	cloves garlic, halved	4
	Mustard seeds	

1. Cut tip ends of asparagus into lengths about ¾ inch (2 cm) shorter than the height of jars. Reserve bottom ends for another use.
2. In a large pot of boiling salted water, in batches as necessary, blanch asparagus spears for about 30 seconds or until bright green. Immediately plunge into a large bowl or sink of ice water and let stand until well chilled, refreshing water as necessary to keep cold, for at least 30 minutes or for up to 1 hour.
3. Meanwhile, prepare canner, jars and lids (see pages 7 to 8).
4. Remove asparagus from water and spread out on towel-lined baking sheets to drain.
5. In a large pot, combine sugar, salt, vinegar and water. Bring to a boil over medium-high heat, stirring often until sugar and salt are dissolved. Boil for 1 minute. Add asparagus and simmer until heated through. Remove from heat.
6. Place 2 garlic halves and ½ tsp (2 mL) mustard seeds in each hot jar. Carefully pack asparagus, tips down, into jars, leaving room for liquid. Pour in hot pickling liquid, leaving ½ inch (1 cm) headspace. Remove air bubbles and adjust headspace as necessary by adding hot pickling liquid. Wipe rim and place hot lid disc on jar. Screw band down until fingertip-tight.
7. Place jars in canner and return to a boil. Process for 10 minutes. Turn off heat, remove canner lid and let jars stand in water for 5 minutes. Transfer jars to a towel-lined surface and let stand for 24 hours. Check lids and refrigerate any jars that are not sealed.

Dill Pickled Asparagus

In Ontario, where I live, the local asparagus is ready long before the big, flavorful dill heads are in bloom, so I created this recipe to capture the dill flavor from dried seeds combined with the freshness of parsley.

Makes about four pint (500 mL) jars

● ● ●

Tip

Use the ends of the asparagus to make soup or trim off the tough ends and sauté the tender pieces to serve as a side dish.

Serving Suggestion

Add chopped drained asparagus spears to potato salad.

● **Baking sheets or trays, lined with lint-free towels**

4 lbs	asparagus	2 kg
¼ cup	granulated sugar	50 mL
2 tbsp	pickling or canning salt	25 mL
1 tbsp	dill seeds	15 mL
3½ cups	cider vinegar	875 mL
2½ cups	water	625 mL
8	sprigs parsley	8

1. Cut tip ends of asparagus into lengths about ¾ inch (2 cm) shorter than the height of jars. Reserve bottom ends for another use.
2. In a large pot of boiling salted water, in batches as necessary, blanch asparagus spears for about 30 seconds or until bright green. Immediately plunge into a large bowl or sink of ice water and let stand until well chilled, refreshing water as necessary to keep cold, for at least 30 minutes or for up to 1 hour.
3. Meanwhile, prepare canner, jars and lids (see pages 7 to 8).
4. Remove asparagus from water and spread out on towel-lined baking sheets to drain.
5. In a large pot, combine sugar, salt, dill seeds, vinegar and water. Bring to a boil over medium-high heat, stirring often until sugar and salt are dissolved. Boil for 1 minute. Add asparagus and simmer until heated through. Remove from heat.
6. Place 2 sprigs of parsley in each hot jar. Carefully pack asparagus, tips down, into jars, leaving room for liquid. Pour in hot pickling liquid, leaving ½ inch (1 cm) headspace. Remove air bubbles and adjust headspace as necessary by adding hot pickling liquid. Wipe rim and place hot lid disc on jar. Screw band down until fingertip-tight.
7. Place jars in canner and return to a boil. Process for 10 minutes. Turn off heat, remove canner lid and let jars stand in water for 5 minutes. Transfer jars to a towel-lined surface and let stand for 24 hours. Check lids and refrigerate any jars that are not sealed.

Pepper and Thyme Pickled Asparagus

Sweet bell peppers, black pepper and fresh thyme combine to add Provençal flair to tender-crisp pickled asparagus.

Makes about four pint (500 mL) jars

● ● ● ●

Tip

When adding asparagus to the pickling liquid, arrange all the tips in the same direction to make it quicker to pick them up and pack them into jars. Silicone-coated tongs are perfect for this job.

Serving Suggestions

Add drained asparagus spears to a Niçoise salad instead of green beans, using the pickling liquid, whisked with olive oil and Dijon mustard, for the dressing.

Serve on a platter of cheeses, olives and pâtés for an easy appetizer.

● Baking sheets or trays, lined with lint-free towels

4 lbs	asparagus	2 kg
2 tbsp	pickling or canning salt	25 mL
2 tbsp	granulated sugar	25 mL
2 tsp	black peppercorns	10 mL
3 cups	water	750 mL
2 cups	white vinegar	500 mL
1 cup	white wine vinegar	250 mL
1	red bell pepper, cut lengthwise into thin strips (about 36)	1
16	sprigs thyme	16

1. Cut tip ends of asparagus into lengths about ¾ inch (2 cm) shorter than the height of jars. Reserve bottom ends for another use.
2. In a large pot of boiling salted water, in batches as necessary, blanch asparagus spears for about 30 seconds or until bright green. Immediately plunge into a large bowl or sink of ice water and let stand until well chilled, refreshing water as necessary to keep cold, for at least 30 minutes or for up to 1 hour.
3. Meanwhile, prepare canner, jars and lids (see pages 7 to 8).
4. Remove asparagus from water and spread out on towel-lined baking sheets to drain.
5. In a large pot, combine salt, sugar, peppercorns, water, white vinegar and white wine vinegar. Bring to a boil over medium-high heat, stirring often until salt and sugar are dissolved. Boil for 1 minute. Add asparagus and red pepper strips; simmer until heated through. Remove from heat.
6. Place 4 thyme sprigs in each hot jar. Carefully pack asparagus, tips down, and red pepper strips into jars, leaving room for liquid. Pour in hot pickling liquid, leaving ½ inch (1 cm) headspace and dividing peppercorns as evenly as possible. Remove air bubbles and adjust headspace as necessary by adding hot pickling liquid. Wipe rim and place hot lid disc on jar. Screw band down until fingertip-tight.
7. Place jars in canner and return to a boil. Process for 10 minutes. Turn off heat, remove canner lid and let jars stand in water for 5 minutes. Transfer jars to a towel-lined surface and let stand for 24 hours. Check lids and refrigerate any jars that are not sealed.

Spicy Pickled Green Beans

This recipe was inspired by the pickled green beans that are served in place of celery sticks in Bloody Caesar cocktails at the Fairmont Jasper Park Lodge in Alberta. They are also terrific in martinis or served as part of a pickle assortment or as a burger garnish.

Makes about six pint (500 mL) jars

• • •

Tip

For a slightly spicy pickled bean, use 3 chile peppers. Use up to 6 to increase the heat. Keep in mind that Scotch bonnet peppers will add quite a bit of heat — go for it if you like them fiery!

3 lbs	green beans	1.5 kg
1½ cups	granulated sugar	375 mL
3 tbsp	pickling or kosher salt	45 mL
1 tbsp	celery seeds	15 mL
1 tbsp	mustard seeds	15 mL
1½ tsp	cumin seeds	7 mL
4 cups	white vinegar	1 L
2½ cups	water	625 mL
1¼ cups	white wine vinegar	300 mL
3 to 6	hot chile peppers (such as long red chile, jalapeño or Scotch bonnet), seeded and quartered	3 to 6

1. Prepare canner, jars and lids (see pages 7 to 8).
2. Cut stems from green beans and discard any imperfect beans. Set aside.
3. In a large pot, combine sugar, salt, celery seeds, mustard seeds, cumin seeds, white vinegar, water and white wine vinegar. Bring to a boil over medium heat, stirring often until sugar and salt are dissolved. Increase heat to medium-high. Add beans and return to a boil, pressing occasionally to immerse beans in liquid. Remove from heat.
4. Divide chile pepper pieces among hot jars. Add beans, packing lightly but leaving room for liquid and leaving 1 inch (2.5 cm) headspace. Pour in hot pickling liquid, leaving ½ inch (1 cm) headspace. Remove air bubbles and adjust headspace as necessary by adding hot pickling liquid. Wipe rim and place hot lid disc on jar. Screw band down until fingertip-tight.
5. Place jars in canner and return to a boil. Process for 10 minutes. Turn off heat, remove canner lid and let jars stand in water for 5 minutes. Transfer jars to a towel-lined surface and let stand for 24 hours. Check lids and refrigerate any jars that are not sealed.

Sweet and Tangy Green Beans

Green beans are one of those crops that sometimes outperforms a gardener's expectations. Capture that bumper crop in this sweet, lightly spiced pickle to enjoy well after the summer harvest.

Makes about six pint (500 mL) jars

• • •

Tips

Silicone-coated tongs work well to handle the hot beans when packing the jars.

Six quarts (6 L) of green beans will give you about 3 lbs (1.5 kg).

3 lbs	green beans	1.5 kg
3	sticks cinnamon (each 3 inches/7.5 cm long), broken in half	3
2½ cups	granulated sugar	625 mL
2 tbsp	pickling or canning salt	25 mL
2 tbsp	mustard seeds	25 mL
1 tbsp	celery seeds	15 mL
1 tsp	whole allspice	5 mL
5 cups	cider vinegar	1.25 L
1½ cups	water	375 mL

1. Prepare canner, jars and lids (see pages 7 to 8).
2. Cut stems from green beans and discard any imperfect beans. Set aside.
3. In a large pot, combine cinnamon sticks, sugar, salt, mustard seeds, celery seeds, allspice, vinegar and water. Bring to a boil over medium heat, stirring often until sugar and salt are dissolved. Increase heat to medium-high. Add beans and return to a boil, pressing occasionally to immerse beans in liquid. Remove from heat.
4. Place half a cinnamon stick in each hot jar. Add beans, packing lightly but leaving room for liquid and leaving 1 inch (2.5 cm) headspace. Pour in hot pickling liquid, leaving ½ inch (1 cm) headspace. Remove air bubbles and adjust headspace as necessary by adding hot pickling liquid. Wipe rim and place hot lid disc on jar. Screw band down until fingertip-tight.
5. Place jars in canner and return to a boil. Process for 10 minutes. Turn off heat, remove canner lid and let jars stand in water for 5 minutes. Transfer jars to a towel-lined surface and let stand for 24 hours. Check lids and refrigerate any jars that are not sealed.

Mustard Pickled Green Beans

The old-fashioned version of this recipe had a thick, somewhat stodgy liquid and beans that were cooked until well-done. This modernized version has tender-crisp beans in a thin pickling liquid (allowing for better heat penetration during processing). Best of all, they still have that classic zesty and sweet taste you remember.

Makes about six pint (500 mL) jars

• • •

Tips

A mixture of green and yellow (wax) beans is nice in these pickles.

Because this is a lightly thickened liquid, upon standing it may separate slightly. Just stir the beans and liquid after opening the jar.

3 lbs	green beans	1.5 kg
3 cups	packed brown sugar	750 mL
⅓ cup	dry mustard	75 mL
1 tbsp	pickling or canning salt	15 mL
2 tsp	celery seeds	10 mL
2 tsp	ground turmeric	10 mL
3½ cups	white vinegar	875 mL
1½ cups	water	375 mL
1 cup	finely chopped onion	250 mL
¼ cup	cornstarch	50 mL
¼ cup	cold water	50 mL

1. Prepare canner, jars and lids (see pages 7 to 8).
2. Cut stems from green beans and discard any imperfect beans. Cut on a diagonal into 1- to 2-inch (2.5 to 5 cm) lengths, depending on the size of the beans. Set aside.
3. In a large pot, whisk together brown sugar, mustard, salt, celery seeds and turmeric. Gradually whisk in vinegar and 1½ cups (375 mL) water until smooth. Stir in onion. Bring to a boil over medium heat, stirring often until sugar and salt are dissolved. Increase heat to medium-high. Stir in beans and return to a boil, stirring occasionally.
4. Meanwhile, in a small bowl, whisk cornstarch into cold water. Stir into bean mixture and cook, stirring, for 2 minutes or until mixture is slightly thickened and liquid is no longer cloudy. Remove from heat.
5. Using a slotted spoon, pack beans into hot jars, leaving 1 inch (2.5 cm) headspace. Pour in hot pickling liquid, leaving ½ inch (1 cm) headspace. Remove air bubbles and adjust headspace as necessary by adding hot pickling liquid. Wipe rim and place hot lid disc on jar. Screw band down until fingertip-tight.
6. Place jars in canner and return to a boil. Process for 10 minutes. Turn off heat, remove canner lid and let jars stand in water for 5 minutes. Transfer jars to a towel-lined surface and let stand for 24 hours. Check lids and refrigerate any jars that are not sealed.

Dill Pickled Green and Yellow Beans

Crispy green beans take on dill flavor beautifully in these simple pickles. If you prefer, you can use all green or all yellow beans instead of a mixture.

Makes about six pint (500 mL) jars

• • •

Tip

Use mature beans for the best texture, but avoid tough, stringy ones. If the beans are too young, they may be limp after pickling. If they are over-mature (when the seeds bulge in the bean pod), they will be quite tough after pickling.

Serving Suggestion

Chop these pickles up and add to tuna salad, potato salad or a three-bean salad, using some of the pickling liquid for the dressing.

3 lbs	mixed green and yellow (wax) beans	1.5 kg
⅓ cup	granulated sugar	75 mL
2 tbsp	pickling or kosher salt	25 mL
6 cups	white vinegar	1.5 L
2¾ cups	water	675 mL
6	cloves garlic, quartered	6
6	dill sprigs	6
6	dill heads	6
	Dill seeds	

1. Prepare canner, jars and lids (see pages 7 to 8).
2. Cut stems from green beans and discard any imperfect beans. Set aside.
3. In a large pot, combine sugar, salt, vinegar and water. Bring to a boil over medium heat, stirring often until sugar and salt are dissolved. Increase heat to medium-high. Add beans and return to a boil, pressing occasionally to immerse beans in liquid. Remove from heat.
4. Place 4 garlic pieces, 1 dill sprig, 1 dill head and ¼ tsp (1 mL) dill seeds in each hot jar. Add beans, packing lightly but leaving room for liquid and leaving 1 inch (2.5 cm) headspace. Pour in hot pickling liquid, leaving ½ inch (1 cm) headspace. Remove air bubbles and adjust headspace as necessary by adding hot pickling liquid. Wipe rim and place hot lid disc on jar. Screw band down until fingertip-tight.
5. Place jars in canner and return to a boil. Process for 10 minutes. Turn off heat, remove canner lid and let jars stand in water for 5 minutes. Transfer jars to a towel-lined surface and let stand for 24 hours. Check lids and refrigerate any jars that are not sealed.

Spiced Pickled Baby Beets

Baby beets take a little more time to prepare, but they look like little glistening jewels once they're pickled. These have touch of spice and sweetness, with just enough tang that everyone will love them.

Makes seven or eight pint (500 mL) jars

● ● ●

Tips

If you have two large pots, in step 1, cook the beets in two batches for better control and even cooking.

This version is mildly spiced if you discard the spices. If you prefer a more pronounced spice flavor, open the spice bag and divide the whole spices among the jars before adding the liquid.

Variations

Hotly Spiced Pickled Baby Beets: Omit the cloves and add 2 tbsp (25 mL) chopped gingerroot, 1 tsp (5 mL) black peppercorns and a pinch of hot pepper flakes to the spice bag.

Spiced Pickled Beet Slices: Use medium beets (2- to 2½-inch/ 5 to 6 cm diameter) and follow step 1 on page 54 to cook and cut into slices. Proceed with step 2 in this recipe.

6 lbs	baby beets (1- to 1½-inch/2.5 to 4 cm diameter)	3 kg
3	sticks cinnamon (each 3 inches/7.5 cm long), broken in half	3
2 tsp	whole allspice	10 mL
1 tsp	whole cloves	5 mL
1¾ cups	packed brown sugar	425 mL
1 tbsp	pickling or canning salt	15 mL
4 cups	cider vinegar	1 L
2 cups	water	500 mL

1. Trim beets and place in a large pot (see tip, at left). Cover with cold water and bring to a boil over medium-high heat. Reduce heat and boil gently for about 30 minutes or until fork-tender. Immediately plunge into a large bowl or sink of cold water and let stand until well chilled, refreshing water as necessary to keep cold, for at least 30 minutes or for up to 1 hour. Peel off skins and set beets aside.
2. Meanwhile, prepare canner, jars and lids (see pages 7 to 8).
3. Place cinnamon sticks, allspice and cloves in the center of a square of triple-layered cheesecloth and tie into a spice bag.
4. In a clean large pot, combine spice bag, brown sugar, salt, vinegar and water. Bring to a boil over medium heat, stirring often until sugar and salt are dissolved. Reduce heat to low, cover and simmer for about 5 minutes or until liquid is flavorful. Increase heat to medium, add beets and return to a boil. Remove from heat and discard spice bag.
5. Using a slotted spoon, pack beets into hot jars, leaving about 1 inch (2.5 cm) headspace. Pour in hot pickling liquid, leaving ½ inch (1 cm) headspace. Remove air bubbles and adjust headspace as necessary by adding hot pickling liquid. Wipe rim and place hot lid disc on jar. Screw band down until fingertip-tight.
6. Place jars in canner and return to a boil. Process for 30 minutes. Turn off heat, remove canner lid and let jars stand in water for 5 minutes. Transfer jars to a towel-lined surface and let stand for 24 hours. Check lids and refrigerate any jars that are not sealed.

Classic Pickled Beet Slices

Beets are certainly the stars here — their natural sweetness and rich flavor comes through in this simple pickle.

Makes about seven pint (500 mL) jars

• • •

Tips

Medium beets, 2 to 2½ inches (5 to 6 cm) in diameter, work best because they are less tedious to peel and slice than small beets and the slices fit nicely in the mouth of the canning jars. If you have larger beets, cut the slices into half-moons, cut lengthwise in wedges so they fit better or use wide-mouth canning jars.

If you have two large pots, in step 1, cook the beets in two batches for better control and even cooking.

Variation

Pickled Beets with Onions: Reduce beets to 5½ lbs (2.75 kg) and add 1 lb (500 g) onions (about 4), halved and thinly sliced, with the sugar in step 3.

6 lbs	beets (see tip, at left)	3 kg
1⅓ cups	granulated sugar	325 mL
2 tsp	pickling or canning salt	10 mL
4 cups	white vinegar	1 L
2 cups	water	500 mL

1. Trim beets and place in a large pot (see tip, at left). Cover with cold water and bring to a boil over high heat. Reduce heat and boil gently for about 40 minutes or until fork-tender. Immediately plunge into a large bowl or sink of cold water and let stand until well chilled, refreshing water as necessary to keep cold, for at least 30 minutes or for up to 1 hour. Peel off skins and cut beets crosswise into ¼-inch (1 cm) slices. Set aside.

2. Meanwhile, prepare canner, jars and lids (see pages 7 to 8).

3. In a clean large pot, combine sugar, salt, vinegar and water. Bring to a boil over medium heat, stirring often until sugar and salt are dissolved. Boil for 1 minute. Increase heat to medium, add beets and return to a boil. Remove from heat.

4. Using a slotted spoon, pack beets into hot jars, leaving about 1 inch (2.5 cm) headspace. Pour in hot pickling liquid, leaving ½ inch (1 cm) headspace. Remove air bubbles and adjust headspace as necessary by adding hot pickling liquid. Wipe rim and place hot lid disc on jar. Screw band down until fingertip-tight.

5. Place jars in canner and return to a boil. Process for 30 minutes. Turn off heat, remove canner lid and let jars stand in water for 5 minutes. Transfer jars to a towel-lined surface and let stand for 24 hours. Check lids and refrigerate any jars that are not sealed.

Pretty Beet and Radish Pickles

Everyone's first reaction when they see these pickles is, "Ooh, pretty," The reaction when they taste the combination of sweet beets and a little heat from the radishes is, "Mmmmmm."

Makes five to six pint (500 mL) jars

• • •

Tips

Use evenly sized medium beets to make sure they cook in the same amount of time and fit nicely in the jars.

Depending on the size of the beet and radish wedges and how tightly you pack them, you may get 5 or 6 pint (500 mL) jars. Prepare an 8-ounce (250 mL) jar as well, in case you don't have enough to fill the sixth pint.

Serving Suggestion

Add to salads or as a garnish for hamburgers or sandwiches.

2½ lbs	beets (about 8)	1.25 kg
½ cup	granulated sugar	125 mL
1 tbsp	pickling or canning salt	15 mL
2¾ cups	white vinegar	675 mL
2½ cups	water	625 mL
1¼ lbs	red radishes, cut into thin wedges (about 4 cups/1 L)	625 g

1. Trim beets and place in a large pot. Cover with cold water and bring to a boil over medium-high heat. Reduce heat and boil gently for about 40 minutes or until fork-tender. Immediately plunge into a large bowl or sink of cold water and let stand until well chilled, refreshing water as necessary to keep cold, for at least 30 minutes or for up to 1 hour. Peel off skins and cut beets into thin wedges. Measure 6 cups (1.5 L).

2. Meanwhile, prepare canner, jars and lids (see pages 7 to 8).

3. In a clean large pot, combine sugar, salt, vinegar and water. Bring to a boil over medium-high heat, stirring often until sugar and salt are dissolved. Boil for 1 minute. Add beets and radishes; simmer until heated through. Remove from heat.

4. Using a slotted spoon, pack beets and radishes into hot jars, leaving about 1 inch (2.5 cm) headspace. Pour in hot pickling liquid, leaving ½ inch (1 cm) headspace. Remove air bubbles and adjust headspace as necessary by adding hot pickling liquid. Wipe rim and place hot lid disc on jar. Screw band down until fingertip-tight.

5. Place jars in canner and return to a boil. Process for 30 minutes. Turn off heat, remove canner lid and let jars stand in water for 5 minutes. Transfer jars to a towel-lined surface and let stand for 24 hours. Check lids and refrigerate any jars that are not sealed.

Pickled Coleslaw

This recipe is based on my favorite coleslaw, which my mom makes. The fresh coleslaw is terrific made ahead, so I figured it could easily be converted to a pickle recipe. Now you can have almost-ready coleslaw on hand all the time.

Makes about six pint (500 mL) or three quart (1 L) jars

• • •

Tips

Choose a cabbage that is heavy for its size and is very firm. Remove a couple of the outer layers to make sure you're using only the best leaves.

Use the coarse side of a box cheese grater to shred the carrots or use the shredding plate on a food processor.

When filling jars with liquid, pour it in a steady stream. When jar is half-full, use the bubble remover or spatula to press down cabbage mixture to make sure the liquid is getting to the bottom and there are no large air pockets.

• **Baking sheets or trays, lined with lint-free towels**

Day 1

4 lbs	green cabbage (about 1)	2 kg
4 cups	shredded carrots (about 8)	1 L
¼ cup	pickling or canning salt	50 mL

Day 2

3¾ cups	granulated sugar	925 mL
2 tbsp	celery seeds	25 mL
2 tbsp	mustard seeds	25 mL
½ tsp	freshly ground black pepper	2 mL
5 cups	cider vinegar	1.25 L

To Serve

Vegetable oil

Dijon mustard (optional)

Day 1

1. Cut cabbage lengthwise into 4 or 6 wedges. Cut out core. Cut each wedge crosswise into very thin slices. You should have about 22 cups (5.5 L).
2. In a large non-reactive bowl, combine cabbage, carrots and salt. Place a plate on top to weigh down vegetables. Cover and let stand at a cool room temperature for at least 12 hours or for up to 24 hours.

Day 2

1. Prepare canner, jars and lids (see pages 7 to 8).
2. In a colander, working in batches, drain vegetables and rinse well. Drain again, squeezing out as much liquid as possible. Spread out on towel-lined baking sheets to drain any remaining water.
3. In a pot, combine sugar, celery seeds, mustard seeds, pepper and vinegar. Bring to a boil over medium heat, stirring often until sugar is dissolved. Boil for 1 minute. Reduce heat to low and keep liquid hot.

4. Working with one jar at a time, pack vegetables into hot jars, leaving room for liquid and leaving 1 inch (2.5 cm) headspace. Pour in hot pickling liquid, leaving $\frac{1}{2}$ inch (1 cm) headspace. Remove air bubbles and adjust headspace as necessary by adding hot pickling liquid. Wipe rim and place hot lid disc on jar. Screw band down until fingertip-tight.

5. Place jars in canner and return to a boil. Process pint (500 mL) jars for 15 minutes and quart (1 L) jars for 20 minutes. Turn off heat, remove canner lid and let jars stand in water for 5 minutes. Transfer jars to a towel-lined surface and let stand for 24 hours. Check lids and refrigerate any jars that are not sealed.

To Serve

1. For every pint (500 mL) pickled coleslaw, stir in $\frac{1}{4}$ cup (50 mL) vegetable oil and 1 tsp (5 mL) Dijon mustard (if using) just before serving.

Serving Suggestions

Drain coleslaw and add it to a panini sandwich with corned beef or pastrami and Swiss cheese.

Add julienned red bell peppers and thinly sliced sweet onion to coleslaw just before serving to vary the flavor.

Classic Sauerkraut

Making your own sauerkraut does take time, but, amazingly, with just two ingredients, some water and natural fermentation, you can create a unique flavor that can't be beat.

Makes five to six pint (500 mL) jars

● ● ●

Tips

If you want to make a larger batch of sauerkraut, feel free to multiply the recipe in batches of 5 lbs (2.5 kg), up to 5 times. Just make sure you have a container large enough to allow for plenty of liquid and bubbling action above the cabbage during fermentation. The raw-pack method is best for larger batches; fill jars in batches that will fit into the canner.

To weigh down the plate, you can use sterilized glass jars with tight-fitting lids full of water or a large, heavy-duty sealable plastic bag filled with cooled extra brine (don't use water, just in case it leaks, because water would dilute the brine and ruin the fermentation).

Use a cotton apron instead of a towel to cover the crock — use the ties on the apron to wrap around the crock and secure the apron.

6 tbsp	pickling or canning salt, divided	90 mL
8 cups	water	2 L
5 lbs	green cabbage (about 1 large)	2.5 kg

Day 1

1. In a pot, combine 3 tbsp (45 mL) of the salt and the water. Bring to a boil over medium-high heat, stirring often until salt is dissolved. Boil for 1 minute. Let cool to room temperature.
2. Meanwhile, cut cabbage lengthwise into 6 or 8 wedges. Cut out core. Cut each wedge crosswise into very thin slices. You should have about 28 cups (7 L).
3. In a large crock, glass bowl or other non-reactive container, combine cabbage and the remaining salt; let stand for about 15 minutes or until wilted.
4. Pour brine over wilted cabbage, pressing to immerse cabbage. The liquid should cover the cabbage by at least 1 inch (2.5 cm). Add extra brine (see tip, page 60), if necessary. Place a plate on top to weigh down cabbage. Fill a couple of glass jars with water (see tip, at left) and place on plate to keep it weighted. Cover with a lint-free towel or several layers of cheesecloth. Let stand at room temperature (70°F to 75°F/21°C to 23°C) for 3 to 6 weeks.

During Fermentation

1. Check every few days to make sure cabbage is fermenting. You should see bubbles form, and the aroma will change. Skim off any scum that forms and add extra brine (see tip, page 60) if necessary to make sure cabbage is covered. If there are any signs of mold or a foul aroma, discard cabbage and liquid. Let ferment until bubbles stop and sauerkraut is well flavored.

Final Day

1. Prepare canner, jars and lids (see pages 7 to 8).

Raw Pack

1. Pack sauerkraut and brine into hot jars, packing sauerkraut lightly but ensuring that there is enough brine to keep it moist, leaving ½ inch (1 cm) headspace. Add extra brine (see tip, page 60) if necessary to fill jars. Remove air bubbles and adjust headspace as necessary by adding brine. Wipe rim and place hot lid disc on jar. Screw band down until fingertip-tight.

2. Place jars in canner and return to a boil. Process for 20 minutes. Turn off heat, remove canner lid and let jars stand in water for 5 minutes. Transfer jars to a towel-lined surface and let stand for 24 hours. Check lids and refrigerate any jars that are not sealed.

Hot Pack

1. In a large pot, heat sauerkraut and brine over medium-high heat, stirring often, just until brine starts to simmer. Do not boil. Remove from heat.

2. Pack hot sauerkraut and brine into hot jars, packing sauerkraut lightly but ensuring that there is enough brine to keep it moist, leaving ½ inch (1 cm) headspace. Add heated extra brine (see tip, page 60) if necessary to fill jars. Remove air bubbles and adjust headspace as necessary by adding hot brine. Wipe rim and place hot lid disc on jar. Screw band down until fingertip-tight.

3. Place jars in canner and return to a boil. Process for 10 minutes. Turn off heat, remove canner lid and let jars stand in water for 5 minutes. Transfer jars to a towel-lined surface and let stand for 24 hours. Check lids and refrigerate any jars that are not sealed.

Tip

Successful fermentation requires the correct air temperature. If the air is too cool, fermentation will be very slow or may not occur at all, which can allow mold to form. If the air is too warm, the sauerkraut can become over-fermented and have a soft, unpleasant texture and flavor. Place a thermometer next to the crock and check it often, relocating the sauerkraut if necessary.

Variation

Hot Pepper Sauerkraut: On the final day, trim stems from 6 long hot red chile peppers and cut in half lengthwise. Remove core and seeds. Cut peppers crosswise into thin slices. Stir into sauerkraut until evenly distributed. Proceed with filling and processing jars. Let sauerkraut stand for 1 week before serving to allow hot pepper flavor to blend.

Purple Sauerkraut

This version of the classic made from red cabbage — or purple cabbage, as it's sometimes called — is really a bright fuchsia color because of the reaction between the pigment in the cabbage and the acid formed during fermentation. It is sure to perk up your Reuben sandwich, hot dog or grilled sausage.

Makes five to six pint (500 mL) jars

● ● ●

Tips

You may need extra brine to cover the cabbage, to add later in the fermenting process if too much evaporates or is skimmed off, or when canning. Use 1½ tbsp (22 mL) pickling or canning salt and 4 cups (1 L) water, prepared according to step 1 (or multiply in the same proportions for more). Extra brine can be stored in an airtight container in the refrigerator for up to 2 months. Let warm to room temperature before adding to crock.

Red cabbage is drier than green cabbage, so tossing it with salt as you do for traditional sauerkraut doesn't create as much liquid. It is better to make a stronger brine to make sure there is enough salt and liquid to facilitate fermentation.

6 tbsp	pickling or canning salt	90 mL
16 cups	water	4 L
5 lbs	red (purple) cabbage (about 2)	2.5 kg

Day 1

1. In a pot, combine salt and water. Bring to a boil over medium-high heat, stirring often until salt is dissolved. Boil for 1 minute. Let cool to room temperature.
2. Meanwhile, cut cabbages lengthwise into 4 or 6 wedges. Cut out core. Cut each wedge crosswise into very thin slices. You should have about 28 cups (7 L).
3. In a large crock, glass bowl or other non-reactive container, pour brine over cabbage, pressing to immerse cabbage. The liquid should cover the cabbage by at least 1 inch (2.5 cm). Add extra brine (see tip, at left), if necessary. Place a plate on top to weigh down cabbage. Fill a couple of glass jars with water (see tip, at right) and place on plate to keep it weighted. Cover with a lint-free towel or several layers of cheesecloth. Let stand at room temperature (70°F to 75°F/21°C to 23°C) for 3 to 6 weeks.

During Fermentation

1. Check every few days to make sure cabbage is fermenting. You should see bubbles form, and the aroma will change. Skim off any scum that forms and add extra brine (see tip, at left) if necessary to make sure cabbage is covered. If there are any signs of mold or a foul aroma, discard cabbage and liquid. Let ferment until bubbles stop and sauerkraut is well flavored.

Final Day

1. Prepare canner, jars and lids (see pages 7 to 8).

Raw Pack

1. Pack sauerkraut and brine into hot jars, packing sauerkraut lightly but ensuring that there is sufficient brine to keep it moist, leaving ½ inch (1 cm) headspace. Add extra brine (see tip, at left) if necessary to fill jars. Remove air bubbles and adjust headspace as necessary by adding brine. Wipe rim and place hot lid disc on jar. Screw band down until fingertip-tight.

2. Place jars in canner and return to a boil. Process for 20 minutes. Turn off heat, remove canner lid and let jars stand in water for 5 minutes. Transfer jars to a towel-lined surface and let stand for 24 hours. Check lids and refrigerate any jars that are not sealed.

Hot Pack

1. In a large pot, heat sauerkraut and brine over medium-high heat, stirring often, just until brine starts to simmer. Do not boil. Remove from heat.

2. Pack hot sauerkraut with brine into hot jars, packing sauerkraut lightly but ensuring that there is sufficient brine to keep it moist, leaving ½ inch (1 cm) headspace. Add heated extra brine (see tip, at left) if necessary to fill jars. Remove air bubbles and adjust headspace as necessary by adding hot brine. Wipe rim and place hot lid disc on jar. Screw band down until fingertip-tight.

3. Place jars in canner and return to a boil. Process for 10 minutes. Turn off heat, remove canner lid and let jars stand in water for 5 minutes. Transfer jars to a towel-lined surface and let stand for 24 hours. Check lids and refrigerate any jars that are not sealed.

Tips

Use an old plate that you're not particularly fond of to weigh down the cabbage. The pigment from the cabbage can stain the plate, especially if there are any cracks in the finish. Alternatively, place the plate in a large resealable plastic bag and seal it, squeezing out any air, to protect it.

To weigh down the plate, you can use sterilized glass jars with tight-fitting lids full of water or a large, heavy-duty sealable plastic bag filled with cooled extra brine (don't use water, just in case it leaks, because water would dilute the brine and ruin the fermentation).

Sweet and Sour Pickled Cabbage

Cabbage is popular in many Eastern European cuisines as the base for delicious salads. This pickle is like cabbage salad in a jar. The recipe was suggested by a friend and fellow professional home economist, Teresa Makarewicz, who remembers pickles like this from her Polish family gatherings.

Makes about six pint (500 mL) or three quart (1 L) jars

● ● ●

Tips

To make a spice bag, cut a 4-inch (10 cm) square piece of triple-layered cheesecloth. Place the pickling spice in the center of the square and bring the edges together into a bundle. Tie tightly with kitchen string. Alternatively, use a large mesh tea ball.

When filling jars with liquid, pour it in a steady stream. When jar is half-full, use the bubble remover or spatula to press down cabbage mixture to make sure the liquid is getting to the bottom and there are no large air pockets.

- Baking sheets or trays, lined with lint-free towels

Day 1

3½ lbs	green cabbage (about 1)	1.75 kg
3 cups	diced celery	750 mL
3 cups	thinly sliced red or green bell peppers	750 mL
2 cups	thinly sliced onions	500 mL
¼ cup	pickling or canning salt	50 mL

Day 2

½ cup	minced hot red or green chile peppers	125 mL
4 cups	granulated sugar	1 L
3 tbsp	pickling spice, tied in a spice bag (see tip, at left)	45 mL
1 tsp	ground turmeric	5 mL
5 cups	white vinegar	1.25 L

Day 1

1. Cut cabbage lengthwise into 4 or 6 wedges. Cut out core. Cut each wedge crosswise into very thin slices. You should have about 18 cups (4.5 L).
2. In a large non-reactive bowl, combine cabbage, celery, bell peppers, onions and salt. Place a plate on top to weigh down vegetables. Cover and let stand at a cool room temperature for at least 12 hours or for up to 24 hours.

Day 2

1. Prepare canner, jars and lids (see pages 7 to 8).
2. In a colander, working in batches, drain vegetables and rinse well. Drain again, squeezing out as much liquid as possible. Spread out on towel-lined baking sheets to drain any remaining water.
3. In a pot, combine chile peppers, sugar, pickling spice, turmeric and vinegar. Bring to a boil over medium heat, stirring often until sugar is dissolved. Boil for 1 minute. Reduce heat to low, cover and simmer for 5 minutes or until liquid is flavorful. Discard spice bag. Keep liquid hot.

4. Working with one jar at a time, pack vegetables into hot jars, leaving room for liquid and leaving 1 inch (2.5 cm) headspace. Pour in hot pickling liquid, leaving $\frac{1}{2}$ inch (1 cm) headspace and dividing chile peppers as evenly as possible. Remove air bubbles and adjust headspace as necessary by adding hot pickling liquid. Wipe rim and place hot lid disc on jar. Screw band down until fingertip-tight.

5. Place jars in canner and return to a boil. Process pint (500 mL) jars for 15 minutes and quart (1 L) jars for 20 minutes. Turn off heat, remove canner lid and let jars stand in water for 5 minutes. Transfer jars to a towel-lined surface and let stand for 24 hours. Check lids and refrigerate any jars that are not sealed.

Serving Suggestions

Use instead of sauerkraut on hot dogs or sausages or in grilled Reuben or other panini sandwiches.

Serve as a salad with grilled meats or poultry.

Pickled Red Cabbage and Apple

This pickle is perfect to serve cold, or heated up for a ready-made braised cabbage dish.

Makes about eight pint (500 mL) jars

● ● ●

Tips

To julienne apples, use a julienne vegetable peeler or the julienne blade on a mandoline. Alternatively, you can cut apples into thin slices around the core, then stack 3 or 4 slices at a time and cut crosswise into thin strips. You'll need about 5 large apples to get 4 cups (1 L) julienned.

When filling jars with liquid, pour it in a steady stream. When jar is half-full, use the bubble remover or spatula to press down cabbage mixture to make sure the liquid is getting to the bottom and there are no large air pockets.

Serving Suggestion

In a large skillet, heat a thin layer of vegetable oil over medium-high heat. Add drained pickled cabbage and apples; sauté until hot, adding a little of the pickling liquid to moisten.

● Baking sheets or trays, lined with lint-free towels

Day 1

4 lbs	red cabbage (about 2)	2 kg
¼ cup	pickling or canning salt	50 mL

Day 2

4 cups	julienned peeled tart cooking apples	1 L
2⅔ cups	granulated sugar	650 mL
1½ tsp	caraway seeds (optional)	7 mL
1½ tsp	freshly ground black pepper	7 mL
5¼ cups	white vinegar	1.3 L
2⅔ cups	water	650 mL

Day 1

1. Cut cabbages lengthwise into 4 or 6 wedges. Cut out cores. Cut each wedge crosswise into very thin slices. You should have about 22 cups (5.5 L).
2. In a large non-reactive bowl, combine cabbage and salt. Place a plate on top to weigh down cabbage. Cover and let stand at a cool room temperature for 12 to 24 hours.

Day 2

1. Prepare canner, jars and lids (see pages 7 to 8).
2. In a colander, working in batches, drain cabbage and rinse well. Drain again, squeezing out as much liquid as possible. Spread out on towel-lined baking sheets to drain any remaining water. Sprinkle apples over cabbage, dividing as evenly as possible, and mix gently to combine. Set aside.
3. In a pot, combine sugar, caraway seeds (if using), pepper, vinegar and water. Bring to a boil over medium heat, stirring often until sugar is dissolved. Boil for 1 minute. Reduce heat to low and keep liquid hot.
4. Working with one jar at a time, pack cabbage and apples into hot jars, leaving room for liquid and leaving 1 inch (2.5 cm) headspace. Pour in hot pickling liquid, leaving ½ inch (1 cm) headspace. Remove air bubbles and adjust headspace as necessary by adding hot pickling liquid. Wipe rim and place hot lid disc on jar. Screw band down until fingertip-tight.
5. Place jars in canner and return to a boil. Process for 15 minutes. Turn off heat, remove canner lid and let jars stand in water for 5 minutes. Transfer jars to a towel-lined surface and let stand for 24 hours. Check lids and refrigerate any jars that are not sealed.

Dill Pickled Carrot Sticks

These are among the easiest pickles to make, and you'll be delighted with what the dilly taste and tangy crunch do to a humble carrot stick.

Makes about six pint (500 mL) jars

3½ lbs	carrots (15 to 20)	1.75 kg
⅓ cup	granulated sugar	75 mL
2 tbsp	pickling or kosher salt	25 mL
6 cups	white vinegar	1.5 L
2¾ cups	water	675 mL
6	dill heads	6
6	dill sprigs	6
	Dill seeds	

Tips

When cutting the carrots, it is easiest to cut them crosswise into 4-inch (10 cm) lengths and then into sticks. You may just need to cut the narrow end of the carrot in half lengthwise; it's okay not to have squared-off sticks.

Avoid very large carrots, which often have a woody core and make unpleasant pickles.

The combination of dill sprigs, dill heads and dill seeds gives these pickles a good dilly flavor. If you don't have dill heads, use 2 large dill sprigs per jar.

1. Prepare canner, jars and lids (see pages 7 to 8).
2. Cut carrots into 4- by ½- by ½-inch (10 by 1 by 1 cm) sticks, or the length that will fit in jars allowing for 1 inch (2.5 cm) headspace. Set aside.
3. In a pot, combine sugar, salt, vinegar and water. Bring to a boil over medium-high heat, stirring often until sugar and salt are dissolved. Boil for 1 minute. Reduce heat to low and keep liquid hot.
4. Working with one jar at a time, place 1 dill head in hot jar. Pack carrot sticks into jar, leaving room for liquid. Add 1 dill sprig and ¼ tsp (1 mL) dill seeds. Pour in hot pickling liquid, leaving ½ inch (1 cm) headspace. Remove air bubbles and adjust headspace as necessary by adding hot pickling liquid. Wipe rim and place hot lid disc on jar. Screw band down until fingertip-tight.
5. Place jars in canner and return to a boil. Process for 10 minutes. Turn off heat, remove canner lid and let jars stand in water for 5 minutes. Transfer jars to a towel-lined surface and let stand for 24 hours. Check lids and refrigerate any jars that are not sealed.

Spicy Carrot Pickles

These pickles have just enough spice and tang to add interest, but not so much that they overpower the natural sweetness of fresh-picked carrots.

Makes six to seven pint (500 mL) jars

● ● ●

Tips

Avoid very large carrots, which often have a woody core and make unpleasant pickles.

The garlic may turn blue in the pickling liquid. It's perfectly safe to eat; the color change is just a reaction between the minerals in the garlic and the acid from the vinegar.

5 lbs	carrots (22 to 30)	2.5 kg
2	bay leaves	2
1 cup	granulated sugar	250 mL
2 tbsp	mustard seeds	25 mL
1 tbsp	pickling or canning salt	15 mL
½ tsp	hot pepper flakes	2 mL
5 cups	cider vinegar	1.25 L
2¼ cups	water	550 mL
6 or 7	cloves garlic, halved	6 or 7

1. Prepare canner, jars and lids (see pages 7 to 8).
2. Cut carrots crosswise on a slight diagonal into ¼-inch (1 cm) slices. Cut any slices that are larger than a quarter into half-moons. You should have about 12 cups (3 L). Set aside.
3. In a large pot, combine bay leaves, sugar, mustard seeds, salt, hot pepper flakes, vinegar and water. Bring to a boil over medium heat, stirring often until sugar is dissolved. Increase heat to medium-high. Add carrots and return to a simmer. Remove from heat. Discard bay leaves.
4. Place 1 piece of garlic in each hot jar. Using a slotted spoon, pack carrots into jars, leaving room for liquid and leaving 1 inch (2.5 cm) headspace. Add another piece of garlic. Pour in hot pickling liquid, leaving ½ inch (1 cm) headspace. Remove air bubbles and adjust headspace as necessary by adding hot pickling liquid. Wipe rim and place hot lid disc on jar. Screw band down until fingertip-tight.
5. Place jars in canner and return to a boil. Process for 10 minutes. Turn off heat, remove canner lid and let jars stand in water for 5 minutes. Transfer jars to a towel-lined surface and let stand for 24 hours. Check lids and refrigerate any jars that are not sealed.

Classic Pickled Cauliflower

Tender-crisp cauliflower florets take on mildly spiced pickling liquid wonderfully in this classic pickle. They are sure to add interest to a pickle assortment or as part of a salad.

Makes about six pint (500 mL) jars

● ● ●

Tip

The cauliflower may turn pink once pickled. There is nothing wrong with the pickles; it's just a reaction between the acid and the pigment in the cauliflower.

Serving Suggestion

Add drained pickled cauliflower to a pasta salad or a bean salad, using some of the pickling liquid whisked with oil as the dressing.

2	large heads cauliflower (about 5 lbs/2.5 kg)	2
2½ cups	granulated sugar	625 mL
2 tbsp	mustard seeds	25 mL
1 tbsp	pickling or canning salt	15 mL
2 tsp	celery seeds	10 mL
¼ tsp	hot pepper flakes	1 mL
5 cups	white vinegar	1.25 L
1 cup	water	250 mL

1. Prepare canner, jars and lids (see pages 7 to 8).
2. Trim off all leaves from heads of cauliflower. Cut cauliflower into 1- to 1½-inch (2.5 to 4 cm) florets, trimming off thick stems. You should have about 18 cups (4.5 L). Set aside.
3. In a large pot, combine sugar, mustard seeds, salt, celery seeds, hot pepper flakes, vinegar and water. Bring to a boil over medium heat, stirring often until sugar and salt are dissolved. Boil for 1 minute. Add cauliflower and return to a boil, pressing occasionally to immerse cauliflower in liquid as it wilts. Remove from heat.
4. Using a slotted spoon, pack cauliflower into hot jars, leaving 1 inch (2.5 cm) headspace. Pour in hot pickling liquid, leaving ½ inch (1 cm) headspace. Remove air bubbles and adjust headspace as necessary by adding hot pickling liquid. Wipe rim and place hot lid disc on jar. Screw band down until fingertip-tight.
5. Place jars in canner and return to a boil. Process for 10 minutes. Turn off heat, remove canner lid and let jars stand in water for 5 minutes. Transfer jars to a towel-lined surface and let stand for 24 hours. Check lids and refrigerate any jars that are not sealed.

Curry Pickled Cauliflower

Curry and cauliflower are a famous flavor combination, so it's a natural for this pleasantly spiced pickle.

Makes about six pint (500 mL) jars

● ● ●

Variation

If you like a touch of heat with your curry, add ½ tsp (2 mL) hot pepper flakes with the spices or use 3 long hot green or red chile peppers, seeded and halved lengthwise, and add one half to each jar with the garlic in step 4.

Serving Suggestion

Add chopped drained cauliflower to tuna salad or whole florets to a potato salad, using some of the pickling liquid mixed with mayonnaise for the dressing.

2	large heads cauliflower (about 5 lbs/2.5 kg)	2
6	cloves garlic, halved	6
1 tbsp	finely chopped gingerroot	15 mL
1 cup	granulated sugar	250 mL
1 tbsp	pickling or canning salt	15 mL
2 tsp	curry powder	10 mL
½ tsp	cumin seeds	2 mL
⅛ tsp	ground turmeric	0.5 mL
5 cups	white vinegar	1.25 L
2¼ cups	water	550 mL

1. Prepare canner, jars and lids (see pages 7 to 8).

2. Trim off all leaves from heads of cauliflower. Cut cauliflower into 1- to 1½-inch (2.5 to 4 cm) florets, trimming off thick stems. You should have about 18 cups (4.5 L). Set aside.

3. In a large pot, combine garlic, ginger, sugar, salt, curry powder, cumin seeds, turmeric, vinegar and water. Bring to a boil over medium heat, stirring often until sugar and salt are dissolved. Reduce heat to low, cover and simmer for 5 minutes or until liquid is flavorful. Increase heat to medium-high. Add cauliflower and return to a boil, pressing occasionally to immerse cauliflower in liquid as it wilts. Remove from heat.

4. Using a slotted spoon, pack cauliflower into hot jars, leaving 1 inch (2.5 cm) headspace and adding 2 pieces of garlic to each jar. Pour in hot pickling liquid, leaving ½ inch (1 cm) headspace. Remove air bubbles and adjust headspace as necessary by adding hot pickling liquid. Wipe rim and place hot lid disc on jar. Screw band down until fingertip-tight.

5. Place jars in canner and return to a boil. Process for 10 minutes. Turn off heat, remove canner lid and let jars stand in water for 5 minutes. Transfer jars to a towel-lined surface and let stand for 24 hours. Check lids and refrigerate any jars that are not sealed.

Pickled Baby Corn

Pickling baby corn was once a way to use up "sucker" cobs that grew on a stalk and were picked off to allow the big cobs to develop. Most commercially grown corn varieties don't have sucker cobs now, but if you grown your own or find a farm that will sell you some baby cobs, this pickle is a lovely, simple way to preserve them.

Makes about six pint (500 mL) jars

• • •

Tips

For tender cobs, baby corn should be harvested the day the silk appears. The cobs should be no longer than 4 inches (10 cm) and no thicker than ½ inch (1 cm) in diameter.

You'll need about 15 baby cobs per pint (500 mL) jar, but it is handy to have a few extra prepared just in case you can fit more into the jars.

When working in batches to blanch the corn in step 3, be sure to let the water return to a boil before adding the next batch.

90	baby corn cobs, (approx., see tips, at left)	90
2½ cups	granulated sugar	625 mL
2 tbsp	pickling or canning salt	25 mL
5½ cups	white vinegar	1.375 L
1¼ cups	water	300 mL

1. Prepare canner, jars and lids (see pages 7 to 8).
2. Carefully shuck husks from corn cobs, being careful not to break the tender cobs. Remove silks and trim ends.
3. In a large pot of boiling water, in batches, blanch corn for 3 minutes. Immediately plunge into a large bowl or sink of ice-cold water and let stand until well chilled, refreshing water as necessary to keep cold. In a colander, working in batches, drain well. Set aside.
4. In a clean pot, combine sugar, salt, vinegar and water. Bring to a boil over medium heat, stirring often until sugar and salt are dissolved. Boil for 1 minute. Reduce heat to low and keep liquid hot.
5. Working with one jar at a time, pack corn into hot jars, alternating tips up and down to pack tightly but leaving room for liquid and leaving 1 inch (2.5 cm) headspace. Pour in hot pickling liquid, leaving ½ inch (1 cm) headspace. Remove air bubbles and adjust headspace as necessary by adding hot pickling liquid. Wipe rim and place hot lid disc on jar. Screw band down until fingertip-tight.
6. Place jars in canner and return to a boil. Process for 15 minutes. Turn off heat, remove canner lid and let jars stand in water for 5 minutes. Transfer jars to a towel-lined surface and let stand for 24 hours. Check lids and refrigerate any jars that are not sealed.

Herb-Pickled Eggplant

This recipe is based on one given to me by a friend, Airin Stephens. The original, passed down for generations, had no quantities and fairly vague instructions. This is my interpretation of the Italian favorite.

Makes about six pint (500 mL) jars

● ● ●

Tips

Small or medium eggplants are best for pickling. If they are too large, they tend to get spongy and have large seeds.

To weigh down the plate, you can use sterilized glass jars with tight-fitting lids full of water or a large, heavy-duty sealable plastic bag filled with cooled extra brine (don't use water, just in case it leaks, because water would dilute the brine and ruin the fermentation). To make brine to fill bags, in a pot, combine 3 tbsp (45 mL) pickling or canning salt and 8 cups (2 L) water. Bring to a boil over medium-high heat, stirring until salt is dissolved. Boil for 1 minute, then let cool to room temperature.

● Baking sheets or trays, lined with lint-free towels

Day 1

7½ lbs	eggplants (about 6)	3.75 kg
⅓ cup	pickling or canning salt	75 mL

Day 2

½ cup	finely chopped hot red chile peppers (preferably pepperoncini)	125 mL
2 tbsp	minced garlic (about 6 cloves)	25 mL
4 cups	white vinegar	1 L
1 cup	water	250 mL
½ cup	chopped fresh mint	125 mL
½ cup	chopped fresh oregano	125 mL

Day 1

1. Trim off stems and peel eggplants. Cut lengthwise into ½-inch (1 cm) slices. Cut crosswise into ½-inch (1 cm) strips.
2. In a large non-reactive bowl, toss about one-third of the eggplant with one-third of the salt. Add half of the remaining eggplant and salt and toss to combine. Repeat with the remaining eggplant and salt, pressing to help release the liquid. Place a plate on top to weigh down eggplant. Fill a couple of glass jars with water (see tip, at left) and place on plate to keep it weighted. Cover and let stand at a cool room temperature for at least 12 hours or for up to 24 hours.

Day 2

1. In a colander, working in batches, drain eggplant, squeezing out as much liquid as possible, and rinse under running water. Drain again. Place on a lint-free towel and squeeze out excess moisture, using a dry towel for subsequent batches. Spread out on towel-lined baking sheets to drain any remaining water.
2. Prepare canner, jars and lids (see pages 7 to 8).

3. In a large pot, combine chile peppers, garlic, vinegar and water. Bring to a boil over medium-high heat. Add eggplant and return to a boil. Stir in mint and oregano. Remove from heat.

4. Using a slotted spoon, pack eggplant into hot jars, leaving room for liquid and leaving 1 inch (2.5 cm) headspace. Pour in hot pickling liquid, leaving ½ inch (1 cm) headspace. Remove air bubbles and adjust headspace as necessary by adding hot pickling liquid. Wipe rim and place hot lid disc on jar. Screw band down until fingertip-tight.

5. Place jars in canner and return to a boil. Process for 15 minutes. Turn off heat, remove canner lid and let jars stand in water for 5 minutes. Transfer jars to a towel-lined surface and let stand for 24 hours. Check lids and refrigerate any jars that are not sealed.

Tip

For the best flavor, these pickles benefit from standing for at least a week before serving.

Variation

Replace 1 cup (250 mL) of the white vinegar with red wine vinegar or balsamic vinegar (the final color will be darker, but different vinegars add a nice flavor).

Sliced Fennel Pickles

The delicate licorice flavor of fennel is captured with a touch of tang and sweetness in this simple pickle. Add the optional orange zest for an added touch.

Makes about four pint (500 mL) jars

● ● ●

Tip
Use small fennel bulbs for the best texture. The big bulbs with thick layers can be tough and stringy.

Serving Suggestion
Add drained pickled fennel to sautéed vegetables for a pasta dish, or add to risotto.

4 lbs	small fennel bulbs	2 kg
1½ cups	granulated sugar	375 mL
1 tbsp	pickling or canning salt	15 mL
3⅔ cups	white vinegar	900 mL
1 cup	water	250 mL
12	black peppercorns	12
4	strips (each 2- by 1-inch/5 by 2.5 cm) orange zest (optional)	4

1. Prepare canner, jars and lids (see pages 7 to 8).
2. Trim stalks and bottom from fennel bulbs. Cut each in half lengthwise and cut out cores. Place cut side down and cut crosswise into ¼-inch (1 cm) slices. You should have about 15 cups (3.75 L). Set aside.
3. In a large pot, combine sugar, salt, vinegar and water. Bring to a boil over medium heat, stirring often until sugar and salt are dissolved. Boil for 1 minute. Add fennel and return to a boil, pressing occasionally to immerse fennel in liquid. Remove from heat.
4. Place 3 peppercorns in each hot jar. Using a slotted spoon, pack fennel into jars, leaving room for liquid and leaving 1 inch (2.5 cm) headspace. Add orange zest (if using). Pour in hot pickling liquid, leaving ½ inch (1 cm) headspace. Remove air bubbles and adjust headspace as necessary by adding hot pickling liquid. Wipe rim and place hot lid disc on jar. Screw band down until fingertip-tight.
5. Place jars in canner and return to a boil. Process for 15 minutes. Turn off heat, remove canner lid and let jars stand in water for 5 minutes. Transfer jars to a towel-lined surface and let stand for 24 hours. Check lids and refrigerate any jars that are not sealed.

Pickled Fiddleheads

The woodsy, green flavor of fiddleheads makes them a springtime delicacy. Their season is very short, so catch them while you can and capture their unique flavor in these pickles to enjoy throughout the year.

Makes about six pint (500 mL) jars

• • •

Tips

If you plan to forage for fiddleheads in the wild, pick only those shoots that you know are ostrich ferns. Other similar-looking shoots may be from ferns that are not edible varieties. If you're not sure, it's best to purchase fiddleheads from a reputable supplier. Also, avoid over-picking an area, so you don't destroy the natural population.

One pound (500 g) of raw fiddleheads gives you about 5 cups (1.25 L).

• **Baking sheet or trays, lined with lint-free towels**

4 lbs	fiddleheads (see tips, at left and page 74)	2 kg
¼ cup	granulated sugar	50 mL
2 tbsp	pickling or canning salt	25 mL
3½ cups	white vinegar	875 mL
2½ cups	water	625 mL
1 cup	white wine vinegar	250 mL
	Black peppercorns	

1. Trim off the stem end of fiddleheads to within 1 to 2 inches (2.5 to 5 cm) of the coil, or where it starts to get tough and fibrous.
2. In a large pot of boiling salted water, in batches, blanch fiddleheads for 1 minute or until bright green. Immediately plunge into a large bowl or sink of ice water. Place a plate on top to submerge fiddleheads and let stand until well chilled, refreshing water as necessary to keep cold, for at least 30 minutes or for up to 1 hour.
3. Meanwhile, prepare canner, jars and lids (see pages 7 to 8).
4. In a colander, working in batches, drain fiddleheads well. Spread out on towel-lined baking sheet to drain any remaining water.
5. In a large pot, combine sugar, salt, white vinegar, water and white wine vinegar. Bring to a boil over medium-high heat, stirring often until sugar and salt are dissolved. Boil for 1 minute. Add fiddleheads and simmer until heated through. Remove from heat.
6. Place ¼ tsp (1 mL) peppercorns in each hot jar. Using a slotted spoon, pack fiddleheads into jars, leaving room for liquid and leaving 1 inch (2.5 cm) headspace. Pour in hot pickling liquid, leaving ½ inch (1 cm) headspace. Remove air bubbles and adjust headspace as necessary by adding hot pickling liquid. Wipe rim and place hot lid disc on jar. Screw band down until fingertip-tight.
7. Place jars in canner and return to a boil. Process for 10 minutes. Turn off heat, remove canner lid and let jars stand in water for 5 minutes. Transfer jars to a towel-lined surface and let stand for 24 hours. Check lids and refrigerate any jars that are not sealed.

Curry Pickled Fiddleheads

Fiddleheads are the tender shoots of the ostrich fern and are named for their shape, which resembles the carved handle on a fiddle. A zesty curry seasoning works well with the flavor of fiddleheads. These pickles are a nice addition to salads or tossed with hot cooked rice for a side dish.

Makes about six pint (500 mL) jars

● ● ●

Tip

The easiest way to make sure the sand is washed out of fiddleheads without breaking the coil is to hold the fiddlehead under cool running water and gently insert your forefinger into the center of the coil from underneath to push up and loosen without completely unraveling the coil. Flip the fiddlehead over and repeat with the other side, then press the coil flat again.

- Baking sheet or trays, lined with lint-free towels

4 lbs	fiddleheads (see tips, at left and page 73)	2 kg
1	stick cinnamon (about 3 inches/7.5 cm long), broken in half	1
1 tbsp	curry powder	15 mL
1 tsp	cumin seeds	5 mL
3	cardamom pods, crushed (optional)	3
¾ cup	granulated sugar	175 mL
2 tbsp	pickling or canning salt	25 mL
4 cups	white vinegar	1 L
2 cups	water	500 mL
⅓ cup	freshly squeezed lime or lemon juice	75 mL
3	cloves garlic, halved	3
	Black peppercorns	

1. Trim off the stem end of fiddleheads to within 1 to 2 inches (2.5 to 5 cm) of the coil, or where it starts to get tough and fibrous.
2. In a large pot of boiling salted water, blanch fiddleheads for 1 minute or until bright green. Immediately plunge into a large bowl or sink of ice water. Place a plate on top to submerge fiddleheads and let stand until well chilled, refreshing water as necessary to keep cold, for at least 30 minutes or for up to 1 hour.
3. Meanwhile, prepare canner, jars and lids (see pages 7 to 8).
4. In a colander, working in batches, drain fiddleheads well. Spread out on towel-lined baking sheet to drain any remaining water.
5. In a small dry skillet, over medium heat, toast cinnamon, curry powder and cumin, stirring constantly, for about 30 seconds or until slightly darker and fragrant. Immediately transfer to a bowl and let cool.

6. In a large pot, combine toasted spices, cardamom pods (if using), sugar, salt, vinegar and water. Bring to a boil over medium-high heat, stirring often until sugar and salt are dissolved. Reduce heat to low, cover and simmer for 5 minutes or until liquid is flavorful. Add fiddleheads and simmer until heated through. Remove from heat. Discard cardamom pods and cinnamon stick.

7. Place 1 piece of garlic and ¼ tsp (1 mL) peppercorns in each hot jar. Using a slotted spoon, pack fiddleheads into jars, leaving room for liquid and leaving 1 inch (2.5 cm) headspace. Pour in hot pickling liquid, leaving ½ inch (1 cm) headspace. Remove air bubbles and adjust headspace as necessary by adding hot pickling liquid. Wipe rim and place hot lid disc on jar. Screw band down until fingertip-tight.

8. Place jars in canner and return to a boil. Process for 10 minutes. Turn off heat, remove canner lid and let jars stand in water for 5 minutes. Transfer jars to a towel-lined surface and let stand for 24 hours. Check lids and refrigerate any jars that are not sealed.

Variation

For some extra kick, add 1 or 2 hot green chile peppers, minced, with the fiddleheads in step 6.

Classic Pickled Garlic

The classic French seasoning makes the garlic as delicious on its own as it is in recipes.

Makes five to six 8-ounce (250 mL) jars

● ● ●

Tips

You can often find peeled garlic cloves in containers or bags in the produce section at supermarkets and warehouse stores. These certainly save a lot of time and effort, but be sure they are very fresh. Rinse and drain them well and trim off the tough root end before adding in step 3 of Day 1.

The garlic may turn blue in the pickling liquid. It's perfectly safe to eat; the color change is just a reaction between the minerals in the garlic and the acid from the vinegar.

Serving Suggestions

Serve with meats or cheeses on an appetizer platter.

Use in place of fresh garlic in a pasta sauce or soup, adding some of the pickling liquid in place of any wine or vinegar in the recipe.

7 cups	garlic cloves (about 21 heads)	1.75 L
5	each small bay leaves and sprigs thyme	5
5	1-inch (2.5 cm) pieces rosemary sprigs	5
1 tbsp	black peppercorns	15 mL
2 tbsp	granulated sugar	25 mL
1 tsp	pickling or canning salt	5 mL
3 cups	white wine vinegar	750 mL
1 cup	dry white wine	250 mL

Day 1

1. In a large pot of boiling water, blanch garlic cloves for 30 seconds. Drain and immediately plunge into a sink of cold water. Let stand until chilled, about 15 minutes. Using a paring knife, trim off root end and slip off skins. Set garlic aside.

2. Place bay leaves, thyme, rosemary and peppercorns in the center of a square of triple-layered cheesecloth and tie into a spice bag.

3. In a clean large pot, combine spice bag, sugar, salt, vinegar and wine. Bring to a boil over medium-high heat, stirring often until sugar and salt are dissolved. Add garlic and return to a boil. Boil for 1 minute. Remove from heat and let cool. Cover and let stand at a cool room temperature for at least 12 hours or for up to 24 hours.

Day 2

1. Prepare canner, jars and lids (see pages 7 to 8).

2. Remove spice bag from garlic mixture, squeezing out excess liquid. Untie bag and reserve herbs and spices.

3. Return garlic mixture to medium heat and bring to a boil. Boil for 1 minute. Remove from heat.

4. Divide reserved herbs and spices evenly among hot jars, breaking small pieces off to add to sixth jar if necessary. Using a slotted spoon, pack garlic into jars, leaving room for liquid and leaving 1 inch (2.5 cm) headspace. Pour in hot pickling liquid, leaving ½ inch (1 cm) headspace. Remove air bubbles and adjust headspace as necessary by adding hot pickling liquid. Wipe rim and place hot lid disc on jar. Screw band down until fingertip-tight.

5. Place jars in canner and return to a boil. Process for 10 minutes. Turn off heat, remove canner lid and let jars stand in water for 5 minutes. Transfer jars to a towel-lined surface and let stand for 24 hours. Check lids and refrigerate any jars that are not sealed.

Hot and Spicy Pickled Garlic

These are definitely for people who like their pickles bold! Use them to spike a martini, salad dressing or pasta arrabbiata.

Makes five to six 8-ounce (250 mL) jars

• • •

Tips

Be sure to use very fresh garlic. The heads should be firm with tight skins and no signs of mold or sprouting. You'll need about 2¼ lbs (1.125 kg) heads of garlic to get 7 cups (1.75 L) of cloves.

Fresh chile peppers can vary in heat, but the small dried red ones are sure to be fiery, making them better for these pickles. The little flakes of red even make the pickles *look* spicy.

7 cups	garlic cloves (about 21 heads)	1.75 L
5	small dried hot red chile peppers, crumbled	5
2 tbsp	pickling spice	25 mL
¼ cup	granulated sugar	50 mL
1 tsp	pickling or canning salt	5 mL
4 cups	white vinegar or white wine vinegar	1 L

Day 1

1. In a large pot of boiling water, blanch garlic cloves for 30 seconds. Drain and immediately plunge into a large bowl or sink of cold water. Let stand until well chilled, about 15 minutes. Using a paring knife, trim off root end and slip off skins. Set garlic aside.
2. Place chile peppers and pickling spice in the center of a square of triple-layered cheesecloth and tie into a spice bag.
3. In a clean large pot, combine spice bag, sugar, salt and vinegar. Bring to a boil over medium-high heat, stirring often until sugar and salt are dissolved. Add garlic and return to a boil. Boil for 1 minute. Remove from heat and let cool. Cover and let stand at a cool room temperature for at least 12 hours or for up to 24 hours.

Day 2

1. Prepare canner, jars and lids (see pages 7 to 8).
2. Remove spice bag from garlic mixture, squeezing out excess liquid. Untie bag and reserve chile peppers and pickling spice.
3. Return garlic mixture to medium heat and bring to a boil. Boil for 1 minute. Remove from heat.
4. Divide reserved chile peppers and pickling spice evenly among hot jars. Using a slotted spoon, pack garlic into jars, leaving room for liquid and leaving 1 inch (2.5 cm) headspace. Pour in hot pickling liquid, leaving ½ inch (1 cm) headspace. Remove air bubbles and adjust headspace as necessary by adding hot pickling liquid. Wipe rim and place hot lid disc on jar. Screw band down until fingertip-tight.
5. Place jars in canner and return to a boil. Process for 10 minutes. Turn off heat, remove canner lid and let jars stand in water for 5 minutes. Transfer jars to a towel-lined surface and let stand for 24 hours. Check lids and refrigerate any jars that are not sealed.

Warmly Spiced Pickled Garlic

The combination of sweet spices, a touch of sugar and zesty garlic gives these pickles a well-rounded burst of flavor. Serve them as you would any sweet pickles: with sharp cheeses, pâté or sandwiches.

Makes five to six 8-ounce (250 mL) jars

• • •

Tips

You can often find peeled garlic cloves in containers or bags in the produce section at supermarkets and warehouse stores. These certainly save a lot of time and effort, but be sure they are very fresh. Rinse and drain them well and trim off the tough root end before adding in step 3 of Day 1.

The garlic may turn blue in the pickling liquid. It's perfectly safe to eat; the color change is just a reaction between the minerals in the garlic and the acid from the vinegar.

These pickles benefit from standing for at least 1 to 2 weeks after processing to allow the flavors to blend.

7 cups	garlic cloves (about 21 heads)	1.75 L
1 cup	granulated sugar	250 mL
1 tsp	pickling or canning salt	5 mL
½ tsp	ground cinnamon	2 mL
½ tsp	ground ginger	2 mL
¼ tsp	ground cloves or allspice	1 mL
3½ cups	cider vinegar	875 mL

1. Prepare canner, jars and lids (see pages 7 to 8).
2. In a large pot of boiling water, blanch garlic cloves for 30 seconds. Drain and immediately plunge into a large bowl or sink of cold water. Let stand until well chilled, about 15 minutes. Using a paring knife, trim off root end and slip off skins. Set garlic aside.
3. In a large pot, combine sugar, salt, cinnamon, ginger, cloves and vinegar. Bring to a boil over medium heat, stirring often until sugar and salt are dissolved. Boil for 1 minute. Add garlic and return to a boil. Boil for 2 minutes or until garlic is heated through. Remove from heat
4. Using a slotted spoon, pack garlic into hot jars, leaving room for liquid and leaving 1 inch (2.5 cm) headspace. Pour in hot pickling liquid, leaving ½ inch (1 cm) headspace. Remove air bubbles and adjust headspace as necessary by adding hot pickling liquid. Wipe rim and place hot lid disc on jar. Screw band down until fingertip-tight.
5. Place jars in canner and return to a boil. Process for 10 minutes. Turn off heat, remove canner lid and let jars stand in water for 5 minutes. Transfer jars to a towel-lined surface and let stand for 24 hours. Check lids and refrigerate any jars that are not sealed.

Pickled Garlic Scapes

Garlic scapes are the seed stalks that shoot up from the growing head of garlic in spring. They are often removed to concentrate the plant's energy toward the garlic head so it grows larger. They have a fresh garlic flavor and a texture similar to asparagus or green beans. This lightly seasoned pickle is a nice way to preserve them.

Makes about three pint (500 mL) jars

● ● ●

Tip

Harvest garlic scapes when they are still tender, start to curl or have just one loop and the seed pod is small and tender.

Serving Suggestions

Serve as garnish in a Bloody Caesar or Bloody Mary.

Chop drained pickled scapes and add to potato or pasta salad, using some of the liquid in the dressing.

Serve with sharp cheese, such as blue cheese, Stilton or extra-old (sharp) Cheddar.

1 lb	garlic scapes	500 g
¼ cup	pickling or canning salt	50 mL
2 tsp	mustard seeds	10 mL
1 tsp	dill seeds	5 mL
2¾ cups	white vinegar	675 mL
2¾ cups	water	675 mL

1. Trim off tough or dry ends from garlic scapes. Cut scapes into 4- to 6-inch (10 to 15 cm) lengths and/or tie the thinner end into a knot. Set aside.
2. Prepare canner, jars and lids (see pages 7 to 8).
3. In a pot, combine salt, mustard seeds, dill seeds, vinegar and water. Bring to a boil over medium heat, stirring often until sugar and salt are dissolved. Boil for 1 minute. Reduce heat to low and keep liquid hot.
4. Pack scapes into hot jars, leaving room for liquid and leaving 1 inch (2.5 cm) headspace. Pour in hot pickling liquid, leaving ½ inch (1 cm) headspace. Remove air bubbles and adjust headspace as necessary by adding hot pickling liquid. Wipe rim and place hot lid disc on jar. Screw band down until fingertip-tight.
5. Place jars in canner and return to a boil. Process for 10 minutes. Turn off heat, remove canner lid and let jars stand in water for 5 minutes. Transfer jars to a towel-lined surface and let stand for 24 hours. Check lids and refrigerate any jars that are not sealed.

Herb and Garlic Pickled Mushrooms

These are just like the mushrooms sold in fancy bottles at gourmet shops. Now, you can make them at home!

Makes about five pint (500 mL) jars

● ● ●

Variation

Peppery Herb and Garlic Pickled Mushrooms: Add ¼ long hot red chile pepper to each jar with the herbs.

Serving Suggestions

Turn these into a Marinated Mushroom Salad by whisking in ¼ cup (50 mL) olive oil and 1 tsp (5 mL) Dijon mustard for each pint (500 mL) of mushrooms. Add chopped fresh herbs as garnish.

Drain mushrooms, slice and sauté in butter for a quick side dish or topping for grilled steak.

● Baking sheets or trays, lined with lint-free towels

8 lbs	small mushrooms (1 to 1½ inches/ 2.5 to 4 cm)	4 kg
9 cups	water, divided	2.25 L
½ cup	freshly squeezed lemon juice	125 mL
5	cloves garlic, halved	5
5	small bay leaves	5
2 tbsp	pickling or canning salt	25 mL
2 cups	white vinegar	750 mL
2 cups	white wine vinegar	500 mL
5	sprigs thyme (each 4 inches/10 cm long)	5
5	1-inch (2.5 cm) pieces rosemary sprigs	5
	Black peppercorns	

1. Prepare canner, jars and lids (see pages 7 to 8).
2. Trim mushroom stems to about ¼ inch (0.5 cm) below cap.
3. In a large pot, combine 8 cups (2 L) of the water and the lemon juice. Bring to a boil over high heat. Add mushrooms, reduce heat and boil gently for about 5 minutes or until mushrooms are tender. Drain and spread out on towel-lined baking sheets to drain any remaining water.
4. In a pot, combine garlic, bay leaves, salt, white vinegar, white wine vinegar and the remaining water. Bring to a boil over medium-high heat, stirring often until salt is dissolved. Boil for 1 minute. Reduce heat to low and keep liquid hot.
5. Working with one jar at a time, place 1 thyme sprig, 1 piece of rosemary and ¼ tsp (1 mL) peppercorns into hot jar. Using a slotted spoon, transfer 2 pieces of garlic and 1 bay leaf to jar. Pack mushrooms into jar, leaving room for liquid and leaving 1 inch (2.5 cm) headspace. Pour in hot pickling liquid, leaving ½ inch (1 cm) headspace. Remove air bubbles and adjust headspace as necessary by adding hot pickling liquid. Wipe rim and place hot lid disc on jar. Screw band down until fingertip-tight.
6. Place jars in canner and return to a boil. Process for 20 minutes. Turn off heat, remove canner lid and let jars stand in water for 5 minutes. Transfer jars to a towel-lined surface and let stand for 24 hours. Check lids and refrigerate any jars that are not sealed.

Dill Pickled Mushrooms

Fresh dill and mushrooms are a fabulous flavor combination. Use them in place of fresh mushrooms in salads or casseroles for an interesting twist.

Makes about five pint (500 mL) jars

● ● ●

Tip

Small mushrooms are best for pickling — they fit better into the jars, and the stems are more tender.

Variation

Garlic Dill Pickled Mushrooms: Add 1 clove garlic, halved, to each jar with the dill head.

● Baking sheets or trays, lined with lint-free towels

8 lbs	small mushrooms (1 to 1½ inches/ 2.5 to 4 cm)	4 kg
9½ cups	water, divided	2.375 L
½ cup	white vinegar or freshly squeezed lemon juice	125 mL
¼ cup	granulated sugar	50 mL
2 tbsp	pickling or kosher salt	25 mL
3½ cups	cider vinegar	875 mL
5	dill heads	5
5	dill sprigs	5
	Dill seeds	

1. Prepare canner, jars and lids (see pages 7 to 8).
2. Trim mushroom stems to about ¼ inch (0.5 cm) below cap.
3. In a large pot, combine 8 cups (2 L) of the water and the white vinegar. Bring to a boil over high heat. Add mushrooms, reduce heat and boil gently for about 5 minutes or until mushrooms are tender. Drain and spread out on towel-lined baking sheets to drain any remaining water.
4. In a saucepan, combine sugar, salt, cider vinegar and the remaining water. Bring to a boil over medium-high heat, stirring often until sugar and salt are dissolved. Boil for 1 minute. Reduce heat to low and keep liquid hot.
5. Working with one jar at a time, place 1 dill head in hot jar. Pack mushrooms into jar, leaving room for liquid and leaving 1 inch (2.5 cm) headspace. Add 1 dill sprig and ¼ tsp (1 mL) dill seeds. Pour in hot pickling liquid, leaving ½ inch (1 cm) headspace. Remove air bubbles and adjust headspace as necessary by adding hot pickling liquid. Wipe rim and place hot lid disc on jar. Screw band down until fingertip-tight.
6. Place jars in canner and return to a boil. Process for 20 minutes. Turn off heat, remove canner lid and let jars stand in water for 5 minutes. Transfer jars to a towel-lined surface and let stand for 24 hours. Check lids and refrigerate any jars that are not sealed.

Fennel-Scented Pickled Exotic Mushrooms

There are many varieties of mushrooms available these days. They are often called "wild," though they are, in fact, cultivated, so the term "exotic" is more accurate. Exotic mushrooms have a deep, woodsy flavor, which this pickle enhances with a touch of fennel and garlic.

Makes about four pint (500 mL) jars

● ● ●

Tips

Do not use true, foraged wild mushrooms for pickling. They can harbor bacteria, which increases the risk of spoilage.

Use a mixture of your favorite mushrooms, or all one variety. Steer clear of portobello mushrooms, though, because the dark gills will cause the pickling liquid to turn black.

Because the shape and size of the mushrooms will vary, you may have some left over after filling the jars. Simply toss them with some vinegar, olive oil and chopped fresh herbs and season with salt and pepper for a salad.

* Baking sheets or trays, lined with lint-free towels

6 lbs	exotic mushrooms	3 kg
⅓ cup	freshly squeezed lemon juice	75 mL
2 tbsp	granulated sugar	25 mL
4 tsp	pickling or kosher salt	20 mL
2 tsp	fennel seeds	10 mL
3¼ cups	white wine vinegar	800 mL
4	cloves garlic, halved	4

1. Prepare canner, jars and lids (see pages 7 to 8).
2. Trim mushroom stems to about ¼ inch (0.5 cm) below cap (if using shiitakes, trim stem even with cap). Cut any mushrooms that are larger than 2 inches (5 cm) in diameter into halves or quarters.
3. In a large pot, combine 7 cups (1.75 L) water and the lemon juice. Bring to a boil over high heat. Working in batches, one variety at a time, add mushrooms, reduce heat and boil gently for 3 to 5 minutes or until mushrooms are tender. Using a slotted spoon, transfer mushrooms to a colander and drain. Spread out on towel-lined baking sheets to drain any remaining water.
4. In a saucepan, combine sugar, salt, fennel seeds, vinegar and 1 cup (250 mL) water. Bring to a boil over medium-high heat, stirring often until sugar and salt are dissolved. Boil for 1 minute. Reduce heat to low and keep liquid hot.
5. Working with one jar at a time, place 1 piece of garlic in hot jar. Pack mushrooms into jar, leaving room for liquid and leaving 1 inch (2.5 cm) headspace. Add another piece of garlic. Pour in hot pickling liquid, leaving ½ inch (1 cm) headspace and dividing fennel seeds as evenly as possible. Remove air bubbles and adjust headspace as necessary by adding hot pickling liquid. Wipe rim and place hot lid disc on jar. Screw band down until fingertip-tight.
6. Place jars in canner and return to a boil. Process for 20 minutes. Turn off heat, remove canner lid and let jars stand in water for 5 minutes. Transfer jars to a towel-lined surface and let stand for 24 hours. Check lids and refrigerate any jars that are not sealed.

Pickled Okra and Hot Peppers

Okra has a unique texture, with a crispy outside and a soft interior. The spicy tang of this pickle will have you crunching and munching until they disappear. This flavor combination is popular in several cuisines around the world, from Louisiana to Turkey.

Makes about five pint (500 mL) jars

● ● ●

Tip

Use okra as soon after harvest or purchase as possible. The ridges and tips tend to get soft and dark quickly, giving the pickles an unpleasant texture.

Variation

Mild Pickled Okra: Omit the hot peppers and add ½ clove garlic per jar, if desired.

2 lbs	okra	1 kg
¼ cup	pickling or canning salt	50 mL
3½ cups	white vinegar	875 mL
2½ cups	water	625 mL
	Celery seeds	
	Mustard seeds	
5	long red hot chile peppers, halved lengthwise	5

1. Prepare canner, jars and lids (see pages 7 to 8).
2. Trim stems from okra pods, being sure not to cut into the pod and expose the seeds. Set aside.
3. In a saucepan, combine salt, vinegar and water. Bring to a boil over medium-high heat, stirring often until salt is dissolved. Boil for 1 minute. Reduce heat to low and keep liquid hot.
4. Working with one jar at a time, place ½ tsp (2 mL) each celery seeds and mustard seeds in hot jar. Pack okra and 2 chile pepper halves into jar, leaving room for liquid. Pour in hot pickling liquid, leaving ½ inch (1 cm) headspace. Remove air bubbles and adjust headspace as necessary by adding hot pickling liquid. Wipe rim and place hot lid disc on jar. Screw band down until fingertip-tight.
5. Place jars in canner and return to a boil. Process for 15 minutes. Turn off heat, remove canner lid and let jars stand in water for 5 minutes. Transfer jars to a towel-lined surface and let stand for 24 hours. Check lids and refrigerate any jars that are not sealed.

Dill Pickled Okra

The fresh "green" flavor of okra pairs very nicely with dill. The texture and interesting look is a welcome addition to a pickle platter in place of traditional cucumber dills.

• • •

2 lbs	okra	1 kg
2 tbsp	granulated sugar	25 mL
2 tbsp	pickling or canning salt	25 mL
3½ cups	cider vinegar	875 mL
2½ cups	water	625 mL
5	cloves garlic, halved	5
5	dill sprigs	5
	Dill seeds	

1. Prepare canner, jars and lids (see pages 7 to 8).
2. Trim stems from okra pods, being sure not to cut into the pod and expose the seeds. Set aside.
3. In a saucepan, combine sugar, salt, vinegar and water. Bring to a boil over medium-high heat, stirring often until sugar and salt are dissolved. Boil for 1 minute. Reduce heat to low and keep liquid hot.
4. Working with one jar at a time, place 2 pieces of garlic and 1 dill sprig in hot jar. Pack okra into jar, leaving room for liquid. Add ½ tsp (2 mL) dill seeds. Pour in hot pickling liquid, leaving ½ inch (1 cm) headspace. Remove air bubbles and adjust headspace as necessary by adding hot pickling liquid. Wipe rim and place hot lid disc on jar. Screw band down until fingertip-tight.
5. Place jars in canner and return to a boil. Process for 15 minutes. Turn off heat, remove canner lid and let jars stand in water for 5 minutes. Transfer jars to a towel-lined surface and let stand for 24 hours. Check lids and refrigerate any jars that are not sealed.

Martini Olives

Be ready for a dirty martini at a moment's notice — these drunken olives are a welcome addition to any cocktail hour, in a drink or just to nibble on. Curing fresh olives is a long and involved process, so this recipe uses store-bought cured olives for simplicity and enhances them with classic martini flavor.

Makes about four 8-ounce (250 mL) jars

3½ cups	drained plain brine-cured green olives	875 mL
1¾ cups	gin	425 mL
¼ cup	dry vermouth	50 mL

● ● ●

Tips

Choose olives that have as few ingredients on the label as possible (no seasonings and no added oil) to make sure they absorb the martini flavor.

Olives with pits hold their shape better when heated, but you can use pitted olives if you prefer.

Variations

Martini Olives with a Twist: Add one 1-inch (2.5 cm) strip lemon peel (yellow part only) to each jar.

Hot Martini Olives: Add ¼ tsp (1 mL) hot pepper flakes to each jar.

Vodka Martini Olives: Replace the gin with vodka.

1. Prepare canner, jars and lids (see pages 7 to 8).
2. In a colander, rinse olives under running water and drain well. Using a toothpick or a fork, pierce olives several times. Set aside.
3. In a deep pot, combine gin and vermouth. Bring just to a simmer over medium heat, making sure the flame on a gas burner is well away from the liquid and the alcohol does not get hot enough to ignite. Add olives and simmer just until heated through. Remove from heat.
4. Using a slotted spoon, pack olives into hot jars, leaving 1 inch (2.5 cm) headspace. Pour in hot pickling liquid, leaving ½ inch (1 cm) headspace. Remove air bubbles and adjust headspace as necessary by adding hot pickling liquid. Wipe rim and place hot lid disc on jar. Screw band down until fingertip-tight.
5. Place jars in canner and return to a boil. Process for 10 minutes. Turn off heat, remove canner lid and let jars stand in water for 5 minutes. Transfer jars to a towel-lined surface and let stand for 24 hours. Check lids and refrigerate any jars that are not sealed.

Spiced Pearl Onions

Warm spices and a touch of sweetness will remind you why these pickles are a timeless classic.

Makes about six pint (500 mL) jars

● ● ●

Tip

Be sure not to boil the onions too long in step 1 on Day 1. You only want to loosen the skins, not cook the onions.

Variation

English Pub-Style Pickled Onions: Replace the cider vinegar with 2½ cups (625 mL) white vinegar and 2 cups (500 mL) malt vinegar, and replace the gingerroot with 1 tsp (5 mL) whole allspice.

Day 1

3½ lbs	¾- to 1-inch (2 to 2.5 cm) pearl (pickling) onions (about 14 cups/3.5 L)	1.75 kg
¼ cup	pickling or canning salt	50 mL

Day 2

6	whole cloves	6
3	sticks cinnamon (each 3 inches/7.5 cm long), broken in half	3
3	thin slices gingerroot, halved	3
1 tsp	black peppercorns	5 mL
½ cup	granulated sugar	125 mL
4½ cups	cider vinegar	1.125 L
2 cups	water	500 mL

Day 1

1. In a large pot of boiling water, in batches as necessary, blanch onions for 2 to 3 minutes or until skins start to loosen. Immediately plunge into a large bowl or sink of cold water. Let stand until well chilled, about 15 minutes. Using a paring knife, trim off root end and slip off skins.
2. In a large non-reactive bowl, combine onions and salt. Add cold water to cover by at least 1 inch (2.5 cm). Place a plate on top to weigh down onions. Cover and let stand at a cool room temperature for at least 12 hours or for up to 24 hours.

Day 2

1. Prepare canner, jars and lids (see pages 7 to 8).
2. In a colander, working in batches, drain onions and rinse well. Drain again and set aside.
3. Place cloves, cinnamon sticks, ginger and peppercorns in the center of a square of triple-layered cheesecloth and tie into a spice bag.
4. In a pot, combine spice bag, sugar, vinegar and water. Bring to a boil over medium-high heat, stirring often until sugar is dissolved. Reduce heat to low, cover and simmer for 5 minutes or until liquid is flavorful. Remove spice bag, squeezing out excess liquid. Untie bag and reserve spices.

5. Working with one jar at a time, add reserved spices to hot jar, dividing evenly. Pack onions into jar, leaving room for liquid and leaving 1 inch (2.5 cm) headspace. Pour in hot pickling liquid, leaving $\frac{1}{2}$ inch (1 cm) headspace. Remove air bubbles and adjust headspace as necessary by adding hot pickling liquid. Wipe rim and place hot lid disc on jar. Screw band down until fingertip-tight.

6. Place jars in canner and return to a boil. Process for 10 minutes. Turn off heat, remove canner lid and let jars stand in water for 5 minutes. Transfer jars to a towel-lined surface and let stand for 24 hours. Check lids and refrigerate any jars that are not sealed.

Serving Suggestions

These are essential for the classic ploughman's lunch of cold meats, sharp cheese and crusty bread.

Skewer with cubes of extra-old (sharp) Cheddar cheese for easy hors d'oeuvres.

Fire and Spice Pearl Onions

With plenty of kick, these pickles add spice to cocktail time, whether served on their own, broiled with bacon on skewers or as garnish for cocktails.

Makes about six pint (500 mL) jars

• • •

Tips

Use only very fresh onions for pickling. The papery skins should be tight, with no signs of mold, and the onions should be plump and firm, with no sprouting in the center.

Be sure not to boil the onions too long in step 1 on Day 1. You only want to loosen the skins, not cook the onions.

Day 1

3½ lbs	¾- to 1-inch (2 to 2.5 cm) pearl (pickling) onions (about 14 cups/3.5 L)	1.75 kg
¼ cup	pickling or canning salt	50 mL

Day 2

6	dried hot red chile peppers, crumbled	6
3	bay leaves, broken in half	3
1 tbsp	mustard seeds	15 mL
1 tsp	coriander seeds	5 mL
1 tsp	cumin seeds (optional)	5 mL
2 tbsp	granulated sugar	25 mL
4½ cups	white vinegar	1.125 L
2 cups	water	500 mL

Day 1

1. In a large pot of boiling water, in batches as necessary, blanch onions for 2 to 3 minutes or until skins start to loosen. Immediately plunge into a large bowl or sink of cold water. Let stand until well chilled, about 15 minutes. Using a paring knife, trim off root end and slip off skins.
2. In a large non-reactive bowl, combine onions and salt. Add cold water to cover by at least 1 inch (2.5 cm). Place a plate on top to weigh down onions. Cover and let stand at a cool room temperature for at least 12 hours or for up to 24 hours.

Day 2

1. Prepare canner, jars and lids (see pages 7 to 8).
2. In a colander, working in batches, drain onions and rinse well. Drain again and set aside.
3. In a pot, combine chile peppers, bay leaves, mustard seeds, coriander seeds, cumin seeds (if using), sugar, vinegar and water. Bring to a boil over medium-high heat, stirring often until sugar is dissolved. Reduce heat to low, cover and simmer for 5 minutes or until liquid is flavorful.

4. Working with one jar at a time, pack onions into hot jars, leaving room for liquid and leaving 1 inch (2.5 cm) headspace. Pour in hot pickling liquid, leaving $\frac{1}{2}$ inch (1 cm) headspace and dividing spices as evenly as possible. Remove air bubbles and adjust headspace as necessary by adding hot pickling liquid. Wipe rim and place hot lid disc on jar. Screw band down until fingertip-tight.

5. Place jars in canner and return to a boil. Process for 10 minutes. Turn off heat, remove canner lid and let jars stand in water for 5 minutes. Transfer jars to a towel-lined surface and let stand for 24 hours. Check lids and refrigerate any jars that are not sealed.

Tip

Use the small dried red chile peppers, often available at Asian grocers or the international foods section at supermarkets, to make sure you get a good fiery heat for these pickles.

Juniper and Gin Pickled Onions

With a double hit of juniper from the berries and the gin, these onions are flavorful.

Makes about six 8-ounce (250 mL) or three pint (500 mL) jars

● ● ● ●

Tip

Juniper berries can be found at specialty spice stores, health food stores or bulk food stores.

Serving Suggestions

Use these as a classic garnish for a gimlet cocktail.

Add pickled onions, either whole or chopped, to salads.

Serve with strong cheeses, such as blue, washed-rind cheeses or aged Cheddar.

Day 1

1¾ lbs	¾- to 1-inch (2 to 2.5 cm) pearl (pickling) onions (about 7 cups/1.75 L)	875 kg
2 tbsp	pickling or canning salt	25 mL

Day 2

2 tsp	juniper berries	10 mL
1 tsp	celery seeds	5 mL
1½ cups	white vinegar	375 mL
1 cup	water	250 mL
½ cup	gin	125 mL

Day 1

1. In a large pot of boiling water, in batches as necessary, blanch onions for 2 to 3 minutes or until skins start to loosen. Immediately plunge into a large bowl or sink of cold water. Let stand until well chilled, about 15 minutes. Using a paring knife, trim off root end and slip off skins.
2. In a large non-reactive bowl, combine onions and salt. Add cold water to cover by at least 1 inch (2.5 cm). Place a plate on top to weigh down onions. Cover and let stand at a cool room temperature for at least 12 hours or for up to 24 hours.

Day 2

1. Prepare canner, jars and lids (see pages 7 to 8).
2. In a colander, working in batches, drain onions and rinse well. Drain again and set aside.
3. In a pot, combine juniper berries, celery seeds, vinegar and water. Bring to a boil over medium-high heat. Reduce heat to low, cover and simmer for 5 minutes or until liquid is flavorful. Stir in gin.
4. Working with one jar at a time, pack onions into hot jars, leaving room for liquid and leaving 1 inch (2.5 cm) headspace. Pour in hot pickling liquid, leaving ½ inch (1 cm) headspace and dividing spices as evenly as possible. Remove air bubbles and adjust headspace as necessary by adding hot pickling liquid. Wipe rim and place hot lid disc on jar. Screw band down until fingertip-tight.
5. Place jars in canner and return to a boil. Process for 10 minutes. Turn off heat, remove canner lid and let jars stand in water for 5 minutes. Transfer jars to a towel-lined surface and let stand for 24 hours. Check lids and refrigerate any jars that are not sealed.

Sweet Pickled Onion Rings

Pungent, freshly harvested onions are tamed in this sweet and savory pickle. They're tasty as a topping for burgers, hot dogs and sandwiches, or alongside roast beef.

Makes about six pint (500 mL) jars

• • •

Tip

For nice rings that fit into the jars, small onions work best. If using larger onions, cut them in half lengthwise, then cut lengthwise into ¼-inch (0.5 cm) slices and separate layers.

Variation

Sweet Pickled Red Onion Rings: Substitute red (purple) onions for the regular onions and add a 3-inch (7.5 cm) sprig of fresh thyme to each jar.

3 lbs	2- to 3-inch (5 to 7.5 cm) onions	1.5 kg
2½ cups	granulated sugar	625 mL
1 tbsp	mustard seeds	15 mL
1 tsp	pickling or canning salt	5 mL
1 tsp	celery seeds	5 mL
¼ tsp	ground turmeric	1 mL
⅛ tsp	ground cloves (optional)	0.5 mL
5 cups	cider vinegar	1.25 L

1. Prepare canner, jars and lids (see pages 7 to 8).
2. Peel onions, cut crosswise into slices about ¼ inch (0.5 cm) thick and separate into rings. You should have about 15 cups (3.75 L). Set aside.
3. In a pot, combine sugar, mustard seeds, salt, celery seeds, turmeric, cloves (if using) and vinegar. Bring to a boil over medium heat, stirring often until sugar and salt are dissolved. Boil for 1 minute. Reduce heat to low and keep liquid hot.
4. Working with one jar at a time, pack onions into hot jars, leaving 1 inch (2.5 cm) headspace. Pour in hot pickling liquid, leaving ½ inch (1 cm) headspace and dividing spices as evenly as possible. Remove air bubbles and adjust headspace as necessary by adding hot pickling liquid. Wipe rim and place hot lid disc on jar. Screw band down until fingertip-tight.
5. Place jars in canner and return to a boil. Process for 10 minutes. Turn off heat, remove canner lid and let jars stand in water for 5 minutes. Transfer jars to a towel-lined surface and let stand for 24 hours. Check lids and refrigerate any jars that are not sealed.

Dill Pickled Onion Rings

A triple burst of dill in these tangy onions brings burger garnish to new heights. Try them on top of a grilled steak or fish fillet too!

Makes about six pint (500 mL) jars

• • •

Tip

For maximum flavor, these pickles benefit from standing for at least 2 to 3 weeks after processing.

3 lbs	2- to 3-inch (5 to 7.5 cm) onions	1.5 kg
¼ cup	granulated sugar	50 mL
1 tbsp	pickling or kosher salt	15 mL
5 cups	white vinegar	1.25 L
2¼ cups	water	550 mL
6	dill heads	6
6	dill sprigs	6
	Dill seeds	

1. Prepare canner, jars and lids (see pages 7 to 8).
2. Peel onions, cut crosswise into slices about ¼ inch (0.5 cm) thick and separate into rings. You should have about 15 cups (3.75 L). Set aside.
3. In a pot, combine sugar, salt, vinegar and water. Bring to a boil over medium-high heat, stirring often until sugar and salt are dissolved. Boil for 1 minute. Reduce heat to low and keep liquid hot.
4. Working with one jar at a time, place 1 dill head in hot jar. Pack onions into jar, leaving 1 inch (2.5 cm) headspace. Add 1 dill sprig and ¼ tsp (1 mL) dill seeds. Pour in hot pickling liquid, leaving ½ inch (1 cm) headspace. Remove air bubbles and adjust headspace as necessary by adding hot pickling liquid. Wipe rim and place hot lid disc on jar. Screw band down until fingertip-tight.
5. Place jars in canner and return to a boil. Process for 10 minutes. Turn off heat, remove canner lid and let jars stand in water for 5 minutes. Transfer jars to a towel-lined surface and let stand for 24 hours. Check lids and refrigerate any jars that are not sealed.

Tangy Parsnip and Carrot Pickles

Contrasting colors and flavors add interest to these easy-to-make pickles. Serve them alongside sandwiches or on a veggie platter with dip.

Makes about six pint (500 mL) jars

● ● ●

Tips

It's best to have a few extra parsnips on hand in case you find the thick ends too thick and tough to use.

When cutting the carrots and parsnips, it is easiest to cut them crosswise into 4-inch (10 cm) lengths and then into sticks. You may just need to cut the narrow end in half lengthwise; it's okay not to have squared-off sticks.

Avoid very large carrots and parsnips, which often have a woody core and make unpleasant pickles.

2 lbs	carrots (8 to 10)	1 kg
2 lbs	parsnips (10 to 12)	1 kg
¼ cup	granulated sugar	50 mL
2 tbsp	pickling or kosher salt	25 mL
1 tbsp	mustard seeds	15 mL
¼ tsp	hot pepper flakes	1 mL
6 cups	cider vinegar	1.5 L
2¾ cups	water	675 mL

1. Prepare canner, jars and lids (see pages 7 to 8).
2. Cut carrots and parsnips into 4- by ½- by ½-inch (10 by 1 by 1 cm) sticks, or the length that will fit in jars allowing for 1 inch (2.5 cm) headspace. (If the thick ends of parsnips are very thick and tough, trim them off and reserve for another use.) Set aside.
3. In a pot, combine sugar, salt, mustard seeds, hot pepper flakes, vinegar and water. Bring to a boil over medium-high heat, stirring often until sugar and salt are dissolved. Boil for 1 minute. Reduce heat to low and keep liquid hot.
4. Working with one jar at a time, pack carrot and parsnip sticks into hot jars, leaving room for liquid. Pour in hot pickling liquid, leaving ½ inch (1 cm) headspace and dividing spices as evenly as possible. Remove air bubbles and adjust headspace as necessary by adding hot pickling liquid. Wipe rim and place hot lid disc on jar. Screw band down until fingertip-tight.
5. Place jars in canner and return to a boil. Process for 10 minutes. Turn off heat, remove canner lid and let jars stand in water for 5 minutes. Transfer jars to a towel-lined surface and let stand for 24 hours. Check lids and refrigerate any jars that are not sealed.

Pickled Hot Pepper Rings

Fiery peppers are the stars in these simple pickles. They'll spice up any summer barbecue or winter sandwich.

2 lbs	hot banana peppers (about 12)	1 kg
1½ lbs	cayenne peppers (about 18)	750 g
4 tsp	pickling or canning salt	20 mL
6½ cups	white vinegar	1.625 L
2 cups	water	500 mL

1. Prepare canner, jars and lids (see pages 7 to 8).
2. Trim off stems and cut out seeds from banana and cayenne peppers, keeping peppers intact. Cut crosswise into ¼-inch (0.5 cm) slices. You should have about 14 cups (3.5 L) total. Set aside.
3. In a pot, combine salt, vinegar and water. Bring to a boil over medium-high heat, stirring often until salt is dissolved. Boil for 1 minute. Reduce heat to low and keep liquid hot.
4. Working with one jar at a time, pack peppers into hot jars, leaving room for liquid and leaving 1 inch (2.5 cm) headspace. Pour in hot pickling liquid, leaving ½ inch (1 cm) headspace. Remove air bubbles and adjust headspace as necessary by adding hot pickling liquid. Wipe rim and place hot lid disc on jar. Screw band down until fingertip-tight.
5. Place jars in canner and return to a boil. Process for 10 minutes. Turn off heat, remove canner lid and let jars stand in water for 5 minutes. Transfer jars to a towel-lined surface and let stand for 24 hours. Check lids and refrigerate any jars that are not sealed.

Sweet and Hot Pickled Rainbow Peppers

If you've picked a peck of peppers, this is the recipe to make! Well, it doesn't use a whole peck, but you can make a second or third batch. The combination of sweet peppers and varying degrees of hot peppers gives a different taste sensation to each bite.

Makes about six pint (500 mL) jars

• • •

Tips

Shepherd peppers are sweet like bell peppers but are longer and narrower and have a thinner skin and flesh that are nice in these pickles.

Yellow wax peppers are often labeled as hot banana peppers. They look very similar to sweet banana peppers, so it's best to taste a small piece to make sure you have hot peppers.

To avoid burns, wear disposable rubber gloves when handling hot peppers and be sure to wash all utensils and the cutting board well after preparing the peppers.

1 lb	yellow wax (hot banana) peppers (about 6)	500 g
1 lb	sweet red shepherd and/or banana peppers (about 5)	500 g
1 lb	cubanelle peppers (about 4)	500 g
8 oz	cayenne peppers (about 6)	250 g
⅓ cup	granulated sugar	75 mL
1 tbsp	pickling or canning salt	15 mL
5 cups	white vinegar	1.25 L
3⅓ cups	water	825 mL

1. Prepare canner, jars and lids (see pages 7 to 8).
2. Trim off stems and cut out seeds from hot banana, sweet banana, cubanelle and cayenne peppers, keeping peppers intact. Cut crosswise into ¼-inch (0.5 cm) slices. You should have about 14 cups (3.5 L) total. Set aside.
3. In a pot, combine sugar, salt, vinegar and water. Bring to a boil over medium-high heat, stirring often until sugar and salt are dissolved. Boil for 1 minute. Reduce heat to low and keep liquid hot.
4. Working with one jar at a time, pack peppers into hot jars, leaving room for liquid and leaving 1 inch (2.5 cm) headspace. Pour in hot pickling liquid, leaving ½ inch (1 cm) headspace. Remove air bubbles and adjust headspace as necessary by adding hot pickling liquid. Wipe rim and place hot lid disc on jar. Screw band down until fingertip-tight.
5. Place jars in canner and return to a boil. Process for 10 minutes. Turn off heat, remove canner lid and let jars stand in water for 5 minutes. Transfer jars to a towel-lined surface and let stand for 24 hours. Check lids and refrigerate any jars that are not sealed.

Vodka-Soaked Pickled Cherry Peppers

Bright red cherry-like peppers look sweet and innocent until you take a bite! The vodka sneaks up on you after the tang from the vinegar subsides, causing a second zing.

**Makes about four
pint (500 mL) jars**

● ● ●

Variation

*Vodka-Soaked Hot
and Sweet Pickled
Peppers:* Replace half
of the sweet peppers
with serrano or
jalapeño peppers.

Serving
Suggestions

For an hors d'oeuvre,
slit open drained
peppers on one side,
scrape out seeds and
stuff each with soft
goat cheese or feta
cheese and a whole
blanched almond.

Mince drained
peppers, discarding
stem and seeds, and
add to pasta sauce or
a salad.

2 lbs	sweet Hungarian cherry peppers	1 kg
2 tsp	pickling or canning salt	10 mL
2 cups	white vinegar	500 mL
½ cup	water	125 mL
1 cup	vodka	250 mL

1. Prepare canner, jars and lids (see pages 7 to 8).
2. Trim off all but ¼ inch (0.5 cm) of the stems from peppers. Using the tip of a sharp paring knife, cut 4 slits in the sides of each pepper, keeping peppers intact. Set aside.
3. In a pot, combine salt, vinegar and water. Bring to a boil over medium-high heat, stirring often until salt is dissolved. Boil for 1 minute. Stir in vodka. Reduce heat to low and keep liquid hot.
4. Working with one jar at a time, pack peppers into hot jars, leaving room for liquid and leaving 1 inch (2.5 cm) headspace. Pour in hot pickling liquid, leaving ½ inch (1 cm) headspace. Remove air bubbles and adjust headspace as necessary by adding hot pickling liquid. Wipe rim and place hot lid disc on jar. Screw band down until fingertip-tight.
5. Place jars in canner and return to a boil. Process for 10 minutes. Turn off heat, remove canner lid and let jars stand in water for 5 minutes. Transfer jars to a towel-lined surface and let stand for 24 hours. Check lids and refrigerate any jars that are not sealed.

Pickled Red Radishes

These are lovely to look at and a delight to eat, whether on their own or added to salads in place of fresh radishes. You'll enjoy the zip of this spring root in each bite.

Makes about five pint (500 mL) jars

• • • •

Tips

Use a mandoline or other slicer for thin, even slices.

You'll need 40 to 48 medium radishes (about 3½ lbs/ 1.75 kg) to get 12 cups (3 L).

Serving Suggestion

Use as garnish for salads, hamburgers or sandwiches.

2 tbsp	granulated sugar	25 mL
1 tbsp	pickling or canning salt	15 mL
1 tbsp	mustard seeds	15 mL
2 tsp	celery seeds	10 mL
2¾ cups	white vinegar	675 mL
2¾ cups	water	675 mL
12 cups	thinly sliced radishes	3 L

1. Prepare canner, jars and lids (see pages 7 to 8).
2. In a large pot, combine sugar, salt, mustard seeds, celery seeds, vinegar and water. Bring to a boil over medium-high heat, stirring often until sugar and salt are dissolved. Boil for 1 minute. Add radishes and simmer until heated through. Remove from heat.
3. Using a slotted spoon, pack radishes into hot jars, leaving room for liquid. Pour in hot pickling liquid, leaving ½ inch (1 cm) headspace and dividing spices as evenly as possible. Remove air bubbles and adjust headspace as necessary by adding hot pickling liquid. Wipe rim and place hot lid disc on jar. Screw band down until fingertip-tight.
4. Place jars in canner and return to a boil. Process for 10 minutes. Turn off heat, remove canner lid and let jars stand in water for 5 minutes. Transfer jars to a towel-lined surface and let stand for 24 hours. Check lids and refrigerate any jars that are not sealed.

Sweet Pickled Rhubarb

If you have a rhubarb plant, you'll get more new shoots throughout the season if you continue to pick them. So, after you've made pies, muffins and coffee cakes, make these sweet and tangy pickles as well, and keep your plant growing.

Makes about four pint (500 mL) jars

• • •

Tips

Use stalks that are no thicker than ½ inch (1 cm). Thicker stalks tend to be tough and stringy. You'll need about thirty 12-inch (30 cm) long rhubarb stalks to get 2 lbs (1 kg).

Processing rhubarb stalks in a boiling-water canner does make them soft. If you prefer a crisper texture, omit the processing. Cover with lids as directed, let filled jars cool to room temperature, then refrigerate for at least 3 days to let the flavors blend. Unprocessed pickles should be kept in the refrigerator and used within 2 months.

Serving Suggestion

Serve on an appetizer platter with other sweet and savory pickles.

2 lbs	rhubarb stalks (leaves removed)	1 kg
	Ice water	
4	1-inch (2.5 cm) pieces cinnamon stick	4
4	thin slices gingerroot	4
2	whole cloves	2
3¾ cups	granulated sugar	925 mL
1 tsp	pickling or canning salt	5 mL
3 cups	cider vinegar	750 mL
1⅓ cups	water	325 mL

1. Trim ends from rhubarb and cut into 4-inch (10 cm) lengths, or the length that will fit in jars allowing for 1 inch (2.5 cm) headspace.
2. In a large bowl, combine rhubarb and ice water to cover. Let stand for at least 30 minutes or for up to 1 hour.
3. Meanwhile, prepare canner, jars and lids (see pages 7 to 8 and tip, at left).
4. In a colander, working in batches, drain rhubarb. Set aside.
5. In a pot, combine cinnamon sticks, ginger, cloves, sugar, salt, vinegar and water. Bring to a boil over medium heat, stirring often until sugar and salt are dissolved. Boil for 1 minute. Reduce heat to low and keep liquid hot.
6. Working with one jar at time, place 1 cinnamon stick and 1 slice of ginger in hot jar; discard cloves. Pack rhubarb into jar, leaving room for liquid. Pour in hot pickling liquid, leaving ½ inch (1 cm) headspace. Remove air bubbles and adjust headspace as necessary by adding hot pickling liquid. Wipe rim and place hot lid disc on jar. Screw band down until fingertip-tight.
7. Place jars in canner and return to a boil. Process for 10 minutes. Turn off heat, remove canner lid and let jars stand in water for 5 minutes. Transfer jars to a towel-lined surface and let stand for 24 hours. Check lids and refrigerate any jars that are not sealed.

Spicy Pickled Rhubarb

Rhubarb usually gets a sweet treatment in desserts because of its ultra-tart nature. This pickle keeps it on the savory side, making for a nice change.

Makes about four pint (500 mL) jars

● ● ●

Tip

Use stalks that are no thicker than $\frac{1}{2}$ inch (1 cm). Thicker stalks tend to be tough and stringy. You'll need about thirty 12-inch (30 cm) long rhubarb stalks to get 2 lbs (1 kg).

Serving Suggestions

Serve alongside roasted meat or with spicy curries.

Drain pickles and cut into small pieces. Sprinkle on top of a green salad, along with pieces of a rich cheese such as Brie, Camembert or Gorgonzola.

2 lbs	rhubarb stalks (leaves removed)	1 kg
	Ice water	
2½ cups	granulated sugar	625 mL
1 tbsp	mustard seeds	15 mL
1½ tsp	pickling or canning salt	7 mL
½ tsp	black peppercorns	2 mL
⅛ tsp	hot pepper flakes	0.5 mL
3 cups	white vinegar	750 mL
2¼ cups	water	550 mL

1. Trim ends from rhubarb and cut into 4-inch (10 cm) lengths, or the length that will fit in jars allowing for 1 inch (2.5 cm) headspace.
2. In a large bowl, combine rhubarb and ice water to cover. Let stand for at least 30 minutes or for up to 1 hour.
3. Meanwhile, prepare canner, jars and lids (see pages 7 to 8 and tip, page 98).
4. In a colander, working in batches, drain rhubarb. Set aside.
5. In a pot, combine sugar, mustard seeds, salt, peppercorns, hot pepper flakes, vinegar and water. Bring to a boil over medium heat, stirring often until sugar and salt are dissolved. Boil for 1 minute. Reduce heat to low and keep liquid hot.
6. Working with one jar at time, pack rhubarb into jar, leaving room for liquid. Pour in hot pickling liquid, leaving ½ inch (1 cm) headspace and dividing spices as evenly as possible. Remove air bubbles and adjust headspace as necessary by adding hot pickling liquid. Wipe rim and place hot lid disc on jar. Screw band down until fingertip-tight.
7. Place jars in canner and return to a boil. Process for 10 minutes. Turn off heat, remove canner lid and let jars stand in water for 5 minutes. Transfer jars to a towel-lined surface and let stand for 24 hours. Check lids and refrigerate any jars that are not sealed.

Dilly Green Tomato Pickles

Some years there don't seem to be enough recipes to use up all of the unripe tomatoes picked before frost sets in. This is another one to add to the list, and you'll be happy for the excuse to make them.

Makes about five pint (500 mL) jars

• • •

Tips

Some heirloom tomato varieties are still green when ripe. Don't use that type for these pickles — you want firm, unripened tomatoes for the right taste and texture.

Tomatoes that are 2 to 3 inches (5 to 7.5 cm) in diameter work best for these pickles, as they fit nicely through the mouth of the jar. If you have larger tomatoes, you may want to cut them in half lengthwise, then slice crosswise for smaller pieces or slice lengthwise into $\frac{1}{4}$-inch (0.5 cm) wedges.

Day 1

5 lbs	green tomatoes	2.5 kg
$\frac{1}{4}$ cup	pickling or canning salt	50 mL

Day 2

$\frac{1}{3}$ cup	granulated sugar	75 mL
1 tbsp	dill seeds	15 mL
6 cups	white vinegar	1.5 L
$2\frac{3}{4}$ cups	water	675 mL
5	cloves garlic, quartered	5
5	dill heads	5
5	dill sprigs	5

Day 1

1. Using a sharp paring knife, remove core from tomatoes. Cut crosswise into $\frac{1}{4}$-inch (0.5 cm) slices. You should have about 15 cups (3.75 L).
2. In a large non-reactive bowl, layer tomato slices and salt, using about one-quarter of each per layer. Place a plate on top to weigh down tomatoes. Cover and let stand at a cool room temperature for at least 12 hours or for up to 24 hours.

Day 2

1. In a colander, working in batches, drain tomatoes and rinse well. Drain again, gently shaking off excess moisture. Rinse bowl and return tomatoes to the bowl. Add cold water to cover by about 1 inch (2.5 cm). Cover bowl and let stand for 3 hours.
2. Meanwhile, prepare canner, jars and lids (see pages 7 to 8).
3. In a colander, working in batches, drain tomatoes well and set aside.
4. In a large pot, combine sugar, dill seeds, vinegar and water. Bring to a boil over medium heat, stirring often until sugar is dissolved. Add tomatoes and bring to a simmer. Reduce heat and simmer, pressing occasionally to immerse tomatoes in liquid, for about 30 minutes or until tomatoes are translucent. Remove from heat.

5. Place 2 pieces of garlic and 1 dill head in each hot jar. Using a slotted spoon, pack tomatoes into jars, leaving 1 inch (2.5 cm) headspace, and top with 2 pieces of garlic and 1 dill sprig. Pour in hot pickling liquid, leaving $\frac{1}{2}$ inch (1 cm) headspace. Remove air bubbles and adjust headspace as necessary by adding hot pickling liquid. Wipe rim and place hot lid disc on jar. Screw band down until fingertip-tight.

6. Place jars in canner and return to a boil. Process for 10 minutes. Turn off heat, remove canner lid and let jars stand in water for 5 minutes. Transfer jars to a towel-lined surface and let stand for 24 hours. Check lids and refrigerate any jars that are not sealed.

Tip

If you don't have dill heads when you're ready to pickle these tomatoes, use all dill sprigs or use 5 parsley sprigs instead and increase the dill seeds to 2 tbsp (25 mL).

Bread-and-Butter Green Tomato Pickles

Rather than being disappointed that tomatoes didn't ripen, take advantage of their firm texture and tangy flavor and turn them into these delicious pickles.

Makes about five pint (500 mL) jars

● ● ●

Tips

When draining and rinsing the tomato slices, handle them gently so they maintain their shape.

Tomatoes that are 2 to 3 inches (5 to 7.5 cm) in diameter work best for these pickles, as they fit nicely through the mouth of the jar. If you have larger tomatoes, you may want to cut them in half lengthwise, then slice crosswise for smaller pieces or slice lengthwise into ¼-inch (0.5 cm) wedges.

Serving Suggestions

These are sublime when paired with well-aged (sharp) Cheddar cheese and crackers.

Make tangy BLT sandwiches using these pickles instead of fresh tomatoes.

Day 1		
5 lbs	green tomatoes	2.5 kg
¼ cup	pickling or canning salt	50 mL
Day 2		
2½ cups	granulated sugar	625 mL
2 tbsp	pickling spice	25 mL
5 cups	cider vinegar	1.25 L

Day 1

1. Using a sharp paring knife, remove core from tomatoes. Cut crosswise into ¼-inch (0.5 cm) slices. You should have about 15 cups (3.75 L).
2. In a large non-reactive bowl, layer tomato slices and salt, using about one-quarter of each per layer. Place a plate on top to weigh down tomatoes. Cover and let stand at a cool room temperature for at least 12 hours or for up to 24 hours.

Day 2

1. In a colander, working in batches, drain tomatoes and rinse well. Drain again, gently shaking off excess moisture. Rinse bowl and return tomatoes to the bowl. Add cold water to cover by about 1 inch (2.5 cm). Cover and let stand for 3 hours.
2. Meanwhile, prepare canner, jars and lids (see pages 7 to 8).
3. In a colander, working in batches, drain tomatoes well and set aside.
4. In a large pot, combine sugar, pickling spice and vinegar. Bring to a boil over medium heat, stirring often until sugar is dissolved. Add tomatoes and bring to a simmer. Reduce heat and simmer, pressing occasionally to immerse tomatoes in liquid, for about 30 minutes or until tomatoes are translucent. Remove from heat.
5. Using a slotted spoon, pack tomatoes into hot jars, leaving 1 inch (2.5 cm) headspace. Pour in hot pickling liquid, leaving ½ inch (1 cm) headspace and dividing spices as evenly as possible. Remove air bubbles and adjust headspace as necessary by adding hot pickling liquid. Wipe rim and place hot lid disc on jar. Screw band down until fingertip-tight.
6. Place jars in canner and return to a boil. Process for 10 minutes. Turn off heat, remove canner lid and let jars stand in water for 5 minutes. Transfer jars to a towel-lined surface and let stand for 24 hours. Check lids and refrigerate any jars that are not sealed.

Hot and Spicy Zucchini Pickles

These perky pickles are crisp and tangy, with a little punch. Add them to a crudités platter to liven up the party, or serve alongside a simple sandwich.

Makes about six pint (500 mL) jars

● ● ● ●

Tips

Zucchini that are larger than 2 inches (5 cm) in diameter tend to have softer, pulpy centers and can have large seeds; these qualities tend to make them fall apart when they're pickled.

Ten to 12 medium zucchini will give you 4 lbs (2 kg).

If you have zucchini that are slightly longer than 4 or 8 inches (10 or 20 cm) and have short pieces left over after cutting the sticks, keep them separate after draining in step 2 and make one jar of small pieces.

4 lbs	zucchini (no larger than 2 inches/ 5 cm in diameter)	2 kg
4 cups	ice cubes	1 L
¼ cup	pickling or canning salt	50 mL
1 cup	granulated sugar	250 mL
4½ cups	white vinegar	1.125 L
2 cups	water	500 mL
6	long hot red, orange or yellow chile peppers, cut lengthwise into thin strips	6
6	bay leaves	6
	Mustard seeds	

1. Trim ends from zucchini and cut into 4- by ½- by ½-inch (10 by 1 by 1 cm) sticks, or the length that will fit in jars allowing for 1 inch (2.5 cm) headspace, discarding any pieces that are just the interior seed portion.

2. In a large non-reactive bowl, layer zucchini, ice cubes and salt, using about one-third of each per layer. Add cold water to cover by about 1 inch (2.5 cm). Place a plate on top to weigh down zucchini. Cover and let stand at a cool room temperature for 3 hours.

3. Meanwhile, prepare canner, jars and lids (see pages 7 to 8).

4. In a colander, working in batches, drain zucchini well. Set aside.

5. In a saucepan, combine sugar, vinegar and 2 cups (500 mL) water. Bring to a boil over medium heat, stirring often until sugar is dissolved. Boil for 1 minute. Reduce heat to low and keep liquid hot.

6. Working with one jar at a time, pack zucchini and one-sixth of the hot pepper strips into each hot jar, leaving 1 inch (2.5 cm) headspace. Add 1 bay leaf and ½ tsp (2 mL) mustard seeds. Pour in hot pickling liquid, leaving ½ inch (1 cm) headspace. Remove air bubbles and adjust headspace as necessary by adding hot pickling liquid. Wipe rim and place hot lid disc on jar. Screw band down until fingertip-tight.

7. Place jars in canner and return to a boil. Process for 10 minutes. Turn off heat, remove canner lid and let jars stand in water for 5 minutes. Transfer jars to a towel-lined surface and let stand for 24 hours. Check lids and refrigerate any jars that are not sealed.

Mixed Vegetable Mustard Pickles

This combination of crunchy vegetables in sweet and tangy mustard is sure to bring back memories of family picnics and classic relish trays. The thinner sauce in this version allows for better heat penetration in processing and more reliable preserving.

Makes about six pint (500 mL) jars

● ● ●

Tips

It may seem as though there isn't enough liquid when you add the vegetables in step 3 of Day 2, but as they wilt they will become immersed. In fact, you may have pickling liquid left over after filling the jars. Use it to dress a three-bean salad, whisking in a little vegetable oil if desired.

Brown sugar gives a nice depth of flavor but does make the color darker. Substitute granulated sugar if you prefer a brighter color.

● **Baking sheets or trays, lined with lint-free towels**

Day 1

1	large head cauliflower (about 2.5 lbs/1.25 kg)	1
½ cup	pickling or canning salt, divided	125 mL
2 lbs	pickling cucumbers	1 kg
2 lbs	carrots (8 to 10)	1 kg
2 cups	chopped onions	500 mL

Day 2

2¾ cups	packed brown sugar	675 mL
½ cup	dry mustard	125 mL
1 tbsp	celery seeds	15 mL
1 tbsp	ground turmeric	15 mL
½ tsp	hot pepper flakes	2 mL
3¼ cups	white vinegar, divided	800 mL
¼ cup	cornstarch	50 mL

Day 1

1. Trim off all leaves from cauliflower. Cut cauliflower into 1- to 1½-inch (2.5 to 4 cm) florets, trimming off thick stems. You should have about 8 cups (2 L). Place in a large bowl and sprinkle with about one-third of the salt.
2. Scrub cucumbers gently under running water. Cut crosswise into ½-inch (1 cm) slices, trimming off ⅛ inch (3 mm) from each end. You should have about 6 cups (1.5 L). Layer over cauliflower in bowl and sprinkle with about one-third of the salt.
3. Cut carrots crosswise on a slight diagonal into ½-inch (1 cm) slices. Cut any slices that are larger than a quarter into half-moons. You should have about 5 cups (1.25 L). In a separate bowl, combine carrots, onions and the remaining salt.
4. To both bowls, add cold water to cover by about 1 inch (2.5 cm). Place a plate on top of each to weigh down vegetables. Cover and let stand at a cool room temperature for at least 12 hours or for up to 24 hours.

Day 2

1. Prepare canner, jars and lids (see pages 7 to 8).
2. In a colander, working in batches, drain vegetables and rinse well. Drain again. Spread cauliflower and cucumbers out on towel-lined baking sheets to drain any remaining water. Set carrots and onions aside in colander.
3. In a large pot, whisk together brown sugar, mustard, celery seeds, turmeric and hot pepper flakes. Gradually whisk in 3 cups (750 mL) of the vinegar until smooth. Bring to a boil over medium heat, stirring often until sugar is dissolved. Increase heat to medium-high. Stir in vegetables and return to a boil, gently stirring often.
4. Meanwhile, in a small bowl, whisk cornstarch into the remaining vinegar. Stir into vegetable mixture and cook, stirring, for 2 minutes or until mixture is slightly thickened and liquid is no longer cloudy. Remove from heat.
5. Using a slotted spoon, pack vegetables into hot jars, leaving 1 inch (2.5 cm) headspace. Pour in hot pickling liquid, leaving $\frac{1}{2}$ inch (1 cm) headspace. Remove air bubbles and adjust headspace as necessary by adding hot pickling liquid. Wipe rim and place hot lid disc on jar. Screw band down until fingertip-tight.
6. Place jars in canner and return to a boil. Process for 15 minutes. Turn off heat, remove canner lid and let jars stand in water for 5 minutes. Transfer jars to a towel-lined surface and let stand for 24 hours. Check lids and refrigerate any jars that are not sealed.

Variation

If you don't like one of the vegetables included in this recipe, feel free to substitute an equal volume of one of the other vegetables. If replacing the onions, use only 1 cup (250 mL) of the replacement vegetable, as cauliflower, cucumbers and carrots don't pack as tightly as onions.

Curry Zucchini Pickles

The zucchini absorbs the wonderful curry spices in these pickles, and the flavor is further enhanced by the tang of vinegar and a touch of lime.

Makes about four pint (500 mL) jars

● ● ●

Tips

Toasting the spices prevents the curry flavor from being harsh, so don't skip that step.

Avoid using curry paste for this recipe, as pastes contain oil and are not safe to use in boiling-water canning.

About 12 medium zucchini will give you 4½ lbs (2.25 kg).

- Baking sheets or trays, lined with lint-free towels

4½ lbs	zucchini (no larger than 2 inches/5 cm in diameter)	2.25 kg
¼ cup	pickling or canning salt	50 mL
2 tsp	curry powder	10 mL
½ tsp	cumin seeds	2 mL
¾ cup	granulated sugar	175 mL
⅛ tsp	ground cinnamon	0.5 mL
2¾ cups	white vinegar	675 mL
1¼ cups	water	300 mL
⅓ cup	freshly squeezed lime juice	75 mL

1. Trim ends from zucchini and cut in half lengthwise. Cut crosswise on a slight diagonal into ⅛-inch (3 mm) slices. You should have about 16 cups (4 L).
2. In a large non-reactive bowl, layer zucchini and salt, using about one-quarter of each per layer. Place a plate on top to weigh down zucchini. Cover and let stand at a cool room temperature for 3 hours or until zucchini is wilted and liquid is released.
3. In a colander, working in batches, drain zucchini and rinse well. Drain again. Spread out on towel-lined baking sheets to drain for at least 30 minutes or for up to 1 hour.
4. Meanwhile, prepare canner, jars and lids (see pages 7 to 8).
5. In a small dry skillet, over medium heat, toast curry powder and cumin seeds, stirring constantly, for about 30 seconds or until slightly darker and fragrant. Immediately transfer to a bowl and let cool.
6. In a large pot, combine toasted spices, sugar, cinnamon, vinegar and water. Bring to a boil over medium-high heat, stirring often until sugar is dissolved. Boil for 1 minute. Add lime juice and zucchini and return to a simmer. Reduce heat and simmer for about 10 minutes or until zucchini is translucent. Remove from heat.

7. Using a slotted spoon, pack zucchini into hot jars, leaving 1 inch (2.5 cm) headspace. Pour in hot pickling liquid, leaving $\frac{1}{2}$ inch (1 cm) headspace. Remove air bubbles and adjust headspace as necessary by adding hot pickling liquid. Wipe rim and place hot lid disc on jar. Screw band down until fingertip-tight.

8. Place jars in canner and return to a boil. Process for 10 minutes. Turn off heat, remove canner lid and let jars stand in water for 5 minutes. Transfer jars to a towel-lined surface and let stand for 24 hours. Check lids and refrigerate any jars that are not sealed.

Serving Suggestions

Serve as a salad with an Indian meal, or even slightly warmed as a side dish.

Add to cold meat sandwiches spread with a touch of mayonnaise, to liven up your lunch.

Sweet and Tangy Zucchini Pickles

Zucchini takes on the mild spices and sweet and tangy flavors of this bread-and-butter-style pickle nicely. This is a terrific way to use up this vigorous vegetable when you tire of zucchini loaf!

Makes about five pint (500 mL) jars

• • •

Tip

About 14 medium zucchini will give you 5 lbs (2.5 kg).

Serving Suggestion

Add zucchini to a pasta salad or a hot pasta, using some of the liquid for the dressing or sauce.

• **Baking sheets or trays, lined with lint-free towels**

5 lbs	zucchini (1 to 1½ inches/2.5 to 4 cm in diameter)	2.5 kg
¼ cup	pickling or canning salt	50 mL
2½ cups	granulated sugar	625 mL
1 tbsp	pickling spice	15 mL
1 tbsp	mustard seeds	15 mL
1 tsp	celery seeds	5 mL
5 cups	cider vinegar	1.25 L

1. Trim ends from zucchini and cut crosswise into ¼-inch (0.5 cm) slices. You should have about 15 cups (3.75 L).
2. In a large non-reactive bowl, layer zucchini and salt, using about one-quarter of each per layer. Place a plate on top to weigh down zucchini. Cover and let stand at a cool room temperature for 3 hours or until zucchini is wilted and liquid is released.
3. In a colander, working in batches, drain zucchini and rinse well. Drain again. Spread out on towel-lined baking sheets to drain for at least 30 minutes or for up to 1 hour.
4. Meanwhile, prepare canner, jars and lids (see pages 7 to 8).
5. In a large pot, combine sugar, pickling spice, mustard seeds, celery seeds and vinegar. Bring to a boil over medium heat, stirring often until sugar is dissolved. Cover, reduce heat to low and simmer for 5 minutes or until liquid is flavorful. Increase heat to medium-high. Add zucchini and return to a simmer. Reduce heat and simmer for about 10 minutes or until zucchini is translucent. Remove from heat.
6. Using a slotted spoon, pack zucchini into hot jars, leaving 1 inch (2.5 cm) headspace. Pour in hot pickling liquid, leaving ½ inch (1 cm) headspace and dividing spices as evenly as possible. Remove air bubbles and adjust headspace as necessary by adding hot pickling liquid. Wipe rim and place hot lid disc on jar. Screw band down until fingertip-tight.
7. Place jars in canner and return to a boil. Process for 10 minutes. Turn off heat, remove canner lid and let jars stand in water for 5 minutes. Transfer jars to a towel-lined surface and let stand for 24 hours. Check lids and refrigerate any jars that are not sealed.

Fruit Pickles

• • •

Fruit Pickle Basics

Pickling lets you take advantage of in-season fruits in a different way than standard jams and jellies. Fruit pickles are generally quick and easy to make, look beautiful in the jars and can liven up meals throughout the winter as savory condiments for appetizers and main courses. Some can even serve a dual purpose and be used in desserts.

Some of the traditional recipes were originally made to ensure that every morsel of food was preserved for the long winter. Classic Sweet Watermelon Rind Pickles (page 134) and Classic Spiced Pickled Crabapples (page 118) use fruits that wouldn't be eaten raw but are a luscious treat once pickled. Other classics capture fruits that spoil easily and are available for only a short time, such as peaches and quince. In modern times, pickle recipes have been developed to preserve locally grown or imported fruits, such as strawberries, pears and pineapple, when they are in season.

Just-ripe fruits are best for pickling, as their texture is far superior to fruits that are overripe and soft. Overripe fruits may also have undetectable spots of rot that can ruin a batch of pickles. Planning ahead is one key to making fruit pickles. If the fruit is very underripe, let it ripen at room temperature, preferably in a single layer on a tray, and check it daily for ripeness. Be sure to make the pickles as soon as the fruit is fragrant and starting to ripen. The exceptions are berries, cherries and grapes; these won't ripen further once picked and should be pickled as soon as possible after harvest.

Most fruit pickles are packed into jars using the hot-pack method. The fruit is added to the boiling pickling liquid in the pot and either heated just until the liquid returns to a boil or boiled or simmered long enough to cook the fruit and infuse the liquid into the fruit. The fruit is then packed into the jars and the hot liquid is added. These pickles can be packed in an assembly-line fashion. Use a slotted spoon to place the fruit in the jars, dividing them evenly between the jars, then use a ladle or a heatproof measuring cup to scoop liquid out of the pot and pour it over the fruit. With this method, it is easier to avoid ending up with one jar that is only partially filled. You do, however, need to work quickly enough to prevent the jars and food from cooling down.

Occasionally, the raw-pack method is used for fruit. Cold fruit is packed into hot jars just before a boiling hot pickling liquid is added. It is best to pack and fill raw-pack jars one at a time so that the cold fruit pieces don't cool the jars down too much before the liquid is added. Raw-pack pickles sometimes require more time in the canner than hot-pack pickles, to make sure the food is heated to a high enough temperature to destroy any microorganisms.

Raw-pack pickle recipes can generally be doubled easily, as long as the filled jars will all fit in your canner at once. Hot-pack pickle recipes aren't as easy to double, because the food may take too long to heat if there is too much in the pot (the bottom pieces of fruit will get mushy before the top ones are heated through). If you want to double hot-pack recipes, make two batches simultaneously in two pots, but only if you can fit all the jars in the canner at once. If you will have too many jars to fit in the canner, delay the start of your second batch by about 10 minutes longer than the processing time of the recipe to give you time to handle the first batch.

Fruit does tend to float in the jars because its tender flesh has tiny air pockets. Heating the fruit helps to reduce floating but won't prevent it completely. Packing the jars full helps to reduce floating as well, but take care not to fill the jars too full — the fruit must be covered by the pickling liquid. Use a spatula to gently poke down floating fruit as you top up the pickling liquid, to make sure the fruit will be covered. Maintaining the correct headspace is important so there is sufficient room for the vacuum seal to work. Use a bubble remover or spatula to remove any trapped air bubbles between pieces of fruit and help reduce floating.

Floating fruit can lead to siphoning, which is the leakage of liquid from the jars after processing. A tiny bit of siphoning is not a worry, as long as it happens immediately after jars are removed from the canner and the lid seals tightly upon cooling. If the headspace in a jar is reduced by too much liquid leaking out, consider it an unsealed jar and refrigerate upon cooling. Use the pickles within 3 weeks.

Some of the fruit pickle recipes will have liquid left over after the jars are filled, but don't be tempted to use less. The extra liquid is required to provide enough to cover the fruit when it's being heated; in addition, juice comes out of the fruit and adds volume to the liquid but isn't necessarily required to fill the jars. Extra liquid can be used to poach other fruit or can be turned into salad dressing. It should not be used again for pickles if the fruit has been immersed in it.

Fruit Pickle Pointers

- Don't alter the amounts of vinegar, water, salt and sugar. The balance of these essential ingredients is important for preserving. The recipes in this book have been carefully created for optimal flavor balance as well.
- The type of vinegar used can be adjusted according to taste as long as the strength of the acetic acid is the same. Five percent white vinegar, cider vinegar, white wine vinegar and red wine vinegar are interchangeable.
- Spices and seasonings (except for salt and sugar) can be adjusted according to taste. Feel free to get creative, but keep in mind that the flavors will be stronger after the pickles stand for a while. If you prefer mild spicing, discard any whole spices before packing jars.
- When working with heated fruit, which is very soft, use a slotted spoon with a smooth edge to lift the fruit carefully and avoid cutting or crushing it.
- Keep a separate cutting board exclusively for fruit so the flavor of strong vegetables, such as onions, doesn't transfer to the fruit.
- When working with fruits with flesh that browns upon exposure to air, soak them in lemon juice and water as soon as they are peeled. You can use a commercial ascorbic acid fruit protector, diluted according to package directions, if you prefer.
- For more pickling pointers, see Vegetable Pickle Pointers (page 24).

Gingery Cantaloupe Pickles

Ginger and ripe melon are a delicious combination. These soft and flavorful pickles are a natural to pair with spicy Asian foods or to add to salads.

Makes about six 8-ounce (250 mL) or three pint (500 mL) jars

• • •

Tip

Use a ripe but not soft melon for the best texture. Ripe cantaloupe has a sweet aroma at the stem end, and the skin under the mesh will have turned from green to beige.

Day 1

2	firm ripe cantaloupes (about 5 lbs/2.5 kg)	2
1 tbsp	pickling or canning salt	15 mL
4 cups	ice cubes	1 L
6	thin slices gingerroot	6
2 cups	granulated sugar	500 mL
1 cup	white vinegar	250 mL
½ cup	rice vinegar	125 mL
½ cup	water	125 mL

Day 1

1. Using a serrated knife, cut rind from cantaloupes. Cut in half lengthwise and scoop out seeds. Cut each half lengthwise into thirds. Cut each wedge crosswise into slices about ½ inch (1 cm) thick. You should have about 9 cups (2.25 L).

2. In a large non-reactive bowl, layer cantaloupe, salt and ice cubes, using about one-third of each per layer. Let stand at a cool room temperature for about 1 hour or until ice is melted. Drain and return cantaloupe to bowl.

3. Meanwhile, in a saucepan, combine ginger, sugar, white vinegar, rice vinegar and water. Bring to a boil over medium heat, stirring often until sugar is dissolved. Boil for 1 minute. Pour over cantaloupe and let cool. Place a plate on top to weigh down cantaloupe. Cover and let stand at a cool room temperature for at least 8 hours or for up to 18 hours.

Day 2

1. Set a colander over a large pot and drain liquid from cantaloupe into pot. Set cantaloupe aside. Bring liquid to a boil over medium-high heat. Boil for 5 minutes. Gently add cantaloupe, reduce heat and simmer, gently stirring occasionally, for about 45 minutes or until melon is translucent and looks glassy. Remove from heat.

2. Meanwhile, prepare canner, jars and lids (see pages 7 to 8).

3. Divide ginger slices evenly among hot jars. Using a slotted spoon, carefully pack cantaloupe into jars, leaving room for liquid and leaving 1 inch (2.5 cm) headspace. Pour in hot pickling liquid, leaving $\frac{1}{2}$ inch (1 cm) headspace. Remove air bubbles and adjust headspace as necessary by adding hot pickling liquid. Wipe rim and place hot lid disc on jar. Screw band down until fingertip-tight.

4. Place jars in canner and return to a boil. Process for 10 minutes. Turn off heat, remove canner lid and let jars stand in water for 5 minutes. Transfer jars to a towel-lined surface and let stand for 24 hours. Check lids and refrigerate any jars that are not sealed.

Serving Suggestions

Serve as a salad with spicy chicken, shrimp or pork satay.

Thread onto skewers with thin slices of prosciutto, Chinese barbecued pork or smoked duck for elegant appetizers.

Pickled Sweet Cherries

This plain and simple recipe lets the natural flavor of cherries shine through.

Makes six to seven 8-ounce (250 mL) jars

● ● ●

Tips

This is a tangy pickle, but you can add more sugar to the cherries just before serving if you want to use them for a dessert.

If you don't have a cherry pitter, use a firm plastic straw or chopstick and press through the cherry from stem to bottom to remove pit.

Serving Suggestions

Serve with roast pork or poultry.

Serve drained cherries on a salad with crumbled blue cheese and toasted pecans.

● Cherry pitter (see tip, at left)

3 lbs	sweet cherries (about 7 cups/1.75 L)	1.5 kg
⅓ cup	granulated sugar	75 mL
2 tsp	pickling or canning salt	10 mL
2 cups	cider vinegar	500 mL
2 cups	water	500 mL

1. Prepare canner, jars and lids (see pages 7 to 8).
2. Using cherry pitter, remove pits. Using a toothpick, pierce the skin of each cherry a few times.
3. In a large pot, combine sugar, salt, vinegar and water. Bring to a boil over medium-high heat, stirring often until sugar and salt are dissolved. Increase heat to high, add cherries and heat just until mixture returns to a boil and cherries are heated through. Remove from heat.
4. Using a slotted spoon, pack cherries into hot jars, leaving 1 inch (2.5 cm) headspace. Pour in hot pickling liquid, leaving ½ inch (1 cm) headspace. Remove air bubbles and adjust headspace as necessary by adding hot pickling liquid. Wipe rim and place hot lid disc on jar. Screw band down until fingertip-tight.
5. Place jars in canner and return to a boil. Process for 15 minutes. Turn off heat, remove canner lid and let jars stand in water for 5 minutes. Transfer jars to a towel-lined surface and let stand for 24 hours. Check lids and refrigerate any jars that are not sealed.

Lightly Spiced Pickled Sour Cherries

Warm spices and sweet brown sugar turn sour cherries into something special.

• Cherry pitter (see tip, page 114)

Makes six to seven 8-ounce (250 mL) jars

● ● ●

3 lbs	sour cherries (about 7 cups/1.75 L)	1.5 kg
2 cups	packed brown sugar	500 mL
½ tsp	pickling or canning salt	2 mL
¼ tsp	ground cinnamon	1 mL
¼ tsp	ground ginger	1 mL
¼ tsp	freshly ground black pepper	1 mL
1⅓ cups	cider vinegar	325 mL
⅓ cup	water	75 mL

1. Prepare canner, jars and lids (see pages 7 to 8).
2. Using cherry pitter, remove pits. Using a toothpick, pierce the skin of each cherry a few times.
3. In a large pot, combine brown sugar, salt, cinnamon, ginger, pepper, vinegar and water. Bring to a boil over medium heat, stirring often until sugar and salt are dissolved. Boil for 1 minute. Increase heat to high, add cherries and heat just until mixture returns to a boil and cherries are heated through. Remove from heat.
4. Using a slotted spoon, pack cherries into hot jars, leaving 1 inch (2.5 cm) headspace. Pour in hot pickling liquid, leaving ½ inch (1 cm) headspace. Remove air bubbles and adjust headspace as necessary by adding hot pickling liquid. Wipe rim and place hot lid disc on jar. Screw band down until fingertip-tight.
5. Place jars in canner and return to a boil. Process for 15 minutes. Turn off heat, remove canner lid and let jars stand in water for 5 minutes. Transfer jars to a towel-lined surface and let stand for 24 hours. Check lids and refrigerate any jars that are not sealed.

Tips

Sour cherries may be labeled "tart cherries" or "pie cherries." There are different varieties, the best known being the Montmorency cherry, which is often used to make dried cherries. Watch for them at farmers' markets and fruit stands, and buy them as soon as you see them. The season is very short.

Sour (tart) cherries are sometimes sold pre-pitted in buckets, packed with a small amount of sugar. These can be used for pickles but will have a softer texture than fresh ones you pit yourself. Drain them well before measuring.

Serving Suggestions

Serve with whipped cream as a topping on cheesecake or pound cake.

Serve with roast ham, poultry or pâté.

Marsala and White Balsamic Pickled Figs

Fresh figs get a decadent treatment with the addition of sweetly fragrant Marsala and pungent balsamic vinegar. These pickles are equally suited to both sweet and savory dishes.

Makes six pint (500 mL) jars

● ● ●

Tips

The figs get quite soft and tender once simmered in the sugar mixture, so be sure to keep the liquid just at a simmer, with bubbles just breaking the surface, and handle the figs carefully when working with them to prevent breaking the skin and splitting them open.

If you have two large pots, it is easier to divide the ingredients in half and cook two smaller batches at the same time. This prevents the delicate figs from getting squished.

Use any leftover liquid to poach other fruit or to drizzle on fruit salad. It freezes well for up to 6 months.

Day 1

48	fresh figs (about 4 lbs/2 kg)	48
	Boiling water	
3 cups	granulated sugar, divided	750 mL
1 tsp	pickling or canning salt	5 mL
6 cups	water	1.5 L
2 cups	white balsamic vinegar	500 mL

Day 2

1 cup	dry Marsala	250 mL

Day 1

1. In a large heatproof bowl, cover figs with boiling water. Let stand for 10 minutes. Drain figs well. Using a toothpick, gently pierce each fig a few times.
2. In a large pot, combine 2 cups (500 mL) of the sugar, the salt and 6 cups (1.5 L) water. Bring to a simmer over medium heat, stirring often until sugar and salt are dissolved. Stir in figs. Reduce heat and simmer gently, flipping occasionally, for about 30 minutes or until fig skins are translucent and easily pierced with a toothpick. (If figs are different sizes, you may need to remove them as they are done. Use a slotted spoon to transfer figs to a bowl and set aside. Add back to pot once all figs are ready.)
3. Stir in the remaining sugar and the vinegar. Remove from heat and let cool to room temperature. Cover and refrigerate for at least 12 hours or for up to 24 hours.

Day 2

1. Prepare canner, jars and lids (see pages 7 to 8).
2. Using a slotted spoon, carefully transfer figs to a bowl, reserving liquid; set figs aside. Measure 5 cups (1.25 L) of the liquid and return to the pot. (Reserve any remaining liquid; see tip, at left.) Stir in Marsala and return figs to the pot. Place pot over medium-low heat and heat, gently stirring occasionally, for about 30 minutes or until liquid is simmering and figs are heated through. Remove from heat.

3. Using a slotted spoon, gently pack 8 figs into each hot jar, leaving 1 inch (2.5 cm) headspace. Pour in hot pickling liquid, leaving ½ inch (1 cm) headspace. Carefully remove air bubbles and adjust headspace as necessary by adding hot pickling liquid. Wipe rim and place hot lid disc on jar. Screw band down until fingertip-tight.

4. Place jars in canner and return to a boil. Process for 20 minutes. Turn off heat, remove canner lid and let jars stand in water for 5 minutes. Transfer jars to a towel-lined surface and let stand for 24 hours. Check lids and refrigerate any jars that are not sealed.

Serving Suggestions

Fig and Prosciutto Hors d'Oeuvres: Drain figs and wrap with a thin slice of prosciutto; secure with a toothpick. Grill over medium heat or broil, turning often, just until heated through.

Slice figs and serve on top of cheesecake, drizzled with the pickling liquid.

Classic Spiced Pickled Crabapples

When I was growing up, crystal bowls of these tiny red apples on the table were a sure sign of a special occasion. Much to my delight, one bite of the warm spices and sweet tang still elicits happy memories of holiday dinners with family.

Makes about six pint (500 mL) jars

● ● ●

Tips

Crabapples don't keep very long once picked, so pickle them as soon as possible after harvest. Don't use apples that have fallen to the ground — they are not fresh enough for preserving. You'll need about seventy 1½ inch (4 cm) crabapples.

For the best flavor and texture, these pickles benefit from standing for 2 to 3 weeks after processing.

For mild spicing, discard the spices after step 4. For bolder spicing, add them to the jars in step 5.

Serving Suggestions

Serve with roast turkey or chicken or with ham.

Slice drained pickled crabapples, discarding cores, and add to meat or cheese sandwiches.

3¾ lbs	crabapples	1.875 kg
6	whole cloves	6
3	sticks cinnamon (each 3 inches/7.5 cm long), broken in half	3
5 cups	granulated sugar	1.25 L
2¾ cups	cider vinegar	675 mL
1 cup	water	250 mL

1. Prepare canner, jars and lids (see pages 7 to 8).
2. Cut stems from crabapples and, using a fork, prick each apple all over.
3. Place cloves and cinnamon sticks in the center of a square of triple-layered cheesecloth and tie into a spice bag.
4. In a large pot, combine spice bag, sugar, vinegar and water. Bring to a boil over medium heat, stirring often until sugar is dissolved. Cover, reduce heat to low and simmer for 5 minutes or until liquid is flavorful. Increase heat to medium-high, add crabapples and return to a boil. Reduce heat and simmer for 2 to 5 minutes or until apples are tender. Remove from heat. Remove spice bag, squeezing out excess liquid. If desired, untie bag and reserve spices.
5. Divide reserved spices (if using) evenly among hot jars. Using a slotted spoon, pack crabapples into jars, leaving 1 inch (2.5 cm) headspace. Pour in hot pickling liquid, leaving ½ inch (1 cm) headspace. Remove air bubbles and adjust headspace as necessary by adding hot pickling liquid. Wipe rim and place hot lid disc on jar. Screw band down until fingertip-tight.
6. Place jars in canner and return to a boil. Process for 20 minutes. Turn off heat, remove canner lid and let jars stand in water for 5 minutes. Transfer jars to a towel-lined surface and let stand for 24 hours. Check lids and refrigerate any jars that are not sealed.

Sweet and Tangy Pickled Grapes

The mild spices are just enough to add interest but don't overwhelm the sweet and tangy flavor of these pickles. Use them to add zest to a cheese platter or nibble them with sandwiches.

Makes about six 8-ounce (250 mL) jars

Tip

Table grapes that have taut skin and a firm texture are best suited to pickling.

6 cups	seedless grapes (about 2¼ lbs/1.125 kg)	1.5 L
3 cups	packed brown sugar	750 mL
½ tsp	pickling or canning salt	2 mL
¼ tsp	ground cinnamon	1 mL
¼ tsp	ground allspice	1 mL
1½ cups	cider vinegar	375 mL

1. Prepare canner, jars and lids (see pages 7 to 8).
2. Using a toothpick, pierce the skin of each grape a few times.
3. In a large pot, combine brown sugar, salt, cinnamon, allspice and vinegar. Bring to a boil over medium heat, stirring often until sugar and salt are dissolved. Boil for 1 minute. Increase heat to high, add grapes and heat just until mixture returns to a boil and grapes are heated through. Remove from heat.
4. Using a slotted spoon, pack grapes into hot jars, leaving 1 inch (2.5 cm) headspace. Pour in hot pickling liquid, leaving ½ inch (1 cm) headspace. Remove air bubbles and adjust headspace as necessary by adding hot pickling liquid. Wipe rim and place hot lid disc on jar. Screw band down until fingertip-tight.
5. Place jars in canner and return to a boil. Process for 10 minutes. Turn off heat, remove canner lid and let jars stand in water for 5 minutes. Transfer jars to a towel-lined surface and let stand for 24 hours. Check lids and refrigerate any jars that are not sealed.

Spiced Pickled Grapes

A blend of sweet and savory spices and a touch of heat make these grapes so tasty you won't be able to eat just one. A cheese and cracker platter will never again be the same without them.

**Makes about
six 8-ounce
(250 mL) jars**

• • •

Tip

To make a spice bag, cut a 4-inch (10 cm) square piece of triple-layered cheesecloth. Place the pickling spice in the center of the square and bring the edges together into a bundle. Tie tightly with kitchen string. Alternatively, use a large mesh tea ball.

**Serving
Suggestions**

Serve with a curry in place of chutney.

Serve with meats, cheeses, sweet vegetable pickles and crusty bread.

6 cups	seedless grapes (about 2¼ lbs/1.125 kg)	1.5 L
2¼ cups	granulated sugar	550 mL
1 tbsp	pickling spice, tied in a spice bag (see tip, at left)	15 mL
½ tsp	pickling or canning salt	2 mL
¼ tsp	hot pepper flakes	1 mL
1½ cups	white vinegar	375 mL
½ cup	water	125 mL

1. Prepare canner, jars and lids (see pages 7 to 8).
2. Using a toothpick, pierce the skin of each grape a few times.
3. In a large pot, combine sugar, pickling spice, salt, hot pepper flakes, vinegar and water. Bring to a boil over medium heat, stirring often until sugar and salt are dissolved. Reduce heat to low, cover and simmer for 5 minutes or until liquid is flavorful. Increase heat to high, add grapes and heat just until mixture returns to a boil and grapes are heated through. Remove from heat.
4. Using a slotted spoon, pack grapes into hot jars, leaving 1 inch (2.5 cm) headspace. Pour in hot pickling liquid, leaving ½ inch (1 cm) headspace. Remove air bubbles and adjust headspace as necessary by adding hot pickling liquid. Wipe rim and place hot lid disc on jar. Screw band down until fingertip-tight.
5. Place jars in canner and return to a boil. Process for 10 minutes. Turn off heat, remove canner lid and let jars stand in water for 5 minutes. Transfer jars to a towel-lined surface and let stand for 24 hours. Check lids and refrigerate any jars that are not sealed.

Old-Fashioned Sweet Pickled Peaches

My family enjoys these pickles with baked ham. They're also lovely served on cheesecake.

Makes about six pint (500 mL) jars

● ● ●

Tips

To make a spice bag, cut a piece of triple-layered cheesecloth about 4-inches (10 cm) square. Place the spices in the center of the square and bring edges together into a bundle. Tie tightly with kitchen string. Alternatively, use a large mesh tea ball.

If using larger peaches, cut them lengthwise into quarters instead of halves so they will fit easily through the mouths of the jars.

If you prefer a subtle spice flavor, discard the spices before filling the jars. If you like a bolder spice flavor, add the spices to the jars in step 6.

Variations

Add ¼ vanilla bean, split in half lengthwise, to the spice bag. Discard before packing jars.

Add 1 tbsp (15 mL) heated brandy to each jar before adding the peaches.

6	whole cloves	6
3	sticks cinnamon (each 3 inches/7.5 cm long), broken in half	3
1	2-inch (5 cm) piece gingerroot, cut into 6 pieces	1
5 cups	granulated sugar	1.25 L
3⅓ cups	cider vinegar	825 mL
8 cups	water	2 L
¼ cup	freshly squeezed lemon juice	50 mL
6 lbs	small firm ripe peaches (about 30)	3 kg

1. Place cloves, cinnamon sticks and ginger in the center of a square of triple-layered cheesecloth and tie into a spice bag.

2. In a large pot, combine spice bag, sugar and vinegar. Bring to a boil over medium heat, stirring often until sugar is dissolved. Remove from heat, cover and let stand for 1 hour to infuse spices.

3. Meanwhile, prepare canner, jars and lids (see pages 7 to 8).

4. In a large bowl, combine water and lemon juice. Peel peaches (see page 16). Using a small paring knife, starting at the stem and the natural indent in the peach, cut in half around the pit. Insert both thumbs into the dent at the stem and gently pry apart into halves, discarding pit. Add peaches to the lemon water as they are peeled and cut.

5. Return pot of pickling liquid to medium-high heat and bring to a boil. Drain peaches, discarding soaking water, and add to pot. Return to a boil. Reduce heat and simmer, gently stirring occasionally, for about 5 minutes or until peaches are tender when pierced with the tip of a knife. Remove from heat. Remove spice bag, squeezing out excess liquid. If desired, untie bag and reserve spices.

6. Divide reserved spices (if using) evenly among hot jars. Using a slotted spoon, pack peaches into jars, rounded side down, leaving 1 inch (2.5 cm) headspace. Pour in hot pickling liquid, leaving ½ inch (1 cm) headspace. Remove air bubbles and adjust headspace as necessary by adding hot pickling liquid. Wipe rim and place hot lid disc on jar. Screw band down until fingertip-tight.

7. Place jars in canner and return to a boil. Process for 20 minutes. Turn off heat, remove canner lid and let jars stand in water for 5 minutes. Transfer jars to a towel-lined surface and let stand for 24 hours. Check lids and refrigerate any jars that are not sealed.

Spiced Pickled Peaches

This pickle is a savory treatment for peaches that highlights their natural fruity flavor and adds a bit of kick.

Makes about 6 pint (500 mL) jars

• • •

Tip

Packing the peaches rounded side down reduces the chance of air pockets getting trapped in the hollow where the pit was removed.

Serving Suggestions

Peach Bruschetta: Dice drained peaches and combine with diced tomatoes, minced garlic and chopped fresh basil. Serve on top of toasted baguette slices.

Serve slightly warmed with grilled pork or veal or roast duck.

10 cups	water, divided	2.5 L
¼ cup	freshly squeezed lemon juice	50 mL
6 lbs	firm ripe peaches (about 24)	3 kg
3	bay leaves	3
3	small dried hot red chile peppers, crumbled	3
1 cup	granulated sugar	250 mL
4 tsp	pickling or kosher salt	20 mL
1 tbsp	mustard seeds	15 mL
3½ cups	white vinegar	875 mL
1¾ cups	water	425 mL

1. Prepare canner, jars and lids (see pages 7 to 8).
2. In a large bowl, combine 8 cups (2 L) of the water and the lemon juice. Peel peaches (see page 16). Using a small paring knife, starting at the stem and the natural indent in the peach, cut in half around the pit. Insert both thumbs into the dent at the stem and gently pry apart into halves. Cut each half lengthwise in two, discarding pit. Add peaches to the lemon water as they are peeled and cut. Set aside.
3. In a large pot, combine bay leaves, chile peppers, sugar, salt, mustard seeds, vinegar and the remaining water. Bring to a boil over medium heat, stirring often until sugar and salt are dissolved. Boil for 1 minute.
4. Drain peaches, discarding soaking water. Increase heat to medium-high, add peaches to pot and return to a boil. Reduce heat and simmer, gently stirring twice, for about 5 minutes or until peaches are tender when pierced with the tip of a knife. Remove from heat. Discard bay leaves.
5. Using a slotted spoon, pack peaches into hot jars, rounded side down, leaving 1 inch (2.5 cm) headspace. Pour in hot pickling liquid, leaving ½ inch (1 cm) headspace and dividing spices as evenly as possible. Remove air bubbles and adjust headspace as necessary by adding hot pickling liquid. Wipe rim and place hot lid disc on jar. Screw band down until fingertip-tight.
6. Place jars in canner and return to a boil. Process for 20 minutes. Turn off heat, remove canner lid and let jars stand in water for 5 minutes. Transfer jars to a towel-lined surface and let stand for 24 hours. Check lids and refrigerate any jars that are not sealed.

Sweet and Tangy Pickled Pears

Fragrant pears take on light spices, sweetness and tang in these pickles. They're special enough to serve with your holiday turkey, or serve them any day with pork chops.

Makes about six pint (500 mL) jars

● ● ●

Tips

Use small, firm pears that are suited for cooking and canning, such as Seckel, Bartlett or Kieffer.

For a lighter spice flavor, discard the spices instead of adding them to the jars.

Packing the pears rounded side down reduces the chance of air pockets getting trapped in the hollow where the core was removed.

You will likely have some of the pickling liquid left over after filling the jars. Use it to poach other fruit or turn it into a salad dressing by whisking in a little vegetable oil, Dijon mustard and chopped fresh basil.

9 cups	water, divided	2.25 L
¼ cup	freshly squeezed lemon juice	50 mL
6 lbs	small pears (about 24)	3 kg
3	sticks cinnamon (each 3 inches/7.5 cm long), broken in half	3
4 cups	granulated sugar	1 L
1 cup	packed brown sugar	250 mL
1 tsp	whole allspice	5 mL
3 cups	cider vinegar	750 mL

1. Prepare canner, jars and lids (see pages 7 to 8).
2. In a large bowl, combine 8 cups (2 L) of the water and the lemon juice. Peel pears and cut in half lengthwise. Remove core and stems. Add pears to the lemon water as they are peeled and cut. Set aside.
3. In a large pot, combine cinnamon sticks, granulated sugar, brown sugar, allspice, vinegar and the remaining water. Bring to a boil over medium heat, stirring often until sugar is dissolved. Reduce heat to low, cover and simmer for 5 minutes or until liquid is flavorful. Increase heat to medium and return to a boil.
4. Drain pears, discarding soaking water, and add to pot. Simmer, gently turning pears occasionally, for 5 to 15 minutes or until pears are tender when pierced with the tip of a knife, adjusting heat as necessary to keep the liquid at a simmer. Remove from heat.
5. Using a slotted spoon, pack pears into hot jars, rounded side down, leaving 1 inch (2.5 cm) headspace. Pour in hot pickling liquid, leaving ½ inch (1 cm) headspace and dividing spices as evenly as possible. Remove air bubbles and adjust headspace as necessary by adding hot pickling liquid. Wipe rim and place hot lid disc on jar. Screw band down until fingertip-tight.
6. Place jars in canner and return to a boil. Process for 20 minutes. Turn off heat, remove canner lid and let jars stand in water for 5 minutes. Transfer jars to a towel-lined surface and let stand for 24 hours. Check lids and refrigerate any jars that are not sealed.

Pinot-Poached Pears with Rosemary and Vanilla

Classic poached pears get an update with fragrant rosemary and vanilla. It's an exotic flavor combination that enhances pears and wine amazingly well.

Makes about four pint (500 mL) jars

● ● ●

Tip

Use a wine that you enjoy drinking by the glass. Don't be tempted to use a lower-quality wine that you don't like! The flavors will intensify after cooking, and bad flavors certainly won't improve.

7 cups	water, divided	1.75 L
3 tbsp	freshly squeezed lemon juice	45 mL
4 lbs	small pears (about 16)	2 kg
1	sprig rosemary (about 3 inches/7.5 cm long)	1
1	1-inch (2.5 cm) piece vanilla bean, split lengthwise	1
3 cups	granulated sugar	750 mL
1½ cups	Pinot Noir or other light fruity red wine	375 mL
½ cup	white wine vinegar	125 mL

1. Prepare canner, jars and lids (see pages 7 to 8).
2. In a large bowl, combine 6 cups (1.5 L) of the water and the lemon juice. Peel pears and cut in half lengthwise. Remove core and stems. Add pears to the lemon water as they are peeled and cut. Set aside.
3. In a large pot, combine rosemary, vanilla bean, sugar, wine, vinegar and the remaining water. Bring to a boil over medium heat, stirring often until sugar is dissolved. Reduce heat to low, cover and simmer for 5 minutes or until liquid is flavorful. Increase heat to medium and return to a boil.
4. Drain pears, discarding soaking water, and add to pot. Simmer, gently turning pears occasionally, for 5 to 15 minutes or until pears are tender when pierced with the tip of a knife, adjusting heat as necessary to keep the liquid at a simmer. Using a slotted spoon, transfer pears to a bowl; cover and keep hot.
5. Increase heat to high and boil liquid for about 10 minutes or until reduced by about one-third and syrupy. Skim off any foam. Reduce heat to low and keep liquid hot. Discard rosemary and vanilla bean.

6. Using a slotted spoon, pack pears into hot jars, rounded side down, leaving 1 inch (2.5 cm) headspace. Pour in hot pickling liquid, leaving $\frac{1}{2}$ inch (1 cm) headspace. Remove air bubbles and adjust headspace as necessary by adding hot pickling liquid. Wipe rim and place hot lid disc on jar. Screw band down until fingertip-tight.

7. Place jars in canner and return to a boil. Process for 20 minutes. Turn off heat, remove canner lid and let jars stand in water for 5 minutes. Transfer jars to a towel-lined surface and let stand for 24 hours. Check lids and refrigerate any jars that are not sealed.

Serving Suggestions

Slice drained pear halves lengthwise and place on top of a baked tart shell filled with custard.

Serve drained pears on a salad with smoked duck or chicken and crumbled sharp cheese. Whisk the pickling liquid with some olive oil to make a dressing.

Five-Spice Pickled Pears

This aromatic pear recipe is adapted from one my friend and colleague Kate Gammal created for Canadian Living *magazine when we worked in the test kitchen there. I've enhanced the pickle character, making it suitable to serve with Asian curries or as an exotic dessert.*

Makes about six pint (500 mL) jars

● ● ●

Tips

Use small, firm pears that are suited for cooking and canning, such as Seckel, Bartlett or Kieffer.

Keep the liquid at a simmer, not a boil, when cooking the pears to make sure the outside doesn't get too soft before the inside is tender.

If you prefer a subtle spice flavor, discard the spices before filling the jars. If you like a bolder spice flavor, add the spices to the jars in step 7.

6	strips (each 1½ by 1 inch/4 by 2.5 cm) lemon zest	6
6	thin slices gingerroot	6
6	whole star anise	6
6	whole cloves	6
6	whole green cardamom pods, lightly crushed	6
½ tsp	black peppercorns	2 mL
10 cups	water, divided	2.5 L
¼ cup	freshly squeezed lemon juice	50 mL
6 lbs	small pears (about 24)	3 kg
6 cups	granulated sugar	1.5 L
2 tsp	pickling or canning salt	10 mL
2 cups	white vinegar	500 mL
1 cup	rice vinegar	250 mL

1. Prepare canner, jars and lids (see pages 7 to 8).
2. Place lemon zest, ginger, star anise, cloves, cardamom and peppercorns in the center of a square of triple-layered cheesecloth and tie into a spice bag. Set aside.
3. In a large bowl, combine 8 cups (2 L) of the water and the lemon juice. Peel pears and cut in half lengthwise. Remove core and stems. Add pears to the lemon water as they are peeled and cut. Set aside.
4. In a large pot, combine spice bag, sugar, salt, white vinegar, rice vinegar and the remaining water. Bring to a boil over medium heat, stirring often until sugar and salt are dissolved. Boil for 5 minutes.
5. Drain pears, discarding soaking water, and add to pot. Reduce heat and simmer, gently turning pears occasionally, for 5 to 15 minutes or until pears are tender when pierced with the tip of a knife, adjusting heat as necessary to keep the liquid at a simmer. Using a slotted spoon, transfer pears to a bowl; cover and keep hot.
6. Increase heat to high and boil liquid for about 10 minutes or until reduced by about one-third and syrupy. Skim off any foam. Reduce heat to low and keep liquid hot. Remove spice bag, squeezing out excess liquid. If desired, untie bag and reserve spices.

7. Divide reserved spices (if using) evenly among hot jars. Pack pears into jars, rounded side down, leaving 1 inch (2.5 cm) headspace. Pour in hot pickling liquid, leaving $\frac{1}{2}$ inch (1 cm) headspace. Remove air bubbles and adjust headspace as necessary by adding hot pickling liquid. Wipe rim and place hot lid disc on jar. Screw band down until fingertip-tight.

8. Place jars in canner and return to a boil. Process for 20 minutes. Turn off heat, remove canner lid and let jars stand in water for 5 minutes. Transfer jars to a towel-lined surface and let stand for 24 hours. Check lids and refrigerate any jars that are not sealed.

Serving Suggestions

Slice drained pears and add at the end of a stir-fry.

Serve pears with ice cream or a baked custard, drizzled with a little of the liquid, for dessert.

Pickled Pineapple Spears

Just a touch of spice accents pineapple spears nicely and makes these sweet and tangy pickles very versatile.

Variations

Rum-Spiked Pineapple Spears: Add 2 tbsp (25 mL) heated dark rum to each jar before adding the pineapple.

Spiced Pickled Pineapple: Tie the cinnamon sticks in a spice bag with ½ tsp (2 mL) each whole allspice and cloves and a ¼-inch (0.5 cm) piece whole nutmeg.

Serving Suggestions

Chop drained pineapple and add diced bell and hot chile peppers for a quick salsa.

Serve with a Caribbean curry or, sliced, on roti or other wraps.

Gently heat pineapple and some of the pickling liquid in a saucepan and serve over ice cream.

2	pineapples (about 8 lbs/4 kg)	2
2	sticks cinnamon (each 3 inches/7.5 cm long)	2
3 cups	granulated sugar	750 mL
½ tsp	pickling or kosher salt	2 mL
3 cups	cider vinegar	750 mL
1 cup	water	250 mL

1. Prepare canner, jars and lids (see pages 7 to 8).
2. Twist off leaves from pineapples. Using a serrated knife, trim off top and bottom. Place flat side down on cutting board and, using a sawing motion, cut off peel in strips. Using a small paring knife, cut out any eyes that remain in fruit. Cut in half lengthwise, then cut each half lengthwise into quarters. Cut off core and discard. Cut pineapple into wedge-shaped spears, each about 2 by 1 by 1 inch (5 by 2.5 by 2.5 cm).
3. In a large pot, combine cinnamon sticks, sugar, salt, vinegar and water. Bring to a boil over medium heat, stirring often until sugar and salt are dissolved. Reduce heat to low, cover and simmer for about 5 minutes or until liquid is flavorful. Increase heat to medium-high, add pineapple and heat just until mixture returns to a boil and pineapple is heated through. Remove from heat. Discard cinnamon sticks.
4. Using a slotted spoon, pack pineapple into hot jars, leaving room for liquid and leaving 1 inch (2.5 cm) headspace. Pour in hot pickling liquid, leaving ½ inch (1 cm) headspace. Remove air bubbles and adjust headspace as necessary by adding hot pickling liquid. Wipe rim and place hot lid disc on jar. Screw band down until fingertip-tight.
5. Place jars in canner and return to a boil. Process for 10 minutes. Turn off heat, remove canner lid and let jars stand in water for 5 minutes. Transfer jars to a towel-lined surface and let stand for 24 hours. Check lids and refrigerate any jars that are not sealed.

Hot and Sweet Pickled Pineapple

Tang, spice and zing make these pickles just the thing to serve with a Thai or Indian meal.

Tips

Peeled, cored pineapples are often available and save a lot of time. Just be sure the pineapple is very fresh and that the entire core was removed. Trim off any tough core that may be left, as it makes for stringy pickles.

You may not have enough pineapple to fill the fifth pint jar, depending on how it packs down. Prepare an 8-ounce (250 mL) jar just in case. Alternatively, refrigerate the partially filled jar for 1 week to blend the flavors and use it first.

Serving Suggestions

Thread pineapple onto skewers with fresh mint leaves to serve as appetizers.

Dice drained pineapple and toss with shredded carrots and sliced green onions for a quick salad. Whisk a little of the pickling liquid with vegetable oil for the dressing.

2	pineapples (about 8 lbs/4 kg)	2
6	thin slices gingerroot	6
5	small dried hot red chile peppers, crumbled	5
2 cups	granulated sugar	500 mL
2 tsp	pickling or kosher salt	10 mL
½ tsp	ground cumin	2 mL
2 cups	white vinegar	500 mL
1 cup	rice vinegar	250 mL
1½ cups	water	375 mL

1. Prepare canner, jars and lids (see pages 7 to 8).
2. Twist off leaves from pineapples. Using a serrated knife, trim off top and bottom. Place flat side down on cutting board and, using a sawing motion, cut off peel in strips. Using a small paring knife, cut out any eyes that remain in fruit. Cut in half lengthwise, then cut each half lengthwise into quarters. Cut off core and discard. Cut pineapple into about 1¼-inch (3 cm) chunks. You should have about 10 cups (2.5 L).
3. In a large pot, combine ginger, chile peppers, sugar, salt, cumin, white vinegar, rice vinegar and water. Bring to a boil over medium heat, stirring often until sugar and salt are dissolved. Increase heat to medium-high, add pineapple and heat just until mixture returns to a boil and pineapple is heated through. Remove from heat.
4. Using a slotted spoon, pack pineapple into hot jars, leaving room for liquid and leaving 1 inch (2.5 cm) headspace. Pour in hot pickling liquid, leaving ½ inch (1 cm) headspace and dividing spices as evenly as possible. Remove air bubbles and adjust headspace as necessary by adding hot pickling liquid. Wipe rim and place hot lid disc on jar. Screw band down until fingertip-tight.
5. Place jars in canner and return to a boil. Process for 10 minutes. Turn off heat, remove canner lid and let jars stand in water for 5 minutes. Transfer jars to a towel-lined surface and let stand for 24 hours. Check lids and refrigerate any jars that are not sealed.

Gingery Pickled Plums

Deep purple plums take on a zingy ginger flavor in this simple pickle. Serve them with roasted or grilled meats or add to a stir-fry for a punch of flavor.

Makes about seven 8-ounce (250 mL) jars

● ● ●

Tip

Use natural rice vinegar for this recipe. "Seasoned" rice vinegar contains added sugar and salt, which would throw off the balance of ingredients.

3 lbs	prune (blue) plums (55 to 60)	1.5 kg
1/3 cup	thin slices gingerroot	75 mL
2 cups	granulated sugar	500 mL
1/4 tsp	pickling or canning salt	1 mL
1 cup	white vinegar	250 mL
1/2 cup	rice vinegar	125 mL
1/4 cup	water	50 mL

1. Prepare canner, jars and lids (see pages 7 to 8).
2. Using a fork, prick plums all over. Using a small paring knife, starting at the stem and the natural indent in the plum, cut in half around the pit. Twist each half in the opposite direction and separate halves. Discard pit.
3. In a large pot, combine ginger, sugar, salt, white vinegar, rice vinegar and water. Bring to a boil over medium heat, stirring often until sugar and salt are dissolved. Boil for 1 minute. Increase heat to high, add plums and heat just until mixture returns to a boil and plums are heated through and slightly tender.
4. Using a slotted spoon, pack plums into hot jars, leaving room for liquid and leaving 1 inch (2.5 cm) headspace, dividing slices of ginger evenly among jars. Pour in hot pickling liquid, leaving 1/2 inch (1 cm) headspace. Remove air bubbles and adjust headspace as necessary by adding hot pickling liquid. Wipe rim and place hot lid disc on jar. Screw band down until fingertip-tight.
5. Place jars in canner and return to a boil. Process for 20 minutes. Turn off heat, remove canner lid and let jars stand in water for 5 minutes. Transfer jars to a towel-lined surface and let stand for 24 hours. Check lids and refrigerate any jars that are not sealed.

Spiced Pickled Plums

In this pickle, plums are preserved in the tradition of spiced peaches and crabapples, taking on sweet, warm spices.

Makes about seven 8-ounce (250 mL) jars

3 lbs	prune (blue) plums (55 to 60)	1.5 kg
14	whole cloves	14
7	thin slices gingerroot	7
3	sticks cinnamon (each 3 inches/7.5 cm long), broken into 7 pieces in total	3
2 tsp	whole allspice	10 mL
2 cups	granulated sugar	500 mL
½ tsp	pickling or canning salt	2 mL
1⅓ cups	cider vinegar	325 mL
⅓ cup	water	75 mL

Tips

Choose firm plums for this recipe. If they are too soft, they'll become mushy when heated.

For a mildly spiced pickle, discard the spices at the end of step 4. For bolder spicing, add them to the jars in step 5.

Serving Suggestions

Serve with baked ham or roast poultry.

Purée plums with pickling liquid and vegetable oil for a richly flavored salad dressing.

1. Prepare canner, jars and lids (see pages 7 to 8).
2. Using a fork, prick plums all over. Using a small paring knife, starting at the stem and the natural indent in the plum, cut in half around the pit. Twist each half in the opposite direction and separate halves. Discard pit. Set aside.
3. Place cloves, ginger and cinnamon sticks and allspice in the center of a square of triple-layered cheesecloth and tie into a spice bag.
4. In a large pot, combine spice bag, sugar, salt, vinegar and water. Bring to a boil over medium heat, stirring often until sugar and salt are dissolved. Cover, reduce heat to low and simmer for about 5 minutes or until liquid is flavorful. Increase heat to high, add plums and heat just until mixture returns to a boil and plums are heated through and slightly tender. Remove from heat. Remove spice bag, squeezing out excess liquid. If desired, untie bag and reserve spices.
5. Divide reserved spices (if using) evenly among hot jars. Using a slotted spoon, pack plums into jars, leaving room for liquid and leaving 1 inch (2.5 cm) headspace. Pour in hot pickling liquid, leaving ½ inch (1 cm) headspace. Remove air bubbles and adjust headspace as necessary by adding hot pickling liquid. Wipe rim and place hot lid disc on jar. Screw band down until fingertip-tight.
6. Place jars in canner and return to a boil. Process for 20 minutes. Turn off heat, remove canner lid and let jars stand in water for 5 minutes. Transfer jars to a towel-lined surface and let stand for 24 hours. Check lids and refrigerate any jars that are not sealed.

Sweetly Spiced Pickled Strawberries

The texture of the pickled berries is quite soft, so don't be alarmed. The mixture of delicate spices and fruity flavor is lovely, whether you use these berries in savory or sweet dishes.

Makes about eight 8-ounce (250 mL) jars

● ● ●

Tips

For best results, use berries that are uniform in size. If some are much smaller or much larger, the final texture won't be as nice.

Use a wide pot to keep the strawberries in as few layers as possible so they'll heat quickly and won't get crushed.

Soaking the strawberries overnight helps to infuse them with the pickling liquid and reduce floating in the jars.

Serving Suggestions

Serve with whipped cream on top of biscuits, shortcake or pound cake for a twist on strawberry short cake.

Add to fruit salad, using a little of the pickling liquid for the dressing.

Serve as a condiment with rich meats or pâté.

12 cups	hulled strawberries	3 L
3 cups	granulated sugar	750 mL
1 tsp	pickling or canning salt	5 mL
½ tsp	ground cinnamon	2 mL
¼ tsp	ground cloves	1 mL
Pinch	ground allspice	Pinch
2 cups	cider vinegar	500 mL

1. Prick strawberries all over with a toothpick and cut any large ones in half.
2. In a saucepan, combine sugar, salt, cinnamon, cloves, allspice and vinegar. Bring to a boil over medium heat, stirring often until sugar and salt are dissolved. Remove from heat and let cool slightly. Add strawberries and toss gently to coat. Cover and let stand at a cool room temperature for at least 6 hours or for up to 18 hours, swirling pot occasionally to coat berries.
3. Prepare canner, jars and lids (see pages 7 to 8).
4. Place pot over medium-low heat, gently stirring occasionally, until strawberries are heated through but still hold their shape.
5. Ladle strawberries and hot pickling liquid into hot jars, leaving ½ inch (1 cm) headspace. Remove air bubbles and adjust headspace as necessary by adding hot pickling liquid. Wipe rim and place hot lid disc on jar. Screw band down until fingertip-tight.
6. Place jars in canner and return to a boil. Process for 10 minutes. Turn off heat, remove canner lid and let jars stand in water for 5 minutes. Transfer jars to a towel-lined surface and let stand for 24 hours. Check lids and refrigerate any jars that are not sealed.

White Balsamic and Pepper Pickled Strawberries

This recipe takes the classic union of balsamic vinegar, black pepper and strawberries and turns it into an exotic addition to your summer preserves. Strawberries become soft when pickled, but their intense flavor and brilliant color make up for it.

Makes about five 8-ounce (250 mL) jars

● ● ●

10 cups	sliced strawberries (¼ inch/0.5 cm thick slices)	2.5 L
2 cups	granulated sugar	500 mL
1 tsp	pickling or canning salt	5 mL
1 tsp	black peppercorns	5 mL
1 cup	white balsamic vinegar	250 mL

Tips

Use a wide pot to keep the strawberries in as few layers as possible so they'll heat quickly and won't get crushed.

Strawberries will float in the jars because of their soft, airy texture. Floating fruit can cause siphoning — the leaking of liquid from the jar after processing. If more than a little trickle of liquid leaks, the jar may not be sealed properly; it is best to refrigerate it and use it within 3 weeks.

Serving Suggestions

Serve with a selection of sharp and/or creamy cheeses as a starter or as a cheese course.

Serve as a topping on cheesecake or ice cream.

1. In a large pot or bowl, sprinkle strawberries with sugar and salt. Cover and let stand at a cool room temperature for at least 6 hours, until berries are very juicy and sugar is dissolved, or overnight.
2. Prepare canner, jars and lids (see pages 7 to 8).
3. Transfer strawberry mixture to a large pot, if necessary. Gently stir in peppercorns and vinegar. Place pot over medium-low heat, gently stirring occasionally, until strawberries are heated through but still hold their shape.
4. Ladle strawberries and hot pickling liquid into hot jars, leaving ½ inch (1 cm) headspace and dividing peppercorns as evenly as possible. Remove air bubbles and adjust headspace as necessary by adding hot pickling liquid. Wipe rim and place hot lid disc on jar. Screw band down until fingertip-tight.
5. Place jars in canner and return to a boil. Process for 10 minutes. Turn off heat, remove canner lid and let jars stand in water for 5 minutes. Transfer jars to a towel-lined surface and let stand for 24 hours. Check lids and refrigerate any jars that are not sealed.

Classic Sweet Watermelon Rind Pickles

After you've enjoyed the juicy fruit of the watermelon, use the firm white rind to make these sweet and tangy spiced pickles. Not only is it the ultimate in conservation, but they're delicious too!

Makes about four pint (500 mL) jars

● ● ●

Tips

If you prefer a mild touch of spice, discard the whole spices instead of adding them to the jars.

Many watermelons these days have a thinner rind than they used to. If you have a melon with thin rind and don't have 16 cups (4 L) of cubes, you can reduce the recipe by half.

Day 1

16 cups	cubed peeled watermelon rind (about 1 large melon, rind cut into 1-inch/2.5 cm cubes)	4 L
½ cup	pickling or canning salt	125 mL

Day 2

2	sticks cinnamon (each 3 inches/7.5 cm long), broken in half	2
4 cups	granulated sugar	1 L
½ tsp	whole cloves	2 mL
½ tsp	ground nutmeg	2 mL
2 cups	cider vinegar	500 mL
2 cups	water	500 mL

Day 1

1. In a large non-reactive bowl, layer watermelon rind and salt, using about one-third of each per layer. Place a plate on top to weigh down rind. Cover and refrigerate for at least 12 hours or for up to 24 hours.

Day 2

1. In a colander, working in batches, drain rind and rinse well. Drain again.
2. In a large pot, combine rind and enough cold water to cover by about 1 inch (2.5 cm). Bring to a boil over medium-high heat. Reduce heat and boil gently for about 10 minutes or until fork-tender. Drain well and set aside.
3. In a clean large pot, combine cinnamon sticks, sugar, cloves, nutmeg, vinegar and 2 cups (500 mL) water. Bring to a boil over medium heat, stirring often until sugar is dissolved. Add rind and simmer, gently stirring occasionally, for 1 to 1½ hours or until rind is translucent and looks glassy. Remove from heat.

4. Meanwhile, prepare canner, jars and lids (see pages 7 to 8).

5. Using a slotted spoon, pack rind and whole spices into hot jars, leaving 1 inch (2.5 cm) headspace and dividing spices as evenly as possible. Pour in hot pickling liquid, leaving $\frac{1}{2}$ inch (1 cm) headspace. Remove air bubbles and adjust headspace as necessary by adding hot pickling liquid. Wipe rim and place hot lid disc on jar. Screw band down until fingertip-tight.

6. Place jars in canner and return to a boil. Process for 10 minutes. Turn off heat, remove canner lid and let jars stand in water for 5 minutes. Transfer jars to a towel-lined surface and let stand for 24 hours. Check lids and refrigerate any jars that are not sealed.

Variation

For a deeper flavor, replace all or half of the granulated sugar with packed brown sugar. The color of the pickles will be a dark caramel.

Spicy Watermelon Rind Pickles

A spicy, savory twist on a classic adds new life to a pickle platter.

Makes about 4 pint (500 mL) jars

• • •

Tips

To prepare the rind for this recipe, cut watermelon into 1-inch (2.5 cm) thick slices and cut out red fruit, reserving for another use. Using a vegetable peeler, trim green skin from the rind. Cut rind into 2- to 3-inch (5 to 7.5 cm) sticks.

Chill these pickles before serving for the best texture.

Serving Suggestions

Serve with pork, beef or chicken satay.

Add drained watermelon pickles at the end of a stir-fry.

Day 1

16 cups	peeled watermelon rind sticks (see tip, at left)	4 L
½ cup	pickling or canning salt	125 mL

Day 2

¼ cup	granulated sugar	50 mL
3½ cups	white vinegar	875 mL
2½ cups	water	625 mL
4	long hot red or green chile peppers, halved lengthwise	4
4	cloves garlic, halved	4

Day 1

1. In a large non-reactive bowl, layer watermelon and salt, using about one-third of each per layer. Place a plate on top to weigh down rind. Cover and refrigerate for at least 12 hours or for up to 24 hours.

Day 2

1. In a colander, working in batches, drain rind and rinse well. Drain again.
2. In a large pot, combine rind and enough cold water to cover by about 1 inch (2.5 cm). Bring to a boil over medium-high heat. Reduce heat and boil gently for about 10 minutes or until fork-tender. Drain well and set aside.
3. In a clean large pot, combine sugar, vinegar and 2½ cups (625 mL) water. Bring to a boil over medium-high heat, stirring often until sugar is dissolved. Add rind and simmer, gently stirring occasionally, for 1 to 1½ hours or until rind is translucent and looks glassy. Add chile peppers and garlic; simmer for 5 minutes. Remove from heat.
4. Meanwhile, prepare canner, jars and lids (see pages 7 to 8).
5. Using a slotted spoon, pack rind, chile peppers and garlic into hot jars, leaving 1 inch (2.5 cm) headspace. Pour in hot pickling liquid, leaving ½ inch (1 cm) headspace. Remove air bubbles and adjust headspace as necessary by adding hot pickling liquid. Wipe rim and place hot lid disc on jar. Screw band down until fingertip-tight.
6. Place jars in canner and return to a boil. Process for 10 minutes. Turn off heat, remove canner lid and let jars stand in water for 5 minutes. Transfer jars to a towel-lined surface and let stand for 24 hours. Check lids and refrigerate any jars that are not sealed.

Savory Pickled Watermelon with Basil

This pickle is inspired by a delicious salad my husband, Jay, makes at our gourmet food shop, In A Nuttshell. It seems like an unusual combination of flavors, and you have to try it to believe how tasty it is. Once pickled, the watermelon has a soft texture and becomes quite different from the fresh fruit.

Makes about three pint (500 mL) jars

● ● ●

Tips

There will be pickling liquid left over after you fill the jars. Use it to dress a fruit salad or whisk in a little vegetable oil and honey for a salad dressing.

Soaking the watermelon pieces in the liquid helps reduce floating, but they will still float somewhat because of their soft, airy texture. Floating fruit can cause siphoning — the leaking of liquid from the jar after processing. If more than a little trickle of liquid leaks, the jar may not be sealed properly; it is best to refrigerate it and use it within 3 weeks.

Serving Suggestion

Drain watermelon and toss with chopped tomatoes and crumbled feta cheese, then drizzle with a little pickling liquid for a wonderful salad.

Day 1

2 cups	granulated sugar	500 mL
2 tbsp	pickling or canning salt	25 mL
½ tsp	freshly ground black pepper	2 mL
2 cups	red wine vinegar	500 mL
1 cup	water	250 mL
12 cups	cubed seedless watermelon (1-inch/2.5 cm cubes)	3 L

Day 2

¼ cup	chopped fresh basil	50 mL

Day 1

1. In a pot, combine sugar, salt, pepper, vinegar and water. Bring to a boil over medium heat, stirring often until sugar and salt are dissolved.
2. Place watermelon in a large, heatproof, non-reactive bowl and pour in hot liquid. Let cool, cover and refrigerate for 12 hours.

Day 2

1. Prepare canner, jars and lids (see pages 7 to 8).
2. Set a colander over a large pot and drain liquid from watermelon into pot. Set watermelon aside. Bring liquid to a boil over medium-high heat. Boil for 5 minutes. Add watermelon, reduce heat and simmer for about 5 minutes or just until heated through.
3. Using a slotted spoon, pack watermelon into hot jars, leaving 1 inch (2.5 cm) headspace, and divide basil evenly among jars. Pour in hot pickling liquid, leaving ½ inch (1 cm) headspace. Remove air bubbles and adjust headspace as necessary by adding hot pickling liquid. Wipe rim and place hot lid disc on jar. Screw band down until fingertip-tight.
4. Place jars in canner and return to a boil. Process for 10 minutes. Turn off heat, remove canner lid and let jars stand in water for 5 minutes. Transfer jars to a towel-lined surface and let stand for 24 hours. Check lids and refrigerate any jars that are not sealed.

Pickled Quince

This ages-old fruit is virtually inedible when raw but turns into a beautiful, aromatic delicacy once pickled. Pickled quince was a tradition in medieval times as an accompaniment to roast meats. No feast was complete without it. Quince are available for just a short time in the fall, so capture them in these pickles while you can.

Makes about seven 8-ounce (250 mL) jars

● ● ●

Tips

Quince resemble pale green pears but are hard, astringent and almost potato-like inside when raw. A natural chemical reaction between the fruit, heat and acid alters the pigments and therefore the flavor compounds when they're cooked, making them sweet and rosy-colored — it seems like magic.

Some quince have a coating of fuzz, like peaches, and others don't. If there is fuzz, it is easily rubbed off under water; there's no need to peel the quince.

For a mildly spiced pickle, discard the spices at the end of step 3. For bolder spicing, add them to the jars in step 5.

3 lbs	quince (about 5)	1.5 kg
4	thin slices gingerroot	4
4	whole cloves	4
½ tsp	black peppercorns	2 mL
4½ cups	granulated sugar	1.125 L
1½ tsp	pickling or canning salt	7 mL
2 cups	cider vinegar	500 mL
1 cup	white vinegar	250 mL

1. Gently rinse quince under cold running water, rubbing to remove any fuzz, if necessary. Cut in half lengthwise and then into quarters. Remove cores and stems and cut lengthwise into thin slices. You should have about 10 cups (2.5 L). Set aside.

2. Place ginger, cloves and peppercorns in the center of a square of triple-layered cheesecloth and tie into a spice bag.

3. In a large pot, combine spice bag, sugar, salt, cider vinegar and white vinegar. Bring to a boil over medium heat, stirring often until sugar and salt are dissolved. Increase heat to medium-high, add quince and return to a boil, stirring gently. Reduce heat and simmer, stirring occasionally, for about 1 hour or until quince are very tender and a translucent, deep rosy-peach color. Remove from heat. Remove spice bag, squeezing out excess liquid. If desired, untie bag and reserve spices.

4. Meanwhile, prepare canner, jars and lids (see pages 7 to 8).

5. Divide reserved spices (if using) evenly among hot jars. Using a slotted spoon, pack quince into jars, leaving 1 inch (2.5 cm) headspace. Pour in hot pickling liquid, leaving ½ inch (1 cm) headspace. Remove air bubbles and adjust headspace as necessary by adding hot pickling liquid. Wipe rim and place hot lid disc on jar. Screw band down until fingertip-tight.

6. Place jars in canner and return to a boil. Process for 20 minutes. Turn off heat, remove canner lid and let jars stand in water for 5 minutes. Transfer jars to a towel-lined surface and let stand for 24 hours. Check lids and refrigerate any jars that are not sealed.

Chili Sauces, Salsas and Other Sauces

continued on next page

Sauce Basics

Sauces are, in general, among the easiest preserves to make. If you can chop, measure and boil, you can make a sauce. They may take a little more time than other preserves, but much of that is spent boiling the ingredients on the stove, and the only effort required during that time is stirring. That stage has the benefit of the soothing bubbling sound and the glorious aroma that fills the house, so an hour or two really doesn't seem all that bad. Some smooth sauces benefit from being passed through a food mill or a Victorio strainer, which is an extra step but still not a difficult one.

When making sauces, especially tomato-based ones, you need to measure the ingredients very precisely. In pH level, tomatoes are on the border between high acid and low acid (see page 6 for more information), and where they fall can vary by variety and growing season. Therefore, to make sure your sauce is high enough in acid to be safe for preserving, you must use ingredients in the proportions specified in a tested recipe. The pH is lowered by adding other high-acid ingredients, including other fruits or vegetables and vinegar or lemon juice. Tomato sauces are also processed in the boiling water canner for a longer period of time to ensure that a high enough temperature is reached for long enough to destroy any lingering microorganisms that could lead to spoilage.

When cooking sauces, you will need to keep an eye on the heat on the stove and adjust it periodically to keep the sauce at a gentle boil. As the sauce thickens, you'll need to reduce the heat and stir more frequently to prevent sticking or scorching.

Plan your preparation wisely to make sure you have time to finish the sauce without being up until the wee hours of the night. If necessary, some ingredients can be chopped a day ahead, covered and refrigerated overnight. Just be sure to let them come to room temperature before adding them to the pot, to avoid slowing the cooking process. Ingredients that hold well for 1 day are bell peppers, chile peppers, celery and onions (very well wrapped). It's best to prepare tomatoes and other fruits just before you're going to cook them.

Sauce-Making Tips

- Good tomato-based sauces rely heavily on good-tasting, perfectly ripe tomatoes. Ripe tomatoes yield slightly when gently pressed and have an even color; they will give your sauce or salsa the best flavor and texture. Underripe tomatoes won't have a good flavor and can be dry, causing a pulpy texture.

- If you buy a large quantity of tomatoes, it is best to spread them out to provide air circulation and reduce deterioration. Line shallow boxes with clean newspaper and arrange tomatoes in a single layer, or a maximum of two layers. Store out of the sun, in a cool place such as a garage or basement (but not in the refrigerator), and check daily to remove any that have started to spoil.

- I prefer to chop all of the ingredients for sauces by hand, because I like the texture and that's part of the experience for me. Some people use a food processor to save time, and that's fine; just make sure you don't chop ingredients too finely before measuring (using the pulse function helps), because it can throw off the balance if too much of an ingredient is packed into the measuring cup, or the mixture can get too wet and won't cook to the right consistency.

- The yield for sauces will vary depending on how long you boil them. For that reason, they may not make exactly the same amount as the yield stated in the recipe. Prepare an extra jar or two (including one 4-ounce/ 125 mL or 8-ounce/250 mL jar) in case you have extra. Alternatively, let the extra cool, store it in a covered container in the refrigerator and use it up first. It's best to use unprocessed sauces within a week or two.

- Homemade tomato sauces and barbecue sauces for canning are thinner than commercial sauces. This allows for better heat penetration in processing and a safer product. Don't be tempted to cook the sauces until they're very thick. You can thicken sauce just before serving by simmering it in a saucepan until reduced or by stirring in a little tomato paste.

- The seeds in chile peppers can get quite bitter when simmered for a long time, so it's best to remove them before chopping peppers for use in cooked sauces.

The Family Chili Sauce

This recipe has been passed around my mom's side of the family for a few generations (that we know of). We eat the classic sweet and spicy sauce with all kinds of things, from scrambled eggs and sandwiches to traditional tourtière, hamburgers and meatloaf, to name a few.

Makes about seven pint (500 mL) jars

● ● ●

Tips

This recipe was created to use a 6-quart (6 L) basket of tomatoes. Traditionally, it was made with regular field (globe) tomatoes, but I like to use half field and half plum (Roma) tomatoes for a chunkier texture (and keep it to the shorter side of the cooking time). You'll need about 9 lbs (4.5 kg) tomatoes.

For instructions on peeling tomatoes, see page 17.

13 cups	chopped peeled tomatoes (see tip, at left)	3.25 L
6 cups	chopped onions	1.5 L
2½ cups	diced red and/or green bell peppers	625 mL
1 cup	chopped celery	250 mL
4 cups	granulated sugar	1 L
2 tbsp	pickling or canning salt	25 mL
1 tsp	ground allspice	5 mL
1 tsp	ground cinnamon	5 mL
1 tsp	ground ginger	5 mL
1 tsp	ground nutmeg	5 mL
½ tsp	ground cloves	2 mL
⅛ tsp	cayenne pepper	0.5 mL
1 cup	white vinegar	250 mL

1. In a large pot, combine tomatoes, onions, red peppers, celery, sugar, salt, allspice, cinnamon, ginger, nutmeg, cloves and cayenne. Bring to a boil over medium-high heat, stirring often. Reduce heat and boil gently, stirring often, for 2 to 2½ hours or until chili sauce is reduced by about half and is thick enough to mound on a spoon.
2. Meanwhile, prepare canner, jars and lids (see pages 7 to 8).
3. Stir vinegar into chili sauce and boil gently, stirring often, for 5 minutes.
4. Ladle hot chili sauce into hot jars, leaving ½ inch (1 cm) headspace. Remove air bubbles and adjust headspace as necessary by adding hot chili sauce. Wipe rim and place hot lid disc on jar. Screw band down until fingertip-tight.
5. Place jars in canner and return to a boil. Process for 20 minutes. Turn off heat and remove canner lid. Let jars stand in water for 5 minutes. Transfer jars to a towel-lined surface and let stand for 24 hours. Check lids and refrigerate any jars that are not sealed.

Jen's Pepped-Up Chili Sauce

Over the years, I've made adjustments to the Family Chili Sauce recipe and have come up with this version. It's got a bit of heat, a little less sweetness and a little more tang.

Tips

For instructions on peeling tomatoes, see page 17.

Yellow wax peppers are often called hot banana peppers because they look so similar to sweet banana peppers. Make sure you do have hot peppers and not sweet ones by tasting a tiny bit before using; otherwise, your sauce won't have much pep.

Variation

This has just a touch of heat. If you prefer a hot chili sauce, use an extra yellow wax pepper or add a jalapeño pepper too.

12 cups	chopped peeled plum (Roma) tomatoes	3 L
8 cups	chopped onions	2 L
2 cups	chopped red bell peppers	500 mL
2 cups	chopped celery	500 mL
2	yellow wax (hot banana) peppers, seeded and chopped	2
3 cups	granulated sugar	750 mL
2 tbsp	pickling or canning salt	25 mL
1 tsp	ground allspice	5 mL
1 tsp	ground cinnamon	5 mL
1 tsp	ground ginger	5 mL
1 tsp	ground nutmeg	5 mL
½ tsp	ground cloves	2 mL
½ tsp	hot pepper flakes	2 mL
1½ cups	cider vinegar	375 mL

1. In a large pot, combine tomatoes, onions, red peppers, celery, yellow wax peppers, sugar, salt, allspice, cinnamon, ginger, nutmeg, cloves, hot pepper flakes and vinegar. Bring to a boil over medium-high heat, stirring often. Reduce heat and boil gently, stirring often, for 2 to 2½ hours or until chili sauce is reduced by about half and is thick enough to mound on a spoon.
2. Meanwhile, prepare canner, jars and lids (see pages 7 to 8).
3. Ladle hot chili sauce into hot jars, leaving ½ inch (1 cm) headspace. Remove air bubbles and adjust headspace as necessary by adding hot chili sauce. Wipe rim and place hot lid disc on jar. Screw band down until fingertip-tight.
4. Place jars in canner and return to a boil. Process for 20 minutes. Turn off heat and remove canner lid. Let jars stand in water for 5 minutes. Transfer jars to a towel-lined surface and let stand for 24 hours. Check lids and refrigerate any jars that are not sealed.

Peach and Roasted Sweet Pepper Chili Sauce

When peaches are ripe and tomatoes and peppers are abundant, mix them all together in this sweet chili sauce, which has nice depth from the roasted peppers.

Makes about six pint (500 mL) jars

• • •

Tips

For instructions on peeling tomatoes and peaches, see pages 17 and 16.

Add any extra roasted peppers to pasta salad or to a sandwich.

Serving Suggestions

Serve on grilled or roasted pork or poultry.

Spread on ham or smoked turkey sandwiches.

Serve on top of toasted baguette slices as a change from bruschetta.

8 cups	chopped peeled plum (Roma) tomatoes	2 L
6 cups	chopped peeled peaches	1.5 L
3 cups	chopped onions	750 mL
2½ cups	packed brown sugar	625 mL
4 tsp	pickling or canning salt	20 mL
1 tsp	ground cinnamon	5 mL
1 tsp	ground ginger	5 mL
½ tsp	hot pepper flakes	2 mL
2 cups	cider vinegar	500 mL
4	large red bell peppers	4
3	large green bell peppers	3

1. In a large pot, combine tomatoes, peaches, onions, brown sugar, salt, cinnamon, ginger, hot pepper flakes and vinegar. Bring to a boil over medium-high heat, stirring often. Reduce heat and boil gently, stirring often, for 2 to 2½ hours or until chili sauce is reduced by about half and is thick enough to mound on a spoon.

2. Meanwhile, preheat broiler or preheat barbecue grill to medium. If using broiler, place bell peppers on a baking sheet. Broil or grill, turning often, for about 20 minutes or until blackened on all sides. Transfer to a bowl, cover with plastic wrap and let cool completely. Peel off skins and remove stems, cores and seeds. Discard any accumulated liquid. Chop red peppers and measure 2¼ cups (550 mL). Chop green peppers and measure 1½ cups (375 mL). Reserve any remaining peppers for another use.

3. Meanwhile, prepare canner, jars and lids (see pages 7 to 8).

4. Stir roasted peppers into chili sauce and boil gently, stirring often, for 10 minutes to blend the flavors.

5. Ladle hot chili sauce into hot jars, leaving ½ inch (1 cm) headspace. Remove air bubbles and adjust headspace as necessary by adding hot chili sauce. Wipe rim and place hot lid disc on jar. Screw band down until fingertip-tight.

6. Place jars in canner and return to a boil. Process for 20 minutes. Turn off heat and remove canner lid. Let jars stand in water for 5 minutes. Transfer jars to a towel-lined surface and let stand for 24 hours. Check lids and refrigerate any jars that are not sealed.

Tender Fruit Chili Sauce

Tomatoes are botanically fruit, so this combination is a natural, capturing the fruits of the late summer harvest in a sweetly spiced sauce.

Makes four to five pint (500 mL) jars

• • •

Tips

Some pear varieties lose their flavor when heated, so choose a variety suited to cooking, such as Bartlett, Bosc or Packham.

To make a spice bag, cut a 4-inch (10 cm) square piece of triple-layered cheesecloth. Place the pickling spice in the center of the square and bring the edges together into a bundle. Tie tightly with kitchen string. Alternatively, use a large mesh tea ball.

Serving Suggestions

Serve spooned on top of crackers spread with cream cheese for a change from red pepper jelly.

Spread on a sandwich stacked with ham and old Cheddar cheese.

6 cups	chopped peeled plum (Roma) tomatoes	1.5 L
4 cups	chopped peeled peaches	1 L
3 cups	chopped peeled pears	750 mL
2 cups	chopped purple, blue or red plums	500 mL
2 cups	chopped onions	500 mL
1 cup	chopped green bell pepper	250 mL
2 cups	granulated sugar	500 mL
1 tbsp	pickling or canning salt	15 mL
1 tbsp	pickling spice, tied in a spice bag (see tip, at left)	15 mL
1 tsp	ground cinnamon	5 mL
1/2 tsp	ground mace or nutmeg	2 mL
1/4 tsp	ground cloves	1 mL
2 cups	white vinegar	500 mL

1. In a large pot, combine tomatoes, peaches, pears, plums, onions, green pepper, sugar, salt, pickling spice, cinnamon, mace, cloves and vinegar. Bring to a boil over medium-high heat, stirring often. Reduce heat and boil gently, stirring often, for 2 to 2½ hours or until chili sauce is reduced by about half and is thick enough to mound on a spoon. Discard spice bag.
2. Meanwhile, prepare canner, jars and lids (see pages 7 to 8).
3. Ladle hot chili sauce into hot jars, leaving ½ inch (1 cm) headspace. Remove air bubbles and adjust headspace as necessary by adding hot chili sauce. Wipe rim and place hot lid disc on jar. Screw band down until fingertip-tight.
4. Place jars in canner and return to a boil. Process for 20 minutes. Turn off heat and remove canner lid. Let jars stand in water for 5 minutes. Transfer jars to a towel-lined surface and let stand for 24 hours. Check lids and refrigerate any jars that are not sealed.

Smoky Pepper Chili Sauce

A thick and rich chili sauce, spiked with heat and smokiness from chipotle peppers, will certainly perk up scrambled eggs, burgers or meat pies.

Makes six to seven pint (500 mL) jars

● ● ●

Tips

Ancho chile peppers are dried poblano peppers. They add a touch of toasted flavor without much heat. Dried ancho chile peppers are often available in the produce section of supermarkets and at specialty food stores.

Chipotle peppers are smoked jalapeño peppers. They pack quite a punch of heat and smoky flavor. Chipotles are often sold in cans in a thick sauce, called adobo sauce, and are available in the international section of well-stocked supermarkets and at specialty food stores.

12 cups	chopped peeled plum (Roma) tomatoes	3 L
4 cups	chopped onions	1 L
3 cups	chopped red bell peppers	750 mL
2 cups	finely chopped celery	500 mL
2 tbsp	minced garlic	25 mL
3 cups	packed brown sugar	750 mL
2 tbsp	pickling or canning salt	25 mL
1 tsp	ground allspice	5 mL
1 tsp	ground cinnamon	5 mL
1 tsp	ground cumin	5 mL
1½ cups	cider vinegar	375 mL
2	dried ancho or mild New Mexico chile peppers	2
1 cup	boiling water	250 mL
2	drained chipotle peppers in adobo sauce, minced	2
2 tbsp	adobo sauce	25 mL

1. In a large pot, combine tomatoes, onions, red peppers, celery, garlic, brown sugar, salt, allspice, cinnamon, cumin and vinegar. Bring to a boil over medium-high heat, stirring often. Reduce heat and boil gently, stirring often, for 2 to 2½ hours or until chili sauce is reduced by about half and is thick enough to mound on a spoon.

2. Meanwhile, prepare canner, jars and lids (see pages 7 to 8).

3. In a heatproof bowl, combine dried chile peppers and boiling water. Let stand for about 30 minutes or until peppers are softened. Remove peppers from liquid and discard liquid. Discard stem and seeds and finely chop peppers. Stir into chili sauce with chipotles and adobo sauce and boil gently, stirring often, for 10 minutes to blend the flavors.

4. Ladle hot chili sauce into hot jars, leaving ½ inch (1 cm) headspace. Remove air bubbles and adjust headspace as necessary by adding hot chili sauce. Wipe rim and place hot lid disc on jar. Screw band down until fingertip-tight.

5. Place jars in canner and return to a boil. Process for 20 minutes. Turn off heat and remove canner lid. Let jars stand in water for 5 minutes. Transfer jars to a towel-lined surface and let stand for 24 hours. Check lids and refrigerate any jars that are not sealed.

Gilly Macrae's Chili Sauce

Gilly is a faithful customer at our store, In A Nuttshell, and she graciously shared this recipe with me. The apple adds a nice touch to the classic flavors and makes this chili sauce wonderfully suited to serving with pork, ham or poultry.

Makes about nine pint (500 mL) jars

● ● ●

Tips

This recipe was created to use a 6-quart (6 L) basket of tomatoes. Traditionally, it was made with regular field (globe) tomatoes, but I like to use half field and half plum (Roma) tomatoes for a chunkier texture (and keep it to the shorter side of the cooking time). You'll need about 9 lbs (4.5 kg) tomatoes.

If you prefer a smoother sauce, use a tart apple variety that softens when cooked, such as McIntosh, Empire or Idared. If you prefer a chunkier sauce, use a variety that holds its shape, such as Granny Smith, Crispin (Mutsu), Northern Spy or Cortland.

13 cups	chopped peeled ripe tomatoes	3.25 L
4 cups	chopped onions	1 L
3¼ cups	chopped peeled tart apples (see tip, at left)	800 mL
2½ cups	finely chopped celery	625 mL
2½ cups	granulated sugar	625 mL
2½ tbsp	pickling or canning salt	32 mL
1½ tsp	ground cinnamon	7 mL
¾ tsp	ground cloves	3 mL
⅛ tsp	cayenne pepper	0.5 mL
2 cups	cider vinegar	500 mL

1. In a large pot, combine tomatoes, onions, apples, celery, sugar, salt, cinnamon, cloves, cayenne and vinegar. Bring to a boil over medium-high heat, stirring often. Reduce heat and boil gently, stirring often, for 2 to 2½ hours or until chili sauce is reduced by about one-third and is almost thick enough to mound on a spoon.
2. Meanwhile, prepare canner, jars and lids (see pages 7 to 8).
3. Ladle hot chili sauce into hot jars, leaving ½ inch (1 cm) headspace. Remove air bubbles and adjust headspace as necessary by adding hot chili sauce. Wipe rim and place hot lid disc on jar. Screw band down until fingertip-tight.
4. Place jars in canner and return to a boil. Process for 20 minutes. Turn off heat and remove canner lid. Let jars stand in water for 5 minutes. Transfer jars to a towel-lined surface and let stand for 24 hours. Check lids and refrigerate any jars that are not sealed.

Classic Mild Tomato Salsa

If you like to incorporate salsa into your cooking and eat it on its own, this is the recipe to make. It's pleasantly seasoned, and its simple flavors make it versatile for use in dishes that call for a salsa touch.

Makes about ten 8-ounce (250 mL) or five pint (500 mL) jars

• • •

Tips

For instructions on peeling tomatoes, see page 17.

If you use 8-ounce (250 mL) jars, they may not all fit in your canner at once. Let extra jars cool, then refrigerate them and use them up first. To avoid this problem, I like to pack some in pint (500 mL) jars and some in 8-ounce (250 mL) jars. That way, I also have different sizes and can open the size I know I'll use up within a few weeks.

14 cups	chopped peeled plum (Roma) tomatoes	3.5 L
3 cups	chopped onions	750 mL
2 cups	chopped red bell peppers	500 mL
1 cup	chopped green bell pepper	250 mL
2 tbsp	finely chopped seeded jalapeño pepper	25 mL
1 tbsp	minced garlic	15 mL
2 tbsp	granulated sugar	25 mL
2 tsp	pickling or canning salt	10 mL
1½ tsp	ground cumin	7 mL
¼ tsp	freshly ground black pepper	1 mL
1¾ cups	cider vinegar	425 mL
¼ cup	chopped fresh cilantro or oregano (optional)	50 mL

1. In a large pot, combine tomatoes, onions, red and green peppers, jalapeño, garlic, sugar, salt, cumin, black pepper and vinegar. Bring to a boil over medium-high heat, stirring often. Reduce heat and boil gently, stirring often, for about 1 hour or until salsa is reduced by about half and is thick enough to mound on a spoon. Stir in cilantro (if using).
2. Meanwhile, prepare canner, jars and lids (see pages 7 to 8).
3. Ladle hot salsa into hot jars, leaving ½ inch (1 cm) headspace. Remove air bubbles and adjust headspace as necessary by adding hot salsa. Wipe rim and place hot lid disc on jar. Screw band down until fingertip-tight.
4. Place jars in canner and return to a boil. Process for 20 minutes. Turn off heat and remove canner lid. Let jars stand in water for 5 minutes. Transfer jars to a towel-lined surface and let stand for 24 hours. Check lids and refrigerate any jars that are not sealed.

Fiery Pepper Salsa

Mixing several varieties of hot peppers into a simple tomato salsa turns up the heat and adds lots of flavor. This one is certainly for the heat-seeking salsa lover!

Makes about eight 8-ounce (250 mL) or four pint (500 mL) jars

• • • •

Tips

For instructions on peeling tomatoes, see page 17.

To avoid burns, wear disposable rubber gloves when handling hot peppers and be sure to wash all utensils and the cutting board well after preparing the peppers.

Serving Suggestion

Purée this salsa and use it as a marinade and baste for hot salsa chicken wings or barbecued pork ribs.

12 cups	chopped peeled plum (Roma) tomatoes	3 L
2 cups	chopped onions	500 mL
1 cup	chopped seeded yellow wax (hot banana) peppers	250 mL
1/2 cup	finely chopped seeded cayenne or other hot red chile peppers	125 mL
1/2 cup	finely chopped seeded jalapeño peppers	125 mL
1 tbsp	minced seeded habanero or Scotch bonnet chile peppers	15 mL
2 tbsp	minced garlic	25 mL
3 tbsp	granulated sugar	45 mL
2 tsp	pickling or canning salt	10 mL
1/2 tsp	freshly ground black pepper	2 mL
1 1/4 cups	white vinegar	300 mL

1. In a large pot, combine tomatoes, onions, yellow wax peppers, cayenne peppers, jalapeños, habanero, garlic, sugar, salt, black pepper and vinegar. Bring to a boil over medium-high heat, stirring often. Reduce heat and boil gently, stirring often, for about 1 hour or until salsa is reduced by about half and is thick enough to mound on a spoon.

2. Meanwhile, prepare canner, jars and lids (see pages 7 to 8).

3. Ladle hot salsa into hot jars, leaving 1/2 inch (1 cm) headspace. Remove air bubbles and adjust headspace as necessary by adding hot salsa. Wipe rim and place hot lid disc on jar. Screw band down until fingertip-tight.

4. Place jars in canner and return to a boil. Process for 20 minutes. Turn off heat and remove canner lid. Let jars stand in water for 5 minutes. Transfer jars to a towel-lined surface and let stand for 24 hours. Check lids and refrigerate any jars that are not sealed.

Roasted Poblano Tomato Salsa

Roasting the mild but flavorful poblano peppers adds a slight smokiness to the salsa without adding heat. There's a bit of heat from the jalapeño, but you can leave it out for a mild salsa.

Makes about eight 8-ounce (250 mL) or four pint (500 mL) jars

● ● ●

Tips

Poblano peppers have a thicker flesh than many chile peppers, and a slightly more zippy flavor than bell peppers, so they're worth seeking out for this salsa. They're often only available for a short time in the late summer, so catch them while you can.

To avoid burns, wear disposable rubber gloves when handling hot peppers and be sure to wash all utensils and the cutting board well after preparing the peppers.

12 cups	chopped peeled plum (Roma) tomatoes	3 L
3 cups	chopped onions	750 mL
2 tbsp	finely chopped seeded jalapeño pepper	25 mL
3 tbsp	granulated sugar	45 mL
2 tsp	pickling or canning salt	10 mL
½ tsp	ground cumin	2 mL
1¼ cups	cider vinegar	300 mL
8	poblano peppers	8
2 tbsp	chopped fresh oregano	25 mL

1. In a large pot, combine tomatoes, onions, jalapeño, sugar, salt, cumin and vinegar. Bring to a boil over medium-high heat, stirring often. Reduce heat and boil gently, stirring often, for about 1 hour or until salsa is reduced by about half and is thick enough to mound on a spoon.
2. Meanwhile, preheat broiler or preheat barbecue grill to medium. If using broiler, place poblano peppers on a baking sheet. Broil or grill, turning often, for about 15 minutes or until blackened on all sides. Transfer to a bowl, cover with plastic wrap and let cool completely. Peel off skins and remove stems, cores and seeds. Discard any accumulated liquid. Chop and measure 2 cups (500 mL). Reserve any remaining peppers for another use.
3. Meanwhile, prepare canner, jars and lids (see pages 7 to 8).
4. Stir roasted peppers and oregano into salsa and boil gently, stirring often, for 5 minutes to blend the flavors.
5. Ladle hot salsa into hot jars, leaving ½ inch (1 cm) headspace. Remove air bubbles and adjust headspace as necessary by adding hot salsa. Wipe rim and place hot lid disc on jar. Screw band down until fingertip-tight.
6. Place jars in canner and return to a boil. Process for 20 minutes. Turn off heat and remove canner lid. Let jars stand in water for 5 minutes. Transfer jars to a towel-lined surface and let stand for 24 hours. Check lids and refrigerate any jars that are not sealed.

Chipotle Tomato Salsa

A rich, smoky heat from the chipotle peppers gives a different twist to this salsa.

Makes about eight 8-ounce (250 mL) or four pint (500 mL) jars

● ● ●

Tips

For instructions on peeling tomatoes, see page 17.

Chipotle peppers are smoked jalapeño peppers. They pack quite a punch of heat and smoky flavor. Chipotles are often sold in cans in a thick sauce, called adobo sauce, and are available in the international section of well-stocked supermarkets and at specialty food stores.

12 cups	chopped peeled plum (Roma) tomatoes	3 L
3 cups	chopped onions	750 mL
2 cups	chopped red bell peppers	500 mL
2 tbsp	minced garlic	25 mL
2 tbsp	granulated sugar	25 mL
2 tsp	pickling or canning salt	10 mL
1 tsp	ground cumin	5 mL
1¼ cups	white vinegar	300 mL
4	drained chipotle peppers in adobo sauce, minced	4
¼ cup	adobo sauce	50 mL

1. In a large pot, combine tomatoes, onions, red peppers, garlic, sugar, salt, cumin and vinegar. Bring to a boil over medium-high heat, stirring often. Reduce heat and boil gently, stirring often, for about 1 hour or until salsa is reduced by about half and is thick enough to mound on a spoon.
2. Meanwhile, prepare canner, jars and lids (see pages 7 to 8).
3. Stir chipotle peppers and adobo sauce into salsa and boil gently, stirring often, for 5 minutes to blend the flavors.
4. Ladle hot salsa into hot jars, leaving ½ inch (1 cm) headspace. Remove air bubbles and adjust headspace as necessary by adding hot salsa. Wipe rim and place hot lid disc on jar. Screw band down until fingertip-tight.
5. Place jars in canner and return to a boil. Process for 20 minutes. Turn off heat and remove canner lid. Let jars stand in water for 5 minutes. Transfer jars to a towel-lined surface and let stand for 24 hours. Check lids and refrigerate any jars that are not sealed.

Mild Tomato and Sweet Pepper Salsa

Sometimes you want a salsa but don't want the heat. This version uses sweet peppers for that authentic taste without the bite.

Makes about eight 8-ounce (250 mL) or four pint (500 mL) jars

● ● ●

Tip

For instructions on peeling tomatoes, see page 17.

Variation

If sweet banana or cubanelle peppers aren't available, substitute an equal amount of other mild peppers, such as Anaheim, poblano or orange or yellow bell peppers.

10 cups	chopped peeled plum (Roma) tomatoes	2.5 L
2 cups	chopped onions	500 mL
2 cups	chopped red and/or green bell peppers	500 mL
1 cup	chopped sweet banana peppers	250 mL
1 cup	chopped cubanelle pepper	250 mL
2 tbsp	minced garlic	25 mL
2 tbsp	granulated sugar	25 mL
2 tsp	pickling or canning salt	10 mL
1 tsp	ground cumin	5 mL
1¼ cups	cider vinegar	300 mL
2 tbsp	chopped fresh cilantro or oregano	25 mL

1. In a large pot, combine tomatoes, onions, red peppers, banana peppers, cubanelle peppers, garlic, sugar, salt, cumin and vinegar. Bring to a boil over medium-high heat, stirring often. Reduce heat and boil gently, stirring often, for about 1 hour or until salsa is reduced by about half and is thick enough to mound on a spoon. Stir in cilantro.
2. Meanwhile, prepare canner, jars and lids (see pages 7 to 8).
3. Ladle hot salsa into hot jars, leaving ½ inch (1 cm) headspace. Remove air bubbles and adjust headspace as necessary by adding hot salsa. Wipe rim and place hot lid disc on jar. Screw band down until fingertip-tight.
4. Place jars in canner and return to a boil. Process for 20 minutes. Turn off heat and remove canner lid. Let jars stand in water for 5 minutes. Transfer jars to a towel-lined surface and let stand for 24 hours. Check lids and refrigerate any jars that are not sealed.

Hot, Hot, Hot Tomato Salsa

As the name says, this salsa has lots of heat: slow, deep heat from the dried chile peppers and fresh, zingy heat from two varieties of fresh hot peppers. Be sure to label this with flames when storing and serving it so you don't get it confused — it's not for the meek.

Makes about ten 8-ounce (250 mL) or five pint (500 mL) jars

● ● ● ●

Tips

To avoid burns, wear disposable rubber gloves when handling hot peppers and be sure to wash all utensils and the cutting board well after preparing the peppers.

If you use 8-ounce (250 mL) jars, they may not all fit in your canner at once. Let extra jars cool, then refrigerate them and use them up first. To avoid this problem, I like to pack some in pint (500 mL) jars and some in 8-ounce (250 mL) jars. That way, I also have different sizes and can open the size I know I'll use up within a few weeks.

14 cups	chopped peeled plum (Roma) tomatoes	3.5 L
3 cups	chopped onions	750 mL
2 cups	chopped red bell peppers	500 mL
¾ cup	finely chopped seeded yellow wax (hot banana) peppers	175 mL
½ cup	finely chopped seeded jalapeño peppers	125 mL
2 tbsp	minced garlic	25 mL
2 tbsp	granulated sugar	25 mL
2 tsp	pickling or canning salt	10 mL
1 tsp	ground cumin	5 mL
1¾ cups	cider vinegar	425 mL
2	dried hot New Mexico chile peppers	2
1 cup	boiling water	250 mL
2 tbsp	chopped fresh oregano or cilantro (optional)	25 mL

1. In a large pot, combine tomatoes, onions, red peppers, yellow wax peppers, jalapeños, garlic, sugar, salt, cumin and vinegar. Bring to a boil over medium-high heat, stirring often. Reduce heat and boil gently, stirring often, for about 1 hour or until salsa is reduced by about half and is thick enough to mound on a spoon.

2. Meanwhile, prepare canner, jars and lids (see pages 7 to 8).

3. In a heatproof bowl, combine dried chile peppers and boiling water. Let stand for about 30 minutes or until peppers are softened. Remove peppers from liquid and discard liquid. Discard stem and seeds and finely chop peppers. Stir into salsa with oregano (if using) and boil gently, stirring often, for 5 minutes to blend the flavors.

4. Ladle hot salsa into hot jars, leaving ½ inch (1 cm) headspace. Remove air bubbles and adjust headspace as necessary by adding hot salsa. Wipe rim and place hot lid disc on jar. Screw band down until fingertip-tight.

5. Place jars in canner and return to a boil. Process for 20 minutes. Turn off heat and remove canner lid. Let jars stand in water for 5 minutes. Transfer jars to a towel-lined surface and let stand for 24 hours. Check lids and refrigerate any jars that are not sealed.

Grilled Corn and Tomato Salsa

I love adding corn to salsa for its bright color and the contrast in texture with the soft tomatoes. Grilling it first adds a depth of flavor that really comes through. Serve this salsa with blue and yellow tortilla chips for a colorful touch, or spoon it onto fajitas.

Makes five to six pint (500 mL) jars

● ● ●

Tips

Feel free to use 8-ounce (250 mL) jars if you prefer, but it's likely they won't all fit into the canner at once. For that reason, you might want to try mixing smaller and larger jars.

This salsa thickens a fair amount upon cooling and setting because of the starch in the corn, so it's best to stop the cooking when it's a thinner texture than you want the final product to be.

This recipe can have a bit of a kick if the hot peppers are, indeed, hot. Because they vary in heat, you can taste them first (if you're brave); if they're very hot and you prefer a milder salsa, add only ¼ cup (50 mL). Alternatively, start with less, then taste the salsa and add hot pepper sauce at the end or when you open the jar to serve it.

● Preheat barbecue grill to medium

6	cobs corn, shucked	6
10 cups	chopped peeled plum (Roma) tomatoes	2.5 L
2 cups	chopped red bell peppers	500 mL
1½ cups	chopped onions	375 mL
½ cup	finely chopped seeded yellow wax (hot banana) or jalapeño peppers	125 mL
2 tbsp	minced garlic	25 mL
2 tbsp	granulated sugar	25 mL
2 tsp	pickling or canning salt	10 mL
2 cups	cider vinegar	500 mL
2 tbsp	chopped fresh oregano or cilantro (optional)	25 mL

1. Place corn on preheated grill and close the lid. Grill, turning often, for about 15 minutes or until kernels are tender and golden brown (there may be a few dark, charred spots, and that's fine). Transfer to a large dish, cover and let steam until cool. Using a serrated knife, cut kernels from cob and measure 3 cups (750 mL). Reserve any remaining corn for another use.

2. In a large pot, combine corn, tomatoes, red peppers, onions, yellow wax peppers, garlic, sugar, salt and vinegar. Bring to a boil over medium-high heat, stirring often. Reduce heat and boil gently, stirring often, for about 1 hour or until salsa is reduced by about half and is almost thick enough to mound on a spoon. Stir in oregano (if using).

3. Meanwhile, prepare canner, jars and lids (see pages 7 to 8).

4. Ladle hot salsa into hot jars, leaving ½ inch (1 cm) headspace. Remove air bubbles and adjust headspace as necessary by adding hot salsa. Wipe rim and place hot lid disc on jar. Screw band down until fingertip-tight.

5. Place jars in canner and return to a boil. Process for 20 minutes. Turn off heat and remove canner lid. Let jars stand in water for 5 minutes. Transfer jars to a towel-lined surface and let stand for 24 hours. Check lids and refrigerate any jars that are not sealed.

New Mexico Pepper and Tomato Salsa

Dried chile peppers add a different flavor and type of heat than fresh chile peppers. New Mexico chile peppers have a lot of flavor and a moderate heat, making them a nice addition to salsa.

Makes about nine 8-ounce (250 mL) or four to five pint (500 mL) jars

• • •

Tips

Dried New Mexico chile peppers are available in both mild and hot varieties. The hot variety adds a nice pep to this salsa, but you can use mild ones if you prefer.

To avoid burns, wear disposable rubber gloves when handling hot peppers and be sure to wash all utensils and the cutting board well after preparing the peppers.

12 cups	chopped peeled plum (Roma) tomatoes	3 L
3 cups	chopped onions	750 mL
2 cups	chopped green bell peppers	500 mL
2 tbsp	granulated sugar	25 mL
2 tsp	pickling or canning salt	10 mL
2 tsp	dried oregano	10 mL
1½ tsp	ground cumin	7 mL
1¼ cups	cider vinegar	300 mL
3	dried hot New Mexico chile peppers	3
1½ cups	boiling water	375 mL

1. In a large pot, combine tomatoes, onions, green peppers, sugar, salt, oregano, cumin and vinegar. Bring to a boil over medium-high heat, stirring often. Reduce heat and boil gently, stirring often, for about 1 hour or until salsa is reduced by about half and is thick enough to mound on a spoon.
2. Meanwhile, prepare canner, jars and lids (see pages 7 to 8).
3. In a heatproof bowl, combine dried chile peppers and boiling water. Let stand for about 30 minutes or until peppers are softened. Remove peppers from liquid and discard liquid. Discard stem and seeds and finely chop peppers. Stir into salsa and boil gently, stirring often, for 5 minutes to blend the flavors.
4. Ladle hot salsa into hot jars, leaving ½ inch (1 cm) headspace. Remove air bubbles and adjust headspace as necessary by adding hot salsa. Wipe rim and place hot lid disc on jar. Screw band down until fingertip-tight.
5. Place jars in canner and return to a boil. Process for 20 minutes. Turn off heat and remove canner lid. Let jars stand in water for 5 minutes. Transfer jars to a towel-lined surface and let stand for 24 hours. Check lids and refrigerate any jars that are not sealed.

Black Bean Tomato Salsa

When I first started experimenting with making salsas beyond the classic tomato, this was one combination I tried — and, I must say, it's still one of my favorites.

Makes about ten 8-ounce (250 mL) or five pint (500 mL) jars

● ● ●

Tips

If using canned black beans (which I usually do), you'll need one 19-oz (540 mL) can. If you have smaller cans, you'll need two. Don't be tempted to add the extra beans to the salsa — it will alter the acid balance. Add them to a salad, mash them with some salsa to make burritos or freeze them for later use.

If you use 8-ounce (250 mL) jars, they may not all fit in your canner at once. Let extra jars cool, then refrigerate them and use them up first. To avoid this problem, I like to pack some in pint (500 mL) jars and some in 8-ounce (250 mL) jars. That way, I also have different sizes and can open the size I know I'll use up within a few weeks.

2 tsp	cumin seeds	10 mL
12 cups	chopped peeled plum (Roma) tomatoes	3 L
1½ cups	chopped onions	375 mL
1 cup	chopped red bell pepper	250 mL
1 cup	chopped green bell pepper	250 mL
¼ cup	finely chopped seeded jalapeño peppers	50 mL
2 tbsp	minced garlic	25 mL
¼ cup	granulated sugar	50 mL
2 tsp	pickling or canning salt	10 mL
2 cups	cider vinegar	500 mL
2 cups	drained rinsed canned or cooked black beans	500 mL
¼ cup	chopped fresh cilantro or oregano	50 mL

1. In a small dry skillet, over medium heat, toast cumin, stirring constantly, for about 1 minute or until fragrant and slightly darker but not yet popping. Immediately transfer to a large pot.
2. Add tomatoes, onions, red and green peppers, jalapeños, garlic, sugar, salt and vinegar to the pot. Bring to a boil over medium-high heat, stirring often. Reduce heat and boil gently, stirring often, for about 1 hour or until salsa is reduced by about half and is thick enough to mound on a spoon.
3. Meanwhile, prepare canner, jars and lids (see pages 7 to 8).
4. Stir beans into salsa and boil gently, stirring often, for about 10 minutes or until beans are very hot. Stir in cilantro.
5. Ladle hot salsa into hot jars, leaving ½ inch (1 cm) headspace. Remove air bubbles and adjust headspace as necessary by adding hot salsa. Wipe rim and place hot lid disc on jar. Screw band down until fingertip-tight.
6. Place jars in canner and return to a boil. Process for 20 minutes. Turn off heat and remove canner lid. Let jars stand in water for 5 minutes. Transfer jars to a towel-lined surface and let stand for 24 hours. Check lids and refrigerate any jars that are not sealed.

Pineapple Lime Tomato Salsa

Tomatoes get a tangy lift from fresh pineapple and zesty limes in this salsa.

Makes about eight 8-ounce (250 mL) or four pint (500 mL) jars

● ● ●

Tips

Hot peppers range widely in heat. When made with yellow wax or jalapeño peppers, this is on the medium side. If you like it a little more fiery, use a mixture of those milder peppers with some Scotch bonnet or habanero peppers (about 1 tbsp/15 mL will kick up the heat quite a bit).

To avoid burns, wear disposable rubber gloves when handling hot peppers and be sure to wash all utensils and the cutting board well after preparing the peppers.

Serving Suggestions

Serve the classic way, with corn tortilla chips for dipping.

Serve as a topping for grilled fish, poultry or pork.

10 cups	chopped peeled plum (Roma) tomatoes	2.5 L
3 cups	finely chopped fresh pineapple	750 mL
2 cups	chopped onions	500 mL
½ cup	finely chopped seeded hot chile peppers	125 mL
4 tsp	minced garlic	20 mL
¼ cup	granulated sugar	50 mL
2 tsp	pickling or canning salt	10 mL
1 cup	white vinegar	250 mL
2 tsp	grated lime zest	10 mL
¼ cup	freshly squeezed lime juice	50 mL
¼ cup	chopped fresh cilantro (optional)	50 mL

1. In a large pot, combine tomatoes, pineapple, onions, chile peppers, garlic, sugar, salt and vinegar. Bring to a boil over medium-high heat, stirring often. Reduce heat and boil gently, stirring often, for about 1 hour or until salsa is reduced by about half and is thick enough to mound on a spoon.
2. Meanwhile, prepare canner, jars and lids (see pages 7 to 8).
3. Stir lime zest, lime juice and cilantro (if using) into salsa and boil gently, stirring often, for 5 minutes to blend the flavors.
4. Ladle hot salsa into hot jars, leaving ½ inch (1 cm) headspace. Remove air bubbles and adjust headspace as necessary by adding hot salsa. Wipe rim and place hot lid disc on jar. Screw band down until fingertip-tight.
5. Place jars in canner and return to a boil. Process for 20 minutes. Turn off heat and remove canner lid. Let jars stand in water for 5 minutes. Transfer jars to a towel-lined surface and let stand for 24 hours. Check lids and refrigerate any jars that are not sealed.

Chile Orange Tomato Salsa

This salsa has multiple layers of flavor: the tang and zest of orange and tomato, a kick of heat from the fresh chile peppers and a touch of toasted flavor from the dried chiles. When you add it all up, it's delicious!

Makes about eight 8-ounce (250 mL) or four pint (500 mL) jars

• • •

Tips

For instructions on peeling tomatoes, see page 17.

Hot peppers range widely in heat. When made with yellow wax or jalapeño peppers, this is on the medium side. If you like it a little more fiery, use a mixture of those milder peppers with some Scotch bonnet or habanero peppers (about 1 tbsp/15 mL will kick up the heat quite a bit).

Ancho chile peppers are dried poblano peppers. They add a touch of toasted flavor without much heat. They are often available in the produce section of supermarkets and at specialty food stores.

12 cups	chopped peeled plum (Roma) tomatoes	3 L
2 tsp	grated orange zest	10 mL
2 cups	finely chopped peeled seedless oranges	500 mL
1½ cups	chopped onions	375 mL
⅓ cup	finely chopped seeded hot chile peppers	75 mL
2	cloves garlic, minced	2
¼ cup	granulated sugar	50 mL
2 tsp	pickling or canning salt	10 mL
1 cup	white vinegar	250 mL
2	dried ancho or mild New Mexico chile peppers	2
1 cup	boiling water	250 mL

1. In a large pot, combine tomatoes, chopped oranges, onions, chopped chile peppers, garlic, sugar, salt and vinegar. Bring to a boil over medium-high heat, stirring often. Reduce heat and boil gently, stirring often, for about 1 hour or until salsa is reduced by about half and is thick enough to mound on a spoon.

2. Meanwhile, prepare canner, jars and lids (see pages 7 to 8).

3. In a heatproof bowl, combine dried chile peppers and boiling water. Let stand for about 30 minutes or until peppers are softened. Remove peppers from liquid and discard liquid. Discard stem and seeds and finely chop peppers. Stir into salsa with orange zest and boil gently, stirring often, for 5 minutes to blend the flavors.

4. Ladle hot salsa into hot jars, leaving ½ inch (1 cm) headspace. Remove air bubbles and adjust headspace as necessary by adding hot salsa. Wipe rim and place hot lid disc on jar. Screw band down until fingertip-tight.

5. Place jars in canner and return to a boil. Process for 20 minutes. Turn off heat and remove canner lid. Let jars stand in water for 5 minutes. Transfer jars to a towel-lined surface and let stand for 24 hours. Check lids and refrigerate any jars that are not sealed.

Fall Fruit Salsa

A sweet, fruity flavor adds a different taste to this zesty salsa. It's delicious as a dip for chips or on top of grilled fish or poultry.

Makes about eleven 8-ounce (250 mL) or five to six pint (500 mL) jars		
7 cups	chopped peeled plum (Roma) tomatoes	1.75 L
3 cups	chopped peeled tart cooking apples	750 mL
2 cups	chopped onions	500 mL
3	cloves garlic, minced	3
2 tbsp	granulated sugar	25 mL
2 tsp	pickling or canning salt	10 mL
½ tsp	ground cinnamon	2 mL
1¼ cups	cider vinegar	300 mL
2 cups	finely chopped peeled pears	500 mL
2 cups	finely chopped plums	500 mL
½ cup	finely chopped seeded yellow wax (hot banana) or cayenne peppers	125 mL
¼ cup	chopped fresh mint or cilantro (optional)	50 mL

Tips

To avoid burns, wear disposable rubber gloves when handling hot peppers and be sure to wash all utensils and the cutting board well after preparing the peppers.

If you use 8-ounce (250 mL) jars, they may not all fit in your canner at once. Let extra jars cool, then refrigerate them and use them up first. To avoid this problem, I like to pack some in pint (500 mL) jars and some in 8-ounce (250 mL) jars. That way, I also have different sizes and can open the size I know I'll use up within a few weeks.

1. Prepare canner, jars and lids (see pages 7 to 8).
2. In a large pot, combine tomatoes, apples, onions, garlic, sugar, salt, cinnamon and vinegar. Bring to a boil over medium-high heat, stirring often. Reduce heat and boil gently, stirring often, for about 30 minutes or until tomatoes start to break down and salsa is slightly thickened. Stir in pears, plums and yellow wax peppers, increase heat to medium and return to a boil. Boil gently, stirring often, for about 20 minutes or until fruit is translucent and salsa is thick enough to mound on a spoon. Stir in mint (if using).
3. Ladle hot salsa into hot jars, leaving ½ inch (1 cm) headspace. Remove air bubbles and adjust headspace as necessary by adding hot salsa. Wipe rim and place hot lid disc on jar. Screw band down until fingertip-tight.
4. Place jars in canner and return to a boil. Process for 20 minutes. Turn off heat and remove canner lid. Let jars stand in water for 5 minutes. Transfer jars to a towel-lined surface and let stand for 24 hours. Check lids and refrigerate any jars that are not sealed.

Kosher-Style Dill Pickles (page 32)

Classic Icicle Pickles (page 40)

Pickled Red Cabbage and Apple (page 64),
Classic Pickled Asparagus (page 46)
and Curry Pickled Cauliflower (page 68)

Smoky Three-Pepper Cucumber Relish (page 259), Aunt Thelma's Bread-and-Butter Pickles (page 35) and Pickled Red Radishes (page 97)

Sweet and Hot Pickled Rainbow Peppers (page 95)

Marsala and White Balsamic Pickled Figs (page 116)

Spiced Pickled Peaches (page 122) and Five-Spice Pickled Pears (page 126)

Hot and Sweet Pickled Pineapple (page 129)

Mango Cilantro Salsa

I love to make fresh mango salsa to serve on top of grilled fish or barbecued pork. I created this one for those times when I don't have fresh mangos on hand.

Makes about eight 8-ounce (250 mL) or four pint (500 mL) jars

● ● ●

Tips

Mixing the mangos with some of the sugar helps to soften them and reduces the amount of cooking required, keeping the flavor fresher.

Use ripe but firm mangos for the best texture and flavor. You'll need about 6 large mangos to get 8 cups (2 L) finely chopped.

8 cups	finely chopped sweet mangos	2 L
½ cup	granulated sugar, divided	125 mL
1½ cups	finely chopped red onion	375 mL
1 cup	finely chopped orange or red bell pepper	250 mL
¼ cup	finely chopped seeded yellow wax (hot banana) pepper or jalapeño peppers	50 mL
1 tsp	pickling or canning salt	5 mL
½ tsp	ground cumin	2 mL
¾ cup	white vinegar	175 mL
¼ cup	freshly squeezed lime juice	50 mL
¼ cup	chopped fresh cilantro	50 mL

1. Prepare canner, jars and lids (see pages 7 to 8).
2. In a bowl, gently combine mangos and half the sugar. Set aside.
3. In a large pot, combine the remaining sugar, onion, orange pepper, yellow wax pepper, salt, cumin and vinegar. Bring to a boil over medium-high heat, stirring often. Reduce heat and boil gently, stirring often, for about 5 minutes or until onions are almost translucent. Stir in mango mixture and boil gently, stirring often, for about 10 minutes or until mango just starts to break down. Stir in lime juice and cilantro.
4. Ladle hot salsa into hot jars, leaving ½ inch (1 cm) headspace. Remove air bubbles and adjust headspace as necessary by adding hot salsa. Wipe rim and place hot lid disc on jar. Screw band down until fingertip-tight.
5. Place jars in canner and return to a boil. Process for 20 minutes. Turn off heat and remove canner lid. Let jars stand in water for 5 minutes. Transfer jars to a towel-lined surface and let stand for 24 hours. Check lids and refrigerate any jars that are not sealed.

Peach, Jalapeño and Mint Salsa

Where I live in southern Ontario, we're lucky enough to have fabulous peach orchards in the nearby Niagara area. I can never resist buying baskets and baskets of peaches at the market when they're in season. This recipe is a terrific way to capture their fragrant flavor in a savory salsa.

Makes about ten 8-ounce (250 mL) or five pint (500 mL) jars

• • •

Tips

For instructions on peeling peaches, see page 16.

If you use 8-ounce (250 mL) jars, they may not all fit in your canner at once. Let extra jars cool, then refrigerate them and use them up first. To avoid this problem, I like to pack some in pint (500 mL) jars and some in 8-ounce (250 mL) jars. That way, I also have different sizes and can open the size I know I'll use up within a few weeks.

Serving Suggestion

Serve on grilled pork chops, a pork roast or grilled fish.

10 cups	finely chopped peeled peaches	2.5 L
2 cups	finely chopped onions	500 mL
1½ cups	finely chopped red or yellow bell peppers	375 mL
¼ cup	minced seeded jalapeño peppers (see tip, page 163)	50 mL
1 tbsp	minced garlic	15 mL
½ cup	granulated sugar	125 mL
1½ tsp	pickling or canning salt	7 mL
1 tsp	ground cumin	5 mL
¼ tsp	ground cinnamon	1 mL
1 cup	white vinegar	250 mL
2 tbsp	chopped fresh mint	25 mL

1. Prepare canner, jars and lids (see pages 7 to 8).
2. In a large pot, combine peaches, onions, red peppers, jalapeños, garlic, sugar, salt, cumin, cinnamon and vinegar. Bring to a boil over medium-high heat, stirring often. Reduce heat and boil gently, stirring often, for about 20 minutes or until onions are translucent and salsa is slightly thickened. Stir in mint.
3. Ladle hot salsa into hot jars, leaving ½ inch (1 cm) headspace. Remove air bubbles and adjust headspace as necessary by adding hot salsa. Wipe rim and place hot lid disc on jar. Screw band down until fingertip-tight.
4. Place jars in canner and return to a boil. Process for 20 minutes. Turn off heat and remove canner lid. Let jars stand in water for 5 minutes. Transfer jars to a towel-lined surface and let stand for 24 hours. Check lids and refrigerate any jars that are not sealed.

Peppery Strawberry Salsa

I created this recipe when my fervor for strawberry picking outdid my need for jam. The combination of fresh berry flavor and sweet and hot peppers makes this a wonderful addition to your salsa inventory.

Makes about twelve 8-ounce (250 mL) jars or 6 pint (500 mL) jars

• • •

Tips

You'll need about 3 quarts (3 L), or 3½ lbs (1.75 kg), whole strawberries.

For the best consistency, place the strawberries in a single layer in a shallow bowl and use a potato masher to crush them one layer at a time.

The heat level in jalapeño peppers varies quite a bit, so the salsa may turn out milder than you expect. Taste the jalapeño before adding it to the salsa; if it seems mild, add 1 to 2 tbsp (15 to 25 mL) more. If you'd rather err on the side of caution and avoid making it too spicy, you can add fresh minced jalapeños or hot pepper sauce when serving it to kick up the heat.

6 cups	crushed strawberries	1.5 L
4 cups	diced red bell peppers	1 L
2 cups	diced yellow bell peppers	500 mL
1½ cups	chopped onions	375 mL
¼ cup	minced seeded jalapeño peppers	50 mL
2 tsp	pickling or canning salt	10 mL
1 tsp	ground cumin	5 mL
¾ cup	cider vinegar	175 mL
½ cup	liquid honey	125 mL
¼ cup	finely chopped cilantro or mint	50 mL

1. Prepare canner, jars and lids (see pages 7 to 8).
2. If berries are very juicy (they squirt when crushed), spoon 3 cups (750 mL) into a sieve set over a bowl. Let drain for about 30 minutes to remove about ¾ cup (175 mL) excess juice; reserve the juice for another use.
3. In a large pot, combine strawberries, red and yellow peppers, onions, jalapeños, salt, cumin, vinegar and honey. Bring to a boil over medium-high heat, stirring often. Reduce heat and boil gently, stirring often, for about 20 minutes or until onions are translucent and salsa is slightly thickened. Stir in cilantro.
4. Ladle hot salsa into hot jars, leaving ½ inch (1 cm) headspace. Remove air bubbles and adjust headspace as necessary by adding hot salsa. Wipe rim and place hot lid disc on jar. Screw band down until fingertip-tight.
5. Place jars in canner and return to a boil. Process for 15 minutes. Turn off heat and remove canner lid. Let jars stand in water for 5 minutes. Transfer jars to a towel-lined surface and let stand for 24 hours. Check lids and refrigerate any jars that are not sealed.

Grilled Tomatillo and Jalapeño Salsa

This salsa combines slightly charred tart green tomatillos and ripe red tomatoes, with a punch of jalapeño peppers. Serve it as a dip with tortilla chips, as garnish on fajitas or tacos or on a grilled steak.

Makes about eight 8-ounce (250 mL) or four pint (500 mL) jars

● ● ●

Tips

Tomatillos are related to tomatoes but are distinguished by their papery husk. Use firm, green tomatillos with a tightly closed husk. They're available at farmers' markets, specialty produce stores and Latin American markets.

To avoid burns, wear disposable rubber gloves when handling hot peppers and be sure to wash all utensils and the cutting board well after preparing the peppers.

Serving Suggestion

Add some diced avocado to this salsa just before serving to make it even more fabulous.

- Preheat broiler or preheat barbecue grill to medium-high
- Rimmed baking sheet (if using broiler)

2 lbs	tomatillos	1 kg
4 cups	chopped peeled plum (Roma) tomatoes	1 L
1½ cups	chopped onions	375 mL
½ cup	finely chopped seeded jalapeño peppers	125 mL
2 tbsp	finely chopped garlic	25 mL
2 tbsp	granulated sugar	25 mL
2 tsp	pickling or canning salt	10 mL
1 tsp	ground cumin	5 mL
1 cup	white vinegar	250 mL
2 tbsp	chopped fresh oregano	25 mL

1. Peel husks from tomatillos, rinse under running water and pat dry. If using broiler, place on baking sheet. Broil or grill, turning often, for about 10 minutes or until charred on all sides and slightly softened. Transfer to a shallow dish and let cool. Coarsely chop and measure 5 cups (1.25 L).
2. Meanwhile, prepare canner, jars and lids (see pages 7 to 8).
3. In a large pot, combine tomatillos, tomatoes, onions, jalapeños, garlic, sugar, salt, cumin and vinegar. Bring to a boil over medium-high heat, stirring often. Reduce heat and boil gently, stirring often, for about 45 minutes or until salsa is thick enough to mound on a spoon. Stir in oregano.
4. Ladle hot salsa into hot jars, leaving ½ inch (1 cm) headspace. Remove air bubbles and adjust headspace as necessary by adding hot salsa. Wipe rim and place hot lid disc on jar. Screw band down until fingertip-tight.
5. Place jars in canner and return to a boil. Process for 20 minutes. Turn off heat and remove canner lid. Let jars stand in water for 5 minutes. Transfer jars to a towel-lined surface and let stand for 24 hours. Check lids and refrigerate any jars that are not sealed.

Tomatillo and Lime Salsa Verde

Traditional Mexican flavors abound in this tart and perky salsa. In Mexico, salsa verde is usually made fresh, but having a cooked and canned version means you can enjoy it all year long, not just when tomatillos are in season.

Makes about ten 8-ounce (250 mL) or five pint (500 mL) jars

● ● ●

Tips

You'll need about 4 lbs (2 kg) tomatillos to get 12 cups (3 L) chopped.

Peel the husks from tomatillos and rinse under running water to remove the slight stickiness before chopping them.

If you use 8-ounce (250 mL) jars, they may not all fit in your canner at once. Let extra jars cool, then refrigerate them and use them up first. To avoid this problem, I like to pack some in pint (500 mL) jars and some in 8-ounce (250 mL) jars. That way, I also have different sizes and can open the size I know I'll use up within a few weeks.

Variation

If you want a fiery salsa verde, increase the jalapeños to ½ cup (125 mL) or add hot pepper sauce to taste with the cilantro.

12 cups	chopped tomatillos	3 L
3 cups	chopped onions	750 mL
½ cup	finely chopped seeded serrano or long hot green chile peppers	125 mL
¼ cup	finely chopped seeded jalapeño peppers	50 mL
¼ cup	finely chopped garlic (about 12 cloves)	50 mL
4 tsp	pickling or canning salt	20 mL
1 cup	white vinegar	250 mL
1 tsp	grated lime zest	5 mL
½ cup	freshly squeezed lime juice	125 mL
¼ cup	chopped fresh cilantro	50 mL

1. Prepare canner, jars and lids (see pages 7 to 8).
2. In a large pot, combine tomatillos, onions, serranos, jalapeños, garlic, salt, vinegar and lime juice. Bring to a boil over medium-high heat, stirring often. Reduce heat and boil gently, stirring often, for about 20 minutes or until tomatillos and onions are tender and salsa is slightly thickened. Stir in lime zest and cilantro.
3. Ladle hot salsa into hot jars, leaving ½ inch (1 cm) headspace. Remove air bubbles and adjust headspace as necessary by adding hot salsa. Wipe rim and place hot lid disc on jar. Screw band down until fingertip-tight.
4. Place jars in canner and return to a boil. Process for 15 minutes. Turn off heat and remove canner lid. Let jars stand in water for 5 minutes. Transfer jars to a towel-lined surface and let stand for 24 hours. Check lids and refrigerate any jars that are not sealed.

Eric's Green Tomato Salsa

Eric Boudrias was a chef at the café I co-own, Nuttshell Next Door, and he brought me a jar of the salsa he and his mom, Kate, make together every year. After one taste of this vibrant-tasting salsa, I knew I had to include the recipe in this book. Thanks to Eric and Kate for sharing it with me. By the way, it's not for the timid palate!

Makes about eight pint (500 mL) jars

● ● ●

Tips

Eric and Kate recommend using a food processor to chop all of the vegetables for this salsa. Process each vegetable, in batches as necessary, until finely chopped but not puréed, then measure the volume.

To avoid burns, wear disposable rubber gloves when handling hot peppers and be sure to wash all utensils and the cutting board well after preparing the peppers.

13½ cups	very finely chopped green tomatoes (about 6 lbs/3 kg)	3.375 L
3½ cups	very finely chopped red onions (about 1½ lbs/750 g)	875 mL
3 cups	very finely chopped red bell peppers (about 1½ lbs/750 g)	750 mL
1 to 1½ cups	finely chopped jalapeño peppers (8 to 12)	250 to 375 mL
⅓ cup	finely chopped garlic (about 1 large head)	75 mL
3 tbsp	pickling or canning salt	45 mL
1½ cups	red wine vinegar	375 mL
⅓ cup	freshly squeezed lime juice (about 2)	75 mL

1. In a large pot, combine green tomatoes, red onions, red peppers, jalapeños to taste and garlic. Bring to a boil over medium-high heat, stirring often. Reduce heat and boil gently, stirring often, for about 1½ hours or until reduced by about one-third.
2. Meanwhile, prepare canner, jars and lids (see pages 7 to 8).
3. Stir salt, vinegar and lime juice into salsa and boil gently, stirring often, for about 5 minutes or until salt is dissolved and flavors are blended.
4. Ladle hot salsa into hot jars, leaving ½ inch (1 cm) headspace. Remove air bubbles and adjust headspace as necessary by adding hot salsa. Wipe rim and place hot lid disc on jar. Screw band down until fingertip-tight.
5. Place jars in canner and return to a boil. Process for 20 minutes. Turn off heat and remove canner lid. Let jars stand in water for 5 minutes. Transfer jars to a towel-lined surface and let stand for 24 hours. Check lids and refrigerate any jars that are not sealed.

Classic Tomato Sauce

Just as the title says, this sauce is lightly seasoned with classic flavors that really highlight the vine-ripened beauty of freshly harvested tomatoes.

Makes about six pint (500 mL) jars

● ● ●

Tips

Many tomato sauce recipes use bottled lemon juice instead of vinegar. I prefer the flavor of vinegar and offset the acidic taste with a bit of sugar. To sweeten to taste, stir 2 cups (500 mL) sauce with 2 tbsp (25 mL) vinegar, taste and add more sugar, if desired. Then add that much sugar with the vinegar to each jar. If you prefer to use bottled lemon juice, use 1 tbsp (15 mL) per jar. Do not use freshly squeezed lemon juice.

If you don't have a food mill or Victorio strainer, peel, seed and chop the tomatoes before step 1. In step 3, using an immersion blender, purée the sauce until fairly smooth. Proceed with step 4 as directed.

● Food mill, fitted with fine plate, or Victorio strainer (optional, see tip, at left)

10 lbs	plum (Roma) tomatoes, cut into chunks, divided	5 kg
3 cups	chopped onions	750 mL
3 cups	chopped red bell peppers	750 mL
2 cups	chopped celery	500 mL
4	cloves garlic, chopped	4
2	bay leaves	2
½ cup	granulated sugar	125 mL
1 tbsp	pickling or canning salt	15 mL
1 tbsp	dried oregano	15 mL
1 tbsp	dried basil	15 mL
1 tsp	freshly ground black pepper	5 mL
	Red wine vinegar (see tip, at left)	

1. In a large pot, heat half the tomatoes over medium heat, stirring often, until wilted. Add the remaining tomatoes and bring to a boil, stirring often. Add onions, red peppers, celery, garlic, bay leaves, sugar, salt, oregano, basil and pepper; return to a boil, stirring often. Reduce heat and boil gently, stirring occasionally, for about 1½ hours or until vegetables are very soft. Discard bay leaves.

2. Meanwhile, prepare canner, jars and lids (see pages 7 to 8).

3. Working in batches, press sauce through food mill into another large pot or bowl, discarding skins and seeds. Return to pot, if necessary.

4. Return pot to medium-high heat and bring sauce to a boil. Reduce heat and boil gently, stirring often, for about 30 minutes or until thick enough to thinly coat a wooden spoon (it will be thinner than commercial pasta sauce).

5. Place 2 tbsp (25 mL) vinegar in the bottom of each hot jar. Ladle hot sauce into jars, leaving ½ inch (1 cm) headspace. Remove air bubbles and adjust headspace as necessary by adding hot sauce. Wipe rim and place hot lid disc on jar. Screw band down until fingertip-tight.

6. Place jars in canner and return to a boil. Process for 35 minutes. Turn off heat and remove canner lid. Let jars stand in water for 5 minutes. Transfer jars to a towel-lined surface and let stand for 24 hours. Check lids and refrigerate any jars that are not sealed.

Spicy Tomato Sauce

A kick of chile peppers in a traditional tomato sauce will heat up your pasta dishes even on the coldest winter night.

Makes about six pint (500 mL) jars

● ● ●

Tip

Many tomato sauce recipes use bottled lemon juice instead of vinegar. I prefer the flavor of vinegar and offset the acidic taste with a bit of sugar. To sweeten to taste, stir 2 cups (500 mL) sauce with 2 tbsp (25 mL) vinegar, taste and add more sugar, if desired. Then add that much sugar with the vinegar to each jar. If you prefer to use bottled lemon juice, use 1 tbsp (15 mL) per jar. Do not use freshly squeezed lemon juice.

• Food mill, fitted with fine plate, or Victorio strainer (optional, see tip, page 167)

10 lbs	plum (Roma) tomatoes, cut into chunks, divided	5 kg
3 cups	chopped onions	750 mL
2½ cups	chopped red bell peppers	625 mL
2 cups	chopped celery	500 mL
¼ cup	chopped garlic	50 mL
½ cup	granulated sugar	125 mL
1 tbsp	pickling or canning salt	15 mL
1 tbsp	dried oregano	15 mL
1 tbsp	dried basil	15 mL
2 tsp	hot pepper flakes	10 mL
1 tsp	freshly ground black pepper	5 mL
½ cup	finely chopped seeded cayenne or yellow wax (hot banana) peppers	125 mL
	White wine vinegar or red wine vinegar (see tip, at left)	

1. In a large pot, heat half the tomatoes over medium heat, stirring often, until wilted. Add the remaining tomatoes and bring to a boil, stirring often. Add onions, red peppers, celery, garlic, sugar, salt, oregano, basil, hot pepper flakes and black pepper; return to a boil, stirring often. Reduce heat and boil gently, stirring occasionally, for about 1½ hours or until vegetables are very soft.

2. Meanwhile, prepare canner, jars and lids (see pages 7 to 8).

3. Working in batches, press sauce through food mill into another large pot or bowl, discarding skins and seeds. Return to pot, if necessary.

4. Stir in cayenne peppers. Return pot to medium-high heat and bring sauce to a boil. Reduce heat and boil gently, stirring often, for about 30 minutes or until thick enough to thinly coat a wooden spoon (it will be thinner than commercial pasta sauce).

5. Place 2 tbsp (25 mL) vinegar in the bottom of each hot jar. Ladle hot sauce into jars, leaving $\frac{1}{2}$ inch (1 cm) headspace. Remove air bubbles and adjust headspace as necessary by adding hot sauce. Wipe rim and place hot lid disc on jar. Screw band down until fingertip-tight.

6. Place jars in canner and return to a boil. Process for 35 minutes. Turn off heat and remove canner lid. Let jars stand in water for 5 minutes. Transfer jars to a towel-lined surface and let stand for 24 hours. Check lids and refrigerate any jars that are not sealed.

Tip

To avoid burns, wear disposable rubber gloves when handling hot peppers and be sure to wash all utensils and the cutting board well after preparing the peppers.

Olive and Herb Tomato Sauce

Fresh herbs and olives add depth of flavor to ripe red tomatoes in this succulent sauce.

Tips

If you don't have a food mill or Victorio strainer, peel, seed and chop the tomatoes before step 1. In step 3, using an immersion blender, purée the sauce until fairly smooth. Proceed with step 4 as directed.

Use black olives that have been cured and preserved in brine (not oil), to make sure they are high in acid. Drain and rinse well. To chop, place olives narrow end down on a cutting board and, using a sharp paring knife, cut the flesh away from the pit in about 4 slices. Place slices flat side down on board and cut into small pieces. You'll need about 30 large olives.

• **Food mill, fitted with fine plate, or Victorio strainer (optional, see tip, at left)**

10 lbs	plum (Roma) tomatoes, cut into chunks, divided	5 kg
3 cups	chopped onions	750 mL
2 cups	chopped red and/or green bell peppers	500 mL
1 cup	chopped carrots	250 mL
2 tbsp	chopped garlic	25 mL
2	bay leaves	2
½ cup	granulated sugar	125 mL
1 tbsp	pickling or canning salt	15 mL
1 tsp	freshly ground black pepper	5 mL
1 cup	finely chopped drained rinsed brine-cured black olives (see tip, at left)	250 mL
½ cup	chopped fresh basil	125 mL
2 tbsp	chopped fresh rosemary	25 mL
1 tbsp	chopped fresh thyme	15 mL
	Red wine vinegar or balsamic vinegar (see tip, page 168)	

1. In a large pot, heat half the tomatoes over medium heat, stirring often, until wilted. Add the remaining tomatoes and bring to a boil, stirring often. Add onions, red peppers, carrots, garlic, bay leaves, sugar, salt and black pepper; return to a boil, stirring often. Reduce heat and boil gently, stirring occasionally, for about 1½ hours or until vegetables are very soft. Discard bay leaves.
2. Meanwhile, prepare canner, jars and lids (see pages 7 to 8).
3. Working in batches, press sauce through food mill into another large pot or bowl, discarding skins and seeds. Return to pot, if necessary.
4. Return pot to medium-high heat and bring sauce to a boil. Reduce heat and boil gently, stirring often, for about 30 minutes or until thick enough to thinly coat a wooden spoon (it will be thinner than commercial pasta sauce). Stir in olives, basil, rosemary and thyme; boil gently, stirring often, for 5 minutes to blend the flavors.

5. Place 2 tbsp (25 mL) vinegar in the bottom of each hot jar. Ladle hot sauce into jars, leaving $\frac{1}{2}$ inch (1 cm) headspace. Remove air bubbles and adjust headspace as necessary by adding hot sauce. Wipe rim and place hot lid disc on jar. Screw band down until fingertip-tight.

6. Place jars in canner and return to a boil. Process for 35 minutes. Turn off heat and remove canner lid. Let jars stand in water for 5 minutes. Transfer jars to a towel-lined surface and let stand for 24 hours. Check lids and refrigerate any jars that are not sealed.

Serving Suggestion

Heat Olive and Herb Tomato Sauce until simmering and add some sautéed chicken pieces or shrimp. Serve over cooked pasta.

Roasted Garlic Tomato Sauce

Roasting garlic brings out a mellow, almost sweet garlic flavor that is very different from the fresh flavor. You'll be tempted to use this sauce for many things beyond the classic pasta.

Makes about six pint (500 mL) jars

● ● ● ●

Tip

If you don't have a food mill or Victorio strainer, peel, seed and chop the tomatoes before step 1. In step 4, using an immersion blender, purée the sauce until fairly smooth. Proceed with step 5 as directed.

● **Food mill, fitted with fine plate, or Victorio strainer (optional, see tip, at left)**

10 lbs	plum (Roma) tomatoes, cut into chunks, divided	5 kg
4 cups	chopped onions	1 L
2 cups	chopped red and/or green bell peppers	500 mL
2 cups	chopped celery	500 mL
½ cup	granulated sugar	125 mL
2 tbsp	dried basil	25 mL
1 tbsp	pickling or canning salt	15 mL
1 tsp	freshly ground black pepper	5 mL
1 tsp	hot pepper flakes (optional)	5 mL
6	heads garlic, cloves separated and peeled	6
	Red wine vinegar (see tip, page 173)	

1. In a large pot, heat half the tomatoes over medium heat, stirring often, until wilted. Add the remaining tomatoes and bring to a boil, stirring often. Add onions, red peppers, celery, sugar, basil, salt, black pepper and hot pepper flakes (if using); return to a boil, stirring often. Reduce heat and boil gently, stirring occasionally, for about 1½ hours or until vegetables are very soft.

2. Meanwhile, preheat oven to 350°F (180°C). Wrap garlic in a large piece of foil and roast for about 1 hour or until very soft.

3. Prepare canner, jars and lids (see pages 7 to 8).

4. Stir roasted garlic into sauce. Working in batches, press sauce through food mill into another large pot or bowl, discarding skins and seeds. Return to pot, if necessary.

5. Return pot to medium-high heat and bring sauce to a boil. Reduce heat and boil gently, stirring often, for about 30 minutes or until thick enough to thinly coat a wooden spoon (it will be thinner than commercial pasta sauce).

6. Place 2 tbsp (25 mL) vinegar in the bottom of each hot jar. Ladle hot sauce into jars, leaving ½ inch (1 cm) headspace. Remove air bubbles and adjust headspace as necessary by adding hot sauce. Wipe rim and place hot lid disc on jar. Screw band down until fingertip-tight.

7. Place jars in canner and return to a boil. Process for 35 minutes. Turn off heat and remove canner lid. Let jars stand in water for 5 minutes. Transfer jars to a towel-lined surface and let stand for 24 hours. Check lids and refrigerate any jars that are not sealed.

Vodka and Rosemary Tomato Sauce

You'll think you're eating at a fine Italian restaurant when you taste this classic sauce.

Makes about six pint (500 mL) jars

● ● ●

Tip

Many tomato sauce recipes use bottled lemon juice instead of vinegar. I prefer the flavor of vinegar and offset the acidic taste with a bit of sugar. To sweeten to taste, stir 2 cups (500 mL) sauce with 2 tbsp (25 mL) vinegar, taste and add more sugar, if desired. Then add that much sugar with the vinegar to each jar. If you prefer to use bottled lemon juice, use 1 tbsp (15 mL) per jar. Do not use freshly squeezed lemon juice.

Serving Suggestion

When serving sauce, for extra decadence, simmer in a saucepan until slightly thickened, then stir in a little whipping (35%) cream.

● Food mill, fitted with fine plate, or Victorio strainer (optional, see tip, page 167)

10 lbs	plum (Roma) tomatoes, cut into chunks, divided	5 kg
4 cups	chopped onions	1 L
2 cups	chopped celery	500 mL
2 cups	chopped carrots	500 mL
2 tbsp	chopped garlic	25 mL
4	bay leaves	4
½ cup	granulated sugar	125 mL
1 tbsp	pickling or canning salt	15 mL
1 tsp	freshly ground black pepper	5 mL
1 cup	vodka	250 mL
2 tbsp	finely chopped fresh rosemary	25 mL
	White wine vinegar (see tip, at left)	

1. In a large pot, heat half the tomatoes over medium heat, stirring often, until wilted. Add the remaining tomatoes and bring to a boil, stirring often. Add onions, celery, carrots, garlic, bay leaves, sugar, salt and pepper; return to a boil, stirring often. Reduce heat and boil gently, stirring occasionally, for about 1½ hours or until vegetables are very soft. Discard bay leaves.

2. Meanwhile, prepare canner, jars and lids (see pages 7 to 8).

3. Working in batches, press sauce through food mill into another large pot or bowl, discarding skins and seeds. Return to pot, if necessary.

4. Return pot to medium-high heat and bring sauce to a boil. Reduce heat and boil gently, stirring often, for about 30 minutes or until thick enough to thinly coat a wooden spoon (it will be thinner than commercial pasta sauce). Stir in vodka and rosemary; boil gently, stirring often, for 5 minutes to blend flavors.

5. Place 2 tbsp (25 mL) vinegar in the bottom of each hot jar. Ladle hot sauce into jars, leaving ½ inch (1 cm) headspace. Remove air bubbles and adjust headspace as necessary by adding hot sauce. Wipe rim and place hot lid disc on jar. Screw band down until fingertip-tight.

6. Place jars in canner and return to a boil. Process for 35 minutes. Turn off heat and remove canner lid. Let jars stand in water for 5 minutes. Transfer jars to a towel-lined surface and let stand for 24 hours. Check lids and refrigerate any jars that are not sealed.

Classic Barbecue Sauce

When fresh tomatoes are at their peak, make this barbecue sauce; after one taste, you'll never go back to the bottled kind again! It's sweet, tangy and savory, all in one.

Makes about six pint (500 mL) jars

• • •

Tip

As the sauce gets thicker, you'll need to stir more often and reduce the heat to prevent it from scorching and splattering too much.

• **Food mill, fitted with fine plate, or Victorio strainer (optional, see tip, page 175)**

10 lbs	plum (Roma) tomatoes, cut into chunks, divided	5 kg
3 cups	chopped onions	750 mL
2 cups	chopped celery	500 mL
4	cloves garlic, chopped	4
2	bay leaves	2
2 tbsp	pickling or canning salt	25 mL
2 tbsp	dry mustard	25 mL
2 tbsp	chili powder	25 mL
1 tsp	freshly ground black pepper	5 mL
1½ cups	granulated sugar	375 mL
2 cups	white vinegar	500 mL
½ cup	fancy (light) molasses	125 mL

1. In a large pot, heat half the tomatoes over medium heat, stirring often, until wilted. Add the remaining tomatoes and bring to a boil, stirring often. Add onions, celery, garlic, bay leaves, salt, mustard, chili powder and pepper; return to a boil, stirring often. Reduce heat and boil gently, stirring occasionally, for about 1½ hours or until vegetables are very soft. Discard bay leaves.

2. Working in batches, press through food mill into another large pot or bowl, discarding skins and seeds. Return to pot, if necessary, and stir in sugar, vinegar and molasses.

3. Return pot to medium-high heat and bring sauce to a boil. Reduce heat and boil gently, stirring often, for about 2 hours or until thick enough to coat a wooden spoon.

4. Meanwhile, prepare canner, jars and lids (see pages 7 to 8).

5. Ladle hot sauce into hot jars, leaving ½ inch (1 cm) headspace. Remove air bubbles and adjust headspace as necessary by adding hot sauce. Wipe rim and place hot lid disc on jar. Screw band down until fingertip-tight.

6. Place jars in canner and return to a boil. Process for 35 minutes. Turn off heat and remove canner lid. Let jars stand in water for 5 minutes. Transfer jars to a towel-lined surface and let stand for 24 hours. Check lids and refrigerate any jars that are not sealed.

Brown Sugar Barbecue Sauce

*This one is for everyone who loves sweet, sticky sauces. Try it on ribs, chicken or kabobs —
you'll be licking your fingers for sure!*

● ● ●

Tip

If you don't have a
food mill or Victorio
strainer, peel, seed
and chop the tomatoes
before step 1. In
step 2, using an
immersion blender,
purée the sauce until
fairly smooth. Proceed
with step 3 as directed.

● Food mill, fitted with fine plate, or Victorio strainer
(optional, see tip, at left)

10 lbs	plum (Roma) tomatoes, cut into chunks, divided	5 kg
4 cups	chopped onions	1 L
1 cup	chopped celery	250 mL
½ cup	chopped gingerroot	125 mL
4	cloves garlic, chopped	4
2	bay leaves	2
2 tbsp	pickling or canning salt	25 mL
1 tsp	freshly ground black pepper	5 mL
1 tsp	ground cloves or allspice (optional)	5 mL
3 cups	packed brown sugar	750 mL
2 cups	cider vinegar	500 mL

1. In a large pot, heat half the tomatoes over medium heat,
   stirring often, until wilted. Add the remaining tomatoes and
   bring to a boil, stirring often. Add onions, celery, ginger,
   garlic, bay leaves, salt, pepper and cloves (if using); return
   to a boil, stirring often. Reduce heat and boil gently, stirring
   occasionally, for about 1½ hours or until vegetables are very
   soft. Discard bay leaves.
2. Working in batches, press through food mill into another
   large pot or bowl, discarding skins and seeds. Return to pot,
   if necessary, and stir in brown sugar and vinegar.
3. Return pot to medium-high heat and bring sauce to a boil.
   Reduce heat and boil gently, stirring often, for about 2 hours
   or until thick enough to coat a wooden spoon.
4. Meanwhile, prepare canner, jars and lids (see pages 7 to 8).
5. Ladle hot sauce into hot jars, leaving ½ inch (1 cm)
   headspace. Remove air bubbles and adjust headspace as
   necessary by adding hot sauce. Wipe rim and place hot lid
   disc on jar. Screw band down until fingertip-tight.
6. Place jars in canner and return to a boil. Process for
   35 minutes. Turn off heat and remove canner lid. Let jars
   stand in water for 5 minutes. Transfer jars to a towel-lined
   surface and let stand for 24 hours. Check lids and refrigerate
   any jars that are not sealed.

Coffee-Spiked Barbecue Chili Sauce

This is a cross between barbecue sauce and chili sauce — you can leave it chunky or make it smooth (see variation, below). You won't necessarily taste the coffee, but it adds a delightfully rich flavor.

Makes about eight pint (500 mL) jars

• • •

Tip

To make strong brewed coffee, use 2 tbsp (25 mL) ground dark coffee per cup (250 mL) water.

Variation

If you prefer a smooth sauce, use an immersion blender to purée sauce in the pot at the end of step 1, or pass sauce through a food mill, fitted with the fine plate, or a Victorio strainer. Reheat until boiling before ladling into jars.

Serving Suggestions

Use this as a braising sauce for brisket or pork shoulder roast.

Serve on hamburgers, hot dogs or grilled sausages.

12 cups	chopped peeled plum (Roma) tomatoes	3 L
8 cups	chopped onions	2 L
2 cups	chopped red bell peppers	500 mL
2 cups	chopped celery	500 mL
2	yellow wax (hot banana) peppers, seeded and chopped	2
3 cups	packed brown sugar	750 mL
2 tbsp	pickling or canning salt	25 mL
2 tbsp	ground ginger	25 mL
1 tbsp	ground allspice	15 mL
½ tsp	hot pepper flakes	2 mL
2 cups	cider vinegar	500 mL
2 cups	strong brewed coffee	500 mL
½ cup	light (fancy) molasses	125 mL

1. In a large pot, combine tomatoes, onions, red peppers, celery, yellow wax peppers, brown sugar, salt, ginger, allspice, hot pepper flakes, vinegar, coffee and molasses. Bring to a boil over medium-high heat, stirring often. Reduce heat and boil gently, stirring often, for 2 to 2½ hours or until chili sauce is reduced by about half and is almost thick enough to mound on a spoon.

2. Meanwhile, prepare canner, jars and lids (see pages 7 to 8).

3. Ladle hot chili sauce into hot jars, leaving ½ inch (1 cm) headspace. Remove air bubbles and adjust headspace as necessary by adding hot chili sauce. Wipe rim and place hot lid disc on jar. Screw band down until fingertip-tight.

4. Place jars in canner and return to a boil. Process for 35 minutes. Turn off heat and remove canner lid. Let jars stand in water for 5 minutes. Transfer jars to a towel-lined surface and let stand for 24 hours. Check lids and refrigerate any jars that are not sealed.

Smoky Raspberry Barbecue Sauce

Tangy raspberries and rich, smoky chipotle peppers are one of my favorite flavor combinations for barbecue sauce. It may sound odd, but when you smell it simmering, it will likely become your favorite too.

Makes about six pint (500 mL) jars

• • •

Tips

Where I live, local raspberries are past their season well before tomatoes are ripe, so I plan ahead and freeze some to make this sauce. Alternatively, you can buy unsweetened frozen raspberries; they're often cheaper than fresh and taste just as good.

If you don't have a food mill or Victorio strainer, peel, seed and chop the tomatoes before step 1. In step 2, using an immersion blender, purée the sauce until fairly smooth. Proceed with step 3 as directed. Keep in mind that the raspberry seeds will remain in the sauce, so you may want to pass it through a fine-mesh sieve just before serving (don't try it with the whole batch at once — it'll take hours).

• **Food mill, fitted with fine plate, or Victorio strainer (optional, see tip, at left)**

8 lbs	plum (Roma) tomatoes, cut into chunks, divided	4 kg
6 cups	raspberries (about 2¼ lbs/1.125 kg)	1.5 L
3 cups	chopped sweet onions	750 mL
2 tbsp	pickling or canning salt	25 mL
1 tsp	freshly ground black pepper	5 mL
2½ cups	granulated sugar	625 mL
2 cups	white vinegar	500 mL
4	drained chipotle peppers in adobo sauce, minced	4
¼ cup	adobo sauce	50 mL

1. In a large pot, heat half the tomatoes over medium heat, stirring often, until wilted. Add the remaining tomatoes and the raspberries; bring to a boil, stirring often. Add onions, salt and pepper; return to a boil, stirring often. Reduce heat and boil gently, stirring occasionally, for about 1½ hours or until vegetables are very soft.

2. Working in batches, press sauce through food mill into another large pot or bowl, discarding skins and seeds. Return to pot, if necessary, and stir in sugar and vinegar.

3. Return pot to medium-high heat and bring sauce to a boil. Reduce heat and boil gently, stirring often, for about 2 hours or until thick enough to coat a wooden spoon.

4. Meanwhile, prepare canner, jars and lids (see pages 7 to 8).

5. Stir chipotles and adobo into sauce and boil gently, stirring often, for 5 minutes to blend the flavors.

6. Ladle hot sauce into hot jars, leaving ½ inch (1 cm) headspace. Remove air bubbles and adjust headspace as necessary by adding hot sauce. Wipe rim and place hot lid disc on jar. Screw band down until fingertip-tight.

7. Place jars in canner and return to a boil. Process for 35 minutes. Turn off heat and remove canner lid. Let jars stand in water for 5 minutes. Transfer jars to a towel-lined surface and let stand for 24 hours. Check lids and refrigerate any jars that are not sealed.

Apricot Chile Barbecue Sauce

Fresh apricots combined with dried chile peppers make this barbecue sauce extra luscious.

Makes about six pint (500 mL) jars

● ● ●

Tip

Dried New Mexico chile peppers are available in both mild and hot varieties. The hot variety adds a nice pep to this sauce, but you can use mild ones if you prefer. Ancho chile peppers are dried poblano peppers. They add a touch of toasted flavor without much heat. Dried chile peppers are often available in the produce section of supermarkets and at specialty food stores.

- Food mill, fitted with fine plate, or Victorio strainer (optional, see tip, page 175)

8 lbs	plum (Roma) tomatoes, cut into chunks, divided	4 kg
2 lbs	apricots, quartered (or cut into chunks if large)	2 kg
4 cups	chopped onions	1 L
2 tbsp	each chopped garlic and gingerroot	25 mL
2 tbsp	pickling or canning salt	25 mL
1 tsp	freshly ground black pepper	5 mL
2½ cups	granulated sugar	625 mL
2 cups	white vinegar	500 mL
2	dried hot New Mexico chile peppers	2
2	dried ancho chile peppers	2
2 cups	boiling water	500 mL

1. In a large pot, heat half the tomatoes over medium heat, stirring often, until wilted. Add the remaining tomatoes and the apricots; bring to a boil, stirring often. Add onions, garlic, ginger, salt and pepper; return to a boil, stirring often. Reduce heat and boil gently, stirring occasionally, for about 1½ hours or until vegetables are very soft.

2. Working in batches, press sauce through food mill into another large pot or bowl, discarding skins and seeds. Return to pot, if necessary, and stir in sugar and vinegar.

3. Return pot to medium-high heat and bring sauce to a boil. Reduce heat and boil gently, stirring often, for about 2 hours or until thick enough to coat a wooden spoon.

4. Meanwhile, prepare canner, jars and lids (see pages 7 to 8).

5. In a heatproof bowl, combine New Mexico and ancho chile peppers and boiling water. Let stand for about 30 minutes or until peppers are softened. Remove peppers from liquid and discard liquid. Discard stem and seeds and finely chop peppers. Stir into sauce and boil gently, stirring often, for 5 minutes to blend the flavors.

6. Ladle hot sauce into hot jars, leaving ½ inch (1 cm) headspace. Remove air bubbles and adjust headspace as necessary by adding hot sauce. Wipe rim and place hot lid disc on jar. Screw band down until fingertip-tight.

7. Place jars in canner and return to a boil. Process for 35 minutes. Turn off heat and remove canner lid. Let jars stand in water for 5 minutes. Transfer jars to a towel-lined surface and let stand for 24 hours. Check lids and refrigerate any jars that are not sealed.

Homemade Ketchup

Making your own homemade ketchup with tomatoes you grew yourself or bought from a local farm means you know exactly what's in it, so you can feel good when your family wants to squirt it on absolutely everything!

Makes five to six pint (500 mL) jars

• • •

Tips

If you don't have a food mill or Victorio strainer, peel, seed and chop the tomatoes before step 2. In step 3, using an immersion blender, purée the sauce until fairly smooth. Proceed with step 4 as directed.

This will be thinner than commercial ketchup because there is no thickening agent, such as starch.

After opening the jar of ketchup, transfer it to a plastic squeeze bottle for the full traditional ketchup effect.

> • Food mill, fitted with fine plate, or Victorio strainer (optional, see tip, at left)

2	bay leaves	2
2 tbsp	celery seeds	25 mL
2 tsp	whole allspice	10 mL
1 tsp	whole cloves	5 mL
1 tsp	black peppercorns	5 mL
10 lbs	plum (Roma) tomatoes, cut into chunks, divided	5 kg
2 cups	chopped onions	500 mL
2 cups	granulated sugar	500 mL
2 tbsp	pickling or canning salt	25 mL
2 cups	cider vinegar	500 mL

1. Place bay leaves, celery seeds, allspice, cloves and peppercorns in the center of a square of triple-layered cheesecloth and tie into a spice bag.

2. In a large pot, combine spice bag and half the tomatoes; heat over medium heat, stirring often, until wilted. Add the remaining tomatoes and the onions; bring to a boil, stirring often. Reduce heat and boil gently, stirring occasionally, for about 1½ hours or until vegetables are very soft. Discard spice bag.

3. Working in batches, press sauce through food mill into another large pot or bowl, discarding skins and seeds. Return to pot, if necessary, and stir in sugar, salt and vinegar.

4. Return pot to medium-high heat and bring sauce to a boil. Reduce heat and boil gently, stirring often, for about 2 hours or until thick enough to coat a wooden spoon.

5. Meanwhile, prepare canner, jars and lids (see pages 7 to 8).

6. Ladle hot ketchup into hot jars, leaving ½ inch (1 cm) headspace. Remove air bubbles and adjust headspace as necessary by adding hot sauce. Wipe rim and place hot lid disc on jar. Screw band down until fingertip-tight.

7. Place jars in canner and return to a boil. Process for 35 minutes. Turn off heat and remove canner lid. Let jars stand in water for 5 minutes. Transfer jars to a towel-lined surface and let stand for 24 hours. Check lids and refrigerate any jars that are not sealed.

Homemade Spicy Ketchup

If your grilled cheese sandwiches or burgers need a little kick, this ketchup will do the trick.

Makes five to six pint (500 mL) jars

● ● ●

Tips

This will be thinner than commercial ketchup because there is no thickening agent, such as starch.

After opening the jar of ketchup, transfer it to a plastic squeeze bottle for the full traditional ketchup effect.

● Food mill, fitted with fine plate, or Victorio strainer (optional, see tip, page 179)

2	bay leaves	2
2 tbsp	celery seeds	25 mL
1 tbsp	hot pepper flakes	15 mL
2 tsp	whole cloves	10 mL
10 lbs	plum (Roma) tomatoes, cut into chunks, divided	5 kg
2 cups	chopped onions	500 mL
¼ cup	chopped seeded jalapeño peppers	50 mL
2 cups	packed brown sugar	500 mL
2 tbsp	pickling or canning salt	25 mL
2 cups	cider vinegar	500 mL

1. Place bay leaves, celery seeds, hot pepper flakes and cloves in the center of a square of triple-layered cheesecloth and tie into a spice bag.
2. In a large pot, combine spice bag and half the tomatoes; heat over medium heat, stirring often, until wilted. Add the remaining tomatoes and the onions; bring to a boil, stirring often. Reduce heat and boil gently, stirring occasionally, for about 1½ hours or until vegetables are very soft. Discard spice bag.
3. Working in batches, press sauce through food mill into another large pot or bowl, discarding skins and seeds. Return to pot, if necessary, and stir in brown sugar, salt and vinegar.
4. Return pot to medium-high heat and bring sauce to a boil. Reduce heat and boil gently, stirring often, for about 2 hours or until thick enough to coat a wooden spoon.
5. Meanwhile, prepare canner, jars and lids (see pages 7 to 8).
6. Ladle hot ketchup into hot jars, leaving ½ inch (1 cm) headspace. Remove air bubbles and adjust headspace as necessary by adding hot sauce. Wipe rim and place hot lid disc on jar. Screw band down until fingertip-tight.
7. Place jars in canner and return to a boil. Process for 35 minutes. Turn off heat and remove canner lid. Let jars stand in water for 5 minutes. Transfer jars to a towel-lined surface and let stand for 24 hours. Check lids and refrigerate any jars that are not sealed.

Taco Sauce

Make your own taco sauce with vine-ripened tomatoes and fresh-picked jalapeño peppers and you'll be ready to spice up tacos, burritos and fajitas all year long.

Makes five to six pint (500 mL) jars

• • •

Tip

After opening the jar of taco sauce, transfer it to a plastic squeeze bottle so it's ready to serve any time.

Variation

For a mild taco sauce, reduce the jalapeño peppers to ¼ cup (50 mL); for a medium sauce, reduce them to ½ cup (125 mL).

○ **Food mill, fitted with fine plate, or Victorio strainer (optional, see tip, page 175)**

6 lbs	plum (Roma) tomatoes, cut into chunks, divided	3 kg
3 cups	chopped red bell peppers	750 mL
2½ cups	chopped onions	625 mL
1 cup	chopped seeded jalapeño peppers (about 8)	250 mL
¼ cup	chopped garlic	50 mL
2 tsp	ground cumin	10 mL
¼ cup	granulated sugar	50 mL
2 tbsp	pickling or canning salt	25 mL
2 cups	white vinegar	500 mL

1. In a large pot, heat about two-thirds of the tomatoes over medium heat, stirring often, until wilted. Add the remaining tomatoes, red peppers, onions, jalapeños, garlic and cumin; return to a boil, stirring often. Reduce heat and boil gently, stirring occasionally, for about 1½ hours or until vegetables are very soft.

2. Working in batches, press sauce through food mill into another large pot or bowl, discarding skins and seeds. Return to pot, if necessary, and stir in sugar, salt and vinegar.

3. Return pot to medium-high heat and bring sauce to a boil. Reduce heat and boil gently, stirring often, for about 2 hours or until thick enough to coat a wooden spoon.

4. Meanwhile, prepare canner, jars and lids (see pages 7 to 8).

5. Ladle hot sauce into hot jars, leaving ½ inch (1 cm) headspace. Remove air bubbles and adjust headspace as necessary by adding hot sauce. Wipe rim and place hot lid disc on jar. Screw band down until fingertip-tight.

6. Place jars in canner and return to a boil. Process for 35 minutes. Turn off heat and remove canner lid. Let jars stand in water for 5 minutes. Transfer jars to a towel-lined surface and let stand for 24 hours. Check lids and refrigerate any jars that are not sealed.

Eggplant and Tomato Caponata

This is a take on the traditional Sicilian dish, modified for home preserving.

Makes about eight 8-ounce (250 mL) or four pint (500 mL) jars

● ● ●

Tip

The balsamic vinegar does darken the caponata, but the flavor is fantastic. If you prefer a lighter color, use white balsamic vinegar instead; just make sure it is 6% acid.

Serving Suggestions

Just before serving, stir in minced anchovies, drained capers and toasted pine nuts to taste. Serve at room temperature or heat in a saucepan with a little olive oil, if desired.

Serve in a bowl or on an antipasto platter to spoon on top of crackers.

Spoon caponata on top of a bed of mixed greens and drizzle with a little extra-virgin olive oil for a delightful salad.

4 cups	diced peeled eggplant	1 L
2 tbsp	pickling or canning salt	25 mL
10 cups	chopped peeled plum (Roma) tomatoes, divided	2.5 L
2 cups	finely chopped onions	500 mL
1 cup	diced red bell peppers	250 mL
1 cup	diced fennel or celery	250 mL
¼ cup	minced garlic	50 mL
2	bay leaves	2
¾ cup	granulated sugar	175 mL
½ tsp	freshly ground black pepper	2 mL
1¼ cups	white wine vinegar	300 mL
½ cup	balsamic vinegar	125 mL
2 tbsp	chopped fresh basil	25 mL
2 tsp	chopped fresh thyme	10 mL
1 tsp	finely chopped fresh rosemary	5 mL

1. In a colander placed in the sink or over a bowl, toss eggplant with salt; let stand for about 2 hours or until excess liquid is released. Rinse eggplant and squeeze out moisture. Place on a clean lint-free towel to continue draining, squeezing the towel lightly until eggplant is quite dry.

2. Meanwhile, in a food processor or blender, purée 2 cups (500 mL) of the tomatoes until smooth.

3. In a large pot, combine puréed and chopped tomatoes, onions, red peppers, fennel, garlic, bay leaves, sugar, pepper, white wine vinegar and balsamic vinegar. Bring to a boil over medium-high heat, stirring often. Reduce heat and boil gently, stirring often, for about 2 hours or until antipasto is reduced by about half and is thick enough to mound on a spoon.

4. Meanwhile, prepare canner, jars and lids (see pages 7 to 8).

5. Stir eggplant into caponata and boil gently, stirring often, for 10 minutes or until eggplant is hot. Stir in basil, thyme and rosemary. Discard bay leaves.

6. Ladle hot caponata into hot jars, leaving ½ inch (1 cm) headspace. Remove air bubbles and adjust headspace as necessary by adding hot caponata. Wipe rim and place hot lid disc on jar. Screw band down until fingertip-tight.

7. Place jars in canner and return to a boil. Process for 20 minutes. Turn off heat and remove canner lid. Let jars stand in water for 5 minutes. Transfer jars to a towel-lined surface and let stand for 24 hours. Check lids and refrigerate any jars that are not sealed.

Fiery Pepperoncini Antipasto

Pepperoncini is the traditional variety used for Tuscan pickled peppers. In this zesty antipasto, they're combined with hot peppers and juicy red tomatoes. The result is sure to get your taste buds jumping.

Makes about eight 8-ounce (250 mL) or four pint (500 mL) jars

● ● ●

Tip

Red pepperoncini peppers make a nicely colored sauce, but the yellow-green ones will work if you can't find red. If you can't find any pepperoncini peppers, use Hungarian red cherry peppers, Anaheim chiles or sweet banana chiles, or a mixture of these.

Serving Suggestion

Stir in 1 can (6 oz/ 170 g) tuna, drained, per pint (500 mL) jar just before serving. Serve on top of toasted crusty bread.

10 cups	chopped peeled plum (Roma) tomatoes, divided	2.5 L
3 cups	diced seeded pepperoncini peppers (preferably red)	750 mL
1½ cups	finely chopped onions	375 mL
½ cup	diced seeded cayenne peppers	125 mL
2 tbsp	minced garlic	25 mL
2	bay leaves	2
1 cup	granulated sugar	250 mL
1 tbsp	pickling or canning salt	15 mL
1 tbsp	dried basil	15 mL
½ tsp	freshly ground black pepper	2 mL
1½ cups	red wine vinegar or white wine vinegar	375 mL

1. In a food processor or blender, purée 2 cups (500 mL) of the tomatoes until smooth.
2. In a large pot, combine puréed and chopped tomatoes, pepperoncini peppers, onions, cayenne peppers, garlic, bay leaves, sugar, salt, basil, pepper and vinegar. Bring to a boil over medium-high heat, stirring often. Reduce heat and boil gently, stirring often, for about 2 hours or until antipasto is reduced by about half and is thick enough to mound on a spoon. Discard bay leaves.
3. Meanwhile, prepare canner, jars and lids (see pages 7 to 8).
4. Ladle hot antipasto into hot jars, leaving ½ inch (1 cm) headspace. Remove air bubbles and adjust headspace as necessary by adding hot antipasto. Wipe rim and place hot lid disc on jar. Screw band down until fingertip-tight.
5. Place jars in canner and return to a boil. Process for 20 minutes. Turn off heat and remove canner lid. Let jars stand in water for 5 minutes. Transfer jars to a towel-lined surface and let stand for 24 hours. Check lids and refrigerate any jars that are not sealed.

Tomato and Olive Antipasto

With jars of this antipasto in your pantry, you can have appetizers ready in mere minutes. The tangy, savory flavors are a delight on their own or when served with rich cheeses or cured meats.

10 cups	chopped peeled plum (Roma) tomatoes, divided	2.5 L
1½ cups	finely chopped onions	375 mL
1½ cups	diced red bell peppers	375 mL
1 cup	diced green bell pepper	250 mL
1 cup	diced celery	250 mL
2 tbsp	minced garlic	25 mL
2	bay leaves	2
1 cup	granulated sugar	250 mL
1 tbsp	pickling or canning salt	15 mL
1 tbsp	dried basil	15 mL
2 tsp	dried oregano	10 mL
½ tsp	freshly ground black pepper	2 mL
1½ cups	red wine vinegar or white wine vinegar	375 mL
½ cup	drained rinsed brine-cured black olives, slivered (see tip, at left)	125 mL

1. In a food processor or blender, purée 2 cups (500 mL) of the tomatoes until smooth.
2. In a large pot, combine puréed and chopped tomatoes, onions, red and green peppers, celery, garlic, bay leaves, sugar, salt, basil, oregano, pepper and vinegar. Bring to a boil over medium-high heat, stirring often. Reduce heat and boil gently, stirring often, for about 2 hours or until antipasto is reduced by about half and is thick enough to mound on a spoon.
3. Meanwhile, prepare canner, jars and lids (see pages 7 to 8).
4. Stir olives into antipasto and boil gently, stirring often, for 5 minutes to blend the flavors. Discard bay leaves.
5. Ladle hot antipasto into hot jars, leaving ½ inch (1 cm) headspace. Remove air bubbles and adjust headspace as necessary by adding hot antipasto. Wipe rim and place hot lid disc on jar. Screw band down until fingertip-tight.
6. Place jars in canner and return to a boil. Process for 20 minutes. Turn off heat and remove canner lid. Let jars stand in water for 5 minutes. Transfer jars to a towel-lined surface and let stand for 24 hours. Check lids and refrigerate any jars that are not sealed.

Chutneys

continued on next page

Chutney Basics

Chutneys are characterized by a combination of sweet, tangy and savory flavors. Some are quite pungent and spicy; others are milder. Freshly harvested fruits and vegetables make the perfect base for a number of flavor profiles, and these colorful chutneys add interest to meats, poultry, fish, lentil dishes, cheeses, appetizers and sandwiches.

Some chutneys focus the flavor on just one or two fruits and/or vegetables, while others combine several different varieties. They can be very simple, such as Classic Peach Chutney (page 217), made with peaches and a touch of savory seasoning, or they can have a more complex flavor, such as Ploughman's Vegetable Chutney (page 235). You may find you prefer one type over the other, or you may want to make some of each to add variety to your chutney pantry.

Making chutney is quite simple. In general, you just mix the ingredients in the pot and gently boil them until the produce is soft and the mixture is thickened. No fancy equipment is required beyond the basic canning tools. Just be sure you have a large enough pot to allow the mixture to bubble up and a long spoon that will reach the bottom of the pot.

I don't recommend doubling chutney recipes, because the food may take too long to cook if there is too much in the pot. The liquid won't evaporate at the same rate as in a single batch, and the flavor will end up being different. In addition, the acid balance might change in the course of cooking the chutney long enough to reach the right texture. If you want to double chutney recipes, make two batches simultaneously in two pots, but only if you can fit all the jars in the canner at once. If you will have too many jars to fit in the canner, delay the start of your second batch by about 10 minutes longer than the processing time of the recipe to give you time to handle the first batch.

Chutney Pointers

- For the highest-quality finished product, choose fruits and vegetables that are ripe but firm and are free from blemishes or rot.
- The amounts in the recipes are precise to ensure the proper balance of flavors and textures, as well as the acidity level needed for safe preserving. To adjust the flavor, you can add more sugar to taste, but don't reduce the amount of sugar, vinegar or citrus juice.
- For information on how much produce you'll need for the prepared amounts required in recipes, see the Purchase and Preparation Guide on page 322.
- The seeds in chile peppers can get quite bitter when simmered for a long time, so it's best to remove them before chopping peppers for use in chutneys.
- When boiling chutney, it will thicken in the process (that's the goal!), so you may need to adjust the heat periodically to keep the mixture at a gentle boil, particularly near the end of the cooking time. You'll also need to stir more frequently near the end to prevent the thicker mixture from sticking and burning.
- The yield for chutneys will vary depending on how long you boil them and how quickly the liquid evaporates. For that reason, they may not make exactly the same amount as the yield stated in the recipe. Prepare an extra jar or two (including one 4-ounce/125 mL or 8-ounce/250 mL jar) in case you have extra. Alternatively, let the extra cool, store it in a covered container in the refrigerator and use it up first.
- Freshly made chutney will thicken upon cooling, so make sure to stop cooking when it is a little thinner than the final texture you desire.
- The flavors intermingle and get better after a couple of days, so plan ahead for the best results.

Apple Plum Chutney

By using a combination of two types of apples, you get a blend of chunky and saucy textures and, with the addition of cider, a deep apple flavor. The plums add more fruitiness and an attractive color.

Tip

Some cooking apples that keep their shape are Crispin (Mutsu), Granny Smith, Northern Spy and Cortland. The most flavorful soft apple for cooking is the good old McIntosh, but you can also use Empire or Idared.

Variation

In place of unsweetened apple cider, use hard apple cider, often available in individual cans and bottles at liquor stores.

Serving Suggestions

This chutney is a natural with pork, ham or sausage and is also perfect with turkey and chicken.

Try chutney in place of mustard or mayonnaise as a sandwich condiment to liven up your lunch.

6 cups	chopped peeled tart cooking apples	1.5 L
3 cups	chopped peeled tart soft apples	750 mL
1 cup	chopped onion	250 mL
1 tbsp	minced gingerroot	15 mL
1½ cups	granulated sugar	375 mL
2 tsp	pickling or canning salt	10 mL
¼ tsp	hot pepper flakes	1 mL
1 cup	cider vinegar	250 mL
¾ cup	unsweetened apple cider	175 mL
2 cups	chopped purple or red plums	500 mL
¼ cup	chopped fresh basil or mint	50 mL

1. Prepare canner, jars and lids (see pages 7 to 8).
2. In a large pot, combine cooking apples, soft apples, onion, ginger, sugar, salt, hot pepper flakes, vinegar and cider. Bring to a boil over medium heat, stirring often. Reduce heat and boil gently, stirring occasionally, for about 20 minutes or until onions are almost translucent and mixture is slightly thickened. Stir in plums and boil gently, stirring often, for about 20 minutes or until plums are soft and mixture is thickened to a jammy consistency. Stir in basil.
3. Ladle hot chutney into hot jars, leaving ½ inch (1 cm) headspace. Remove air bubbles and adjust headspace as necessary by adding hot chutney. Wipe rim and place hot lid disc on jar. Screw band down until fingertip-tight.
4. Place jars in canner and return to a boil. Process for 10 minutes. Turn off heat and remove canner lid. Let jars stand in water for 5 minutes. Transfer jars to a towel-lined surface and let stand for 24 hours. Check lids and refrigerate any jars that aren't sealed.

Apple Raisin Chutney

India is the home of chutney, and this savory apple version uses some of the spices that are integral to that country's exotic cuisine. This is, of course, suited to serving with curries or to spice up plain chicken or turkey.

Makes about seven 8-ounce (250 mL) jars

● ● ●

Tips

Purchase spices at a bulk food store, natural foods store or other spice emporium that has a high turnover and the freshest spices. Buy small amounts of those you use infrequently to be sure they don't go stale.

Fenugreek seeds are small, golden brown, irregular-shaped seeds that add a characteristic bitterness to Indian curries.

8 cups	chopped peeled tart cooking apples	2 L
2 cups	chopped onions	500 mL
¼ cup	finely chopped gingerroot	50 mL
1½ cups	raisins	375 mL
1½ cups	packed brown sugar	375 mL
1 tbsp	mustard seeds	15 mL
1 tbsp	coriander seeds, crushed	15 mL
1 tsp	pickling or canning salt	5 mL
1 tsp	cumin seeds	5 mL
1 tsp	ground cinnamon	5 mL
½ tsp	fenugreek seeds (optional)	2 mL
½ tsp	cayenne pepper	2 mL
2 cups	cider vinegar	500 mL

1. Prepare canner, jars and lids (see pages 7 to 8).
2. In a large pot, combine apples, onions, ginger, raisins, brown sugar, mustard seeds, coriander seeds, salt, cumin seeds, cinnamon, fenugreek (if using), cayenne and vinegar. Bring to a boil over medium heat, stirring often. Reduce heat and boil gently, stirring occasionally, for about 40 minutes or until onions are almost translucent and mixture is thick enough to mound on a spoon.
3. Ladle hot chutney into hot jars, leaving ½ inch (1 cm) headspace. Remove air bubbles and adjust headspace as necessary by adding hot chutney. Wipe rim and place hot lid disc on jar. Screw band down until fingertip-tight.
4. Place jars in canner and return to a boil. Process for 10 minutes. Turn off heat and remove canner lid. Let jars stand in water for 5 minutes. Transfer jars to a towel-lined surface and let stand for 24 hours. Check lids and refrigerate any jars that aren't sealed.

Apple, Onion and Sage Chutney

Serve this chutney to add pizzazz to your Thanksgiving turkey or a Sunday night roast chicken. Leftovers on a sandwich will add gourmet flair to your lunchbox.

Makes about eight 8-ounce (250 mL) jars

Tip

There are many varieties of sweet onions available: look for Vidalia, Oso Sweet, Maui, Walla Walla or Spanish, to name a few.

7 cups	chopped peeled tart cooking apples	1.75 L
3 cups	chopped sweet onions	750 mL
1½ cups	granulated sugar	375 mL
2 tsp	pickling or canning salt	10 mL
½ tsp	freshly ground black pepper	2 mL
1½ cups	white wine vinegar or cider vinegar	375 mL
¼ cup	chopped fresh sage	50 mL

1. Prepare canner, jars and lids (see pages 7 to 8).
2. In a large pot, combine apples, onions, sugar, salt, pepper and vinegar. Bring to a boil over medium heat, stirring often. Reduce heat and boil gently, stirring occasionally, for about 40 minutes or until onions are translucent and mixture is thick enough to mound on a spoon. Stir in sage.
3. Ladle hot chutney into hot jars, leaving ½ inch (1 cm) headspace. Remove air bubbles and adjust headspace as necessary by adding hot chutney. Wipe rim and place hot lid disc on jar. Screw band down until fingertip-tight.
4. Place jars in canner and return to a boil. Process for 10 minutes. Turn off heat and remove canner lid. Let jars stand in water for 5 minutes. Transfer jars to a towel-lined surface and let stand for 24 hours. Check lids and refrigerate any jars that aren't sealed.

Apple Pear Chutney

This simply spiced chutney, which combines two fall fruits, is just the thing to serve with pork or poultry.

Makes about six 8-ounce (250 mL) jars

● ● ●

Tips

Tart cooking apples that hold their shape will make a chunkier chutney; those that soften will make a smoother chutney. The choice is yours.

Choose fragrant but firm pears and use a variety that keeps its flavor when cooked, such as Bartlett, Bosc or Packham.

5 cups	chopped peeled tart apples	1.25 L
4 cups	chopped peeled pears	1 L
1½ cups	chopped onions	375 mL
1½ cups	packed brown sugar	375 mL
1 tsp	pickling or canning salt	5 mL
1 tsp	ground cinnamon	5 mL
1 tsp	ground ginger	5 mL
¼ tsp	ground allspice	1 mL
¼ tsp	freshly ground black pepper	1 mL
1½ cups	cider vinegar	375 mL

1. Prepare canner, jars and lids (see pages 7 to 8).
2. In a large pot, combine apples, pears, onions, brown sugar, salt, cinnamon, ginger, allspice, pepper and vinegar. Bring to a boil over medium heat, stirring often. Reduce heat and boil gently, stirring occasionally, for about 40 minutes or until onions are translucent and mixture is thickened to a jammy consistency.
3. Ladle hot chutney into hot jars, leaving ½ inch (1 cm) headspace. Remove air bubbles and adjust headspace as necessary by adding hot chutney. Wipe rim and place hot lid disc on jar. Screw band down until fingertip-tight.
4. Place jars in canner and return to a boil. Process for 10 minutes. Turn off heat and remove canner lid. Let jars stand in water for 5 minutes. Transfer jars to a towel-lined surface and let stand for 24 hours. Check lids and refrigerate any jars that aren't sealed.

Peach, Jalapeño and Mint Salsa (page 162)

Tomatillo and Lime Salsa Verde (page 165) and Hot, Hot, Hot Tomato Salsa (page 154)

Tomato and Olive Antipasto (page 184)

Blueberry, Tart Apple and Onion Chutney (page 199)

Sweet Mango Chutney (page 211)

Grilled Corn Relish (page 250) and Carrot and Red Pepper Relish (page 263)

Pickled Ginger (page 295) and Pickled Daikon Radish (page 288)

Preserved Lemons (page 318), Preserved Oranges (page 319) and Preserved Limes (page 320)

Apple Walnut Chutney

Apples and walnuts are a classic combination and go together beautifully in this easy chutney. Use a mix of apples that hold their shape and those that soften.

Makes about seven 8-ounce (250 mL) jars

● ● ●

Tips

Some cooking apples that keep their shape are Crispin (Mutsu), Granny Smith and Northern Spy. The most flavorful soft apple for cooking is the good old McIntosh, but you can also use Empire or Idared.

Fresh walnuts are essential for this chutney. Choose walnuts from California that have a sweet aroma, pale brown skin and crisp texture. Older, stale or rancid nuts will impart a bitter flavor.

To toast walnuts, spread walnut halves on a baking sheet and bake in a 375°F (190°C) oven, stirring once, for about 8 minutes or until toasted and fragrant. Let cool, then chop.

Serving Suggestion

Serve on top of a salad with crumbled blue cheese.

6 cups	chopped peeled tart cooking apples	1.5 L
2 cups	chopped peeled tart soft apples	500 mL
2 cups	finely chopped onions	500 mL
1½ cups	packed brown sugar	375 mL
2 tsp	pickling or canning salt	10 mL
½ tsp	freshly ground black pepper	2 mL
½ tsp	ground nutmeg (preferably freshly grated)	2 mL
1½ cups	cider vinegar	375 mL
1 cup	chopped toasted walnuts	250 mL

1. Prepare canner, jars and lids (see pages 7 to 8).
2. In a large pot, combine cooking apples, soft apples, onions, brown sugar, salt, pepper, nutmeg and vinegar. Bring to a boil over medium heat, stirring often. Reduce heat and boil gently, stirring occasionally, for about 40 minutes or until soft apples start to break down and mixture is thick enough to mound on a spoon. Stir in walnuts.
3. Ladle hot chutney into hot jars, leaving ½ inch (1 cm) headspace. Remove air bubbles and adjust headspace as necessary by adding hot chutney. Wipe rim and place hot lid disc on jar. Screw band down until fingertip-tight.
4. Place jars in canner and return to a boil. Process for 10 minutes. Turn off heat and remove canner lid. Let jars stand in water for 5 minutes. Transfer jars to a towel-lined surface and let stand for 24 hours. Check lids and refrigerate any jars that aren't sealed.

Apricot Ginger Chutney

A lovely orange color and a punch of ginger make this softly set chutney shine. It's equally wonderful with curries and atop crackers or toasted baguette slices as a simple appetizer.

Makes about six 8-ounce (250 mL) jars

● ● ●

Tips

If your apricots are quite sweet, you can reduce the sugar to 2 cups (500 mL), reducing the amount added in step 3 to 1½ cups (375 mL).

Be sure to use very fresh gingerroot with taut, shiny skin, juicy flesh and no signs of mold.

6 cups	chopped apricots	1.5 L
2¼ cups	granulated sugar, divided	550 mL
2 cups	finely chopped onions	500 mL
2 tbsp	finely chopped gingerroot	25 mL
1 tsp	pickling or canning salt	5 mL
¼ tsp	freshly ground black pepper	1 mL
1¼ cups	white vinegar	300 mL
½ cup	water	125 mL

1. Prepare canner, jars and lids (see pages 7 to 8).
2. In a bowl, gently combine apricots and ½ cup (125 mL) of the sugar. Set aside.
3. In a large pot, combine the remaining sugar, onions, ginger, salt, pepper, vinegar and water. Bring to a boil over medium heat, stirring often. Reduce heat and boil gently for about 20 minutes or until onion is soft and liquid is slightly reduced. Stir in apricot mixture, increase heat to medium and boil gently, stirring often, for about 20 minutes or until apricots are translucent but still hold their shape.
4. Ladle hot chutney into hot jars, leaving ½ inch (1 cm) headspace. Remove air bubbles and adjust headspace as necessary by adding hot chutney. Wipe rim and place hot lid disc on jar. Screw band down until fingertip-tight.
5. Place jars in canner and return to a boil. Process for 10 minutes. Turn off heat and remove canner lid. Let jars stand in water for 5 minutes. Transfer jars to a towel-lined surface and let stand for 24 hours. Check lids and refrigerate any jars that aren't sealed.

Apricot, Date and Raisin Chutney

Dried fruits combined with fresh onions create a succulent, jammy chutney that you can make any time of the year.

**Makes about
eight 8-ounce
(250 mL) jars**

● ● ●

Tips

The knife will get sticky when you're chopping the apricots and dates. To make chopping easier, wipe the blade periodically with a clean hot cloth.

Check dates for pits before chopping them. Even those labeled "pitted" often have one or two pits still in them.

This chutney thickens quite a bit upon cooling, so stop the cooking when it's thinner than you want the final texture to be.

4 cups	finely chopped onions	1 L
2 cups	chopped dried apricots	500 mL
1½ cups	chopped dates	375 mL
1½ cups	raisins	375 mL
3 tbsp	minced gingerroot	45 mL
¾ cup	packed brown sugar	175 mL
2 tbsp	mustard seeds	25 mL
2 tsp	pickling or canning salt	10 mL
¼ tsp	freshly ground black pepper	1 mL
3 cups	water	750 mL
2 cups	cider vinegar	500 mL

1. Prepare canner, jars and lids (see pages 7 to 8).
2. In a large pot, combine onions, apricots, dates, raisins, ginger, brown sugar, mustard seeds, salt, pepper, water and vinegar. Bring to a boil over medium heat, stirring often. Reduce heat and boil gently, stirring occasionally, for about 30 minutes or until onions are translucent and mixture is just thick enough to mound on a spoon.
3. Ladle hot chutney into hot jars, leaving ½ inch (1 cm) headspace. Remove air bubbles and adjust headspace as necessary by adding hot chutney. Wipe rim and place hot lid disc on jar. Screw band down until fingertip-tight.
4. Place jars in canner and return to a boil. Process for 10 minutes. Turn off heat and remove canner lid. Let jars stand in water for 5 minutes. Transfer jars to a towel-lined surface and let stand for 24 hours. Check lids and refrigerate any jars that aren't sealed.

Beet and Orange Chutney

*Beets and oranges are a classic flavor combination. This vibrant chutney is quite different —
in a good way — from other, mostly fruit-based chutneys.*

**Makes about
seven 8-ounce
(250 mL) jars**

●●●

Tips

The cooking time for
the beets in step 1 is
based on 6 medium
beets. If you have
smaller or larger
beets, adjust the
cooking time in step 1
accordingly.

Cooking the beets
separately ensures
that they get tender
throughout. Vinegar
and other acidic
ingredients can
prevent root vegetables
from getting tender
when cooked together.

2 lbs	beets	1 kg
2 cups	chopped onions	500 mL
2	cloves garlic, minced	2
1½ cups	granulated sugar	375 mL
2 tsp	pickling or canning salt	10 mL
½ tsp	ground cinnamon	2 mL
¼ tsp	ground cloves	1 mL
¼ tsp	hot pepper flakes	1 mL
1 cup	cider vinegar or white wine vinegar	250 mL
2 cups	chopped peeled seedless oranges	500 mL

1. Trim beets and place in a large pot. Cover with cold water
   and bring to a boil over medium-high heat. Reduce heat and
   boil gently for about 40 minutes or until fork-tender (see tip,
   at left). Immediately plunge into a large bowl or sink of cold
   water and let stand until well chilled, refreshing water as
   necessary to keep cold, for at least 30 minutes or for up to
   1 hour. Peel off skins and chop beets. Measure 4 cups (1 L),
   reserving any extra for another use. Set aside.
2. Meanwhile, prepare canner, jars and lids (see pages 7 to 8).
3. In a large pot, combine onions, garlic, sugar, salt, cinnamon,
   cloves, hot pepper flakes and vinegar. Bring to a boil over
   medium heat, stirring often. Reduce heat and boil gently,
   stirring occasionally, for about 20 minutes or until onions
   are almost translucent. Stir in beets and oranges; boil gently,
   stirring often, for about 15 minutes or until mixture is thick
   enough to mound on a spoon.
4. Ladle hot chutney into hot jars, leaving ½ inch (1 cm)
   headspace. Remove air bubbles and adjust headspace as
   necessary by adding hot chutney. Wipe rim and place hot lid
   disc on jar. Screw band down until fingertip-tight.
5. Place jars in canner and return to a boil. Process for
   10 minutes. Turn off heat and remove canner lid. Let jars
   stand in water for 5 minutes. Transfer jars to a towel-lined
   surface and let stand for 24 hours. Check lids and refrigerate
   any jars that aren't sealed.

Black Currant and Apple Chutney

If you're lucky enough to have black currant bushes in your yard or know of a farm where you can pick them, this chutney is a tasty treat to make with the harvest.

Makes about six 8-ounce (250 mL) jars

● ● ●

Tip

Tart cooking apples that hold their shape will make a chunkier chutney; those that soften will make a smoother chutney. The choice is yours.

Serving Suggestions

Spread some of this chutney on the bread when making a grilled cheese sandwich. Try it with Swiss cheese or Gouda.

Toast baguette slices and top with a thin slice of roast beef or Brie cheese and a dollop of chutney for an easy appetizer.

6 cups	stemmed black currants	1.5 L
3 cups	finely chopped peeled tart apples	750 mL
1½ cups	chopped onions	375 mL
2 tbsp	minced gingerroot	25 mL
2	cloves garlic, minced	2
2 cups	granulated sugar	500 mL
1 tbsp	mustard seeds	15 mL
2 tsp	pickling or canning salt	10 mL
1 tsp	coriander seeds, crushed	5 mL
½ tsp	ground cinnamon	2 mL
1½ cups	cider vinegar	375 mL

1. Prepare canner, jars and lids (see pages 7 to 8).

2. In a large pot, combine black currants, apples, onions, ginger, garlic, sugar, mustard seeds, salt, coriander seeds, cinnamon and vinegar. Bring to a boil over medium heat, stirring often. Reduce heat and boil gently, stirring occasionally, for about 40 minutes or until onions are translucent and mixture is thickened to a jammy consistency.

3. Ladle hot chutney into hot jars, leaving ½ inch (1 cm) headspace. Remove air bubbles and adjust headspace as necessary by adding hot chutney. Wipe rim and place hot lid disc on jar. Screw band down until fingertip-tight.

4. Place jars in canner and return to a boil. Process for 10 minutes. Turn off heat and remove canner lid. Let jars stand in water for 5 minutes. Transfer jars to a towel-lined surface and let stand for 24 hours. Check lids and refrigerate any jars that aren't sealed.

Blueberry Peach Chutney

Blueberries and peaches are one of my favorite fruit combinations, so I created this zesty chutney to capture the terrific taste in a jar.

**Makes about
five 8-ounce
(250 mL) jars**

● ● ●

Tips

This recipe works equally well with fresh or frozen blueberries. If using frozen blueberries, let them thaw, saving the juices, before adding to the pot.

For instructions on peeling peaches, see page 16.

This chutney thickens quite a bit upon cooling, so stop the cooking when it's thinner than you want the final texture to be.

Serving Suggestion

Serve with curries, as a dip for chicken or pork satays or simply spooned on top of slices of crusty bread.

6 cups	chopped peeled peaches	1.5 L
2 cups	blueberries (preferably wild)	500 mL
1 cup	finely chopped red onion	250 mL
2 tbsp	minced gingerroot	25 mL
1	jalapeño or hot banana pepper, seeded and minced	1
1	clove garlic, minced	1
1½ cups	packed brown sugar	375 mL
1 tsp	pickling or canning salt	5 mL
1 cup	cider vinegar	250 mL

1. Prepare canner, jars and lids (see pages 7 to 8).
2. In a large pot, combine peaches, blueberries, onion, ginger, jalapeño, garlic, brown sugar, salt and vinegar. Bring to a boil over medium heat, stirring often. Reduce heat and boil gently, stirring occasionally, for about 35 minutes or until onions are translucent and mixture is thickened to a thin jammy consistency.
3. Ladle hot chutney into hot jars, leaving ½ inch (1 cm) headspace. Remove air bubbles and adjust headspace as necessary by adding hot chutney. Wipe rim and place hot lid disc on jar. Screw band down until fingertip-tight.
4. Place jars in canner and return to a boil. Process for 10 minutes. Turn off heat and remove canner lid. Let jars stand in water for 5 minutes. Transfer jars to a towel-lined surface and let stand for 24 hours. Check lids and refrigerate any jars that aren't sealed.

Blueberry, Tart Apple and Onion Chutney

This chutney started out as a small batch of filling for phyllo pastry appetizers, which my husband, Jay, and I love to make for the holidays. We always found ourselves sneaking spoonfuls of the chutney before it made it into the pastry, so we decided to turn it into a big batch to enjoy the rest of the year.

Makes about six 8-ounce (250 mL) jars

● ● ●

Tip

This recipe works equally well with fresh or frozen blueberries. If using frozen blueberries, let them thaw, saving the juices, before adding to the pot.

Serving Suggestions

Wrap into phyllo triangles with a small piece of Brie cheese and bake in a 425°F (220°C) oven for a succulent appetizer.

Spread onto ham or smoked turkey sandwiches.

4 cups	diced peeled tart cooking apples	1 L
4 cups	blueberries	1 L
2 cups	finely chopped onions	500 mL
3	cloves garlic, minced	3
1½ cups	granulated sugar	375 mL
1 tsp	ground ginger	5 mL
1 tsp	pickling or canning salt	5 mL
½ tsp	freshly ground black pepper	2 mL
1 cup	white vinegar	250 mL
1 tsp	grated lemon zest	5 mL
¼ cup	freshly squeezed lemon juice	50 mL

1. Prepare canner, jars and lids (see pages 7 to 8).
2. In a large pot, combine apples, blueberries, onions, garlic, sugar, ginger, salt, pepper and vinegar. Bring to a boil over medium heat, stirring often. Reduce heat and boil gently, stirring occasionally, for about 40 minutes or until onions are translucent and mixture is thickened to a jammy consistency. Stir in lemon zest and juice.
3. Ladle hot chutney into hot jars, leaving ½ inch (1 cm) headspace. Remove air bubbles and adjust headspace as necessary by adding hot chutney. Wipe rim and place hot lid disc on jar. Screw band down until fingertip-tight.
4. Place jars in canner and return to a boil. Process for 10 minutes. Turn off heat and remove canner lid. Let jars stand in water for 5 minutes. Transfer jars to a towel-lined surface and let stand for 24 hours. Check lids and refrigerate any jars that aren't sealed.

Sour Cherry Chutney

This recipe evolved from a classic raisin sauce that my mom, Patricia, always serves with baked ham. For a magazine article featuring an Eastern European–themed Easter dinner menu, I recreated it with sour cherries in place of the raisins. Now, I've turned it into a saucy chutney that is equally fantastic with ham.

Makes four to five 8-ounce (250 mL) jars

● ● ●

Tip

If using sweetened frozen sour cherries, measure when frozen, let thaw and drain off half the juice. Reduce the brown sugar by 2 tbsp (25 mL).

6 cups	chopped pitted sour (tart) cherries	1.5 L
1½ cups	finely chopped red onion	375 mL
2½ cups	packed light brown sugar	625 mL
1 tbsp	dry mustard	15 mL
1 tsp	pickling or canning salt	5 mL
¼ tsp	freshly ground black pepper	1 mL
¼ tsp	ground cloves	1 mL
1 cup	cider vinegar	250 mL

1. Prepare canner, jars and lids (see pages 7 to 8).
2. In a large pot, combine cherries, onion, brown sugar, mustard, salt, pepper, cloves and vinegar. Bring to a boil over medium heat, stirring often. Reduce heat and boil gently, stirring occasionally, for about 40 minutes or until onions are translucent and mixture is slightly thickened.
3. Ladle hot chutney into hot jars, leaving ½ inch (1 cm) headspace. Remove air bubbles and adjust headspace as necessary by adding hot chutney. Wipe rim and place hot lid disc on jar. Screw band down until fingertip-tight.
4. Place jars in canner and return to a boil. Process for 10 minutes. Turn off heat and remove canner lid. Let jars stand in water for 5 minutes. Transfer jars to a towel-lined surface and let stand for 24 hours. Check lids and refrigerate any jars that aren't sealed.

Sweet Cherry and Onion Chutney

Sweet cherries are in season for such a short time, so capture their rich color and flavor in this chutney to enjoy all year long.

Makes four to five 8-ounce (250 mL) jars

● ● ●

Tip

The yield varies slightly depending on how much you cook this down, so it's best to prepare an extra jar — and a small 4-oz (125 mL) jar too — in case you get a little more or a little less.

Serving Suggestions

Serve with baked ham or roasted or grilled poultry.

Spoon on top of a gently warmed wheel of Brie or Camembert and serve with fresh crusty bread.

6 cups	chopped pitted sweet cherries	1.5 L
2 cups	finely chopped sweet onion	500 mL
1 tbsp	minced gingerroot	15 mL
3	cloves garlic, minced	3
1½ cups	granulated sugar	375 mL
1 tsp	pickling or canning salt	5 mL
¼ tsp	ground cinnamon	1 mL
⅛ tsp	ground allspice	0.5 mL
⅛ tsp	ground cardamom (optional)	0.5 mL
1 cup	red wine vinegar	250 mL
¼ cup	freshly squeezed lemon juice	50 mL

1. Prepare canner, jars and lids (see pages 7 to 8).
2. In a large pot, combine cherries, onion, ginger, garlic, sugar, salt, cinnamon, allspice, cardamom (if using) and vinegar. Bring to a boil over medium heat, stirring often. Reduce heat and boil gently, stirring occasionally, for about 40 minutes or until onions are translucent and mixture is thickened to a jammy consistency. Stir in lemon juice.
3. Ladle hot chutney into hot jars, leaving ½ inch (1 cm) headspace. Remove air bubbles and adjust headspace as necessary by adding hot chutney. Wipe rim and place hot lid disc on jar. Screw band down until fingertip-tight.
4. Place jars in canner and return to a boil. Process for 10 minutes. Turn off heat and remove canner lid. Let jars stand in water for 5 minutes. Transfer jars to a towel-lined surface and let stand for 24 hours. Check lids and refrigerate any jars that aren't sealed.

Red Currant, Apple and Sage Chutney

One year I had so many red currants on my bush that I had to get creative to use them all up. Having already stocked my pantry with currant jelly, I decided to experiment with the natural pairing of tart currants with apples and sage. Now you can savor the delicious results.

Tips

Picking red currants is tedious work. I use scissors to efficiently snip the clusters off the bush, then pick the individual currants off the stems in the comfort of my kitchen, with some good music to accompany the task.

This chutney thickens quite a bit upon cooling, so stop the cooking when it's thinner than you want the final texture to be.

Serving Suggestions

Serve as a condiment with roast poultry in place of cranberry sauce or pâté.

Use as a glaze on meatloaf for the last 10 minutes of baking.

6 cups	chopped peeled tart cooking apples	1.5 L
4 cups	red currants	1 L
2 cups	chopped onions	500 mL
2¾ cups	granulated sugar	675 mL
2 tsp	pickling salt	10 mL
½ tsp	freshly ground black pepper	2 mL
2 cups	red wine vinegar	500 mL
2 tbsp	chopped fresh sage	25 mL

1. Prepare canner, jars and lids (see pages 7 to 8).
2. In a large pot, combine apples, red currants, onions, sugar, salt, pepper and vinegar. Bring to a boil over medium heat, stirring often. Reduce heat and boil gently, stirring often, for about 1 hour or until thickened to a thin jammy consistency. Stir in sage.
3. Ladle hot chutney into hot jars, leaving ½ inch (1 cm) headspace. Remove air bubbles and adjust headspace as necessary by adding hot chutney. Wipe rim and place hot lid disc on jar. Screw band down until fingertip-tight.
4. Place jars in canner and return to a boil. Process for 10 minutes. Turn off heat and remove canner lid. Let jars stand in water for 5 minutes. Transfer jars to a towel-lined surface and let stand for 24 hours. Check lids and refrigerate any jars that aren't sealed.

Lemon, Lime and Grapefruit Chutney

Lovers of marmalade are sure to find many uses for this savory version, which is a tasty blend of bitter, tangy and sweet.

Makes about five 8-ounce (250 mL) jars

● ● ●

Tips

You may need more or fewer lemons, grapefruits and limes, depending on their size. The volume measures of the rind and flesh are important for the balance of the recipe. It's best to buy a couple extra of each, just in case.

This chutney thickens quite a bit upon cooling, so stop the cooking when it's thinner than you want the final texture to be.

4	lemons	4
3	grapefruits (yellow or red)	3
3	limes	3
3 cups	water	750 mL
2 cups	chopped onions	500 mL
2	cloves garlic	2
2½ cups	granulated sugar	625 mL
1 tsp	pickling salt	5 mL
1 cup	cider vinegar	250 mL

1. Prepare canner, jars and lids (see pages 7 to 8).
2. Cut lemons in half crosswise and scoop out flesh. Cut rind into thin strips and measure ½ cup (125 mL). Remove any seeds and coarsely chop flesh; measure 1 cup (250 mL). Repeat with grapefruits and limes, keeping each type of rind separate and measuring 1 cup (250 mL) grapefruit rind, 3 cups (750 mL) grapefruit flesh, ⅓ cup (75 mL) lime rind and ½ cup (125 mL) lime flesh. Set flesh aside.
3. In a large pot, combine grapefruit rinds and water. Bring to a simmer over high heat. Reduce heat and simmer for 10 minutes. Stir in lemon and lime rinds; simmer for about 15 minutes or until rinds are very soft. Drain off liquid and return rinds to pot.
4. Add grapefruit, lemon and lime flesh, onions, garlic, sugar, salt and vinegar. Bring to a boil over medium heat, stirring often. Reduce heat and boil gently, stirring occasionally, for about 30 minutes or until onions are translucent and mixture is thickened to a thin jammy consistency.
5. Ladle hot chutney into hot jars, leaving ½ inch (1 cm) headspace. Remove air bubbles and adjust headspace as necessary by adding hot chutney. Wipe rim and place hot lid disc on jar. Screw band down until fingertip-tight.
6. Place jars in canner and return to a boil. Process for 10 minutes. Turn off heat and remove canner lid. Let jars stand in water for 5 minutes. Transfer jars to a towel-lined surface and let stand for 24 hours. Check lids and refrigerate any jars that aren't sealed.

Sangria Citrus Chutney

The famous beverage comes over to the savory side with the addition of red onion to make a tangy chutney that will give you the sensation of the hot Spanish sun any time of year.

Makes five to six 8-ounce (250 mL) jars

● ● ●

Tips

You may need more or fewer oranges, lemons and limes, depending on their size. The volume measures of the rind and flesh are important for the balance of the recipe. It's best to buy a couple extra of each, just in case.

This chutney thickens quite a bit upon cooling, so stop the cooking when it's thinner than you want the final texture to be.

Serving Suggestions

Serve on crackers with Spanish cheese, such as Manchego.

Brush a little chutney on roasted or grilled poultry or pork during the last 5 to 10 minutes of cooking. Serve with more on the side.

6	oranges	6
4	lemons	4
3	limes	3
3 cups	water	750 mL
2 cups	chopped red onion	500 mL
2½ cups	granulated sugar	625 mL
1 tsp	pickling salt	5 mL
1 cup	light, fruity red wine	250 mL
½ cup	red wine vinegar	125 mL
¼ cup	brandy	50 mL

1. Prepare canner, jars and lids (see pages 7 to 8).
2. Cut oranges in half crosswise and scoop out flesh. Cut rind into thin strips and measure 1 cup (250 mL). Remove any seeds and coarsely chop flesh; measure 3 cups (750 mL). Repeat with lemons and limes, measuring ½ cup (125 mL) lemon rind, 1 cup (250 mL) lemon flesh, ⅓ cup (75 mL) lime rind and ½ cup (125 mL) lime flesh. Set flesh aside.
3. In a large pot, combine orange, lemon and lime rinds and water. Bring to a simmer over high heat. Reduce heat and simmer for about 15 minutes or until rinds are very soft. Drain off liquid and return rinds to pot.
4. Add orange, lemon and lime flesh, onion, sugar, salt, wine and vinegar. Bring to a boil over medium heat, stirring often. Reduce heat and boil gently, stirring occasionally, for about 30 minutes or until onions are translucent and mixture is thickened to a thin jammy consistency. Stir in brandy and boil for 1 minute.
5. Ladle hot chutney into hot jars, leaving ½ inch (1 cm) headspace. Remove air bubbles and adjust headspace as necessary by adding hot chutney. Wipe rim and place hot lid disc on jar. Screw band down until fingertip-tight.
6. Place jars in canner and return to a boil. Process for 10 minutes. Turn off heat and remove canner lid. Let jars stand in water for 5 minutes. Transfer jars to a towel-lined surface and let stand for 24 hours. Check lids and refrigerate any jars that aren't sealed.

Clementine Pear Chutney

Tangy, sweet and bitter flavors are combined in this lively chutney. It's perfect to make on a blustery winter afternoon.

Makes about eight 8-ounce (250 mL) jars

● ● ●

Tips

You may need more or fewer clementines or tangerines, depending on their size. The volume measures of the rind and flesh are important for the balance of the recipe. It's best to buy a couple extra, just in case.

Choose flavorful pears that keep their flavor once cooked, such as Bartlett, Bosc or Packham.

Serving Suggestions

Serve with grilled fish or seafood or roasted poultry.

Combine with softened blue cheese and cream cheese for a flavorful cracker spread.

10	clementines or tangerines	10
3 cups	water	750 mL
4 cups	chopped peeled pears	1 L
2 cups	chopped onions	500 mL
3	cloves garlic, minced	3
1½ cups	granulated sugar	375 mL
1 tsp	pickling salt	5 mL
¼ tsp	hot pepper flakes	1 mL
1 cup	cider vinegar	250 mL

1. Prepare canner, jars and lids (see pages 7 to 8).
2. Cut clementines in half crosswise and scoop out flesh. Cut rind into thin strips and measure 2 cups (500 mL). Remove seeds and coarsely chop flesh; measure 3 cups (750 mL) and set aside.
3. In a large pot, combine clementine rind and water. Bring to a simmer over high heat. Reduce heat and simmer for about 10 minutes or until rind is very soft. Drain off liquid and return rind to pot.
4. Add clementine flesh, pears, onions, garlic, sugar, salt, hot pepper flakes and vinegar. Bring to a boil over medium heat, stirring often. Reduce heat and boil gently, stirring occasionally, for about 30 minutes or until pears and onions are translucent and mixture is thick enough to mound on a spoon.
5. Ladle hot chutney into hot jars, leaving ½ inch (1 cm) headspace. Remove air bubbles and adjust headspace as necessary by adding hot chutney. Wipe rim and place hot lid disc on jar. Screw band down until fingertip-tight.
6. Place jars in canner and return to a boil. Process for 10 minutes. Turn off heat and remove canner lid. Let jars stand in water for 5 minutes. Transfer jars to a towel-lined surface and let stand for 24 hours. Check lids and refrigerate any jars that aren't sealed.

Spiced Cranberry Apple Chutney

Ginger and cinnamon, cranberries and apples — this blend of autumn flavors is sure to fill your kitchen with warmth and add delight to your holiday turkey.

Makes about six 8-ounce (250 mL) jars

● ● ●

Tips

Tart cooking apples that hold their shape will make a chunkier chutney; those that soften will make a smoother chutney. The choice is yours.

This chutney thickens quite a bit upon cooling, so stop the cooking when it's thinner than you want the final texture to be.

If you can't find crystallized ginger, substitute 2 tsp (10 mL) ground ginger or 1 tbsp (15 mL) minced gingerroot.

6 cups	cranberries	1.5 L
2 cups	chopped peeled tart apples	500 mL
2 cups	chopped onions	500 mL
2 tbsp	minced crystallized ginger	25 mL
2 cups	granulated sugar	500 mL
¾ cup	packed brown sugar	175 mL
2 tsp	pickling salt	10 mL
1 tsp	freshly ground black pepper	5 mL
½ tsp	ground cinnamon	2 mL
2 cups	cider vinegar	500 mL

1. Prepare canner, jars and lids (see pages 7 to 8).
2. In a large pot, combine cranberries, apples, onions, ginger, granulated sugar, brown sugar, salt, pepper, cinnamon and vinegar. Bring to a boil over medium heat, stirring often. Reduce heat and simmer, stirring often, for about 30 minutes or until thickened to a thin jammy consistency.
3. Ladle hot chutney into hot jars, leaving ½ inch (1 cm) headspace. Remove air bubbles and adjust headspace as necessary by adding hot chutney. Wipe rim and place hot lid disc on jar. Screw band down until fingertip-tight.
4. Place jars in canner and return to a boil. Process for 10 minutes. Turn off heat and remove canner lid. Let jars stand in water for 5 minutes. Transfer jars to a towel-lined surface and let stand for 24 hours. Check lids and refrigerate any jars that aren't sealed.

Classic Cranberry Chutney

A touch of onion and orange and a big burst of cranberry make it clear why this is a classic to serve with roast turkey and chicken.

Makes about five 8-ounce (250 mL) jars

● ● ●

Tip

This chutney thickens quite a bit upon cooling, so stop the cooking when it's thinner than you want the final texture to be.

9 cups	cranberries	2.25 L
1 cup	finely chopped onions	250 mL
2½ cups	granulated sugar	625 mL
1 tsp	pickling salt	5 mL
¼ tsp	freshly ground black pepper	1 mL
1½ cups	cider vinegar	375 mL
2 tsp	grated orange zest	10 mL
2 tbsp	freshly squeezed orange juice	25 mL

1. Prepare canner, jars and lids (see pages 7 to 8).
2. In a large pot, combine cranberries, onions, sugar, salt, pepper and vinegar. Bring to a boil over medium heat, stirring often. Reduce heat and simmer, stirring often, for about 30 minutes or until thickened to a thin jammy consistency. Stir in orange zest and juice.
3. Ladle hot chutney into hot jars, leaving ½ inch (1 cm) headspace. Remove air bubbles and adjust headspace as necessary by adding hot chutney. Wipe rim and place hot lid disc on jar. Screw band down until fingertip-tight.
4. Place jars in canner and return to a boil. Process for 10 minutes. Turn off heat and remove canner lid. Let jars stand in water for 5 minutes. Transfer jars to a towel-lined surface and let stand for 24 hours. Check lids and refrigerate any jars that aren't sealed.

Cranberry Pear Chutney

Pears add a floral sweetness and pleasant balance to the tang of the cranberries.

**Makes about
six 8-ounce
(250 mL) jars**

● ● ●

Tips

Choose fragrant but
firm pears and use a
variety that keeps its
flavor when cooked,
such as Bartlett, Bosc
or Packham.

This chutney thickens
quite a bit upon
cooling, so stop the
cooking when it's
thinner than you want
the final texture to be.

4 cups	cranberries	1 L
4 cups	chopped peeled pears	1 L
1½ cups	finely chopped onions	375 mL
2¼ cups	packed brown sugar	300 mL
2 tsp	pickling salt	10 mL
1 tsp	freshly ground black pepper	5 mL
½ tsp	ground cinnamon	2 mL
¼ tsp	ground nutmeg or ginger	1 mL
1½ cups	cider vinegar	375 mL

1. Prepare canner, jars and lids (see pages 7 to 8).
2. In a large pot, combine cranberries, pears, onions, brown sugar, salt, pepper, cinnamon, nutmeg and vinegar. Bring to a boil over medium heat, stirring often. Reduce heat and simmer, stirring often, for about 30 minutes or until thickened to a thin jammy consistency.
3. Ladle hot chutney into hot jars, leaving ½ inch (1 cm) headspace. Remove air bubbles and adjust headspace as necessary by adding hot chutney. Wipe rim and place hot lid disc on jar. Screw band down until fingertip-tight.
4. Place jars in canner and return to a boil. Process for 10 minutes. Turn off heat and remove canner lid. Let jars stand in water for 5 minutes. Transfer jars to a towel-lined surface and let stand for 24 hours. Check lids and refrigerate any jars that aren't sealed.

Warmly Spiced Cranberry Chutney

This chutney is tangy and sweet, with a spicy heat that sneaks up on you. It makes a good condiment for roast meats and poultry and a zesty topping for cheese and crackers.

Makes about six 8-ounce (250 mL) jars

● ● ●

Tips

This chutney thickens quite a bit upon cooling, so stop the cooking when it's thinner than you want the final texture to be.

Fresh jalapeños and other chile peppers vary in heat. Taste the pepper before adding it; if it seems very hot, you may want to add less. If it's mild, you may want to add another, or some cayenne pepper. If you're not sure, taste the chutney after cooking and add hot pepper sauce to taste before filling jars.

8 cups	cranberries	2 L
3 cups	finely chopped red onions	750 mL
1 tbsp	minced gingerroot	15 mL
3	cloves garlic, minced	3
1	jalapeño pepper or other hot chile pepper, seeded and minced	1
2½ cups	granulated sugar	625 mL
2 tsp	pickling salt	10 mL
1 tsp	ground cinnamon	5 mL
½ tsp	freshly ground black pepper	2 mL
¼ tsp	ground cloves	1 mL
2 cups	cider vinegar or red wine vinegar	500 mL

1. Prepare canner, jars and lids (see pages 7 to 8).
2. In a large pot, combine cranberries, onions, ginger, garlic, jalapeño, sugar, salt, cinnamon, pepper, cloves and vinegar. Bring to a boil over medium heat, stirring often. Reduce heat and simmer, stirring often, for about 30 minutes or until thickened to a thin jammy consistency.
3. Ladle hot chutney into hot jars, leaving ½ inch (1 cm) headspace. Remove air bubbles and adjust headspace as necessary by adding hot chutney. Wipe rim and place hot lid disc on jar. Screw band down until fingertip-tight.
4. Place jars in canner and return to a boil. Process for 10 minutes. Turn off heat and remove canner lid. Let jars stand in water for 5 minutes. Transfer jars to a towel-lined surface and let stand for 24 hours. Check lids and refrigerate any jars that aren't sealed.

Fig, Date and Lemon Chutney

The sweet, exotic flavors of figs and dates are highlighted by fresh lemons. Making this chutney is a super way to spend a cold winter afternoon — you just might feel as though you've been transported to the warm Mediterranean on the aroma.

Makes about seven 8-ounce (250 mL) jars

● ● ●

Tips

You may need more or fewer lemons, depending on their size. The volume measure of the flesh is important for the balance of the recipe. It's best to buy a couple extra, just in case.

The knife will get sticky when you're chopping the figs and dates. To make chopping easier, wipe the blade periodically with a clean hot cloth.

This chutney thickens quite a bit upon cooling, so stop the cooking when it's thinner than you want the final texture to be.

Serving Suggestion

Serve as a condiment for Moroccan tagines or Indian curries.

4	lemons	4
2½ cups	chopped dried figs	625 mL
2½ cups	chopped dates	625 mL
2 cups	finely chopped onions	500 mL
1 cup	packed brown sugar	250 mL
2 tbsp	coriander seeds, crushed	25 mL
2 tsp	pickling or canning salt	10 mL
¼ tsp	hot pepper flakes	1 mL
2½ cups	water	625 mL
1½ cups	cider vinegar	375 mL

1. Prepare canner, jars and lids (see pages 7 to 8).
2. Using a Microplane-style grater or the fine side of a box grater, grate 1 tbsp (15 mL) lemon zest; set aside. Cut lemons in half crosswise and scoop out flesh, discarding rind. Remove any seeds and coarsely chop flesh; measure 2 cups (500 mL).
3. In a large pot, combine lemon flesh, figs, dates, onions, brown sugar, coriander seeds, salt, hot pepper flakes, water and vinegar. Bring to a boil over medium heat, stirring often. Reduce heat and boil gently, stirring occasionally, for about 30 minutes or until onions are translucent and mixture is just thick enough to mound on a spoon. Stir in lemon zest.
4. Ladle hot chutney into hot jars, leaving ½ inch (1 cm) headspace. Remove air bubbles and adjust headspace as necessary by adding hot chutney. Wipe rim and place hot lid disc on jar. Screw band down until fingertip-tight.
5. Place jars in canner and return to a boil. Process for 10 minutes. Turn off heat and remove canner lid. Let jars stand in water for 5 minutes. Transfer jars to a towel-lined surface and let stand for 24 hours. Check lids and refrigerate any jars that aren't sealed.

Sweet Mango Chutney

Simple flavors complement the rich taste of mango in this all-purpose chutney.

Makes about seven 8-ounce (250 mL) jars

● ● ●

Tips

Be sure to use mangos that are ripe but not mushy. The skin should yield slightly when pressed, and the mangos should have a fragrant aroma, particularly at the stem end.

Look for rich-flavored mangos with yellow skin for a wonderful flavor and texture. There are several varieties, such as Ataulfo or Alfonso. You'll need about 12 of these smaller varieties or 5 of the large varieties.

7 cups	chopped peeled sweet mangos	1.75 L
3 cups	chopped red bell peppers	750 mL
1½ cups	chopped onions	375 mL
2 cups	packed brown sugar	500 mL
1 tsp	pickling or canning salt	5 mL
1 tsp	ground cinnamon	5 mL
1 cup	cider vinegar	250 mL
¼ cup	freshly squeezed lime juice	50 mL

1. Prepare canner, jars and lids (see pages 7 to 8).
2. In a large pot, combine mangos, red peppers, onions, brown sugar, salt, cinnamon, and vinegar. Bring to a boil over medium heat, stirring often. Reduce heat and boil gently, stirring occasionally, for about 40 minutes or until onion is soft and mixture is thick enough to mound on a spoon. Stir in lime juice.
3. Ladle hot chutney into hot jars, leaving ½ inch (1 cm) headspace. Remove air bubbles and adjust headspace as necessary by adding hot chutney. Wipe rim and place hot lid disc on jar. Screw band down until fingertip-tight.
4. Place jars in canner and return to a boil. Process for 10 minutes. Turn off heat and remove canner lid. Let jars stand in water for 5 minutes. Transfer jars to a towel-lined surface and let stand for 24 hours. Check lids and refrigerate any jars that aren't sealed.

Major Grey Mango Chutney

Pungent, bitter, spicy, sweet and tangy flavors are the perfect foil for spicy-hot curries.

Makes eight to nine 8-ounce (250 mL) jars

● ● ●

Tip

This chutney thickens quite a bit upon cooling, so stop the cooking when it's thinner than you want the final texture to be.

5 cups	chopped peeled sweet mangos	1.25 L
1½ cups	chopped peeled seedless oranges	375 mL
1 cup	finely chopped onion	250 mL
½ cup	finely chopped lemon (rind and flesh), seeds removed	125 mL
⅓ cup	finely chopped lime (rind and flesh), seeds removed	75 mL
¼ cup	finely chopped gingerroot	50 mL
2 tbsp	minced garlic	25 mL
1 cup	raisins	250 mL
¾ cup	packed brown sugar	175 mL
4 tsp	mustard seeds	20 mL
2 tsp	pickling or canning salt	10 mL
1 tsp	ground cinnamon	5 mL
1 tsp	ground coriander	5 mL
½ tsp	ground cloves	2 mL
¼ tsp	ground cardamom (optional)	1 mL
1 cup	cider vinegar	250 mL
⅔ cup	light (fancy) molasses	150 mL
½ cup	water	125 mL

1. In a large pot, combine mangos, oranges, onion, lemon, lime, ginger, garlic, raisins, brown sugar, mustard seeds, salt, cinnamon, coriander, cloves, cardamom (if using), vinegar, molasses and water. Bring to a boil over medium heat, stirring often. Reduce heat and boil gently, stirring occasionally, for about 1 hour or until onions, lemon and lime rinds are very soft and mixture is just thick enough to mound on a spoon.
2. Meanwhile, prepare canner, jars and lids (see pages 7 to 8).
3. Ladle hot chutney into hot jars, leaving ½ inch (1 cm) headspace. Remove air bubbles and adjust headspace as necessary by adding hot chutney. Wipe rim and place hot lid disc on jar. Screw band down until fingertip-tight.
4. Place jars in canner and return to a boil. Process for 10 minutes. Turn off heat and remove canner lid. Let jars stand in water for 5 minutes. Transfer jars to a towel-lined surface and let stand for 24 hours. Check lids and refrigerate any jars that aren't sealed.

Mango Banana Chutney

Tropical tastes make this chutney a lively accompaniment to Caribbean curries, on roti or with plain grilled or roasted meats that need a boost.

Makes about seven 8-ounce (250 mL) jars

• • •

Tips

If you like it fiery, use a Scotch bonnet pepper. If you like just a little heat, use a long hot green or red chile pepper or a jalapeño pepper.

Whole nutmeg is available at well-stocked bulk or natural foods stores, spice emporiums and some supermarkets. Grate with a very fine grater just before using for a true nutmeg flavor.

5 cups	chopped peeled sweet mangos	1.25 L
1 cup	finely chopped onion	250 mL
1	hot green or red chile pepper, seeded and minced	1
2 cups	packed brown sugar	500 mL
1 tsp	pickling or canning salt	5 mL
$\frac{1}{2}$ tsp	ground nutmeg (preferably freshly grated)	2 mL
$\frac{1}{8}$ tsp	ground allspice	0.5 mL
$1\frac{1}{2}$ cups	cider vinegar	375 mL
1 cup	water	250 mL
2 cups	mashed ripe bananas	500 mL
$\frac{1}{4}$ cup	freshly squeezed lemon juice	50 mL

1. Prepare canner, jars and lids (see pages 7 to 8).
2. In a large pot, combine mangos, onion, chile pepper, brown sugar, salt, nutmeg, allspice, vinegar and water. Bring to a boil over medium heat, stirring often. Reduce heat and boil gently, stirring occasionally, for about 20 minutes or until onion is soft and liquid is slightly reduced. Stir in bananas, increase heat to medium and boil gently, stirring often, for about 15 minutes or until fruit is translucent and mixture is thick enough to mound on a spoon. Stir in lemon juice.
3. Ladle hot chutney into hot jars, leaving $\frac{1}{2}$ inch (1 cm) headspace. Remove air bubbles and adjust headspace as necessary by adding hot chutney. Wipe rim and place hot lid disc on jar. Screw band down until fingertip-tight.
4. Place jars in canner and return to a boil. Process for 10 minutes. Turn off heat and remove canner lid. Let jars stand in water for 5 minutes. Transfer jars to a towel-lined surface and let stand for 24 hours. Check lids and refrigerate any jars that aren't sealed.

Mango, Papaya and Ginger Chutney with Lime

Mixing the mango and papaya with some of the sugar and letting them stand helps to draw out the juices and soften the fruit; they then require less cooking, which gives this chutney an extra-fruity flavor.

Makes about eight 8-ounce (250 mL) jars

● ● ●

Tips

Look for rich-flavored mangos with yellow skin for a wonderful flavor and texture. There are several varieties, such as Ataulfo or Alfonso. You'll need about 10 of these smaller varieties or 4 of the large varieties.

Papayas vary dramatically in size depending on the variety. If using a small variety, you'll need about 1 large. If using a larger variety, you'll need about ½. Sprinkle any extra chopped papaya with lime juice, salt and pepper for a quick salsa.

6 cups	chopped peeled sweet mangos	1.5 L
2 cups	chopped peeled papaya	500 mL
2 cups	packed brown sugar, divided	500 mL
1 cup	finely chopped sweet onion	250 mL
¼ cup	finely chopped gingerroot	50 mL
1 tsp	pickling or canning salt	5 mL
¾ tsp	ground cinnamon	3 mL
¼ tsp	ground nutmeg (preferably freshly grated)	1 mL
⅛ tsp	ground cloves	0.5 mL
1½ cups	cider vinegar	375 mL
1 cup	water	250 mL
2	hot green or red chile peppers, seeded and minced	2
1 tsp	grated lime zest	5 mL
¼ cup	freshly squeezed lime juice	50 mL

1. Prepare canner, jars and lids (see pages 7 to 8).
2. In a large bowl, gently combine mangos, papaya and ½ cup (125 mL) of the brown sugar; set aside.
3. In a large pot, combine the remaining brown sugar, onion, ginger, salt, cinnamon, nutmeg, cloves, vinegar and water. Bring to a boil over medium heat, stirring often. Reduce heat and boil gently, stirring occasionally, for about 20 minutes or until onion is soft and liquid is slightly reduced. Stir in mango mixture and chile peppers, increase heat to medium and boil gently, stirring often, for about 30 minutes or until fruit is translucent but still holds its shape. Stir in lime zest and juice.
4. Ladle hot chutney into hot jars, leaving ½ inch (1 cm) headspace. Remove air bubbles and adjust headspace as necessary by adding hot chutney. Wipe rim and place hot lid disc on jar. Screw band down until fingertip-tight.
5. Place jars in canner and return to a boil. Process for 10 minutes. Turn off heat and remove canner lid. Let jars stand in water for 5 minutes. Transfer jars to a towel-lined surface and let stand for 24 hours. Check lids and refrigerate any jars that aren't sealed.

Orange, Date and Onion Chutney

Oranges and dates are a fabulous flavor combination, and this chutney is a lovely blend of both. It's wonderful with rich meats such as lamb or dark poultry such as duck.

Makes about seven 8-ounce (250 mL) jars

● ● ●

Variation

If you want a deeper orange flavor, use a Microplane-style grater or the fine side of a box grater to grate 1 tsp (5 mL) zest from the oranges before peeling them. Stir the zest into the chutney at the end of step 2.

4 cups	finely chopped onions	1 L
4 cups	chopped dates	1 L
2 cups	chopped peeled seedless oranges	500 mL
2 tbsp	minced gingerroot	25 mL
¾ cup	packed brown sugar	175 mL
2 tbsp	mustard seeds	25 mL
2 tsp	pickling or canning salt	10 mL
¼ tsp	hot pepper flakes	1 mL
1½ cups	cider vinegar	375 mL
1 cup	water	250 mL

1. Prepare canner, jars and lids (see pages 7 to 8).
2. In a large pot, combine onions, dates, oranges, ginger, brown sugar, mustard seeds, salt, hot pepper flakes, vinegar and water. Bring to a boil over medium heat, stirring often. Reduce heat and boil gently, stirring occasionally, for about 30 minutes or until onions are translucent and mixture is thick enough to mound on a spoon.
3. Ladle hot chutney into hot jars, leaving ½ inch (1 cm) headspace. Remove air bubbles and adjust headspace as necessary by adding hot chutney. Wipe rim and place hot lid disc on jar. Screw band down until fingertip-tight.
4. Place jars in canner and return to a boil. Process for 10 minutes. Turn off heat and remove canner lid. Let jars stand in water for 5 minutes. Transfer jars to a towel-lined surface and let stand for 24 hours. Check lids and refrigerate any jars that aren't sealed.

Red Onion and Raisin Chutney

Chopping all of the onions might seem daunting, but don't be tempted to use a power tool for the job. Hand-chopping will give a far superior texture to this versatile chutney.

Makes about seven 8-ounce (250 mL) jars

● ● ●

Tip

You'll need about 5 large red onions, or about 3 lbs (1.5 kg), to get 8 cups (2 L) chopped.

Serving Suggestions

Serve with grilled or smoked salmon.

Use as a condiment with roast beef or a grilled steak.

8 cups	chopped red onions	2 L
3	cloves garlic, minced	3
2 cups 1.5	granulated sugar	500 mL
1½ tsp	pickling or canning salt	7 mL
⅛ tsp	hot pepper flakes	0.5 mL
1 cup	water	250 mL
2 cups	raisins	500 mL
1 cup	red wine vinegar	250 mL
1 tbsp	chopped fresh thyme	15 mL

1. Prepare canner, jars and lids (see pages 7 to 8).
2. In a large pot, combine onions, garlic, sugar, salt, hot pepper flakes and water. Bring to a simmer over medium heat, stirring often. Reduce heat and boil gently, stirring occasionally, for about 20 minutes or until onions are very soft. Stir in raisins, vinegar and thyme; simmer for about 20 minutes or until onions are translucent, raisins are plump and liquid is syrupy.
3. Ladle hot chutney into hot jars, leaving ½ inch (1 cm) headspace. Remove air bubbles and adjust headspace as necessary by adding hot chutney. Wipe rim and place hot lid disc on jar. Screw band down until fingertip-tight.
4. Place jars in canner and return to a boil. Process for 10 minutes. Turn off heat and remove canner lid. Let jars stand in water for 5 minutes. Transfer jars to a towel-lined surface and let stand for 24 hours. Check lids and refrigerate any jars that aren't sealed.

Classic Peach Chutney

Capture fragrant, juicy peaches at the height of their season in this chutney, which is fruity with a touch of spice. Puréeing some of the peaches gives you a chunky chutney with a touch of jamminess.

Makes about eight 8-ounce (250 mL) jars

● ● ●

Tips

Use ripe and fragrant but firm peaches for this chutney. You'll need about 20 medium, or about 4½ lbs (2.25 kg), to get 8 cups (2 L) chopped.

For instructions on peeling peaches, see page 16.

Add the jalapeño if you like a touch of heat in your chutney; leave it out for a mild, fruity version. If you like more heat, add a whole jalapeño.

Serving Suggestions

Serve this chutney with spicy Indian curries to help cool them off.

Spread on roast chicken or ham sandwiches.

8 cups	chopped peeled peaches, divided	2 L
½	jalapeño pepper, minced (optional)	½
2 cups	finely chopped sweet onion	500 mL
1¾ cups	granulated sugar	425 mL
1 tsp	pickling or canning salt	5 mL
1 tsp	ground cinnamon	5 mL
⅛ tsp	ground cloves	0.5 mL
1¼ cups	cider vinegar	300 mL

1. Prepare canner, jars and lids (see pages 7 to 8).
2. Using an immersion blender in a tall cup, or in a food processor or blender, purée 2 cups (500 mL) of the peaches until smooth.
3. In a large pot, combine puréed and chopped peaches, jalapeño (if using), onion, sugar, salt, cinnamon, cloves and vinegar. Bring to a boil over medium heat, stirring often. Reduce heat and boil gently, stirring occasionally, for about 40 minutes or until onions are translucent and mixture is thick enough to mound on a spoon.
4. Ladle hot chutney into hot jars, leaving ½ inch (1 cm) headspace. Remove air bubbles and adjust headspace as necessary by adding hot chutney. Wipe rim and place hot lid disc on jar. Screw band down until fingertip-tight.
5. Place jars in canner and return to a boil. Process for 10 minutes. Turn off heat and remove canner lid. Let jars stand in water for 5 minutes. Transfer jars to a towel-lined surface and let stand for 24 hours. Check lids and refrigerate any jars that aren't sealed.

Peach and Sweet Pepper Chutney

No matter how hot and muggy it is, or how busy I am at the height of peach and pepper season, this is one of the recipes I just have to make. Come February, when it's frigid and I'm really tired of the snow, it gives me a taste of that sunny summer sunshine I long for.

Makes about seven 8-ounce (250 mL) jars

● ● ●

Tips

Use ripe and fragrant but firm peaches for this chutney. You'll need about 18 medium, or about 4 lbs (2 kg), to get 7 cups (1.75 L) chopped.

For instructions on peeling peaches, see page 16.

Serving Suggestions

Serve with spicy coconut milk–based curries.

Serve as a condiment for grilled or roast pork or poultry.

7 cups	chopped peeled peaches	1.75 L
2 cups	finely chopped onions	500 mL
2 cups	finely chopped red bell peppers	500 mL
1 cup	finely chopped yellow bell pepper	250 mL
2 cups	packed brown sugar	500 mL
1 tsp	pickling or canning salt	5 mL
½ tsp	ground cinnamon	2 mL
¼ tsp	freshly ground black pepper	1 mL
1 cup	cider vinegar	250 mL

1. Prepare canner, jars and lids (see pages 7 to 8).
2. In a large pot, combine peaches, onions, red and yellow peppers, brown sugar, salt, cinnamon, pepper and vinegar. Bring to a boil over medium heat, stirring often. Reduce heat and boil gently, stirring occasionally, for about 45 minutes or until onions are translucent and mixture is thick enough to mound on a spoon.
3. Ladle hot chutney into hot jars, leaving ½ inch (1 cm) headspace. Remove air bubbles and adjust headspace as necessary by adding hot chutney. Wipe rim and place hot lid disc on jar. Screw band down until fingertip-tight.
4. Place jars in canner and return to a boil. Process for 10 minutes. Turn off heat and remove canner lid. Let jars stand in water for 5 minutes. Transfer jars to a towel-lined surface and let stand for 24 hours. Check lids and refrigerate any jars that aren't sealed.

Curried Peach Chutney

Toasted fragrant spices combine with sweet peaches and a touch of lime in this chutney. It's perfect for spicing up grilled meats or sharp cheeses, or to stir right into a curry to boost the flavor.

Makes seven to eight 8-ounce (250 mL) jars

• • •

Tips

Don't use a curry paste, which contains oil, for this recipe. Choose a high-quality, fragrant curry powder for the best flavor.

Use ripe and fragrant but firm peaches for this chutney. You'll need about 20 medium, or about 4½ lbs (2.25 kg), to get 8 cups (2 L) chopped.

For instructions on peeling peaches, see page 16.

1 tbsp	curry powder	15 mL
½ tsp	ground cumin	2 mL
¼ tsp	ground cinnamon	2 mL
8 cups	chopped peeled peaches	2 L
1½ cups	chopped onions	375 mL
2 tbsp	finely chopped gingerroot	25 mL
2	cloves garlic, minced	2
2	long hot red or green chile peppers, seeded and minced	2
1½ cups	packed brown sugar	375 mL
1 tsp	pickling or canning salt	5 mL
1 cup	white vinegar	250 mL
¼ cup	freshly squeezed lime juice	50 mL

1. Prepare canner, jars and lids (see pages 7 to 8).
2. In a small dry skillet, over medium heat, toast curry powder, cumin and cinnamon, stirring constantly, for about 1 minute or until spices are fragrant and slightly darker. Immediately transfer to a large pot.
3. Add peaches, onions, ginger, garlic, chile peppers, brown sugar, salt and vinegar to the pot. Bring to a boil over medium heat, stirring often. Reduce heat and boil gently, stirring occasionally, for about 40 minutes or until onions are translucent and mixture is thick enough to mound on a spoon. Stir in lime juice.
4. Ladle hot chutney into hot jars, leaving ½ inch (1 cm) headspace. Remove air bubbles and adjust headspace as necessary by adding hot chutney. Wipe rim and place hot lid disc on jar. Screw band down until fingertip-tight.
5. Place jars in canner and return to a boil. Process for 10 minutes. Turn off heat and remove canner lid. Let jars stand in water for 5 minutes. Transfer jars to a towel-lined surface and let stand for 24 hours. Check lids and refrigerate any jars that aren't sealed.

Major Grey Pear Chutney

Floral, sweet pears are the base for this chutney, which is richly flavored with spices and citrus, with a nice touch of bitterness.

6 cups	chopped peeled pears	1.5 L
1 cup	chopped peeled seedless oranges	250 mL
1 cup	finely chopped onion	250 mL
⅓ cup	finely chopped lemon (rind and flesh), seeds removed	75 mL
¼ cup	finely chopped lime (rind and flesh), seeds removed	50 mL
2 tbsp	finely chopped gingerroot	25 mL
2 tbsp	minced garlic	25 mL
1 cup	raisins	250 mL
¾ cup	packed brown sugar	175 mL
1 tbsp	mustard seeds	15 mL
2 tsp	pickling or canning salt	10 mL
1 tsp	ground cinnamon	5 mL
1 tsp	ground coriander	5 mL
½ tsp	ground cloves	2 mL
¼ tsp	cayenne pepper	1 mL
1 cup	cider vinegar	250 mL
¾ cup	water	175 mL
½ cup	light (fancy) molasses	125 mL

1. In a large pot, combine pears, oranges, onion, lemon, lime, ginger, garlic, raisins, brown sugar, mustard seeds, salt, cinnamon, coriander, cloves, cayenne, vinegar, water and molasses. Bring to a boil over medium heat, stirring often. Reduce heat and boil gently, stirring occasionally, for about 1 hour or until onions, lemon and lime rinds are very soft and mixture is just thick enough to mound on a spoon.

2. Meanwhile, prepare canner, jars and lids (see pages 7 to 8).

3. Ladle hot chutney into hot jars, leaving ½ inch (1 cm) headspace. Remove air bubbles and adjust headspace as necessary by adding hot chutney. Wipe rim and place hot lid disc on jar. Screw band down until fingertip-tight.

4. Place jars in canner and return to a boil. Process for 10 minutes. Turn off heat and remove canner lid. Let jars stand in water for 5 minutes. Transfer jars to a towel-lined surface and let stand for 24 hours. Check lids and refrigerate any jars that aren't sealed.

Five-Spice Pear Chutney

Exotic spices and pears combine to make this fragrant and flavorful chutney. Serve it with Asian stir-fries, grilled marinated meats or stronger-flavored fish.

Makes about six 8-ounce (250 mL) jars

• • •

Tips

Choose fragrant but firm pears and use a variety that keeps its flavor when cooked, such as Bartlett, Bosc or Packham.

Five-spice powder is a blend of warm spices commonly used in Chinese cuisine. The spices used can vary, as can the proportion of each, but the key ingredients are usually cinnamon, cloves, fennel, star anise and Szechuan peppercorns. You can find five-spice powder at Asian grocery stores, spice emporiums and well-stocked supermarkets.

8 cups	chopped peeled pears	2 L
1½ cups	finely chopped onions	375 mL
4	cloves garlic, minced	4
1	hot red or green chile pepper, seeded and minced	1
1½ cups	granulated sugar	375 mL
1½ tsp	pickling or canning salt	7 mL
1½ tsp	Chinese five-spice powder	7 mL
1 cup	white vinegar	250 mL
½ cup	rice vinegar	125 mL

1. Prepare canner, jars and lids (see pages 7 to 8).
2. In a large pot, combine pears, onions, garlic, chile pepper, sugar, salt, five-spice powder, white vinegar and rice vinegar. Bring to a boil over medium heat, stirring often. Reduce heat and boil gently, stirring occasionally, for about 40 minutes or until onions are translucent and mixture is thick enough to mound on a spoon.
3. Ladle hot chutney into hot jars, leaving ½ inch (1 cm) headspace. Remove air bubbles and adjust headspace as necessary by adding hot chutney. Wipe rim and place hot lid disc on jar. Screw band down until fingertip-tight.
4. Place jars in canner and return to a boil. Process for 10 minutes. Turn off heat and remove canner lid. Let jars stand in water for 5 minutes. Transfer jars to a towel-lined surface and let stand for 24 hours. Check lids and refrigerate any jars that aren't sealed.

Pear Mint Chutney

A bit of heat and a touch of cooling mint, with sweet and tangy in between, make this chutney a vibrant addition to your meals.

Makes about seven 8-ounce (250 mL) jars

● ● ●

Tips

Choose fragrant but firm pears and use a variety that keeps its flavor when cooked, such as Bartlett, Bosc or Packham.

If you prefer a more jammy consistency, purée 2 cups (500 mL) of the pears before adding them to the pot and finely chop the onions.

Serving Suggestions

The mint makes this chutney a natural to pair with grilled or roasted lamb.

Serve with fish curries or plain grilled fish.

8 cups	chopped peeled pears	2 L
2 cups	chopped onions	500 mL
1½ cups	diced red bell pepper	375 mL
1	hot red or green chile pepper, seeded and minced	1
3	cloves garlic, minced	3
1½ cups	packed brown sugar	375 mL
1 tsp	pickling or canning salt	5 mL
1½ cups	cider vinegar	375 mL
2 tbsp	chopped fresh mint	25 mL
¼ cup	freshly squeezed lemon juice	50 mL

1. Prepare canner, jars and lids (see pages 7 to 8).
2. In a large pot, combine pears, onions, red pepper, chile pepper, garlic, brown sugar, salt, and vinegar. Bring to a boil over medium heat, stirring often. Reduce heat and boil gently, stirring occasionally, for about 40 minutes or until onions are translucent and mixture is thick enough to mound on a spoon. Stir in mint and lemon juice.
3. Ladle hot chutney into hot jars, leaving ½ inch (1 cm) headspace. Remove air bubbles and adjust headspace as necessary by adding hot chutney. Wipe rim and place hot lid disc on jar. Screw band down until fingertip-tight.
4. Place jars in canner and return to a boil. Process for 10 minutes. Turn off heat and remove canner lid. Let jars stand in water for 5 minutes. Transfer jars to a towel-lined surface and let stand for 24 hours. Check lids and refrigerate any jars that aren't sealed.

Pear and Sweet Onion Chutney

A subtle sherry undertone, mild pears and sweet onions make for a pleasant combination in this easy chutney. The toasted almonds add flavor and a nice contrast in texture to the tender pears.

Makes about seven 8-ounce (250 mL) jars

● ● ●

Tips

Choose fragrant but firm pears and use a variety that keeps its flavor when cooked, such as Bartlett, Bosc or Packham.

To toast almonds, spread on a baking sheet and bake in a 375°F (190°C) oven, stirring once, for about 8 minutes or until toasted and fragrant.

Serving Suggestions

Serve with sharp or creamy cheeses, spice-rubbed chicken or pork or grilled fish.

Top baguette slices with pâté and a spoonful of warmed chutney for a simple appetizer.

8 cups	chopped peeled pears	2 L
2 cups	finely chopped sweet onion	500 mL
1½ cups	packed brown sugar	375 mL
2 tsp	pickling or canning salt	10 mL
½ tsp	freshly ground black pepper	2 mL
1½ cups	white wine vinegar	375 mL
½ cup	dry sherry	125 mL
1 cup	chopped toasted almonds	250 mL

1. Prepare canner, jars and lids (see pages 7 to 8).
2. In a large pot, combine pears, onion, brown sugar, salt, pepper and vinegar. Bring to a boil over medium heat, stirring often. Reduce heat and boil gently, stirring occasionally, for about 35 minutes or until onions are translucent and mixture is thick enough to mound on a spoon. Stir in sherry and almonds.
3. Ladle hot chutney into hot jars, leaving ½ inch (1 cm) headspace. Remove air bubbles and adjust headspace as necessary by adding hot chutney. Wipe rim and place hot lid disc on jar. Screw band down until fingertip-tight.
4. Place jars in canner and return to a boil. Process for 10 minutes. Turn off heat and remove canner lid. Let jars stand in water for 5 minutes. Transfer jars to a towel-lined surface and let stand for 24 hours. Check lids and refrigerate any jars that aren't sealed.

Pear Fig Chutney

Fresh figs don't last long once picked, so make sure your pears are ripe and ready to make this mild but fruity chutney when you get the figs.

Makes about seven 8-ounce (250 mL) jars

● ● ●

Tips

Choose fragrant but firm pears and use a variety that keeps its flavor when cooked, such as Bartlett, Bosc or Packham.

Yellow-green Calimyrna figs make a pretty, light-colored chutney, but any fresh figs will work. You'll need about 10 large, or about 1½ lbs (750 g), to get 3 cups (750 mL) chopped.

This chutney thickens quite a bit upon cooling, so stop the cooking when it's thinner than you want the final texture to be.

Serving Suggestions

Spread crackers or toasted baguette slices with blue cheese and top with a spoonful of chutney for a classic flavor pairing.

Serve with grilled fish, poultry or veal.

6 cups	chopped peeled pears	1.5 L
3 cups	chopped fresh figs	750 mL
1½ cups	finely chopped sweet onion	375 mL
1	clove garlic, minced	1
1½ cups	granulated sugar	375 mL
1 tsp	pickling or canning salt	5 mL
¼ tsp	freshly ground black pepper	1 mL
1 cup	white wine vinegar	250 mL
½ tsp	grated lemon zest	2 mL
2 tbsp	freshly squeezed lemon juice	25 mL

1. Prepare canner, jars and lids (see pages 7 to 8).
2. In a large pot, combine pears, figs, onion, garlic, sugar, salt, pepper and vinegar. Bring to a boil over medium heat, stirring often. Reduce heat and boil gently, stirring occasionally, for about 30 minutes or until pears and onion are translucent and mixture is thickened to a thin jammy consistency. Stir in lemon zest and juice.
3. Ladle hot chutney into hot jars, leaving ½ inch (1 cm) headspace. Remove air bubbles and adjust headspace as necessary by adding hot chutney. Wipe rim and place hot lid disc on jar. Screw band down until fingertip-tight.
4. Place jars in canner and return to a boil. Process for 10 minutes. Turn off heat and remove canner lid. Let jars stand in water for 5 minutes. Transfer jars to a towel-lined surface and let stand for 24 hours. Check lids and refrigerate any jars that aren't sealed.

Pineapple Coconut Chutney

The tropical flavor of this chutney will transport you to warm, balmy climes where pineapples and coconut grow in abundance — well, in your imagination anyway.

Makes about five 8-ounce (250 mL) jars

• • •

Tips

Peel off the brown layer from the coconut before grating it. You can grate it on the coarse side of a box grater or, for a finer texture, by pulsing it in a food processor.

In place of the fresh coconut, you can use thawed frozen unsweetened grated coconut, commonly available at Asian and Caribbean grocery stores.

Serving Suggestions

Serve with Thai-marinated meats, chicken or shrimp satays, or spicy Caribbean or Indian curries.

Spread on top of grilled fish for the last couple of minutes of cooking for a warm glaze.

6 cups	chopped fresh pineapple	1.5 L
1 cup	lightly packed grated fresh coconut	250 mL
2	cloves garlic, minced	2
1½ cups	granulated sugar	375 mL
1 tsp	pickling or canning salt	5 mL
½ tsp	ground cardamom	2 mL
½ tsp	ground nutmeg (preferably freshly grated)	2 mL
⅛ tsp	hot pepper flakes	0.5 mL
1 cup	white vinegar	250 mL

1. Prepare canner, jars and lids (see pages 7 to 8).
2. In a large pot, combine pineapple, coconut, garlic, sugar, salt, cardamom, nutmeg, hot pepper flakes and vinegar. Bring to a boil over medium heat, stirring often. Reduce heat and boil gently, stirring occasionally, for about 20 minutes or until pineapple is translucent and mixture is thick enough to mound on a spoon.
3. Ladle hot chutney into hot jars, leaving ½ inch (1 cm) headspace. Remove air bubbles and adjust headspace as necessary by adding hot chutney. Wipe rim and place hot lid disc on jar. Screw band down until fingertip-tight.
4. Place jars in canner and return to a boil. Process for 10 minutes. Turn off heat and remove canner lid. Let jars stand in water for 5 minutes. Transfer jars to a towel-lined surface and let stand for 24 hours. Check lids and refrigerate any jars that aren't sealed.

Pineapple Ginger Chutney

The ginger adds a touch of heat to sweet and tangy pineapple. You can increase the heat by including the chile pepper, if you like. Either way, this is a bright, fresh-tasting chutney.

Makes five to six 8-ounce (250 mL) jars

● ● ●

Tip

You'll need about 2 large pineapples, peeled, cored and chopped, to get 6 cups (1.5 L).

Serving Suggestions

Serve with shrimp, chicken or pork satay.

Spoon chutney on top of a fish fillet for the last few minutes of grilling or baking.

6 cups	chopped fresh pineapple	1.5 L
1½ cups	finely chopped onions	375 mL
2 tbsp	finely chopped gingerroot	25 mL
1	hot red or green chile pepper (optional), seeded and minced	1
1¾ cups	packed brown sugar	425 mL
1 tsp	pickling or canning salt	5 mL
½ tsp	ground cinnamon	2 mL
1¼ cups	cider vinegar	300 mL

1. Prepare canner, jars and lids (see pages 7 to 8).
2. In a large pot, combine pineapple, onions, ginger, chile pepper (if using), brown sugar, salt, cinnamon and vinegar. Bring to a boil over medium heat, stirring often. Reduce heat and boil gently, stirring occasionally, for about 25 minutes or until mixture is thick enough to mound on a spoon.
3. Ladle hot chutney into hot jars, leaving ½ inch (1 cm) headspace. Remove air bubbles and adjust headspace as necessary by adding hot chutney. Wipe rim and place hot lid disc on jar. Screw band down until fingertip-tight.
4. Place jars in canner and return to a boil. Process for 10 minutes. Turn off heat and remove canner lid. Let jars stand in water for 5 minutes. Transfer jars to a towel-lined surface and let stand for 24 hours. Check lids and refrigerate any jars that aren't sealed.

Pineapple Mint Chutney

Pineapple and mint are two flavors that just seem natural together. This chutney is equally at home with Indian curries, Thai foods and Caribbean foods, or with plain grilled meats, poultry and fish.

Makes about six 8-ounce (250 mL) jars

• • •

Tips

There are many varieties of sweet onions available: look for Vidalia, Oso Sweet, Maui, Walla Walla or Spanish, to name a few.

The rice vinegar adds a pleasant sweet tang, but you can use all white vinegar if you prefer.

6 cups	chopped fresh pineapple	1.5 L
1½ cups	finely chopped sweet onion	375 mL
1 cup	finely chopped red bell pepper	250 mL
2	cloves garlic, minced	2
1¾ cups	granulated sugar	425 mL
1½ tsp	pickling or canning salt	7 mL
¼ tsp	hot pepper flakes	1 mL
1 cup	white vinegar	250 mL
½ cup	rice vinegar	125 mL
2 tbsp	chopped fresh mint	25 mL

1. Prepare canner, jars and lids (see pages 7 to 8).
2. In a large pot, combine pineapple, onion, red pepper, garlic, sugar, salt, hot pepper flakes, white vinegar and rice vinegar. Bring to a boil over medium heat, stirring often. Reduce heat and boil gently, stirring occasionally, for about 25 minutes or until pineapple is translucent and mixture is thick enough to mound on a spoon. Stir in mint.
3. Ladle hot chutney into hot jars, leaving ½ inch (1 cm) headspace. Remove air bubbles and adjust headspace as necessary by adding hot chutney. Wipe rim and place hot lid disc on jar. Screw band down until fingertip-tight.
4. Place jars in canner and return to a boil. Process for 10 minutes. Turn off heat and remove canner lid. Let jars stand in water for 5 minutes. Transfer jars to a towel-lined surface and let stand for 24 hours. Check lids and refrigerate any jars that aren't sealed.

Plum, Pear and Ginger Chutney

When plums and pears are ready for harvest, combine them in this jewel-colored chutney, which has a pleasant kick from the ginger.

Makes about six 8-ounce (250 mL) jars

● ● ●

Tips

I prefer blue (Italian-style) or purple plums for their firmer, drier texture, which makes a jammy chutney. The skins are a bit thicker, but they add interest to the overall texture.

Be sure to use very fresh gingerroot with taut, shiny skin, juicy flesh and no signs of mold.

5 cups	chopped blue or purple plums	1.25 L
3 cups	chopped peeled pears	750 mL
1 cup	finely chopped onion	250 mL
¼ cup	finely chopped gingerroot	50 mL
2	cloves garlic, minced	2
1½ cups	granulated sugar	375 mL
1 tsp	pickling salt	5 mL
¼ tsp	freshly ground black pepper	1 mL
1¼ cups	cider vinegar	300 mL
¼ cup	freshly squeezed lemon juice	50 mL

1. Prepare canner, jars and lids (see pages 7 to 8).
2. In a large pot, combine plums, pears, onion, ginger, garlic, sugar, salt, pepper and vinegar. Bring to a boil over medium heat, stirring often. Reduce heat and boil gently, stirring occasionally, for about 40 minutes or until onions are translucent and mixture is thickened to a jammy consistency. Stir in lemon juice.
3. Ladle hot chutney into hot jars, leaving ½ inch (1 cm) headspace. Remove air bubbles and adjust headspace as necessary by adding hot chutney. Wipe rim and place hot lid disc on jar. Screw band down until fingertip-tight.
4. Place jars in canner and return to a boil. Process for 10 minutes. Turn off heat and remove canner lid. Let jars stand in water for 5 minutes. Transfer jars to a towel-lined surface and let stand for 24 hours. Check lids and refrigerate any jars that aren't sealed.

Plum Orange Chutney

Turn your holiday traditions upside down by serving this chutney with roast turkey in place of cranberry sauce. It also goes well with ham and roast pork.

4	seedless oranges	4
2 cups	water	500 mL
6 cups	chopped plums	1.5 L
1½ cups	finely chopped onions	375 mL
2	cloves garlic, minced	2
2 cups	granulated sugar	500 mL
1 tsp	pickling salt	5 mL
½ tsp	ground cinnamon	2 mL
¼ tsp	hot pepper flakes	1 mL
1 cup	white vinegar	250 mL

1. Prepare canner, jars and lids (see pages 7 to 8).
2. Cut oranges in half crosswise and scoop out flesh. Cut rind into thin strips and measure 1 cup (250 mL). Coarsely chop flesh, measure 2 cups (500 mL) and set aside. Reserve any extra for another use.
3. In a large pot, combine orange rind and water. Bring to a simmer over high heat. Reduce heat and simmer for about 15 minutes or until rind is very soft. Drain off liquid and return rind to pot.
4. Add orange flesh, plums, onions, garlic, sugar, salt, cinnamon, hot pepper flakes and vinegar. Bring to a boil over medium heat, stirring often. Reduce heat and boil gently, stirring occasionally, for about 30 minutes or until onions are translucent and mixture is thick enough to mound on a spoon.
5. Ladle hot chutney into hot jars, leaving ½ inch (1 cm) headspace. Remove air bubbles and adjust headspace as necessary by adding hot chutney. Wipe rim and place hot lid disc on jar. Screw band down until fingertip-tight.
6. Place jars in canner and return to a boil. Process for 10 minutes. Turn off heat and remove canner lid. Let jars stand in water for 5 minutes. Transfer jars to a towel-lined surface and let stand for 24 hours. Check lids and refrigerate any jars that aren't sealed.

Mom's Rhubarb Chutney

My mom has been making a version of rhubarb chutney for as long as I can remember. We love to eat it with so many things that the batch size has gotten bigger over the years to make sure we have enough until rhubarb is ready for harvest again.

8 cups	chopped rhubarb	2 L
3½ cups	chopped onions	875 mL
½ cup	minced gingerroot	125 mL
6 cups	packed light brown sugar	1.5 L
3 tbsp	mustard seeds	45 mL
1 tsp	ground cumin	5 mL
1 tsp	pickling or canning salt	5 mL
¼ tsp	hot pepper flakes	1 mL
5 cups	cider vinegar	1.25 L
¼ cup	tamarind concentrate or paste	50 mL

1. In a large pot, combine rhubarb, onions, ginger, brown sugar, mustard seeds, cumin, salt, hot pepper flakes, vinegar and tamarind. Bring to a boil over medium heat, stirring often. Reduce heat and boil gently, stirring occasionally, for about 1 hour or until rhubarb is very soft and mixture is thickened to a jammy consistency.

2. Meanwhile, prepare canner, jars and lids (see pages 7 to 8).

3. Ladle hot chutney into hot jars, leaving ½ inch (1 cm) headspace. Remove air bubbles and adjust headspace as necessary by adding hot chutney. Wipe rim and place hot lid disc on jar. Screw band down until fingertip-tight.

4. Place jars in canner and return to a boil. Process for 10 minutes. Turn off heat and remove canner lid. Let jars stand in water for 5 minutes. Transfer jars to a towel-lined surface and let stand for 24 hours. Check lids and refrigerate any jars that aren't sealed.

Savory Rhubarb Strawberry Chutney

I am lucky enough to have a prolific rhubarb plant in my garden and a strawberry farm near my house, so I often have plenty of both to get creative with. Since I love strawberry rhubarb jam and strawberry rhubarb pie, I thought, hey, why not combine them in a savory chutney, too?

Makes about six 8-ounce (250 mL) jars

• • •

Tip

Mixing some of the rhubarb with the strawberries and sugar softens it slightly and reduces the amount of cooking required, keeping the flavor fresher. The rhubarb that gets cooked for the entire time breaks down and adds a jammy consistency.

Serving Suggestions

Serve as a condiment on grilled fish or with creamy cheeses, such as Brie, Camembert or regular cream cheese, on crackers or crusty bread.

Spoon over a spinach salad instead of dressing and sprinkle with chopped toasted almonds or pecans.

4 cups	chopped rhubarb, divided	1 L
2 cups	diced strawberries	500 mL
1¾ cups	granulated sugar, divided	425 mL
1½ cups	chopped onions	375 mL
1 cup	diced peeled tart cooking apple	250 mL
1 tbsp	minced gingerroot	15 mL
3	cloves garlic, minced	3
1 tsp	pickling or canning salt	5 mL
½ tsp	freshly ground black pepper	2 mL
1½ cups	white wine vinegar or cider vinegar	375 mL
1 tsp	grated lemon zest	5 mL
2 tbsp	freshly squeezed lemon juice	25 mL

1. Prepare canner, jars and lids (see pages 7 to 8).
2. In a bowl, combine half the rhubarb, the strawberries and ¾ cup (175 mL) of the sugar; set aside.
3. In a large pot, combine the remaining rhubarb, the remaining sugar, onions, apple, ginger, garlic, salt, pepper and vinegar. Bring to a boil over medium heat, stirring often. Reduce heat and boil gently, stirring occasionally, for about 20 minutes or until onions are translucent and mixture is thickened. Stir in rhubarb mixture, lemon zest and lemon juice, increase heat to medium and return to a boil, stirring often. Boil for about 1 minute or until strawberries and rhubarb are tender but still hold their shape.
4. Ladle hot chutney into hot jars, leaving ½ inch (1 cm) headspace. Remove air bubbles and adjust headspace as necessary by adding hot chutney. Wipe rim and place hot lid disc on jar. Screw band down until fingertip-tight.
5. Place jars in canner and return to a boil. Process for 15 minutes. Turn off heat and remove canner lid. Let jars stand in water for 5 minutes. Transfer jars to a towel-lined surface and let stand for 24 hours. Check lids and refrigerate any jars that aren't sealed.

Indian Spiced Tomato Chutney

Classic chutney flavors abound in this pleasantly spice-spiked recipe. Serve it with Indian curries, of course, or with grilled steak or even roast beef.

Makes about six 8-ounce (250 mL) jars

● ● ●

Tips

Curry leaves are available fresh or dried at Indian and other Asian grocery stores and at spice emporiums or specialty food stores. They are edible, but some people find the texture disconcerting, so you may prefer to discard them before filling the jars.

For instructions on peeling tomatoes, see page 17. Seeding the tomatoes does take a little extra time, but it reduces the amount of liquid added to the pot and therefore reduces the amount of cooking required, giving the chutney a fresher tomato flavor.

2 tbsp	mustard seeds	25 mL
1 tbsp	cumin seeds	15 mL
1 tsp	coriander seeds	5 mL
8 cups	chopped seeded peeled plum (Roma) tomatoes	2 L
2 cups	chopped onions	500 mL
1/4 cup	minced seeded long hot green or red chile peppers	50 mL
1/4 cup	minced gingerroot	50 mL
2 tbsp	curry leaves (optional)	25 mL
2	cloves garlic, minced	2
1¾ cups	granulated sugar	425 mL
2 tsp	pickling or canning salt	10 mL
1/2 tsp	ground turmeric	2 mL
1½ cups	white vinegar	375 mL

1. Prepare canner, jars and lids (see pages 7 to 8).
2. In a small dry skillet, over medium heat, toast mustard seeds, cumin seeds and coriander seeds, stirring constantly, for about 1 minute or until spices are fragrant and slightly darker but not yet popping. Immediately transfer to a large pot.
3. Add tomatoes, onions, chile peppers, ginger, curry leaves (if using), garlic, sugar, salt, turmeric and vinegar to the pot. Bring to a boil over medium heat, stirring often. Reduce heat and boil gently, stirring occasionally, for about 45 minutes or until onions are translucent and mixture is thick enough to mound on a spoon. Discard curry leaves, if desired.
4. Ladle hot chutney into hot jars, leaving 1/2 inch (1 cm) headspace. Remove air bubbles and adjust headspace as necessary by adding hot chutney. Wipe rim and place hot lid disc on jar. Screw band down until fingertip-tight.
5. Place jars in canner and return to a boil. Process for 20 minutes. Turn off heat and remove canner lid. Let jars stand in water for 5 minutes. Transfer jars to a towel-lined surface and let stand for 24 hours. Check lids and refrigerate any jars that aren't sealed.

Sweet and Spicy Tomato Chutney

This is much like the flavor of chili sauce but not as sweet, and with an accent on the tang and a chunky texture that are characteristics of chutney.

Makes about six 8-ounce (250 mL) jars

● ● ●

Tip

For instructions on peeling tomatoes, see page 17.

Variation

If you like a hot chutney, increase the chile peppers to 2. If you're not sure, just use 1 to start, then add hot pepper sauce to taste after it's cooked, if desired.

8 cups	chopped seeded peeled plum (Roma) tomatoes	2 L
2 cups	chopped onions	500 mL
1 cup	chopped red bell pepper	250 mL
2	cloves garlic, minced	2
1	hot red or green chile pepper, seeded and minced	1
1½ cups	granulated sugar	375 mL
1½ tsp	pickling or canning salt	7 mL
1 tsp	ground cinnamon	5 mL
1 tsp	ground ginger	5 mL
½ tsp	ground allspice	2 mL
1½ cups	cider vinegar	375 mL

1. Prepare canner, jars and lids (see pages 7 to 8).
2. In a large pot, combine tomatoes, onions, red pepper, garlic, chile pepper, sugar, salt, cinnamon, ginger, allspice and vinegar. Bring to a boil over medium heat, stirring often. Reduce heat and boil gently, stirring occasionally, for about 45 minutes or until onions are translucent and mixture is thick enough to mound on a spoon.
3. Ladle hot chutney into hot jars, leaving ½ inch (1 cm) headspace. Remove air bubbles and adjust headspace as necessary by adding hot chutney. Wipe rim and place hot lid disc on jar. Screw band down until fingertip-tight.
4. Place jars in canner and return to a boil. Process for 20 minutes. Turn off heat and remove canner lid. Let jars stand in water for 5 minutes. Transfer jars to a towel-lined surface and let stand for 24 hours. Check lids and refrigerate any jars that aren't sealed.

Tomato Papaya Chutney

This might not be a common flavor combination, but once you taste it you'll be trying to think of more ways to enjoy it.

Makes about eight 8-ounce (250 mL) jars

● ● ●

Tips

Papayas vary dramatically in size depending on the variety. If using a small variety, you'll need about 2. If using a larger variety, you'll need about ⅔. Sprinkle any extra papaya with lime juice, salt and pepper for a quick salsa.

For instructions on peeling tomatoes, see page 17.

Serving Suggestion

Serve with grilled or roast pork or poultry or as a condiment for quiche or other egg dishes.

3 cups	chopped peeled papaya	750 mL
2 cups	granulated sugar, divided	500 mL
5 cups	chopped peeled seeded plum (Roma) tomatoes	1.25 L
1 cup	finely chopped onion	250 mL
1 tbsp	finely chopped gingerroot	15 mL
1 tsp	pickling or canning salt	5 mL
½ tsp	ground cinnamon	2 mL
1¾ cups	cider vinegar	425 mL
1	hot green or red chile pepper, seeded and minced	1

1. Prepare canner, jars and lids (see pages 7 to 8).
2. In a bowl, gently combine papaya and ½ cup (125 mL) of the sugar; set aside.
3. In a large pot, combine the remaining sugar, tomatoes, onion, ginger, salt, cinnamon and vinegar. Bring to a boil over medium heat, stirring often. Reduce heat and boil gently, stirring occasionally, for about 30 minutes or until onion is soft and mixture is slightly thickened. Stir in papaya mixture and chile pepper, increase heat to medium and boil gently, stirring often, for about 15 minutes or until papaya is translucent but still hold its shape.
4. Ladle hot chutney into hot jars, leaving ½ inch (1 cm) headspace. Remove air bubbles and adjust headspace as necessary by adding hot chutney. Wipe rim and place hot lid disc on jar. Screw band down until fingertip-tight.
5. Place jars in canner and return to a boil. Process for 20 minutes. Turn off heat and remove canner lid. Let jars stand in water for 5 minutes. Transfer jars to a towel-lined surface and let stand for 24 hours. Check lids and refrigerate any jars that aren't sealed.

Ploughman's Vegetable Chutney

In England, this Branston Pickle–style chutney is an essential component of any ploughman's lunch or Indian curry meal. The lively bitter, sweet and tangy flavors are the hallmarks of this rich chutney.

Makes about nine 8-ounce (250 mL) jars

● ● ●

Tip

The commercially prepared version often has caramel coloring added, so this version isn't quite as dark.

3 cups	diced carrots	750 mL
2 cups	diced rutabaga	500 mL
2 cups	diced zucchini	500 mL
2 cups	finely chopped onions	500 mL
2 cups	finely chopped cauliflower	500 mL
2 cups	finely chopped tart soft apples	500 mL
1 cup	chopped dates	250 mL
½ cup	diced drained sweet gherkin pickles (store-bought or see recipe, page 38)	125 mL
¼ cup	tomato paste	50 mL
3	cloves garlic, minced	3
2 cups	packed dark brown sugar	500 mL
1 tbsp	mustard seeds	15 mL
1½ tsp	pickling or canning salt	7 mL
1 tsp	ground allspice	5 mL
½ tsp	cayenne pepper (optional)	2 mL
1¾ cups	malt or cider vinegar	425 mL
1½ cups	water	375 mL

1. In a large pot, combine carrots, rutabaga, zucchini, onions, cauliflower, apple, dates, pickles, tomato paste, garlic, brown sugar, mustard seeds, salt, allspice, cayenne (if using), vinegar and water. Bring to a boil over medium heat, stirring often. Reduce heat and boil gently, stirring occasionally, for about 1½ hours or until vegetables are tender and mixture is thick enough to mound on a spoon.
2. Meanwhile, prepare canner, jars and lids (see pages 7 to 8).
3. Ladle hot chutney into hot jars, leaving ½ inch (1 cm) headspace. Remove air bubbles and adjust headspace as necessary by adding hot chutney. Wipe rim and place hot lid disc on jar. Screw band down until fingertip-tight.
4. Place jars in canner and return to a boil. Process for 20 minutes. Turn off heat and remove canner lid. Let jars stand in water for 5 minutes. Transfer jars to a towel-lined surface and let stand for 24 hours. Check lids and refrigerate any jars that aren't sealed.

Sweet and Sour Green Tomato Chutney

If the frost is fast approaching and you know those extra tomatoes just aren't going to ripen, this chutney is a fabulous way to use them up with other fall-harvested produce.

Makes about seven 8-ounce (250 mL) jars

● ● ●

Serving Suggestions

Serve with sharp Cheddar cheese and crackers, or with crusty bread and liver pâté.

Use as a condiment for grilled beef or pork.

6 cups	chopped seeded green tomatoes	1.5 L
2 cups	chopped peeled tart cooking apples	500 mL
1½ cups	chopped onions	375 mL
1 cup	chopped green bell pepper	250 mL
1 cup	chopped red bell pepper	250 mL
¾ cup	raisins	175 mL
2 cups	granulated sugar	500 mL
2 tsp	dry mustard	10 mL
1½ tsp	pickling or canning salt	7 mL
1 tsp	ground cinnamon	5 mL
¼ tsp	ground cloves	1 mL
¼ tsp	freshly ground black pepper	1 mL
1½ cups	cider vinegar	375 mL

1. Prepare canner, jars and lids (see pages 7 to 8).

2. In a large pot, combine tomatoes, apples, onions, green and red peppers, raisins, sugar, mustard, salt, cinnamon, cloves, pepper and vinegar. Bring to a boil over medium heat, stirring often. Reduce heat and boil gently, stirring occasionally, for about 45 minutes or until onions are translucent and mixture is thick enough to mound on a spoon.

3. Ladle hot chutney into hot jars, leaving ½ inch (1 cm) headspace. Remove air bubbles and adjust headspace as necessary by adding hot chutney. Wipe rim and place hot lid disc on jar. Screw band down until fingertip-tight.

4. Place jars in canner and return to a boil. Process for 20 minutes. Turn off heat and remove canner lid. Let jars stand in water for 5 minutes. Transfer jars to a towel-lined surface and let stand for 24 hours. Check lids and refrigerate any jars that aren't sealed.

Autumn Harvest Chutney

In the early autumn, when tree fruits are at their peak and cranberries are fresh from the bogs, mix them all together and make this beautiful, tasty chutney.

Makes about seven 8-ounce (250 mL) jars

● ● ●

Tips

If using frozen cranberries, let them come to room temperature before adding them to the chutney so they don't slow the cooking process too much.

Adding the cranberries at the end keeps their shape a little more intact, so they're visible in the chutney.

This chutney thickens quite a bit upon cooling, so stop the cooking when it's thinner than you want the final texture to be.

4 cups	chopped peeled tart cooking apples	1 L
3 cups	chopped peeled pears	750 mL
2 cups	chopped plums	500 mL
1 cup	finely chopped onion	250 mL
1¾ cups	packed brown sugar	425 mL
1 tsp	pickling or canning salt	5 mL
1 tsp	ground cinnamon	5 mL
1 tsp	ground ginger	5 mL
½ tsp	ground nutmeg	2 mL
¼ tsp	hot pepper flakes	1 mL
1½ cups	cider vinegar	375 mL
2 cups	cranberries	500 mL

1. Prepare canner, jars and lids (see pages 7 to 8).
2. In a large pot, combine apples, pears, plums, onion, brown sugar, salt, cinnamon, ginger, nutmeg, hot pepper flakes and vinegar. Bring to a boil over medium heat, stirring often. Reduce heat and boil gently, stirring occasionally, for about 30 minutes or until onions are translucent and mixture is slightly thickened. Stir in cranberries, increase heat to medium and boil gently, stirring often, for about 10 minutes or until cranberries are tender and starting to pop.
3. Ladle hot chutney into hot jars, leaving ½ inch (1 cm) headspace. Remove air bubbles and adjust headspace as necessary by adding hot chutney. Wipe rim and place hot lid disc on jar. Screw band down until fingertip-tight.
4. Place jars in canner and return to a boil. Process for 10 minutes. Turn off heat and remove canner lid. Let jars stand in water for 5 minutes. Transfer jars to a towel-lined surface and let stand for 24 hours. Check lids and refrigerate any jars that aren't sealed.

Out-of-the-Freezer Chutney

If you have a stockpile of frozen fruit, you can make this chutney any time to replenish your pantry or to while away a winter afternoon. Since frozen fruit is already chopped, and because it's softer than fresh, it cooks faster, so you can have this chutney simmered and in jars in no time.

Makes about five 8-ounce (250 mL) jars

• • •

Tips

Frozen fruits that work well in chutney include peaches, mangos, pineapple, blueberries, cherries, cranberries, raspberries and rhubarb. When you're mixing fruits, just be sure you like the flavor combination. A weird mix won't get better in a chutney.

Depending on the sweetness of the fruit you use, you may need to add more sugar. Taste the cooked chutney, keeping in mind that the flavors will mellow as it stands; if you want to add more sugar, stir it in and cook, stirring, for another 5 minutes or until the sugar is dissolved.

8 cups	chopped mixed frozen fruit (see tip, at left), thawed and drained	2 L
2 cups	finely chopped onions	500 mL
3	cloves garlic, minced	3
1¾ cups	granulated sugar (approx., see tip, at left)	425 mL
1 tsp	pickling or canning salt	5 mL
1 tsp	ground cinnamon	5 mL
½ tsp	hot pepper flakes	2 mL
1¼ cups	cider vinegar	300 mL

1. Prepare canner, jars and lids (see pages 7 to 8).
2. In a large pot, combine fruit, onions, garlic, sugar, salt, cinnamon, hot pepper flakes and vinegar. Bring to a boil over medium heat, stirring often. Reduce heat and boil gently, stirring occasionally, for about 20 minutes or until onions are translucent and mixture is thick enough to mound on a spoon.
3. Ladle hot chutney into hot jars, leaving ½ inch (1 cm) headspace. Remove air bubbles and adjust headspace as necessary by adding hot chutney. Wipe rim and place hot lid disc on jar. Screw band down until fingertip-tight.
4. Place jars in canner and return to a boil. Process for 20 minutes. Turn off heat and remove canner lid. Let jars stand in water for 5 minutes. Transfer jars to a towel-lined surface and let stand for 24 hours. Check lids and refrigerate any jars that aren't sealed.

Relishes and Tapenades

continued on next page

Relish Basics

Relishes consist of finely chopped, grated or shredded vegetables and fruits in a sugar and vinegar pickling liquid — essentially, chopped sweet pickles. They tend to be a little less sweet and, often, more crunchy or crispy than chutneys, but still have that sweet and tangy flavor combination. Most relishes are made with vegetables, but some do combine fruits with the vegetables.

Traditionally, relishes are used as a topping for hamburgers and hot dogs, but their usefulness goes so much further: the wide variety of relishes in this chapter can be used to add interest to fish, poultry, meats, cheeses and salads, and even served on their own as cracker toppings.

As with all pickling, the freshest, highest-quality produce is important for a good-quality, safe relish. Because the produce is finely chopped, you can use vegetables and fruits that are misshapen, slightly too large or, perhaps, not quite perfect enough to pickle whole, but any produce that is past its prime will likely cause spoilage of the relish.

One of the advantages of mixed vegetable and fruit relishes is that you can use up smaller amounts of produce in combination, which is especially handy after you've used larger amounts for single-item pickles. Those last few zucchini and red bell peppers get mixed together to make wonderful Zucchini Red Pepper Relish (page 278), and if you've got extra cucumbers, but not quite enough for another batch of dill pickles, mix them into Corn and Cucumber Relish (page 249) or Hot Dog Relish (page 256).

Relishes generally have a shorter cooking time than chutneys and other sauces, so they are perfect to make on a day when you don't have much time. Many do require soaking the vegetables in salt to remove some of the natural moisture and give a crispier texture, but the active time in the kitchen is relatively short. The soaking (or brining) of the finely chopped produce allows the pickling liquid to infuse into the produce faster and shortens the cooking time, thereby giving a toothsome texture to the relish. All relishes are packed using the hot-pack method and have a shorter processing time than raw-pack products and tomato sauces.

Many older recipes thicken relish with flour or cornstarch to create a texture more similar to commercial relishes. However, thinner mixtures allow for better heat penetration when processing, which is essential to safe home canning, so these older recipes may not be safe to use. In addition, cornstarch can break down during heat processing and is not recommended for home canning. These recipes do not have added starch and are therefore a less cohesive texture than thickened relishes, but once you get used to the difference you probably won't notice.

The wonderful flavors of homemade relish are so superior to most of what you can buy that you'll be thrilled each time you open a jar.

Relish Pointers

- Hand chopping does take time, but for some relishes it gives such a superior texture to the final product that it's worth it. If you have a good, sharp knife, a large cutting board and some good music in the background (or better yet, some kitchen helpers), it can be an enjoyable part of the preparations. Other relishes will not be adversely affected by vegetables chopped in the food processor; information to this effect is noted in the sidebars of relevant recipes. If you do use a food processor to chop your vegetables, just make sure not to purée them.

- When filling jars, the liquid from the relish should cover the solids. If necessary, remove some of the solids from the filled jar to make sure there is liquid on top with the correct $\frac{1}{2}$ inch (1 cm) headspace above it.

- The relatively short cooking time means you really need to make sure the canner, jars and lids are prepared when the relish is ready to go into the jars. It's best to have them ready before you start cooking so the relish doesn't cool at all.

- Due to its short cooking time, the flavor of relish doesn't blend as much as with chutneys and sauces during the initial preparation, so it's best to let the flavors blend and mellow for at least a week — and preferably 2 to 3 weeks — before serving.

- As with all pickling, the amounts and types of produce, sugar and acid ingredients are essential to a safe product. Measure the specified amount of sugar and vinegar carefully. Be sure to measure finely chopped ingredients without packing too tightly or too loosely — moderately packed is the general rule unless otherwise noted.

- The type of vinegar used can be adjusted according to taste as long as the strength of the acetic acid is the same. Five percent white vinegar, cider vinegar, white wine vinegar and red wine vinegar are interchangeable.

- Spices and seasonings (except for salt and sugar) can be adjusted according to taste. Feel free to get creative, but keep in mind that the flavors will be stronger after the relishes stand for a while.

Maple Apple Onion Relish

An accent of pure maple syrup works wonderfully with tart apples and sweet onions. This relish puts a new spin on good old pork chops and applesauce.

Makes about six 8-ounce (250 mL) jars

● ● ●

Tips

There are many varieties of sweet onions available: look for Vidalia, Oso Sweet, Maui, Walla Walla or Spanish, to name a few.

Some cooking apples that keep their shape are Crispin (Mutsu), Granny Smith, Northern Spy and Cortland.

For this relish, I prefer to chop the onions and apples by hand, but you can use the metal blade and pulse function of a food processor if you prefer. Just be sure not to purée them.

2 cups	finely chopped sweet onions	500 mL
1 cup	granulated sugar	250 mL
2 tsp	pickling or canning salt	10 mL
1½ cups	white vinegar	375 mL
½ cup	pure maple syrup	125 mL
6 cups	finely chopped peeled tart cooking apples	1.5 L

1. Prepare canner, jars and lids (see pages 7 to 8).
2. In a large pot, combine onions, sugar, salt, vinegar and maple syrup. Bring to a boil over medium heat, stirring often until sugar and salt are dissolved. Increase heat to medium-high, add apples and return to a boil, stirring often. Reduce heat and boil gently, stirring often, for about 2 minutes or until apples just start to soften but don't break down and mixture is slightly thickened.
3. Ladle hot relish into hot jars, leaving ½ inch (1 cm) headspace. Remove air bubbles and adjust headspace as necessary by adding hot relish. Wipe rim and place hot lid disc on jar. Screw band down until fingertip-tight.
4. Place jars in canner and return to a boil. Process for 10 minutes. Turn off heat and remove canner lid. Let jars stand in water for 5 minutes. Transfer jars to a towel-lined surface and let stand for 24 hours. Check lids and refrigerate any jars that are not sealed.

Apple, Onion and Ale Relish

The malt and hops from the ale add depth to this sweet and savory relish. Serve it with crusty bread, cold ham and old Cheddar cheese for a sublime lunch.

Makes about six 8-ounce (250 mL) jars

● ● ●

Tip

Combining two types of apples helps thicken the relish while keeping a chunky texture. The most flavorful soft apple for cooking is the good old McIntosh, but you can also use Empire or Idared. Some cooking apples that keep their shape are Crispin (Mutsu), Granny Smith, Northern Spy and Cortland.

4 cups	finely chopped onions	1 L
2 tbsp	pickling or canning salt	25 mL
1½ cups	packed brown sugar	375 mL
1 tbsp	mustard seeds	15 mL
¼ tsp	ground cinnamon	1 mL
¼ tsp	ground nutmeg (preferably freshly grated)	1 mL
1 cup	cider vinegar	250 mL
2 cups	finely chopped peeled tart soft apples	500 mL
1 cup	dark ale	250 mL
4 cups	finely chopped peeled tart cooking apples	1 L

1. In a large non-reactive bowl, combine onions and salt. Cover and let stand at a cool room temperature for 2 hours.
2. Meanwhile, prepare canner, jars and lids (see pages 7 to 8).
3. In a colander lined with cheesecloth, working in batches, drain onions and rinse well. Drain again and squeeze out excess liquid. Set aside in colander to continue draining.
4. In a large pot, combine brown sugar, mustard seeds, cinnamon, nutmeg and vinegar. Bring to a boil over medium heat, stirring often until sugar is dissolved. Increase heat to medium-high and add drained onions, soft apples and ale; return to a boil, stirring often. Reduce heat and boil gently, stirring often, for about 10 minutes or until apples start to break down and mixture is slightly thickened. Stir in cooking apples and return to a boil, stirring often. Reduce heat and boil gently, stirring often, for about 2 minutes or until cooking apples just start to soften but don't break down.
5. Ladle hot relish into hot jars, leaving ½ inch (1 cm) headspace. Remove air bubbles and adjust headspace as necessary by adding hot relish. Wipe rim and place hot lid disc on jar. Screw band down until fingertip-tight.
6. Place jars in canner and return to a boil. Process for 10 minutes. Turn off heat and remove canner lid. Let jars stand in water for 5 minutes. Transfer jars to a towel-lined surface and let stand for 24 hours. Check lids and refrigerate any jars that are not sealed.

Apple Horseradish Relish

Zingy horseradish adds a surprising kick to fresh-tasting apples in this relish. It's terrific with poultry and pork, of course, and holds its own with rich roast beef too.

Makes about six 8-ounce (250 mL) jars

• • •

Tips

Horseradish root should be very firm, with tight skin and no soft spots. Peel the skin with a vegetable peeler, then shred the root on the coarse side of a box grater or using the shredding blade of a food processor.

Shred the onions by hand on the coarse side of a box grater.

Wearing goggles while shredding strong ingredients such as onions and horseradish really does help protect your eyes from stinging.

Some cooking apples that keep their shape are Crispin (Mutsu), Granny Smith, Northern Spy and Cortland.

2 cups	shredded horseradish root	500 mL
2 cups	shredded onions	500 mL
2 tbsp	pickling or canning salt	25 mL
2¼ cups	granulated sugar	550 mL
1 tsp	dried thyme	5 mL
2 cups	cider vinegar	500 mL
6 cups	shredded peeled tart cooking apples	1.5 L

1. In a large non-reactive bowl, combine horseradish, onions and salt. Cover and let stand at a cool room temperature for 2 hours.
2. Meanwhile, prepare canner, jars and lids (see pages 7 to 8).
3. In a colander lined with cheesecloth, working in batches, drain vegetables and rinse well. Drain again and squeeze out excess liquid. Set aside in colander to continue draining.
4. In a large pot, combine sugar, thyme and vinegar. Bring to a boil over medium heat, stirring often until sugar is dissolved. Increase heat to medium-high, add drained vegetables and return to a boil, stirring often. Reduce heat and boil gently, stirring often, for about 10 minutes or until vegetables are translucent and mixture is slightly thickened. Stir in apples and return to a boil, stirring often.
5. Ladle hot relish into hot jars, leaving ½ inch (1 cm) headspace. Remove air bubbles and adjust headspace as necessary by adding hot relish. Wipe rim and place hot lid disc on jar. Screw band down until fingertip-tight.
6. Place jars in canner and return to a boil. Process for 10 minutes. Turn off heat and remove canner lid. Let jars stand in water for 5 minutes. Transfer jars to a towel-lined surface and let stand for 24 hours. Check lids and refrigerate any jars that are not sealed.

Red Pepper and Horseradish Relish

The sweetness of bell peppers and the heat of horseradish combine for a lively relish that will dress up roast beef or grilled steak.

Makes about six 8-ounce (250 mL) jars

6 cups	finely chopped red bell peppers	1.5 L
3 cups	shredded horseradish root	750 mL
2 cups	finely chopped onions	500 mL
2 tbsp	pickling or canning salt	25 mL
2½ cups	granulated sugar	625 mL
2 tsp	celery seeds	10 mL
2 cups	cider vinegar	500 mL

Tips

To save time, you can finely chop the red pepper in a food processor using the metal blade and the pulse function — just be sure not to purée it.

Horseradish root should be very firm, with tight skin and no soft spots. Peel the skin with a vegetable peeler, then shred the root on the coarse side of a box grater or using the shredding blade of a food processor.

Wearing goggles while shredding strong ingredients such as horseradish really does help protect your eyes from stinging.

1. In a large non-reactive bowl, combine red peppers, horseradish, onions and salt. Cover and let stand at a cool room temperature for 2 hours.
2. Meanwhile, prepare canner, jars and lids (see pages 7 to 8).
3. In a colander lined with cheesecloth, working in batches, drain vegetables and rinse well. Drain again and squeeze out excess liquid. Set aside in colander to continue draining.
4. In a large pot, combine sugar, celery seeds and vinegar. Bring to a boil over medium heat, stirring often until sugar is dissolved. Increase heat to medium-high, add drained vegetables and return to a boil, stirring often. Reduce heat and boil gently, stirring often, for about 15 minutes or until vegetables are translucent and mixture is slightly thickened.
5. Ladle hot relish into hot jars, leaving ½ inch (1 cm) headspace. Remove air bubbles and adjust headspace as necessary by adding hot relish. Wipe rim and place hot lid disc on jar. Screw band down until fingertip-tight.
6. Place jars in canner and return to a boil. Process for 10 minutes. Turn off heat and remove canner lid. Let jars stand in water for 5 minutes. Transfer jars to a towel-lined surface and let stand for 24 hours. Check lids and refrigerate any jars that are not sealed.

Beet and Horseradish Relish

This Eastern European classic is a must on holiday tables to serve with roast poultry, beef or ham.

Makes about six 8-ounce (250 mL) jars

● ● ●

Tips

The cooking time for the beets in step 1 is based on 12 medium beets. If you have smaller or larger beets, adjust the cooking time in step 1 accordingly.

Shred beets, horseradish and onions by hand on the coarse side of a box grater for the best texture.

Wear disposable gloves when shredding the beets to prevent your hands from getting stained.

Serving Suggestion

Make luxurious hors d'oeuvres by folding some of this relish into unsweetened whipped cream, then spread it on baguette slices and top with shaved roast beef.

4 lbs	beets (about 12)	2 kg
1 cup	shredded horseradish root	250 mL
1 cup	shredded onion	250 mL
2 cups	granulated sugar	500 mL
½ tsp	freshly ground black pepper	2 mL
2 cups	white vinegar	500 mL

1. Trim beets and place in a large pot. Cover with cold water and bring to a boil over high heat. Reduce heat and boil gently for about 30 minutes or until almost fork-tender (see tip, at left). Immediately plunge into a large bowl or sink of cold water and let stand until well chilled, refreshing water as necessary to keep cold, for at least 30 minutes or for up to 1 hour. Peel off skins and shred beets. Measure 6 cups (1.5 L) loosely packed. Reserve any extra beets for another use. Set aside.

2. Meanwhile, in a large non-reactive bowl, combine horseradish, onion and salt. Cover and let stand at a cool room temperature for 2 hours.

3. Prepare canner, jars and lids (see pages 7 to 8).

4. In a colander lined with cheesecloth, working in batches, drain horseradish mixture and rinse well. Drain again and squeeze out excess liquid. Set aside in colander to continue draining.

5. In a large pot, combine sugar, pepper and vinegar. Bring to a boil over medium heat, stirring often until sugar is dissolved. Increase heat to medium-high and add drained horseradish mixture and beets; return to a boil, stirring often. Reduce heat and boil gently, stirring often, for about 15 minutes or until vegetables are tender and mixture is slightly thickened.

6. Ladle hot relish into hot jars, leaving ½ inch (1 cm) headspace. Remove air bubbles and adjust headspace as necessary by adding hot relish. Wipe rim and place hot lid disc on jar. Screw band down until fingertip-tight.

7. Place jars in canner and return to a boil. Process for 15 minutes. Turn off heat and remove canner lid. Let jars stand in water for 5 minutes. Transfer jars to a towel-lined surface and let stand for 24 hours. Check lids and refrigerate any jars that are not sealed.

Harvard Beet Relish

This is a take on the classic side dish of diced beets with a sweet and tangy sauce. Its simplicity is what makes it so wonderful — the flavor of beets really shines.

Makes about five 8-ounce (250 mL) jars

• • •

4 lbs	beets (about 12)	2 kg
2 cups	granulated sugar	500 mL
1 tbsp	pickling or canning salt	15 mL
½ tsp	freshly ground black pepper	2 mL
2 cups	cider vinegar	500 mL

Tip

The cooking time for the beets in step 1 is based on 12 medium beets. If you have smaller or larger beets, adjust the cooking time in step 1 accordingly.

Serving Suggestion

Warm beet relish in a saucepan over medium heat until simmering. Whisk in 2 tsp (10 mL) cornstarch dissolved in 2 tbsp (25 mL) cold water per 8-ounce (250 mL) jar and cook, stirring, for 2 minutes, until thickened. Stir in 1 tbsp (15 mL) butter at the end for a rich finish. Serve as a side dish with baked ham, roast chicken or pork chops.

1. Trim beets and place in a large pot. Cover with cold water and bring to a boil over high heat. Reduce heat and boil gently for about 40 minutes or until fork-tender (see tip, at left). Immediately plunge into a large bowl or sink of cold water and let stand until well chilled, refreshing water as necessary to keep cold, for at least 30 minutes or for up to 1 hour. Peel off skins and finely dice enough beets to make 5 cups (1.25 L). Set aside.

2. In a food processor, purée the remaining beets until smooth. Measure 1 cup (250 mL). Reserve any extra beet purée for another use. Set aside.

3. Meanwhile, prepare canner, jars and lids (see pages 7 to 8).

4. In a large pot, combine sugar, salt, pepper and vinegar. Bring to a boil over medium heat, stirring often until sugar and salt are dissolved. Increase heat to medium-high and add diced and puréed beets; return to a boil, stirring often. Reduce heat and boil gently, stirring often, for about 10 minutes or until mixture is slightly thickened.

5. Ladle hot relish into hot jars, leaving ½ inch (1 cm) headspace. Remove air bubbles and adjust headspace as necessary by adding hot relish. Wipe rim and place hot lid disc on jar. Screw band down until fingertip-tight.

6. Place jars in canner and return to a boil. Process for 15 minutes. Turn off heat and remove canner lid. Let jars stand in water for 5 minutes. Transfer jars to a towel-lined surface and let stand for 24 hours. Check lids and refrigerate any jars that are not sealed.

Corn and Cucumber Relish

When the late summer harvest is at its peak and corn and cucumbers are plentiful, combine them in this colorful, tangy relish. It's perfect on grilled burgers, hot dogs and sausages.

Makes about eleven 8-ounce (250 mL) or five to six pint (500 mL) jars

● ● ●

Tips

To cook the corn, boil it in a large pot of boiling water, in batches as necessary, for about 5 minutes or until kernels are tender. Using tongs, remove from water and drain well. Let cool completely. Using a serrated knife, cut kernels from cob and measure. You'll need about 9 cobs of corn to get 6 cups (1.5 L) kernels.

If you use 8-ounce (250 mL) jars, they may not all fit in your canner at once. Let extra jars cool, then refrigerate them and use them up first. To avoid this problem, I like to pack some in pint (500 mL) jars and some in 8-ounce (250 mL) jars. That way, I also have different sizes and can open the size I know I'll use up within a few weeks.

1¾ cups	granulated sugar	425 mL
2 tbsp	pickling or canning salt	25 mL
2 tbsp	dry mustard	25 mL
1 tbsp	celery seeds	15 mL
1 tsp	ground turmeric	5 mL
¼ tsp	freshly ground black pepper	1 mL
2¾ cups	white vinegar	675 mL
6 cups	cooked corn kernels (see tip, at left)	1.5 L
2 cups	finely chopped onions	500 mL
1 cup	finely chopped celery	250 mL
4 cups	finely chopped pickling cucumbers (see tip, page 254)	1 L
1 cup	finely chopped red or green bell pepper	250 mL

1. Prepare canner, jars and lids (see pages 7 to 8).
2. In a large pot, combine sugar, salt, mustard, celery seeds, turmeric, pepper and vinegar. Bring to a boil over medium heat, stirring often until sugar and salt are dissolved. Increase heat to medium-high and add corn, onions and celery; return to a boil, stirring often. Reduce heat and boil gently, stirring often, for about 20 minutes or until onions and celery are tender. Stir in cucumbers and red pepper; boil gently, stirring often, for about 15 minutes or until cucumbers are translucent and mixture is slightly thickened
3. Ladle hot relish into hot jars, leaving ½ inch (1 cm) headspace. Remove air bubbles and adjust headspace as necessary by adding hot relish. Wipe rim and place hot lid disc on jar. Screw band down until fingertip-tight.
4. Place jars in canner and return to a boil. Process for 15 minutes. Turn off heat and remove canner lid. Let jars stand in water for 5 minutes. Transfer jars to a towel-lined surface and let stand for 24 hours. Check lids and refrigerate any jars that are not sealed.

Grilled Corn Relish

A hint of smoky flavor accents this traditional corn relish, making it perfect to eat in winter, when the grill is buried in snow. The ancho chiles add another layer of smoky flavor without adding heat, but you can leave them out if they're not available.

Makes about eleven 8-ounce (250 mL) or five to six pint (500 mL) jars

● ● ●

Tip

If you use 8-ounce (250 mL) jars, they may not all fit in your canner at once. Let extra jars cool, then refrigerate them and use them up first. To avoid this problem, I like to pack some in pint (500 mL) jars and some in 8-ounce (250 mL) jars. That way, I also have different sizes and can open the size I know I'll use up within a few weeks.

● **Preheat barbecue grill to medium**

12	cobs corn, shucked	12
3	dried ancho chile peppers	3
1 cup	boiling water	250 mL
1¾ cups	granulated sugar	425 mL
2 tbsp	pickling or canning salt	25 mL
1 tbsp	celery seeds	15 mL
¼ tsp	ground turmeric	1 mL
2¾ cups	cider vinegar	675 mL
½ cup	water	125 mL
2 cups	finely chopped onions	500 mL
1½ cups	finely chopped celery	375 mL
1 cup	finely chopped cubanelle or other mild peppers	250 mL

1. Prepare canner, jars and lids (see pages 7 to 8).
2. In a large pot of boiling water, boil corn, in batches as necessary, for about 3 minutes or until just starting to turn bright yellow. Using tongs, remove from water and drain well. Place corn on preheated barbecue grill and close lid. Grill, turning often, for about 10 minutes or until kernels are tender and slightly browned. Let cool completely. Using a serrated knife, cut kernels from cob and measure 8 cups (2 L).
3. Meanwhile, in a heatproof bowl, combine chile peppers and boiling water. Let stand for 30 minutes or until softened. Remove peppers from liquid, discarding liquid. Discard stems and seeds and finely chop peppers.
4. In a large pot, combine sugar, salt, celery seeds, turmeric, vinegar and water. Bring to a boil over medium heat, stirring often until sugar and salt are dissolved. Increase heat to medium-high and add corn, onions, celery and cubanelle peppers; return to a boil, stirring often. Reduce heat and boil gently, stirring often, for about 30 minutes or until onions and celery are tender and mixture is slightly thickened. Stir in chile peppers and boil gently, stirring often, for 1 minute.

5. Ladle hot relish into hot jars, leaving $\frac{1}{2}$ inch (1 cm) headspace. Remove air bubbles and adjust headspace as necessary by adding hot relish. Wipe rim and place hot lid disc on jar. Screw band down until fingertip-tight.

6. Place jars in canner and return to a boil. Process for 15 minutes. Turn off heat and remove canner lid. Let jars stand in water for 5 minutes. Transfer jars to a towel-lined surface and let stand for 24 hours. Check lids and refrigerate any jars that are not sealed.

Variation

If you like a touch of heat, use dried hot New Mexico chile peppers instead of the ancho chiles.

Corn Zucchini Relish

I'm fortunate to live about 3 minutes away from Martin and Linda Jackson's farm, where they grow the most wonderful sweet corn. Martin's mom, Sylvia, generously shared her recipe for corn relish with me. Sylvia makes an enormous batch (starting with 32 cups/8 L of corn kernels) so she has enough to enjoy and to sell at the corn stand. I've scaled the recipe down but kept the fantastic flavor.

Makes about twelve 8-ounce (250 mL) or six pint (500 mL) jars

• • •

Tips

To cook the corn, boil it in a large pot of boiling water, in batches as necessary, for about 5 minutes or until kernels are tender. Using tongs, remove from water and drain well. Let cool completely. Using a serrated knife, cut kernels from cob and measure. You'll need about 12 cobs of corn to get 8 cups (2 L).

If you use 8-ounce (250 mL) jars, they may not all fit in your canner at once. Let extra jars cool, then refrigerate them and use them up first. To avoid this problem, I like to pack some in pint (500 mL) jars and some in 8-ounce (250 mL) jars. That way, I also have different sizes and can open the size I know I'll use up within a few weeks.

8 cups	cooked corn kernels (see tip, at left)	2 L
2 cups	finely chopped zucchini	500 mL
1½ cups	finely chopped onions	375 mL
1½ cups	finely chopped celery	375 mL
1 cup	finely chopped red bell pepper	250 mL
1 cup	finely chopped green bell pepper	250 mL
2 cups	granulated sugar	500 mL
¼ cup	dry mustard	50 mL
2 tbsp	pickling or canning salt	25 mL
1 tbsp	ground ginger	15 mL
1 tbsp	celery seeds	15 mL
1 tsp	ground turmeric	5 mL
½ tsp	hot pepper flakes	2 mL
2½ cups	cider vinegar	625 mL

1. Prepare canner, jars and lids (see pages 7 to 8).
2. In a large pot, combine corn, zucchini, onions, celery, red and green peppers, sugar, mustard, salt, ginger, celery seeds, turmeric, hot pepper flakes and vinegar. Bring to a boil over medium heat, stirring often until sugar and salt are dissolved. Reduce heat and boil gently, stirring often, for about 30 minutes or until onions and celery are tender and mixture is slightly thickened.
3. Ladle hot relish into hot jars, leaving ½ inch (1 cm) headspace. Remove air bubbles and adjust headspace as necessary by adding hot relish. Wipe rim and place hot lid disc on jar. Screw band down until fingertip-tight.
4. Place jars in canner and return to a boil. Process for 15 minutes. Turn off heat and remove canner lid. Let jars stand in water for 5 minutes. Transfer jars to a towel-lined surface and let stand for 24 hours. Check lids and refrigerate any jars that are not sealed.

Corn, Roasted Sweet Pepper and Basil Relish

Sweet corn with roasted red bell peppers and basil is one of my favorite flavor combinations to add to salads and pastas. Here, I took a traditional corn relish and jazzed it up with roasted peppers and basil. The results are just as I'd hoped: fantastic!

Makes about ten 8-ounce (250 mL) or five pint (500 mL) jars

● ● ●

Tip

To cook the corn, boil it in a large pot of boiling water, in batches as necessary, for about 5 minutes or until kernels are tender. Using tongs, remove from water and drain well. Let cool completely. Using a serrated knife, cut kernels from cob and measure. You'll need about 12 cobs of corn to get 8 cups (2 L) kernels.

● **Preheat broiler or preheat barbecue grill to medium**

4	large red bell peppers	4
1¾ cups	granulated sugar	425 mL
2 tbsp	pickling or canning salt	25 mL
1 tbsp	each celery seeds and mustard seeds	15 mL
½ tsp	ground turmeric	2 mL
3 cups	cider vinegar	750 mL
8 cups	cooked corn kernels (see tip, at left)	2 L
1½ cups	finely chopped onions	375 mL
1 cup	finely chopped celery	250 mL
¼ cup	chopped fresh basil	50 mL

1. Prepare canner, jars and lids (see pages 7 to 8).
2. If using broiler, place red peppers on a baking sheet. Broil or grill, turning often, for about 20 minutes or until blackened on all sides. Transfer to a bowl, cover with plastic wrap and let cool completely. Peel off skins and remove stems, cores and seeds. Discard any accumulated liquid. Chop peppers and measure 2 cups (500 mL). Reserve any remaining peppers for another use.
3. Meanwhile, in a large pot, combine sugar, salt, celery seeds, mustard seeds, turmeric and vinegar. Bring to a boil over medium heat, stirring often until sugar and salt are dissolved. Increase heat to medium-high and stir in corn, onions and celery; return to a boil, stirring often. Reduce heat and boil gently, stirring often, for about 30 minutes or until onions and celery are tender and mixture is slightly thickened. Stir in roasted peppers and boil gently, stirring often, for about 5 minutes or until peppers are hot. Stir in basil.
4. Ladle hot relish into hot jars, leaving ½ inch (1 cm) headspace. Remove air bubbles and adjust headspace as necessary by adding hot relish. Wipe rim and place hot lid disc on jar. Screw band down until fingertip-tight.
5. Place jars in canner and return to a boil. Process for 15 minutes. Turn off heat and remove canner lid. Let jars stand in water for 5 minutes. Transfer jars to a towel-lined surface and let stand for 24 hours. Check lids and refrigerate any jars that are not sealed.

Sweet Green Relish

You can't go wrong with this plain and simple, classic green relish.

Makes about seven 8-ounce (250 mL) jars

• • •

Tip

Pickling cucumbers have a nice firm texture for relish. If they aren't available, peeled and seeded field cucumbers can be used instead, though the color of the relish will be pale.

Day 1

10 cups	finely chopped pickling cucumbers (see tip, at left)	2.5 L
1/3 cup	pickling or canning salt	75 mL

Day 2

2 1/2 cups	granulated sugar	625 mL
1/4 tsp	freshly ground black pepper	1 mL
2 cups	white vinegar	500 mL

Day 1

1. In a large non-reactive bowl, combine cucumbers and salt. Add cold water to cover by 1 inch (2.5 cm). Place a plate on top to weigh down cucumbers. Cover and let stand at a cool room temperature for at least 8 hours or for up to 18 hours.

Day 2

1. Prepare canner, jars and lids (see pages 7 to 8).
2. In a colander lined with cheesecloth, working in batches, drain cucumbers and rinse well. Drain again and squeeze out excess liquid. Set aside in colander to continue draining.
3. In a large pot, combine sugar, pepper and vinegar. Bring to a boil over medium heat, stirring often until sugar is dissolved. Increase heat to medium-high, add drained cucumbers and return to a boil, stirring often. Reduce heat and boil gently, stirring often, for about 15 minutes or until cucumbers are translucent and mixture is slightly thickened.
4. Ladle hot relish into hot jars, leaving 1/2 inch (1 cm) headspace. Remove air bubbles and adjust headspace as necessary by adding hot relish. Wipe rim and place hot lid disc on jar. Screw band down until fingertip-tight.
5. Place jars in canner and return to a boil. Process for 10 minutes. Turn off heat and remove canner lid. Let jars stand in water for 5 minutes. Transfer jars to a towel-lined surface and let stand for 24 hours. Check lids and refrigerate any jars that are not sealed.

Dill Cucumber Relish

Dill adds an herby freshness to this tangy relish. It's a natural to serve on grilled burgers or fish.

Makes about seven 8-ounce (250 mL) jars

● ● ●

Tips

Pickling cucumbers have a nice firm texture for relish. If they aren't available, peeled and seeded field cucumbers can be used instead, though the color of the relish will be pale.

Use the feathery fresh dill sprigs, rather than the more mature dill heads, for the best flavor and texture in this relish.

Day 1

8 cups	finely chopped pickling cucumbers (see tip, at left)	2 L
2 cups	finely chopped onions	500 mL
⅓ cup	pickling or canning salt	75 mL

Day 2

1½ cups	granulated sugar	375 mL
1 tbsp	dill seeds	15 mL
2 tsp	mustard seeds	10 mL
3½ cups	white vinegar	875 mL
¼ cup	finely chopped fresh dill	50 mL

Day 1

1. In a large non-reactive bowl, combine cucumbers, onions and salt. Add cold water to cover by 1 inch (2.5 cm). Place a plate on top to weigh down vegetables. Cover and let stand at a cool room temperature for at least 8 hours or for up to 18 hours.

Day 2

1. Prepare canner, jars and lids (see pages 7 to 8).
2. In a colander lined with cheesecloth, working in batches, drain vegetables and rinse well. Drain again and squeeze out excess liquid. Set aside in colander to continue draining.
3. In a large pot, combine sugar, dill seeds, mustard seeds and vinegar. Bring to a boil over medium heat, stirring often until sugar is dissolved. Increase heat to medium-high, add drained vegetables and return to a boil, stirring often. Reduce heat and boil gently, stirring often, for about 15 minutes or until vegetables are translucent and mixture is slightly thickened. Stir in fresh dill and boil gently, stirring, for 1 minute.
4. Ladle hot relish into hot jars, leaving ½ inch (1 cm) headspace. Remove air bubbles and adjust headspace as necessary by adding hot relish. Wipe rim and place hot lid disc on jar. Screw band down until fingertip-tight.
5. Place jars in canner and return to a boil. Process for 10 minutes. Turn off heat and remove canner lid. Let jars stand in water for 5 minutes. Transfer jars to a towel-lined surface and let stand for 24 hours. Check lids and refrigerate any jars that are not sealed.

Hot Dog Relish

Once you taste this slightly zesty, sweet and tangy relish, you'll be using it on much more than hot dogs. Try it on grilled fish, poultry and burgers too.

Makes about eight 8-ounce (250 mL) jars

● ● ●

Tips

Pickling cucumbers have a nice firm texture for relish. If they aren't available, peeled and seeded field cucumbers can be used instead, though the color of the relish will be pale.

For this relish, I prefer to chop the vegetables by hand, but you can use the metal blade and pulse function of a food processor if you prefer. Just be sure not to purée them. Chop each vegetable separately and measure after chopping.

Day 1

1	long hot red chile pepper, seeded and minced	1
4 cups	finely chopped pickling cucumbers (see tip, at left)	1 L
2½ cups	finely chopped celery	625 mL
2 cups	finely chopped onions	500 mL
1½ cups	finely chopped green or red bell peppers	375 mL
⅓ cup	pickling or canning salt	75 mL

Day 2

2½ cups	granulated sugar	625 mL
1 tbsp	celery seeds	15 mL
2 tsp	mustard seeds	10 mL
3 cups	white vinegar	750 mL

Day 1

1. In a large non-reactive bowl, combine chile pepper, cucumbers, celery, onions, green peppers and salt. Add cold water to cover by 1 inch (2.5 cm). Place a plate on top to weigh down vegetables. Cover and let stand at a cool room temperature for at least 8 hours or for up to 18 hours.

Day 2

1. Prepare canner, jars and lids (see pages 7 to 8).
2. In a colander lined with cheesecloth, working in batches, drain vegetables and rinse well. Drain again and squeeze out excess liquid. Set aside in colander to continue draining.
3. In a large pot, combine sugar, celery seeds, mustard seeds and vinegar. Bring to a boil over medium heat, stirring often until sugar is dissolved. Increase heat to medium-high, add drained vegetables and return to a boil, stirring often. Reduce heat and boil gently, stirring often, for about 15 minutes or until vegetables are translucent and mixture is slightly thickened.
4. Ladle hot relish into hot jars, leaving ½ inch (1 cm) headspace. Remove air bubbles and adjust headspace as necessary by adding hot relish. Wipe rim and place hot lid disc on jar. Screw band down until fingertip-tight.
5. Place jars in canner and return to a boil. Process for 10 minutes. Turn off heat and remove canner lid. Let jars stand in water for 5 minutes. Transfer jars to a towel-lined surface and let stand for 24 hours. Check lids and refrigerate any jars that are not sealed.

Mustard and Relish Combo

Save time dressing your burgers and hot dogs with this sweet and tangy blend of mustard and relish in one.

Makes about seven 8-ounce (250 mL) jars

● ● ●

Tip

Pickling cucumbers have a nice firm texture for relish. If they aren't available, peeled and seeded field cucumbers can be used instead, though the color of the relish will be pale.

Variation

For a spicy version, add ½ to 1 tsp (2 to 5 mL) cayenne pepper with the other spices.

Day 1

10 cups	finely chopped pickling cucumbers	2.5 L
⅓ cup	pickling or canning salt	75 mL

Day 2

2 cups	packed brown sugar	500 mL
¼ cup	dry mustard	50 mL
1 tsp	ground turmeric	5 mL
¼ tsp	freshly ground black pepper	1 mL
¼ tsp	paprika	1 mL
2½ cups	cider vinegar	625 mL

Day 1

1. In a large non-reactive bowl, combine cucumbers and salt. Add cold water to cover by 1 inch (2.5 cm). Place a plate on top to weigh down cucumbers. Cover and let stand at a cool room temperature for at least 8 hours or for up to 18 hours.

Day 2

1. Prepare canner, jars and lids (see pages 7 to 8).
2. In a colander lined with cheesecloth, working in batches, drain cucumbers and rinse well. Drain again and squeeze out excess liquid. Set aside in colander to continue draining.
3. In a large pot, combine brown sugar, mustard, turmeric, pepper and paprika. Gradually whisk in vinegar. Bring to a boil over medium heat, stirring often until sugar is dissolved. Increase heat to medium-high, add drained cucumbers and return to a boil, stirring often. Reduce heat and boil gently, stirring often, for about 15 minutes or until cucumbers are translucent and mixture is slightly thickened.
4. Ladle hot relish into hot jars, leaving ½ inch (1 cm) headspace. Remove air bubbles and adjust headspace as necessary by adding hot relish. Wipe rim and place hot lid disc on jar. Screw band down until fingertip-tight.
5. Place jars in canner and return to a boil. Process for 10 minutes. Turn off heat and remove canner lid. Let jars stand in water for 5 minutes. Transfer jars to a towel-lined surface and let stand for 24 hours. Check lids and refrigerate any jars that are not sealed.

Sweet and Hot Pepper Relish

A colorful and flavorful blend of peppers creates a relish with a nice balance of sweetness, tang and heat.

Makes about six 8-ounce (250 mL) jars

• • •

Variations

If sweet banana peppers aren't available, substitute an equal amount of other mild peppers, such as cubanelle, Anaheim or orange or yellow bell peppers.

This version is moderately hot. If you prefer a hotter relish, reduce the banana peppers to 1½ cups (375 mL) and increase cayenne peppers to 1 cup (250 mL).

4 cups	diced red bell peppers	1 L
3 cups	diced green bell peppers	750 mL
2 cups	diced sweet banana peppers	500 mL
1½ cups	finely chopped onions	375 mL
½ cup	finely chopped seeded cayenne or other hot red chile peppers	125 mL
⅓ cup	pickling or canning salt	75 mL
1½ cups	granulated sugar	375 mL
1 tbsp	celery seeds	15 mL
½ tsp	freshly ground black pepper	2 mL
2 cups	cider vinegar	500 mL

1. In a large non-reactive bowl, combine red and green peppers, banana peppers, onions, cayenne peppers and salt. Cover and let stand at a cool room temperature for 4 hours.
2. Meanwhile, prepare canner, jars and lids (see pages 7 to 8).
3. In a colander lined with cheesecloth, working in batches, drain vegetables and rinse well. Drain again and squeeze out excess liquid. Set aside in colander to continue draining.
4. In a large pot, combine sugar, celery seeds, black pepper and vinegar. Bring to a boil over medium heat, stirring often until sugar is dissolved. Increase heat to medium-high, add drained vegetables and return to a boil, stirring often. Reduce heat and simmer gently, stirring often, for about 15 minutes or just until cucumbers are translucent and vegetables are heated through.
5. Ladle hot relish into hot jars, leaving ½ inch (1 cm) headspace. Remove air bubbles and adjust headspace as necessary by adding hot relish. Wipe rim and place hot lid disc on jar. Screw band down until fingertip-tight.
6. Place jars in canner and return to a boil. Process for 10 minutes. Turn off heat and remove canner lid. Let jars stand in water for 5 minutes. Transfer jars to a towel-lined surface and let stand for 24 hours. Check lids and refrigerate any jars that are not sealed.

Smoky Three-Pepper Cucumber Relish

The smokiness and heat from the chipotle add depth and interest to this colorful relish that will tantalize your taste buds.

Makes five to six 8-ounce (250 mL) jars

4 cups	diced seeded cucumbers	1 L
3 cups	diced red bell peppers	750 mL
3 cups	diced cubanelle peppers	750 mL
1 cup	finely chopped onion	250 mL
$\frac{1}{3}$ cup	pickling or canning salt	75 mL
2 cups	white vinegar, divided	500 mL
1	dried chipotle pepper	1
$1\frac{1}{2}$ cups	granulated sugar	375 mL
2 tbsp	mustard seeds	25 mL

Tip

Chipotle peppers are smoked jalapeño peppers. They pack quite a punch of heat and smoky flavor. Dried chipotles are often available in the produce section of well-stocked supermarkets and at specialty food stores.

Serving Suggestions

Use this relish to add pizzazz to hot dogs and hamburgers.

Spread onto flour tortillas and top with cheese for a different twist on a quesadilla.

1. In a large non-reactive bowl, combine cucumbers, red peppers, cubanelle peppers, onion and salt. Cover and let stand at a cool room temperature for 4 hours.

2. Meanwhile, in a saucepan or in the microwave, heat $\frac{1}{2}$ cup (125 mL) of the vinegar until steaming. Add chipotle pepper and let soak for about 2 hours or until very soft. Drain chipotle, reserving liquid. Discard stem and seeds and finely chop. Set aside.

3. Prepare canner, jars and lids (see pages 7 to 8).

4. In a colander lined with cheesecloth, working in batches, drain vegetables and rinse well. Drain again and squeeze out excess liquid. Set aside in colander to continue draining.

5. In a large pot, combine chipotle soaking liquid, the remaining vinegar, sugar and mustard seeds. Bring to a boil over medium heat, stirring often until sugar is dissolved. Increase heat to medium-high and add drained vegetables and chopped chipotle; return to a boil, stirring often. Reduce heat and simmer gently, stirring often, for about 15 minutes or just until cucumbers are translucent and mixture is slightly thickened.

6. Ladle hot relish into hot jars, leaving $\frac{1}{2}$ inch (1 cm) headspace. Remove air bubbles and adjust headspace as necessary by adding hot relish. Wipe rim and place hot lid disc on jar. Screw band down until fingertip-tight.

7. Place jars in canner and return to a boil. Process for 10 minutes. Turn off heat and remove canner lid. Let jars stand in water for 5 minutes. Transfer jars to a towel-lined surface and let stand for 24 hours. Check lids and refrigerate any jars that are not sealed.

Hot and Sweet Pepper Balsamic Relish

I really enjoy a hot and sweet pepper balsamic jelly I make, so I took the same flavors and turned them into a zesty relish.

Makes about five 8-ounce (250 mL) jars

• • • •

Tips

To avoid burns, wear disposable rubber gloves when handling hot peppers and be sure to wash all utensils and the cutting board well after preparing the peppers.

The balsamic vinegar does darken the relish, but the flavor is fantastic. If you prefer a lighter color, use white balsamic vinegar instead; just make sure it is 6% acid.

Serving Suggestions

Spread softened cream cheese on crackers and spoon this relish on top.

Use relish as a glaze during the last minute or two when grilling or broiling fish.

6 cups	finely chopped red bell peppers	1.5 L
2 cups	finely chopped onions	500 mL
1 cup	finely chopped seeded cayenne or other hot red chile peppers	250 mL
¼ cup	pickling or canning salt	50 mL
1¼ cups	granulated sugar	300 mL
½ tsp	freshly ground black pepper	2 mL
1 cup	white vinegar	250 mL
¾ cup	balsamic vinegar	175 mL

1. In a large non-reactive bowl, combine red peppers, onions, cayenne peppers and salt. Cover and let stand at a cool room temperature for 4 hours.

2. Meanwhile, prepare canner, jars and lids (see pages 7 to 8).

3. In a colander lined with cheesecloth, working in batches, drain vegetables and rinse well. Drain again and squeeze out excess liquid. Set aside in colander to continue draining.

4. In a large pot, combine sugar, black pepper, white vinegar and balsamic vinegar. Bring to a boil over medium heat, stirring often until sugar is dissolved. Increase heat to medium-high, add drained vegetables and return to a boil, stirring often. Reduce heat and simmer gently, stirring often, for about 10 minutes or until onions are translucent and mixture is slightly thickened.

5. Ladle hot relish into hot jars, leaving ½ inch (1 cm) headspace. Remove air bubbles and adjust headspace as necessary by adding hot relish. Wipe rim and place hot lid disc on jar. Screw band down until fingertip-tight.

6. Place jars in canner and return to a boil. Process for 10 minutes. Turn off heat and remove canner lid. Let jars stand in water for 5 minutes. Transfer jars to a towel-lined surface and let stand for 24 hours. Check lids and refrigerate any jars that are not sealed.

Carrot and Fennel Relish

The subtle taste of licorice and the sweetness of carrots pair well in this simple relish.

Makes about six 8-ounce (250 mL) jars

● ● ●

Tips

You'll need about 1¾ lbs (875 g) carrots to get 5 cups (1.25 L) shredded.

You'll need a little less than 2 small fennel bulbs to get 5 cups (1.25 L) finely chopped. Any extra fennel can be thinly sliced and sautéed to add to pasta or used raw in a salad.

Serving Suggestions

Serve on grilled poultry or pork.

Top a fish fillet with this relish and bake *en papillote*.

5 cups	shredded carrots	1.25 L
5 cups	finely chopped fennel bulb	1.25 L
1 cup	finely chopped onion	250 mL
2 tbsp	pickling or canning salt	25 mL
2 cups	granulated sugar	500 mL
1 tsp	cracked black peppercorns	5 mL
2 cups	white wine vinegar	500 mL

1. In a large non-reactive bowl, combine carrots, fennel, onion and salt. Cover and let stand at a cool room temperature for 2 hours.
2. Meanwhile, prepare canner, jars and lids (see pages 7 to 8).
3. In a colander lined with cheesecloth, working in batches, drain vegetables and rinse well. Drain again and squeeze out excess liquid. Set aside in colander to continue draining.
4. In a large pot, combine sugar, peppercorns and vinegar. Bring to a boil over medium heat, stirring often until sugar is dissolved. Increase heat to medium-high, add drained vegetables and return to a boil, stirring often. Reduce heat and boil gently, stirring often, for about 15 minutes or until vegetables are translucent and mixture is slightly thickened.
5. Ladle hot relish into hot jars, leaving ½ inch (1 cm) headspace. Remove air bubbles and adjust headspace as necessary by adding hot relish. Wipe rim and place hot lid disc on jar. Screw band down until fingertip-tight.
6. Place jars in canner and return to a boil. Process for 10 minutes. Turn off heat and remove canner lid. Let jars stand in water for 5 minutes. Transfer jars to a towel-lined surface and let stand for 24 hours. Check lids and refrigerate any jars that are not sealed.

Carrot and Onion Relish

When you have a bumper crop of sweet, juicy carrots, this savory relish is a lovely way to capture their flavor.

**Makes about
five 8-ounce
(250 mL) jars**

• • •

Tips

You'll need about
2¾ lbs (1.375 kg)
carrots to get 8 cups
(2 L) shredded.

Make quick work
of shredding the
carrots by using a
food processor
fitted with the large
shredding blade.

**Serving
Suggestions**

Toss this relish with
cooked potatoes and
mayonnaise or sour
cream for a quick
salad.

Serve on burgers for
a twist on traditional
toppings.

8 cups	shredded carrots	2 L
2 cups	finely chopped onions	500 mL
2 tbsp	pickling or canning salt	25 mL
1¾ cups	granulated sugar	425 mL
2 tsp	celery seeds	10 mL
1 tsp	dried thyme	5 mL
½ tsp	freshly ground black pepper	2 mL
2 cups	cider vinegar	500 mL
1 tbsp	minced garlic	15 mL

1. In a large non-reactive bowl, combine carrots, onions and salt. Cover and let stand at a cool room temperature for 2 hours.
2. Meanwhile, prepare canner, jars and lids (see pages 7 to 8).
3. In a colander lined with cheesecloth, working in batches, drain vegetables and rinse well. Drain again and squeeze out excess liquid. Set aside in colander to continue draining.
4. In a large pot, combine sugar, celery seeds, thyme, pepper and vinegar. Bring to a boil over medium heat, stirring often until sugar is dissolved. Increase heat to medium-high and add drained vegetables and garlic; return to a boil, stirring often. Reduce heat and boil gently, stirring often, for about 15 minutes or until vegetables are translucent and mixture is slightly thickened.
5. Ladle hot relish into hot jars, leaving ½ inch (1 cm) headspace. Remove air bubbles and adjust headspace as necessary by adding hot relish. Wipe rim and place hot lid disc on jar. Screw band down until fingertip-tight.
6. Place jars in canner and return to a boil. Process for 10 minutes. Turn off heat and remove canner lid. Let jars stand in water for 5 minutes. Transfer jars to a towel-lined surface and let stand for 24 hours. Check lids and refrigerate any jars that are not sealed.

Carrot and Red Pepper Relish

Sweet carrots and red peppers are a terrific combination. This colorful relish just might become one of your all-purpose condiments. It's delicious on fish, poultry and pork and even as an easy garnish for a green salad, using some of the liquid for the dressing.

Makes about six 8-ounce (250 mL) jars

• • •

Tips

You'll need about 2 lbs (1 kg) carrots to get 6 cups (1.5 L) shredded.

Make quick work of shredding the carrots by using a food processor fitted with the large shredding blade.

The red peppers can be chopped using the metal cutting blade of a food processor, but make sure to use the pulse function and chop them without letting them get juicy.

6 cups	shredded carrots	1.5 L
4 cups	finely chopped red bell peppers	1 L
1 cup	finely chopped onion	250 mL
2 tbsp	pickling or canning salt	25 mL
2 cups	granulated sugar	500 mL
1 tbsp	mustard seeds	15 mL
2 tsp	celery seeds	10 mL
2 cups	cider vinegar	500 mL
1 tbsp	minced gingerroot	15 mL

1. In a large non-reactive bowl, combine carrots, red peppers, onion and salt. Cover and let stand at a cool room temperature for 2 hours.
2. Meanwhile, prepare canner, jars and lids (see pages 7 to 8).
3. In a colander lined with cheesecloth, working in batches, drain vegetables and rinse well. Drain again and squeeze out excess liquid. Set aside in colander to continue draining.
4. In a large pot, combine sugar, mustard seeds, celery seeds and vinegar. Bring to a boil over medium heat, stirring often until sugar is dissolved. Increase heat to medium-high and add drained vegetables and ginger; return to a boil, stirring often. Reduce heat and boil gently, stirring often, for about 15 minutes or until vegetables are translucent and mixture is slightly thickened.
5. Ladle hot relish into hot jars, leaving ½ inch (1 cm) headspace. Remove air bubbles and adjust headspace as necessary by adding hot relish. Wipe rim and place hot lid disc on jar. Screw band down until fingertip-tight.
6. Place jars in canner and return to a boil. Process for 10 minutes. Turn off heat and remove canner lid. Let jars stand in water for 5 minutes. Transfer jars to a towel-lined surface and let stand for 24 hours. Check lids and refrigerate any jars that are not sealed.

Clementine and Sweet Onion Relish

The abundance of clementines when they're in season is too tempting to resist; however, it's always tricky to use them up quickly enough. Make this relish and you'll enjoy the fresh clementine flavor all year long.

Makes about six to seven 8-ounce (250 mL) jars

● ● ●

Tips

There are many varieties of sweet onions available: look for Vidalia, Oso Sweet, Maui, Walla Walla or Spanish, to name a few.

This is one of the few times I prefer the food processor for chopping the fruit. If you don't have one, finely chop the clementines using a sharp serrated knife.

This relish thickens quite a bit upon cooling, so don't worry if it looks thin when the clementine peel is tender.

Serving Suggestion

Serve on grilled fish or poultry, or with curried chicken or beef satay.

4 cups	chopped sweet onions	1 L
2 tbsp	pickling or canning salt	25 mL
12	clementines or tangerines	12
1	bay leaf	1
1½ cups	granulated sugar	375 mL
1 tbsp	mustard seeds	15 mL
½ tsp	dried thyme	2 mL
½ tsp	freshly ground black pepper	2 mL
1 cup	cider vinegar	250 mL

1. Prepare canner, jars and lids (see pages 7 to 8).
2. In a large, non-reactive bowl, combine onions and salt. Cover and let stand at a cool room temperature for 30 minutes. In a colander lined with cheesecloth, working in batches, drain onions and rinse well. Drain again and squeeze out excess liquid. Set aside in colander to continue draining.
3. Cut clementines into quarters and remove seeds. In a food processor, pulse clementines (flesh and peel) until finely chopped. Measure 4 cups (1 L). Reserve any extra for another use.
4. In a large pot, combine clementines, bay leaf, sugar, mustard seeds, thyme, pepper and vinegar. Bring to a boil over medium heat, stirring until sugar is dissolved. Add drained onions and return to a boil, stirring often. Reduce heat and simmer, stirring often, for about 10 minutes or until clementine peel is tender. Discard bay leaf.
5. Ladle hot relish into hot jars, leaving ½ inch (1 cm) headspace. Remove air bubbles and adjust headspace as necessary by adding hot relish. Wipe rim and place hot lid disc on jar. Screw band down until fingertip-tight.
6. Place jars in canner and return to a boil. Process for 10 minutes. Turn off heat and remove canner lid. Let jars stand in water for 5 minutes. Transfer jars to a towel-lined surface and let stand for 24 hours. Check lids and refrigerate any jars that are not sealed.

Cranberry Orange Relish

Draining the juice from the cranberries and onions gives a crunchy, fresh texture to relish that is quite distinct from the jammy texture of cranberry sauce.

Makes about seven 8-ounce (250 mL) jars

● ● ●

Tips

The cranberries can be chopped using the metal cutting blade of a food processor, but make sure to use the pulse function and chop them without letting them get juicy.

Extra finely chopped orange can be added to muffin batter in place of some of the liquid in the recipe.

This relish thickens quite a bit upon cooling, so don't worry if it looks thin when the orange peel is tender.

6 cups	cranberries, chopped	1.5 L
2 cups	finely chopped onions	500 mL
2 tbsp	pickling or canning salt	25 mL
4	seedless oranges	4
2½ cups	granulated sugar	625 mL
½ tsp	freshly ground black pepper	2 mL
½ tsp	ground cinnamon	2 mL
¼ tsp	ground allspice	1 mL
1½ cups	white vinegar	375 mL

1. In a large non-reactive bowl, combine cranberries, onions and salt. Cover and let stand at a cool room temperature for 4 hours.
2. Meanwhile, prepare canner, jars and lids (see pages 7 to 8).
3. In a colander lined with cheesecloth, working in batches, drain cranberry mixture, squeezing out excess liquid. Set aside in colander to continue draining.
4. Cut oranges into quarters. In a food processor, pulse oranges (flesh and peel) until finely chopped. Measure 2 cups (500 mL). Reserve any extra for another use.
5. In a large pot, combine oranges, sugar, pepper, cinnamon, allspice and vinegar. Bring to a boil over medium heat, stirring until sugar is dissolved. Add drained cranberry mixture and return to a boil, stirring often. Reduce heat and boil gently, stirring often, for about 20 minutes or until orange peel is tender and mixture is slightly thickened.
6. Ladle hot relish into hot jars, leaving ½ inch (1 cm) headspace. Remove air bubbles and adjust headspace as necessary by adding hot relish. Wipe rim and place hot lid disc on jar. Screw band down until fingertip-tight.
7. Place jars in canner and return to a boil. Process for 10 minutes. Turn off heat and remove canner lid. Let jars stand in water for 5 minutes. Transfer jars to a towel-lined surface and let stand for 24 hours. Check lids and refrigerate any jars that are not sealed.

Savory Grape and Cranberry Relish

Rich purple grapes and tangy cranberries create a jewel-colored relish that is as vibrant in flavor as it is in color.

Makes about seven 8-ounce (250 mL) jars

• • •

Tips

Concord grapes add a rich grape flavor and deep purple color. If you can find the seedless Coronation variety, use them and avoid the work of seeding. Other juicy purple or red grapes can be used instead.

This relish thickens upon cooling, so don't worry if it looks thin at the end of step 4.

Serving Suggestions

Add to an appetizer platter with creamy cheeses and liver pâté.

Serve with roast turkey in place of plain cranberry sauce.

3 cups	cranberries, chopped	750 mL
3 cups	finely chopped red onions	750 mL
2 tbsp	pickling or canning salt	25 mL
1¾ cups	granulated sugar	425 mL
1 tsp	cracked black peppercorns	5 mL
½ tsp	dried thyme	2 mL
2 cups	red wine vinegar	500 mL
1 tbsp	minced gingerroot	15 mL
4 cups	Concord grapes, halved and seeded	1 L

1. In a large non-reactive bowl, combine cranberries, onions and salt. Cover and let stand at a cool room temperature for 4 hours.
2. Meanwhile, prepare canner, jars and lids (see pages 7 to 8).
3. In a colander lined with cheesecloth, working in batches, drain cranberry mixture, squeezing out excess liquid. Set aside in colander to continue draining.
4. In a large pot, combine sugar, peppercorns, thyme and vinegar. Bring to a boil over medium heat, stirring until sugar is dissolved. Add drained cranberry mixture and ginger; return to a boil, stirring often. Reduce heat and boil gently, stirring often, for about 15 minutes or until onions are translucent. Stir in grapes and boil gently, stirring often, for about 10 minutes or until fruit is soft and mixture is slightly thickened.
5. Ladle hot relish into hot jars, leaving ½ inch (1 cm) headspace. Remove air bubbles and adjust headspace as necessary by adding hot relish. Wipe rim and place hot lid disc on jar. Screw band down until fingertip-tight.
6. Place jars in canner and return to a boil. Process for 10 minutes. Turn off heat and remove canner lid. Let jars stand in water for 5 minutes. Transfer jars to a towel-lined surface and let stand for 24 hours. Check lids and refrigerate any jars that are not sealed.

Fiery Cranberry Jalapeño Relish

This colorful relish is simple to make, and its fiery tang will add zip to burgers or roast pork or poultry.

Makes about six 8-ounce (250 mL) jars

• • •

Tips

The cranberries can be chopped using the metal cutting blade of a food processor, but make sure to use the pulse function and chop them without letting them get juicy.

To avoid burns, wear disposable rubber gloves when handling hot peppers and be sure to wash all utensils and the cutting board well after preparing them.

6 cups	cranberries, chopped	1.5 L
2 cups	finely chopped red onions	500 mL
1 cup	finely chopped seeded jalapeño peppers	250 mL
2 tbsp	pickling or canning salt	25 mL
1¾ cups	granulated sugar	425 mL
1½ cups	white vinegar	375 mL

1. In a large non-reactive bowl, combine cranberries, onions, jalapeños and salt. Cover and let stand at a cool room temperature for 4 hours.
2. Meanwhile, prepare canner, jars and lids (see pages 7 to 8).
3. In a colander lined with cheesecloth, working in batches, drain cranberry mixture, squeezing out excess liquid. Set aside in colander to continue draining.
4. In a large pot, combine sugar and vinegar. Bring to a boil over medium heat, stirring until sugar is dissolved. Add drained cranberry mixture and return to a boil, stirring often. Reduce heat and boil gently, stirring often, for about 20 minutes or until onions are translucent and mixture is slightly thickened.
5. Ladle hot relish into hot jars, leaving ½ inch (1 cm) headspace. Remove air bubbles and adjust headspace as necessary by adding hot relish. Wipe rim and place hot lid disc on jar. Screw band down until fingertip-tight.
6. Place jars in canner and return to a boil. Process for 10 minutes. Turn off heat and remove canner lid. Let jars stand in water for 5 minutes. Transfer jars to a towel-lined surface and let stand for 24 hours. Check lids and refrigerate any jars that are not sealed.

Fennel, Sweet Pepper and Herb Relish

Add the flavor of French country cooking to seared tuna, steamed mussels or roast poultry with this fragrant relish.

Makes about six 8-ounce (250 mL) jars

● ● ●

Tip

You'll need a little less than 2 small fennel bulbs to get 5 cups (1.25 L) finely chopped. Any extra fennel can be thinly sliced and sautéed to add to pasta or used raw in a salad.

Variation

A touch of heat is also nice in this relish. Add ½ tsp (2 mL) hot pepper flakes with the black pepper.

5 cups	finely chopped fennel bulb	1.25 L
5 cups	finely chopped red bell peppers	1.25 L
1 cup	finely chopped onion	250 mL
2 tbsp	pickling or canning salt	25 mL
2 cups	granulated sugar	500 mL
½ tsp	freshly ground black pepper	2 mL
2 cups	white wine vinegar	500 mL
1 tbsp	minced garlic	15 mL
2 tbsp	chopped fresh basil	25 mL
2 tsp	chopped fresh thyme	10 mL
1 tsp	chopped fresh rosemary	5 mL

1. In a large non-reactive bowl, combine fennel, red peppers, onion and salt. Cover and let stand at a cool room temperature for 2 hours.
2. Meanwhile, prepare canner, jars and lids (see pages 7 to 8).
3. In a colander lined with cheesecloth, working in batches, drain vegetables and rinse well. Drain again and squeeze out excess liquid. Set aside in colander to continue draining.
4. In a large pot, combine sugar, pepper and vinegar. Bring to a boil over medium heat, stirring often until sugar is dissolved. Increase heat to medium-high and add drained vegetables and garlic; return to a boil, stirring often. Reduce heat and boil gently, stirring often, for about 15 minutes or until vegetables are translucent and mixture is slightly thickened. Stir in basil, thyme and rosemary.
5. Ladle hot relish into hot jars, leaving ½ inch (1 cm) headspace. Remove air bubbles and adjust headspace as necessary by adding hot relish. Wipe rim and place hot lid disc on jar. Screw band down until fingertip-tight.
6. Place jars in canner and return to a boil. Process for 10 minutes. Turn off heat and remove canner lid. Let jars stand in water for 5 minutes. Transfer jars to a towel-lined surface and let stand for 24 hours. Check lids and refrigerate any jars that are not sealed.

Red Radish Relish

Fast-growing radishes are one of the earliest crops of summer, and it's always exciting when the first ones are ready to be picked. This relish gives you a new way to use them, beyond the usual salads.

Makes about seven 8-ounce (250 mL) jars

● ● ●

Tip

This relish is prettiest when the vegetables are chopped by hand. It does take some time, but the results are worth it.

Serving Suggestions

Add relish to mayonnaise and use as a dressing for potato or tuna salad.

Serve on top of grilled fish.

4 cups	finely chopped red radishes	1 L
3 cups	finely chopped celery	750 mL
2 cups	finely chopped red bell peppers	500 mL
2 cups	finely chopped red onion	500 mL
2 tbsp	pickling or canning salt	25 mL
2 cups	granulated sugar	500 mL
1 tbsp	mustard seeds	15 mL
1 tbsp	dill seeds	15 mL
2 cups	white vinegar	500 mL

1. In a large pot, combine radishes, celery, red peppers, onion and salt. Cover and let stand at a cool room temperature for 1 hour.
2. Meanwhile, prepare canner, jars and lids (see pages 7 to 8).
3. Add sugar, mustard seeds, dill seeds and vinegar to vegetables. Bring to a boil over medium heat, stirring often until sugar is dissolved. Reduce heat and boil gently, stirring often, for about 15 minutes or until radishes and onions are translucent.
4. Ladle hot relish into hot jars, leaving $\frac{1}{2}$ inch (1 cm) headspace. Remove air bubbles and adjust headspace as necessary by adding hot relish. Wipe rim and place hot lid disc on jar. Screw band down until fingertip-tight.
5. Place jars in canner and return to a boil. Process for 10 minutes. Turn off heat and remove canner lid. Let jars stand in water for 5 minutes. Transfer jars to a towel-lined surface and let stand for 24 hours. Check lids and refrigerate any jars that are not sealed.

Mexican Green Tomato Relish

This is different from a salsa because of the firm texture of the vegetables and the sweeter taste, but it can be used to add Mexican flair to tacos, nachos and quesadillas just the same.

Makes about eight 8-ounce (250 mL) jars

● ● ●

Tip

Some heirloom tomato varieties are still green when ripe. Don't use that type for this relish — you want firm, unripened tomatoes for the right taste and texture.

Day 1

8 cups	chopped green tomatoes	2 L
2 cups	each chopped onions and green bell peppers	500 mL
¼ cup	pickling or canning salt	50 mL

Day 2

1 tbsp	cumin seeds	15 mL
1¼ cups	granulated sugar	300 mL
1½ cups	white vinegar	375 mL
½ cup	finely chopped seeded jalapeño peppers	125 mL
2 tbsp	minced garlic	25 mL
⅓ cup	freshly squeezed lime juice	75 mL
2 tbsp	chopped fresh cilantro	25 mL

Day 1

1. In a large non-reactive bowl, combine tomatoes, onions, green peppers and salt. Cover and let stand at a cool room temperature for at least 8 hours or for up to 18 hours.

Day 2

1. Prepare canner, jars and lids (see pages 7 to 8).
2. In a colander lined with cheesecloth, working in batches, drain vegetables and rinse well. Drain again and squeeze out excess liquid. Set aside in colander to continue draining.
3. In a dry skillet, over medium heat, toast cumin seeds, stirring, for about 1 minute or until fragrant and slightly darker but not yet popping. Immediately transfer to a large pot.
4. Add sugar and vinegar to the pot. Bring to a boil over medium heat, stirring often until sugar is dissolved. Increase heat to medium-high and add vegetables, jalapeños and garlic; return to a boil, stirring often. Reduce heat and boil gently, stirring often, for about 30 minutes or until tomatoes are tender and mixture is slightly thickened. Stir in lime juice and cilantro.
5. Ladle hot relish into hot jars, leaving ½ inch (1 cm) headspace. Remove air bubbles and adjust headspace as necessary by adding hot relish. Wipe rim and place hot lid disc on jar. Screw band down until fingertip-tight.
6. Place jars in canner and return to a boil. Process for 10 minutes. Turn off heat and remove canner lid. Let jars stand in water for 5 minutes. Transfer jars to a towel-lined surface and let stand for 24 hours. Check lids and refrigerate any jars that are not sealed.

Green Tomato Chow Chow

Chow chow is another one of those recipes that varies from family to family and region to region. This version uses green tomatoes and cabbage, with a touch of mustard for zest.

Makes about six 8-ounce (250 mL) jars

• • •

Tips

For the best flavor, this relish benefits from mellowing for at least 2 weeks before eating.

Some heirloom tomato varieties are still green when ripe. Don't use that type for this relish — you want firm, unripened tomatoes for the right taste and texture.

Day 1

4 cups	chopped green tomatoes	1 L
4 cups	finely chopped green cabbage	1 L
2 cups	chopped red and green bell peppers	500 mL
1 cup	chopped onion	250 mL
¼ cup	pickling or canning salt	50 mL

Day 2

2 cups	granulated sugar	500 mL
1 tbsp	dry mustard	15 mL
2 tsp	celery seeds	10 mL
½ tsp	ground turmeric	2 mL
¼ tsp	ground allspice	1 mL
2½ cups	cider vinegar	625 mL

Day 1

1. In a large non-reactive bowl, combine green tomatoes, cabbage, red and green peppers, onion and salt. Add cold water to cover by 1 inch (2.5 cm). Place a plate on top to weigh down vegetables. Cover and let stand at a cool room temperature for at least 8 hours or for up to 18 hours.

Day 2

1. Prepare canner, jars and lids (see pages 7 to 8).
2. In a colander lined with cheesecloth, working in batches, drain vegetables and rinse well. Drain again and squeeze out excess liquid. Set aside in colander to continue draining.
3. In a large pot, combine sugar, mustard, celery seeds, turmeric and allspice. Gradually whisk in vinegar. Bring to a boil over medium heat, stirring often until sugar is dissolved. Increase heat to medium-high, add drained vegetables and return to a boil, stirring often. Reduce heat and boil gently, stirring often, for about 45 minutes or until vegetables are translucent and mixture is slightly thickened.
4. Ladle hot relish into hot jars, leaving ½ inch (1 cm) headspace. Remove air bubbles and adjust headspace as necessary by adding hot relish. Wipe rim and place hot lid disc on jar. Screw band down until fingertip-tight.
5. Place jars in canner and return to a boil. Process for 10 minutes. Turn off heat and remove canner lid. Let jars stand in water for 5 minutes. Transfer jars to a towel-lined surface and let stand for 24 hours. Check lids and refrigerate any jars that are not sealed.

Piccalilli Relish

There are many opinions of what makes a piccalilli relish authentic. I've based the flavors of this one on a recipe from an 1899 edition of the White House Cook Book. *Of course, it took quite a bit of modification, since that recipe is written in prose, with rather vague amounts and instructions.*

Makes about six 8-ounce (250 mL) jars

● ● ●

Tip

Some heirloom tomato varieties are still green when ripe. Don't use that type for this relish — you want firm, unripened tomatoes for the right taste and texture.

Day 1

8 cups	chopped green tomatoes	2 L
3 cups	chopped onions	750 mL
½ cup	pickling or canning salt	125 mL

Day 2

4 cups	water	1 L
3 cups	white vinegar, divided	750 mL
1½ cups	granulated sugar	375 mL
2 tbsp	mustard seeds	25 mL
2 tsp	freshly ground black pepper	10 mL
1 tsp	ground cinnamon	5 mL
1 tsp	ground ginger	5 mL
½ tsp	ground cloves	2 mL
½ tsp	ground allspice	2 mL
¼ tsp	cayenne pepper	1 mL

Day 1

1. In a large non-reactive bowl, combine tomatoes, onions and salt. Add cold water to cover by 1 inch (2.5 cm). Place a plate on top to weigh down vegetables. Cover and let stand at a cool room temperature for at least 8 hours or for up to 18 hours.

Day 2

1. Prepare canner, jars and lids (see pages 7 to 8).
2. In a colander, working in batches, drain vegetables and rinse well. Drain again and squeeze out excess liquid. Set aside in colander to continue draining.
3. In a large pot, combine drained vegetables, water and 1 cup (250 mL) of the vinegar. Bring to a boil over medium-high heat. Reduce heat and boil gently, stirring often, for about 20 minutes or until tomatoes start to soften. In a colander, working in batches, drain well, then return to pot.
4. Add the remaining vinegar, sugar, mustard seeds, black pepper, cinnamon, ginger, cloves, allspice and cayenne. Bring to a boil over medium heat, stirring often. Reduce heat and boil gently, stirring often, for about 15 minutes or until tomatoes are tender and mixture is slightly thickened.

5. Ladle hot relish into hot jars, leaving ½ inch (1 cm) headspace. Remove air bubbles and adjust headspace as necessary by adding hot relish. Wipe rim and place hot lid disc on jar. Screw band down until fingertip-tight.

6. Place jars in canner and return to a boil. Process for 10 minutes. Turn off heat and remove canner lid. Let jars stand in water for 5 minutes. Transfer jars to a towel-lined surface and let stand for 24 hours. Check lids and refrigerate any jars that are not sealed.

Serving Suggestions

Serve with roasted meats and fish.

Add to an appetizer platter with cold meats, cheeses and pâté.

Tomato Apple Relish

The fruity flavor of this relish makes for a nice change from straight vegetable relish, yet it's crunchier and tangier than a chutney.

Makes about six 8-ounce (250 mL) jars

● ● ●

Tip

Some cooking apples that keep their shape are Crispin (Mutsu), Granny Smith, Northern Spy and Cortland.

Serving Suggestions

Dollop a spoonful of relish on top of sharp (old) Cheddar cheese or blue cheese on crackers.

Serve on grilled steaks or burgers.

Day 1

4 cups	chopped seeded peeled plum (Roma) tomatoes	1 L
4 cups	finely chopped peeled tart cooking apples	1 L
2 cups	chopped onions	500 mL
1 cup	finely chopped red bell peppers	250 mL
¼ cup	pickling or canning salt	50 mL

Day 2

2 cups	granulated sugar	500 mL
2 tbsp	mustard seeds	25 mL
2 tsp	celery seeds	10 mL
½ tsp	ground ginger	2 mL
2½ cups	white vinegar	625 mL

Day 1

1. In a large non-reactive bowl, combine tomatoes, apples, onions, red peppers and salt. Cover and let stand at a cool room temperature for at least 8 hours or for up to 18 hours.

Day 2

1. Prepare canner, jars and lids (see pages 7 to 8).
2. In a colander lined with cheesecloth, working in batches, drain tomato mixture and rinse well. Drain again and squeeze out excess liquid. Set aside in colander to continue draining.
3. In a large pot, combine sugar, mustard seeds, celery seeds, ginger and vinegar. Bring to a boil over medium heat, stirring often until sugar is dissolved. Increase heat to medium-high, add drained tomato mixture and return to a boil, stirring often. Reduce heat and boil gently, stirring often, for about 15 minutes or until tomatoes are tender and mixture is slightly thickened.
4. Ladle hot relish into hot jars, leaving ½ inch (1 cm) headspace. Remove air bubbles and adjust headspace as necessary by adding hot relish. Wipe rim and place hot lid disc on jar. Screw band down until fingertip-tight.
5. Place jars in canner and return to a boil. Process for 20 minutes. Turn off heat and remove canner lid. Let jars stand in water for 5 minutes. Transfer jars to a towel-lined surface and let stand for 24 hours. Check lids and refrigerate any jars that are not sealed.

Three-Onion Relish

Top a juicy steak with this relish and you'll never go back to a bottled sauce. It's also wonderful as a sandwich spread.

Makes about six 8-ounce (250 mL) jars

• • •

Tips

This relish looks nice if you cut the onions in half lengthwise, then crosswise into thin slices.

Be sure to wash the leeks well to remove all of the sand and grit. Trim off the root end and dark green parts, then cut the white and light green portion in half lengthwise. Rinse well between the layers and drain, then cut crosswise into thin slices.

6 cups	thinly sliced onions	1.5 L
2 cups	sliced leeks (white and light green parts only)	500 mL
¼ cup	pickling or canning salt	50 mL
1½ cups	granulated sugar	375 mL
2 tsp	coriander seeds, crushed	10 mL
1 tsp	dried thyme	5 mL
2¼ cups	cider vinegar	550 mL
2 cups	thinly sliced green onions	500 mL

1. In a large non-reactive bowl, combine onions, leeks and salt. Cover and let stand at a cool room temperature for 2 hours.
2. Meanwhile, prepare canner, jars and lids (see pages 7 to 8).
3. In a colander lined with cheesecloth, working in batches, drain onion mixture and rinse well. Drain again and squeeze out excess liquid. Set aside in colander to continue draining.
4. In a large pot, combine sugar, coriander seeds, thyme and vinegar. Bring to a boil over medium heat, stirring often until sugar is dissolved. Increase heat to medium-high, add drained onions and return to a boil, stirring often. Reduce heat and boil gently, stirring often, for about 15 minutes or until onions are translucent and mixture is slightly thickened. Stir in green onions and return to a boil, stirring often.
5. Ladle hot relish into hot jars, leaving ½ inch (1 cm) headspace. Remove air bubbles and adjust headspace as necessary by adding hot relish. Wipe rim and place hot lid disc on jar. Screw band down until fingertip-tight.
6. Place jars in canner and return to a boil. Process for 10 minutes. Turn off heat and remove canner lid. Let jars stand in water for 5 minutes. Transfer jars to a towel-lined surface and let stand for 24 hours. Check lids and refrigerate any jars that are not sealed.

Caramelized Onion Relish

This takes longer to cook than most relishes, but the deep caramelized flavor is worth every minute.

Makes about four 8-ounce (250 mL) jars

12 cups	chopped onions	3 L
2 cups	granulated sugar	500 mL
2 tsp	pickling or canning salt	10 mL
½ cup	water	125 mL
1½ cups	cider vinegar	375 mL

Tip

Chop the onions by hand for the best texture. Wearing goggles while chopping strong ingredients such as onions really does help protect your eyes from stinging.

Serving Suggestions

Spread over salmon fillets for the last 2 minutes of grilling.

Serve with a smoked salmon and cream cheese platter or spooned onto smoked salmon canapés.

Spoon over roast chicken breasts for the last 10 minutes of roasting, or serve alongside roast poultry.

1. Prepare canner, jars and lids (see pages 7 to 8).
2. In a large pot, combine onions, sugar, salt and water. Bring to a boil over medium heat, stirring often until sugar is dissolved. Cover, reduce heat to low and simmer, stirring occasionally, for about 20 minutes or until onions are softened. Uncover, increase heat to medium-low and boil gently, stirring often, for about 40 minutes or until onions are deeply caramelized. Increase heat to medium-high, add vinegar and return to a boil, stirring often. Reduce heat and boil gently, stirring constantly, for about 5 minutes or until mixture is slightly thickened.
3. Ladle hot relish into hot jars, leaving ½ inch (1 cm) headspace. Remove air bubbles and adjust headspace as necessary by adding hot relish. Wipe rim and place hot lid disc on jar. Screw band down until fingertip-tight.
4. Place jars in canner and return to a boil. Process for 10 minutes. Turn off heat and remove canner lid. Let jars stand in water for 5 minutes. Transfer jars to a towel-lined surface and let stand for 24 hours. Check lids and refrigerate any jars that are not sealed.

Spicy Pear Cucumber Relish

A blend of fragrant pears and fresh cucumbers adds an interesting touch to this sweet relish.

Makes about seven 8-ounce (250 mL) jars

● ● ●

Tips

Pickling cucumbers have a nice firm texture for relish. If they aren't available, peeled and seeded field cucumbers can be used instead, though the color of the relish will be pale.

Some pear varieties lose their flavor when heated, so choose a variety suited to cooking, such as Bartlett, Bosc or Packham.

Serving Suggestions

Spoon on top of sharp (old) Cheddar cheese on crackers.

Serve with grilled poultry or fish.

Spread on ham sandwiches instead of mustard.

Day 1

6 cups	finely chopped pickling cucumbers (see tip, at left)	1.5 L
3 tbsp	pickling or canning salt	45 mL

Day 2

2 tbsp	finely chopped gingerroot	25 mL
2¼ cups	granulated sugar	550 mL
½ tsp	hot pepper flakes	2 mL
¼ tsp	ground cinnamon	1 mL
⅛ tsp	ground cloves	0.5 mL
2 cups	white vinegar	500 mL
4 cups	finely chopped peeled pears	1 L

Day 1

1. In a large non-reactive bowl, combine cucumbers and salt. Add cold water to cover by 1 inch (2.5 cm). Place a plate on top to weigh down cucumbers. Cover and let stand at a cool room temperature for at least 8 hours or for up to 18 hours.

Day 2

1. Prepare canner, jars and lids (see pages 7 to 8).
2. In a colander lined with cheesecloth, working in batches, drain cucumbers and rinse well. Drain again and squeeze out excess liquid. Set aside in colander to continue draining.
3. In a large pot, combine ginger, sugar, hot pepper flakes, cinnamon, cloves and vinegar. Bring to a boil over medium heat, stirring often until sugar is dissolved. Increase heat to medium-high and add drained cucumbers and pears; return to a boil, stirring often. Reduce heat and boil gently, stirring often, for about 15 minutes or until cucumbers and pears are translucent and mixture is slightly thickened.
4. Ladle hot relish into hot jars, leaving ½ inch (1 cm) headspace. Remove air bubbles and adjust headspace as necessary by adding hot relish. Wipe rim and place hot lid disc on jar. Screw band down until fingertip-tight.
5. Place jars in canner and return to a boil. Process for 10 minutes. Turn off heat and remove canner lid. Let jars stand in water for 5 minutes. Transfer jars to a towel-lined surface and let stand for 24 hours. Check lids and refrigerate any jars that are not sealed.

Zucchini Red Pepper Relish

Take advantage of a bumper crop of zucchini by making this easy, tasty relish. Its color is as terrific as its flavor.

Makes about seven 8-ounce (250 mL) jars

● ● ●

Tips

Use small zucchini that are firm and moist. Larger zucchini tend to be spongy and have large seeds, and aren't suitable for preserving.

Use a food processor to chop the zucchini if you like. Just be sure to cut them into chunks and chop them in small batches. Use the pulse function and avoid chopping them to the point where they get juicy. The peppers and onions are best chopped by hand.

Serving Suggestions

Mix this relish with a little mayonnaise and/or plain yogurt for a quick dressing for potato salad or pasta salad.

Serve on grilled sausages, hot dogs or hamburgers.

7 cups	finely chopped zucchini (see tips, at left)	1.75 L
3 cups	finely chopped red bell peppers	750 mL
1½ cups	finely chopped onions	375 mL
⅓ cup	pickling or canning salt	75 mL
2½ cups	granulated sugar	625 mL
2 tsp	celery seeds	10 mL
¼ tsp	ground turmeric	1 mL
2 cups	white vinegar	500 mL

1. In a large non-reactive bowl, combine zucchini, red peppers, onions and salt. Cover and let stand at a cool room temperature for 2 hours.
2. Meanwhile, prepare canner, jars and lids (see pages 7 to 8).
3. In a colander lined with cheesecloth, working in batches, drain vegetables and rinse well. Drain again and squeeze out excess liquid. Set aside in colander to continue draining.
4. In a large pot, combine sugar, celery seeds, turmeric and vinegar. Bring to a boil over medium-high heat, stirring often until sugar is dissolved. Add drained vegetables and return to a boil, stirring often. Reduce heat and boil gently, stirring often, for about 15 minutes or until vegetables are translucent and mixture is slightly thickened.
5. Ladle hot relish into hot jars, leaving ½ inch (1 cm) headspace. Remove air bubbles and adjust headspace as necessary by adding hot relish. Wipe rim and place hot lid disc on jar. Screw band down until fingertip-tight.
6. Place jars in canner and return to a boil. Process for 10 minutes. Turn off heat and remove canner lid. Let jars stand in water for 5 minutes. Transfer jars to a towel-lined surface and let stand for 24 hours. Check lids and refrigerate any jars that are not sealed.

Zucchini Fennel Seed Relish

The Mediterranean flavors of fennel and zucchini combine in harmony in this sweet and fragrant relish.

Makes about six 8-ounce (250 mL) jars

• • •

Variation

For an extra fennel punch, reduce the zucchini to 6 cups (1.5 L) and add 2 cups (500 mL) finely chopped fennel bulb.

Serving Suggestion

Stir a little relish into your tuna salad for an exotic touch.

8 cups	finely chopped zucchini (see tips, page 278)	2 L
1 cup	finely chopped shallots or onions	250 mL
¼ cup	pickling or canning salt	50 mL
2 tbsp	minced garlic	25 mL
2 cups	granulated sugar	500 mL
2 tsp	fennel seeds	10 mL
¼ tsp	hot pepper flakes	1 mL
1 cup	white wine vinegar	250 mL
⅔ cup	white vinegar	150 mL

1. In a large non-reactive bowl, combine zucchini, shallots and salt. Cover and let stand at a cool room temperature for 2 hours.
2. Meanwhile, prepare canner, jars and lids (see pages 7 to 8).
3. In a colander lined with cheesecloth, working in batches, drain vegetables and rinse well. Drain again and squeeze out excess liquid. Set aside in colander to continue draining.
4. In a large pot, combine garlic, sugar, fennel seeds, hot pepper flakes, white wine vinegar and white vinegar. Bring to a boil over medium-high heat, stirring until sugar is dissolved. Add drained vegetables and return to a boil, stirring often. Reduce heat and boil gently, stirring often, for about 15 minutes or until vegetables are translucent and mixture is slightly thickened.
5. Ladle hot relish into hot jars, leaving ½ inch (1 cm) headspace. Remove air bubbles and adjust headspace as necessary by adding hot relish. Wipe rim and place hot lid disc on jar. Screw band down until fingertip-tight.
6. Place jars in canner and return to a boil. Process for 10 minutes. Turn off heat and remove canner lid. Let jars stand in water for 5 minutes. Transfer jars to a towel-lined surface and let stand for 24 hours. Check lids and refrigerate any jars that are not sealed.

Mushroom and Lemon Tapenade

A richly flavored spread made from mushrooms will liven up your appetizers and meals with its zesty taste.

Makes about eight 4-ounce (125 mL) or four 8-ounce (250 mL) jars

2 lbs	mushrooms, halved or quartered if large	1 kg
1 cup	chopped shallots	250 mL
2 tsp	pickling or canning salt	10 mL
2 tsp	grated lemon zest	10 mL
2 tbsp	freshly squeezed lemon juice	25 mL
1 tsp	chopped fresh thyme	5 mL
$\frac{1}{2}$ tsp	freshly ground black pepper	2 mL
$1\frac{1}{2}$ cups	white wine vinegar	375 mL

Tip

When filling the jars, be sure there is enough liquid on top of the tapenade to cover the solids. If necessary, bring more vinegar to a boil and add on top, maintaining the correct headspace.

Serving Suggestions

Spread on toasted baguette slices for quick canapés.

Serve as a condiment for grilled steak or roast beef.

1. Prepare canner, jars and lids (see pages 7 to 8).
2. In a large pot, combine mushrooms, shallots, salt and lemon juice. Cook, stirring often, for about 5 minutes or until mushrooms start to release their liquid. Cover, reduce heat to low and simmer, stirring occasionally, for about 10 minutes or until mushrooms are very soft and mixture is very wet. Uncover, increase heat to medium-high and cook, stirring often, for about 5 minutes or until liquid is almost evaporated. Let cool slightly.
3. In a food processor, working in batches, pulse mushroom mixture until very finely chopped but not puréed. Return to pot and stir in lemon zest, thyme, pepper and vinegar. Bring to a boil over medium-high heat, stirring often. Boil, stirring constantly, for 1 minute.
4. Ladle hot tapenade into hot jars, leaving $\frac{1}{2}$ inch (1 cm) headspace. Remove air bubbles and adjust headspace as necessary by adding hot tapenade. Wipe rim and place hot lid disc on jar. Screw band down until fingertip-tight.
5. Place jars in canner and return to a boil. Process for 10 minutes. Turn off heat and remove canner lid. Let jars stand in water for 5 minutes. Transfer jars to a towel-lined surface and let stand for 24 hours. Check lids and refrigerate any jars that are not sealed.

Roasted Red Pepper Tapenade

Roasted red peppers are divine on their own, but when mixed with fresh herbs and tangy vinegar in this vibrant spread, they get even better.

Makes about eight 4-ounce (125 mL) or four 8-ounce (250 mL) jars

• • •

Tips

It's best to roast your own fresh bell peppers for this tapenade. Commercially prepared roasted peppers are often treated with preservatives, which take away from the fresh, homemade flavor.

Add any extra finely chopped roasted peppers to a vinaigrette salad dressing or a soup.

• **Preheat broiler or preheat barbecue grill to medium**

6	large red bell peppers	6
1 cup	finely chopped red onion	250 mL
2 tbsp	minced garlic	25 mL
1 tbsp	granulated sugar	15 mL
1 tsp	pickling or canning salt	5 mL
1 cup	white wine vinegar or red wine vinegar	250 mL
¼ cup	water	50 mL
1 tbsp	chopped fresh basil	15 mL
1 tsp	chopped fresh rosemary	5 mL

1. Prepare canner, jars and lids (see pages 7 to 8).
2. If using broiler, place red peppers on a baking sheet. Broil or grill, turning often, for about 20 minutes or until blackened on all sides. Transfer to a bowl, cover with plastic wrap and let cool completely. Peel off skins and remove stems, cores and seeds. Discard any accumulated liquid. In a food processor or by hand, finely chop peppers (do not purée). Measure 3 cups (750 mL). Reserve any remaining peppers for another use.
3. In a pot, combine onion, garlic, sugar, salt, vinegar and water. Bring to a boil over medium heat, stirring often until sugar and salt are dissolved. Reduce heat and boil gently, stirring often, for about 10 minutes or until onion is softened. Stir in roasted peppers and return to a boil, stirring often. Boil for 1 minute. Stir in basil and rosemary.
4. Ladle hot tapenade into hot jars, leaving ½ inch (1 cm) headspace. Remove air bubbles and adjust headspace as necessary by adding hot tapenade. Wipe rim and place hot lid disc on jar. Screw band down until fingertip-tight.
5. Place jars in canner and return to a boil. Process for 10 minutes. Turn off heat and remove canner lid. Let jars stand in water for 5 minutes. Transfer jars to a towel-lined surface and let stand for 24 hours. Check lids and refrigerate any jars that are not sealed.

Double Tomato and Herb Tapenade

Fresh and dried tomatoes are combined for an extra punch in this lovely spread.

Makes about eight 4-ounce (125 mL) or four 8-ounce (250 mL) jars

• • •

Tips

For instructions on peeling tomatoes, see page 17. Seeding the tomatoes does take a little extra time, but it reduces the amount of liquid added to the pot and therefore reduces the amount of cooking required, giving the tapenade a fresher tomato flavor.

Use dry-packed dried tomatoes rather than the oil-packed type to make this tapenade safe for home canning.

Serving Suggestions

Spread on cooked chicken breasts, top with a slice of Brie cheese and broil until cheese is melted.

Spread on veal cutlets, roll up jellyroll-style and pan-sear or roast.

Serve spread on toasted baguette slices.

5 cups	chopped seeded peeled plum (Roma) tomatoes	1.25 L
½ cup	chopped onion	125 mL
2	cloves garlic, chopped	2
¼ cup	granulated sugar	50 mL
½ tsp	pickling or canning salt	2 mL
½ tsp	freshly ground black pepper	2 mL
½ cup	dried tomatoes (see tip, at left)	125 mL
1 cup	white wine vinegar or red wine vinegar	250 mL
2 tbsp	chopped fresh basil	25 mL
2 tsp	chopped fresh oregano	10 mL
1 tsp	chopped fresh sage (optional)	5 mL

1. Prepare canner, jars and lids (see pages 7 to 8).
2. In a pot, combine tomatoes, onion, garlic, sugar, salt and pepper. Bring to a boil over medium heat, stirring often. Reduce heat and boil gently, stirring often, for about 30 minutes or until tomatoes are softened. Let cool slightly.
3. Transfer half the tomato mixture to a food processor, in batches, and add dried tomatoes. Pulse until finely chopped but not puréed. Return to the pot.
4. Stir in vinegar and return to a boil over medium heat, stirring often. Reduce heat and boil gently, stirring often, for about 10 minutes or until dried tomatoes are softened and mixture is slightly thickened. Stir in basil, oregano and sage (if using).
5. Ladle hot tapenade into hot jars, leaving ½ inch (1 cm) headspace. Remove air bubbles and adjust headspace as necessary by adding hot tapenade. Wipe rim and place hot lid disc on jar. Screw band down until fingertip-tight.
6. Place jars in canner and return to a boil. Process for 20 minutes. Turn off heat and remove canner lid. Let jars stand in water for 5 minutes. Transfer jars to a towel-lined surface and let stand for 24 hours. Check lids and refrigerate any jars that are not sealed.

World Traveler

Pickles and Condiments from Around the World

• • •

Pickling is a technique used throughout the world by many cultures. Some cultures preserve vegetables to get them through long, cold winters, while others in more temperate climates pickle ingredients purely for flavor. Many pickles from other parts of the world aren't designed for home canning; rather, they're eaten fresh or within a few days or weeks. I've modified many traditional pickles to convert them into recipes that can be processed in a hot-water bath, then stored at room temperature. The texture may change as a result, but I've tried to keep the flavors as true to the traditional as possible.

See Vegetable Pickle Pointers (page 24), Fruit Pickle Pointers (page 111), Sauce-Making Tips (page 142) and Chutney Pointers (page 188) for more information.

Hot Chile Pickled Cucumber and Carrots

Many tropical-climate cuisines combine cooling cucumbers and carrots with fiery chile peppers in salads. Now you can simply pop open a jar of these pickles to add to your Asian-inspired meals.

Makes about seven pint (500 mL) jars

● ● ●

Tips

Fresh chile peppers can vary in heat, but the small dried red ones are sure to be fiery, making them better for these pickles. The little flakes of red even make the pickles *look* spicy.

Use natural rice vinegar for this recipe. "Seasoned" rice vinegar contains added sugar and salt, which would throw off the balance of ingredients.

2 lbs	3½- to 4-inch (8.5 to 10 cm) pickling cucumbers	1 kg
1½ lbs	carrots (6 to 8)	750 g
4 cups	ice cubes	1 L
10	small dried hot red chile peppers, crumbled	10
1½ cups	granulated sugar	375 mL
¼ cup	pickling or canning salt	50 mL
4 cups	white vinegar	1 L
2 cups	rice vinegar	500 mL
1½ cups	water	375 mL
	Mustard seeds	
	Celery seeds	

1. Scrub cucumbers gently under running water. Trim off ⅛ inch (3 mm) from each end and cut cucumbers lengthwise into quarters. Cut carrots into 4- by ½- by ½-inch (10 by 1 by 1 cm) sticks, or the length that will fit in jars allowing for 1 inch (2.5 cm) headspace.
2. In a large bowl, layer cucumbers, carrots and ice cubes, using about one-third of vegetables and ice per layer. Add cold water to cover by about 1 inch (2.5 cm). Place a plate on top to weigh down cucumbers. Cover and let stand at a cool room temperature for 3 hours
3. Meanwhile, prepare canner, jars and lids (see pages 7 to 8).
4. In a colander, working in batches, drain vegetables; set aside.
5. In a pot, combine chile peppers, sugar, salt, white vinegar, rice vinegar and 1½ cups (375 mL) water. Bring to a boil over medium heat, stirring often until sugar and salt are dissolved. Boil for 5 minutes. Reduce heat to low and keep liquid hot.
6. Working with one jar at a time, pack cucumbers and carrots into hot jar, dividing as evenly as possible and leaving 1 inch (2.5 cm) headspace. Add ½ tsp (2 mL) each mustard seeds and celery seeds. Pour in hot pickling liquid, leaving ½ inch (1 cm) headspace. Remove air bubbles and adjust headspace as necessary by adding hot pickling liquid. Wipe rim and place hot lid disc on jar. Screw band down until fingertip-tight.
7. Place jars in canner and return to a boil. Process for 10 minutes. Turn off heat, remove canner lid and let jars stand in water for 5 minutes. Transfer jars to a towel-lined surface and let stand for 24 hours. Check lids and refrigerate any jars that are not sealed.

Lemongrass Cucumber Pickles

The subtle flavor of lemongrass combines with cucumbers and rice vinegar for a fresh-tasting pickle with a twist.

Makes about six pint (500 mL) or three quart (1 L) jars

• • •

Tips

Use cucumbers that are evenly sized and less than 1 inch (2.5 cm) in diameter for the best texture.

Use natural rice vinegar for this recipe. "Seasoned" rice vinegar contains added sugar and salt, which would throw off the balance of ingredients.

Day 1		
4 lbs	pickling cucumbers	2 kg
¼ cup	pickling or canning salt	50 mL
Day 2		
3	stalks lemongrass	3
2 cups	granulated sugar	500 mL
4 cups	white vinegar	1 L
2 cups	water	500 mL
1 cup	rice vinegar	250 mL

Day 1

1. Scrub cucumbers gently under running water. Cut crosswise on a diagonal into ¼-inch (0.5 cm) slices, trimming off ⅛ inch (3 mm) from each end. You should have about 12 cups (3 L).

2. In a large bowl, layer cucumbers and salt, using about one-third of each per layer. Add cold water to cover by about 1 inch (2.5 cm). Place a plate on top to weigh down cucumbers. Cover and let stand at a cool room temperature for at least 12 hours or for up to 18 hours.

Day 2

1. Prepare canner, jars and lids (see pages 7 to 8).

2. In a colander, working in batches, drain cucumbers and rinse well. Drain again and set aside.

3. Trim outer leaves from lemongrass. Cut stalks in half lengthwise. Remove tender portion from center and cut into six 4-inch (10 cm) pieces; set aside. Chop remaining lemongrass finely and tie in a square of cheesecloth to make a spice bag.

4. In a large pot, combine spice bag, sugar, white vinegar, water and rice vinegar. Bring to a boil over medium heat, stirring often until sugar is dissolved. Reduce heat to low, cover and simmer for 10 minutes or until liquid is flavorful. Increase heat to medium-high, add drained cucumbers and return to a boil, pressing occasionally to immerse cucumbers in liquid. Remove from heat. Discard spice bag.

5. Using a slotted spoon, pack cucumbers into hot jars, leaving 1 inch (2.5 cm) headspace. Add 1 piece of reserved lemongrass to each pint (500 mL) jar and 2 pieces to each quart (1 L) jar. Pour in hot pickling liquid, leaving $\frac{1}{2}$ inch (1 cm) headspace. Remove air bubbles and adjust headspace as necessary by adding hot pickling liquid. Wipe rim and place hot lid disc on jar. Screw band down until fingertip-tight.

6. Place jars in canner and return to a boil. Process for 10 minutes. Turn off heat, remove canner lid and let jars stand in water for 5 minutes. Transfer jars to a towel-lined surface and let stand for 24 hours. Check lids and refrigerate any jars that are not sealed.

Serving Suggestions

Make a salad by adding thin slices of red bell pepper and/or green mango and chopped fresh cilantro to pickles. Use a little of the pickling liquid, mixed with Thai fish sauce and Asian chili sauce, for the dressing.

Serve alongside hot Thai curries.

Pickled Daikon Radish

Large white daikon radishes are used in many Asian cuisines. This simple pickle is versatile enough to serve on its own or with sushi, or to add to salads and stir-fries.

Makes four to five 8-ounce (250 mL) jars

• • •

Tips

It is easy to double this recipe if you eat a lot of pickled daikon. Use four to five pint (500 mL) jars.

Use natural rice vinegar for this recipe. "Seasoned" rice vinegar contains added sugar and salt, which would throw off the balance of ingredients.

Variation

Hot Pickled Daikon Radish: Add 4 small dried hot red chile peppers, crumbled, or 1 tsp (5 mL) hot pepper flakes with the sugar.

Day 1		
2 lbs	daikon radishes	1 kg
2 tbsp	pickling or canning salt	25 mL
Day 2		
1 cup	granulated sugar	250 mL
1 cup	rice vinegar	250 mL
¾ cup	water	175 mL

Day 1

1. Peel daikon and trim off ends. Cut lengthwise in half, then cut each half lengthwise to make quarters. Cut each quarter crosswise into ¼-inch (0.5 cm) thick slices. You should have about 6 cups (1. 5 L).

2. In a non-reactive bowl, combine daikon and salt; toss to combine. Add cold water to cover by 1 inch (2.5 cm). Place a plate on top to weigh down daikon. Cover and let stand at a cool room temperature for at least 8 hours or for up to 18 hours.

Day 2

1. Prepare canner, jars and lids (see pages 7 to 8).

2. In a colander, working in batches, drain daikon and rinse well. Drain again.

3. In a pot, combine sugar, vinegar and water. Bring to a boil over medium heat, stirring often to dissolve sugar. Boil for 1 minute. Reduce heat to low and keep liquid hot.

4. Working with one jar at a time, pack daikon into hot jar, leaving 1 inch (2.5 cm) headspace and leaving room for liquid. Pour in hot pickling liquid, leaving ½ inch (1 cm) headspace. Remove air bubbles and adjust headspace as necessary by adding hot pickling liquid. Wipe rim and place hot lid disc on jar. Screw band down until fingertip-tight.

5. Place jars in canner and return to a boil. Process for 10 minutes. Turn off heat, remove canner lid and let jars stand in water for 5 minutes. Transfer jars to a towel-lined surface and let stand for 24 hours. Check lids and refrigerate any jars that are not sealed.

Asian Pickled Eggplant

Eggplant absorbs the pleasant heat of ginger wonderfully in these sweet and tangy pickles. Add them to stir-fries, serve them on a sushi platter or spoon them onto rice crackers as an appetizer.

Makes about four pint (500 mL) jars

● ● ●

Tips

Asian eggplants are the long, slender variety with light or medium-dark purple skin. They are also known as Japanese eggplants or Chinese eggplants. Look for firm eggplants that are heavy for their size and have no signs of shriveling or soft spots.

Asian eggplants tend to have tender, thin skin, which is fine to leave on for pickles. If the skin seems thick — or if you prefer — you can peel the eggplants before slicing.

Use natural rice vinegar for this recipe. "Seasoned" rice vinegar contains added sugar and salt, which would throw off the balance of ingredients.

Serving Suggestion

For a little extra flavor, stir 2 tbsp (25 mL) tamari soy sauce into each pint (500 mL) of pickles after opening them.

● Baking sheets or trays, lined with lint-free towels

5 lbs	Asian eggplants (about 10)	2.5 kg
2 tbsp	thinly sliced gingerroot	25 mL
1 tbsp	minced garlic	15 mL
⅓ cup	granulated sugar	75 mL
2 tsp	pickling or canning salt	10 mL
2 cups	white vinegar	500 mL
2 cups	rice vinegar	500 mL
1 cup	water	250 mL
¼ cup	chopped fresh cilantro	50 mL

1. Prepare canner, jars and lids (see pages 7 to 8).

2. Trim off stems from eggplants and peel if desired (see tip, at left). Cut crosswise into ½-inch (1 cm) slices. You should have about 20 cups (5 L).

3. In a large pot of boiling water, in batches as necessary, boil eggplant for about 2 minutes or until almost fork-tender. Drain well. Spread eggplant out on towel-lined baking sheets to drain any remaining water.

4. In a clean large pot, combine ginger, garlic, sugar, salt, white vinegar, rice vinegar and water. Bring to a boil over medium-high heat, stirring often until sugar and salt are dissolved. Add eggplant and return to a boil, gently pressing occasionally to immerse eggplant in liquid. Remove from heat and gently stir in cilantro.

5. Using a slotted spoon, pack eggplant into hot jars, leaving room for liquid, leaving 1 inch (2.5 cm) headspace and dividing ginger slices as evenly as possible. Pour in hot pickling liquid, leaving ½ inch (1 cm) headspace. Remove air bubbles and adjust headspace as necessary by adding hot pickling liquid. Wipe rim and place hot lid disc on jar. Screw band down until fingertip-tight.

6. Place jars in canner and return to a boil. Process for 15 minutes. Turn off heat, remove canner lid and let jars stand in water for 5 minutes. Transfer jars to a towel-lined surface and let stand for 24 hours. Check lids and refrigerate any jars that are not sealed.

Kimchi-Style Pickled Cabbage

Making traditional kimchi is a true art, and it is often made and stored in a special refrigerator designed for the task. This version is based on the flavors of the traditional style but has been designed for hot-water processing and room temperature storage. My thanks goes to my good friend Annie Walker and her mom, Mrs. Youn, for the coaching.

Makes six to seven pint (500 mL) jars

● ● ●

Tips

If the cabbage is too big to fit in one bowl right away, divide it into two bowls and let it stand for 15 to 30 minutes to let it wilt. Once it's wilted, combine in one large bowl.

To weigh down the plate, you can use sterilized glass jars with tight-fitting lids full of water or other sealed containers. Do not use a plastic bag, as it may leak and ruin the salt concentration of the brine.

Day 1

5 lbs	green cabbage	2.5 kg
½ cup	pickling or canning salt, divided	125 mL
6 cups	water	1.5 L

Day 2

3 cups	coarsely chopped green onions	750 mL
1 cup	garlic cloves	250 mL
½ cup	coarsely chopped seeded long hot red chile peppers	125 mL
½ cup	coarsely chopped gingerroot	125 mL
1 tbsp	granulated sugar	15 mL
1 tbsp	pickling or canning salt	15 mL
1 tbsp	Korean ground chile pepper or cayenne pepper	15 mL

Final Day

3 cups	water	750 mL
1⅓ cups	white vinegar	325 mL

Day 1

1. Cut cabbage lengthwise into 6 or 8 wedges. Trim out core and tough spine pieces. Cut cabbage lengthwise into slices and then crosswise into about 1-inch (2.5 cm) squares. As you chop, layer in a large non-reactive bowl, using ¼ cup (50 mL) of the salt to sprinkle in thin layers over cabbage.

2. In a bowl, combine the remaining salt and water, stirring until salt is dissolved. Pour over cabbage. Place a plate on top to weigh down cabbage. Cover and let stand at a cool room temperature for at least 12 hours or for up to 24 hours.

Day 2

1. In a colander, working in batches, drain cabbage and rinse well. Drain again. Return to rinsed bowl.

2. In a food processor, combine green onions, garlic, chile peppers, ginger, sugar, salt and ground chile pepper. Pulse until finely chopped. Scrape down sides of bowl and purée until mixture is fairly smooth, adding a little water if necessary.

3. Add paste to cabbage and toss to evenly coat cabbage. Pack into a large crock, glass bowl or other non-reactive container. Place a plate on top to weigh down cabbage. Fill a couple of glass jars with water (see tip, page 290) and place on plate to keep it weighted. Cover with a lint-free towel and let stand at a cool room temperature (65°C to 70°F/18°C to 21°C) for at least 5 days or up to 2 weeks.

During Fermentation

1. Check every day to make sure cabbage is fermenting. You should see small bubbles form, and the aroma will change. If there are any signs of mold or a foul aroma, discard cabbage and liquid. After 5 days, taste daily to determine if desired fermented flavor is reached.

Final Day

1. Prepare canner, jars and lids (see pages 7 to 8).

2. In a colander set over a large pot, drain liquid from cabbage mixture into pot. Set cabbage aside. Stir water and vinegar into pot. Bring to a boil over medium-high heat. Add cabbage mixture and return to a simmer, stirring often.

3. Pack hot cabbage mixture and liquid into hot jars, leaving ½ inch (1 cm) headspace. Remove air bubbles and adjust headspace as necessary by adding hot pickling liquid. Wipe rim and place hot lid disc on jar. Screw band down until fingertip-tight.

4. Place jars in canner and return to a boil. Process for 10 minutes. Turn off heat, remove canner lid and let jars stand in water for 5 minutes. Transfer jars to a towel-lined surface and let stand for 24 hours. Check lids and refrigerate any jars that are not sealed.

Tip

The amount of time you allow the kimchi to ferment depends on personal taste. Some people prefer a lightly fermented "green" taste, while others prefer a deeper flavor. Be sure it doesn't over-mature and become soft and overly strong (it shouldn't be as fermented as sauerkraut). The added vinegar in this recipe ensures that the acid level will be safe for preserving.

Serving Suggestions

Traditional kimchi contains anchovies or fish sauce. For a more authentic flavor, you can stir in 2 tsp (10 mL) minced canned anchovies, anchovy paste or fish sauce per pint (500 mL), or to taste, just before serving.

Kimchi is spooned over rice, either as a snack on its own or to accompany a meal.

Pickled Daikon, Carrot and Cucumber with Ginger

Japanese pickles are generally made and eaten right away, rather than being preserved. This pickle is an adaptation of the traditional fresh version, specially created so it can be stored in your pantry.

Makes about six pint (500 mL) jars

● ● ●

Tips

Use cucumbers that are evenly sized and less than 1 inch (2.5 cm) in diameter for the best texture.

Be sure to use very fresh gingerroot with taut, shiny skin, juicy flesh and no signs of mold.

Use a Y-shaped vegetable peeler to peel the skin from gingerroot, then use a mandoline, Microplane-style slicer or sharp knife to cut crosswise into very thin slices.

Day 1

2 lbs	pickling cucumbers	1 kg
1 lb	carrots	500 g
1 lb	daikon radish	500 g
¼ cup	pickling or canning salt	50 mL

Day 2

¼ cup	thinly sliced peeled gingerroot	50 mL
2 cups	granulated sugar	500 mL
5 cups	white vinegar	1.25 L
2 cups	water	500 mL

Day 1

1. Scrub cucumbers gently under running water. Cut crosswise on a diagonal into ¼-inch (0.5 cm) slices, trimming off ⅛ inch (3 mm) from each end. You should have about 6 cups (1.5 L).
2. Cut carrots crosswise on a slight diagonal into ¼-inch (0.5 cm) slices. Cut any slices larger than a quarter into half-moons. You should have about 3 cups (750 mL).
3. Peel daikon and trim off ends. Cut lengthwise in half, then cut each half lengthwise to make quarters. Cut each quarter crosswise into ⅛-inch (3 mm) thick slices. You should have about 3 cups (750 mL).
4. In a large bowl, layer cucumbers, carrots and daikon with salt, using about one-third of the vegetables and salt per layer. Add cold water to cover by about 1 inch (2.5 cm). Place a plate on top to weigh down vegetables. Cover and let stand at a cool room temperature for at least 12 hours or for up to 18 hours.

Day 2

1. Prepare canner, jars and lids (see pages 7 to 8).
2. In a colander, working in batches, drain vegetables and rinse well. Drain again and set aside.

3. In a large pot, combine ginger, sugar, vinegar and water. Bring to a boil over medium heat, stirring until sugar is dissolved. Reduce heat to low, cover and simmer for 10 minutes or until liquid is flavorful. Increase heat to medium-high, add drained vegetables and return to a boil, pressing occasionally to immerse vegetables in liquid. Remove from heat.

4. Using a slotted spoon, pack vegetables into hot jars, dividing as evenly as possible and leaving 1 inch (2.5 cm) headspace. Pour in hot pickling liquid, leaving ½ inch (1 cm) headspace. Remove air bubbles and adjust headspace as necessary by adding hot pickling liquid. Wipe rim and place hot lid disc on jar. Screw band down until fingertip-tight.

5. Place jars in canner and return to a boil. Process for 10 minutes. Turn off heat, remove canner lid and let jars stand in water for 5 minutes. Transfer jars to a towel-lined surface and let stand for 24 hours. Check lids and refrigerate any jars that are not sealed.

Serving Suggestions

These pickles make a nice salad to serve with grilled meats, fish or poultry. Toss with a little vegetable or sesame oil just before serving.

Spiced Pickled Eggplant

Southeast Asian spices are captured in this eggplant pickle, so it's perfect as an accompaniment to curries or as an hors d'oeuvres on crisp flatbreads.

Makes about four pint (500 mL) jars

• • •

Tips

Small or medium eggplants are best for pickling. If they are too large, they tend to be spongy and have large seeds.

For the best flavor, these pickles benefit from standing for at least a week before serving.

Serving Suggestion

Serve with roasted lamb and garlic mashed potatoes.

• **Baking sheets or trays, lined with lint-free towels**

5 lbs	eggplants (about 4)	2.5 kg
3	long hot green chile peppers, seeded and finely chopped	3
1 tbsp	minced garlic	15 mL
¼ cup	granulated sugar	50 mL
2 tbsp	mustard seeds	25 mL
1 tbsp	pickling or canning salt	15 mL
2 tsp	cumin seeds	10 mL
1 tsp	fennel seeds or fenugreek seeds	5 mL
4 cups	white vinegar	1 L
⅔ cup	water	150 mL
2 tbsp	freshly squeezed lime or lemon juice	25 mL

1. Prepare canner, jars and lids (see pages 7 to 8).
2. Trim off stems and peel eggplants. Cut into 1-inch (2.5 cm) cubes. You should have about 20 cups (5 L).
3. In a large pot of boiling water, in batches as necessary, boil eggplant for about 5 minutes or until almost fork-tender. Drain well. Spread eggplant out on towel-lined baking sheets to drain any remaining water.
4. In a clean large pot, combine chile peppers, garlic, sugar, mustard seeds, salt, cumin seeds, fennel seeds, vinegar and water. Bring to a boil over medium-high heat, stirring often until sugar and salt are dissolved. Add eggplant and return to a boil, gently pressing occasionally to immerse eggplant in liquid. Stir in lime juice. Remove from heat.
5. Using a slotted spoon, pack eggplant into hot jars, leaving room for liquid and leaving 1 inch (2.5 cm) headspace. Pour in hot pickling liquid, leaving ½ inch (1 cm) headspace. Remove air bubbles and adjust headspace as necessary by adding hot pickling liquid. Wipe rim and place hot lid disc on jar. Screw band down until fingertip-tight.
6. Place jars in canner and return to a boil. Process for 15 minutes. Turn off heat, remove canner lid and let jars stand in water for 5 minutes. Transfer jars to a towel-lined surface and let stand for 24 hours. Check lids and refrigerate any jars that are not sealed.

Pickled Ginger

Why buy commercially prepared pickled ginger when it's simple to make yourself and the taste is outstanding? The key is to use very fresh gingerroot for the best flavor.

Makes about six 4-ounce (125 mL) or three 8-ounce (250 mL) jars

• • •

Tips

Be sure to use very fresh gingerroot with taut, shiny skin, juicy flesh and no signs of mold.

Use a Y-shaped vegetable peeler to peel the skin from gingerroot, then use a mandoline, Microplane-style slicer or sharp knife to cut crosswise into paper-thin slices. You'll need about 1 lb (500 g) gingerroot to get 3 cups (750 mL).

The ginger may turn pink once it's pickled. There is nothing wrong with the pickles; it's just a reaction between the acid and the pigment in the ginger. Commercially prepared pickled ginger often has food coloring added to make sure it turns pink.

Day 1

3 cups	very thinly sliced peeled gingerroot	750 mL
1 tsp	pickling or canning salt	5 mL

Day 2

½ cup	granulated sugar	125 mL
1½ cups	rice vinegar (see tip, page 296)	375 mL
½ cup	water	125 mL

Day 1

1. In a non-reactive bowl, combine ginger and salt; toss to combine. Cover and refrigerate for at least 8 hours or for up to 24 hours.

Day 2

1. Prepare canner, jars and lids (see pages 7 to 8).
2. In a colander, drain ginger, gently squeezing out excess liquid; set aside.
3. In a pot, combine sugar, vinegar and water. Bring to a boil over medium-high heat, stirring often to dissolve sugar. Boil for 1 minute. Add ginger and simmer until heated through.
4. Using a slotted spoon, pack ginger into hot jars, leaving room for liquid and leaving 1 inch (2.5 cm) headspace. Pour in hot pickling liquid, leaving ½ inch (1 cm) headspace. Remove air bubbles and adjust headspace as necessary by adding hot pickling liquid. Wipe rim and place hot lid disc on jar. Screw band down until fingertip-tight.
5. Place jars in canner and return to a boil. Process for 10 minutes. Turn off heat, remove canner lid and let jars stand in water for 5 minutes. Transfer jars to a towel-lined surface and let stand for 24 hours. Check lids and refrigerate any that are not sealed.

Pickled Lemongrass

Lemongrass adds a floral, almost sweet lemon flavor when simmered in curries and sauces. When you don't have fresh lemongrass on hand but you want the unique flavor it provides, it's great to have a store of pickled lemongrass in your pantry.

Makes about four 8-ounce (250 mL) jars

● ● ●

20	stalks lemongrass	20
½ cup	granulated sugar	125 mL
½ tsp	pickling or canning salt	2 mL
1½ cups	rice vinegar	375 mL
½ cup	water	125 mL

Tips

Use natural rice vinegar for this recipe. "Seasoned" rice vinegar contains added sugar and salt, which would throw off the balance of ingredients.

In general, lemongrass isn't meant to be eaten; rather, you infuse foods with its flavor and then discard it (as with bay leaves).

Serving Suggestions

Drain pickled lemongrass and use in place of fresh lemongrass in recipes. You may want to reduce the other vinegar or acid in the recipe at first, then add more to taste if necessary.

When making chicken stock that you'll use for Asian soups, add a few pieces of drained pickled lemongrass with the other vegetables.

1. Prepare canner, jars and lids (see pages 7 to 8).
2. Trim outer leaves from lemongrass and trim off root ends. Cut crosswise into about 1-inch (2.5 cm) pieces, discarding the hard, tough tips. You should have about 3 cups (750 mL).
3. In a colander, rinse lemongrass pieces under cold running water. Drain well and set aside.
4. In a saucepan, combine sugar, salt, vinegar and water. Bring to a boil over medium-high heat, stirring often until sugar and salt are dissolved. Boil for 1 minute. Reduce heat to low.
5. Pack lemongrass into hot jars, leaving 1 inch (2.5 cm) headspace. Pour in hot pickling liquid, leaving ½ inch (1 cm) headspace. Remove air bubbles and adjust headspace as necessary by adding hot pickling liquid. Wipe rim and place hot lid disc on jar. Screw band down until fingertip-tight.
6. Place jars in canner and return to a boil. Process for 10 minutes. Turn off heat, remove canner lid and let jars stand in water for 5 minutes. Transfer jars to a towel-lined surface and let stand for 24 hours. Check lids and refrigerate any jars that are not sealed.

Pickled Horseradish

In many Eastern European cuisines, pickled horseradish is a staple condiment. It's particularly suited to rich, roasted meats and is an integral ingredient in salads and vegetable dishes.

Makes about four 8-ounce (250 mL) jars

1 cup	granulated sugar	250 mL
1 tbsp	pickling or canning salt	15 mL
2 cups	white vinegar	500 mL
7 cups	lightly packed shredded horseradish root	1.75 L

1. Prepare canner, jars and lids (see pages 7 to 8).
2. In a saucepan, combine sugar, salt and vinegar. Bring to a boil over medium-high heat, stirring often until sugar and salt are dissolved. Add horseradish and return to a boil, pressing occasionally to immerse horseradish in liquid. Remove from heat.
3. Pack hot horseradish and liquid into hot jars, leaving $\frac{1}{2}$ inch (1 cm) headspace. Remove air bubbles and adjust headspace as necessary by adding hot liquid. Wipe rim and place hot lid disc on jar. Screw band down until fingertip-tight.
4. Place jars in canner and return to a boil. Process for 10 minutes. Turn off heat, remove canner lid and let jars stand in water for 5 minutes. Transfer jars to a towel-lined surface and let stand for 24 hours. Check lids and refrigerate any jars that are not sealed.

Tips

Horseradish root should be very firm, with tight skin and no soft spots. Peel the skin with a vegetable peeler, then shred the root on the coarse side of a box grater or using the shredding blade of a food processor. If you have a meat grinder, you can use it to grind the root and make a finer-textured pickle. You'll need about 3 lbs (1.5 kg) whole root to get 7 cups (1.75 L) shredded.

When working with horseradish, be sure to work in a well-ventilated area. Wearing goggles while shredding strong ingredients such as horseradish really does help protect your eyes from stinging.

Serving Suggestion

Add pickled horseradish to the filling for devilled eggs.

Tangy French Cornichons

These tiny, tangy pickles beg for a charcuterie platter with pâté, fine cheeses and Dijon mustard.

Makes about five pint (500 mL) jars

● ● ●

Tip

Tiny cucumbers have thin skins and get soft and deteriorate quickly after they're picked, so make these pickles as soon after harvesting as possible.

Variation

Substitute thyme sprigs for the tarragon sprigs or add thyme sprigs along with the tarragon.

Day 1

3 lbs	1½- to 2-inch (4 to 5 cm) pickling cucumbers	1.5 kg
½ cup	pickling or canning salt	125 mL

Day 2

2¼ cups	white vinegar, divided	550 mL
4 cups	white wine vinegar	1 L
5	bay leaves	5
5	sprigs tarragon (about 3 inches/7.5 cm long)	5
5	small shallots, halved lengthwise	5
	White or black peppercorns	

Day 1

1. Scrub cucumbers gently under running water. Trim off ⅛ inch (3 mm) from the blossom end.
2. In a large bowl, layer cucumbers and salt, using about one-quarter of each per layer. Cover and let stand at a cool room temperature for 24 hours, gently stirring occasionally once the brine forms.

Day 2

1. Prepare canner, jars and lids (see pages 7 to 8).
2. In a colander, working in batches, drain cucumbers and rinse well.
3. In a large bowl, combine 8 cups (2 L) cold water and ¼ cup (50 mL) of the white vinegar. Add cucumbers and stir gently. Drain again and set aside.
4. In a pot, combine the remaining white vinegar and the white wine vinegar. Bring to a boil over medium-high heat. Reduce heat to low and keep liquid hot.
5. Working with one jar at a time, place 1 bay leaf, 1 tarragon sprig, 1 shallot piece and ¼ tsp (1 mL) peppercorns in hot jar. Pack cucumbers into jar, leaving 1 inch (2.5 cm) headspace, and top with another shallot piece. Pour in hot pickling liquid, leaving ½ inch (1 cm) headspace. Remove air bubbles and adjust headspace as necessary by adding hot pickling liquid. Wipe rim and place hot lid disc on jar. Screw band down until fingertip-tight.
6. Place jars in canner and return to a boil. Process for 10 minutes. Turn off heat, remove canner lid and let jars stand in water for 5 minutes. Transfer jars to a towel-lined surface and let stand for 24 hours. Check lids and refrigerate any jars that are not sealed.

Pickled Nasturtium Capers

True capers are the pickled buds of the caper bush, which grows in the Mediterranean, but you can make "poor man's" or, as I like to call them, "faux" capers with the newly formed seed pods of nasturtium plants. Nasturtiums are easy to grow pretty much anywhere the sun shines.

Makes up to one 8-ounce (250 mL) jar

• • •

Tips

The seeds pods develop on the plant gradually, so it's tricky to get a lot at one time unless you have hundreds of plants. For this reason, adding the pods to the pickling liquid gradually is easiest.

Pick seed pods when they first form (after the flower petals fall off) and are tender and green.

Variation

You can use the flower buds of the nasturtium plant instead of, or in addition to, the seed pods. Pick the flower buds when they're green, less than ½ inch (1 cm) long and showing no signs of the flower petals inside. Keep in mind, your plants won't flower or develop seed pods. It's good to primarily use the seed pods, then pick the flower buds at the end of the season when the plants are finishing anyway.

	Nasturtium flower seed pods (up to ¾ cup/175 mL)	
	Boiling water	
½	small shallot, halved lengthwise	½
1 tsp	pickling or canning salt	5 mL
¼ tsp	black peppercorns	1 mL
½ cup	white wine vinegar	125 mL

1. Prepare jar (see page 7), keeping it hot.
2. Place seed pods in a heatproof bowl and pour in just enough boiling water to cover. Immediately transfer to a sieve or colander and drain well. Set aside.
3. In a saucepan, combine shallot, salt, peppercorns and vinegar. Bring to a boil over medium-high heat, stirring often until salt is dissolved. Remove from heat.
4. Add seed pods to hot jar. Pour in hot pickling liquid, leaving at least ½ inch (1 cm) headspace (there will be considerably more space if you have added fewer seed pods).
5. If jar is full, remove air bubbles and adjust headspace as necessary by adding hot pickling liquid. Wipe rim and place hot lid disc on jar. Screw band down until fingertip-tight. Let cool completely. Refrigerate for at least 2 weeks or for up to 6 months.
6. If jar isn't full, let cool, uncovered. Cover with a plastic storage cap or two-piece lid and refrigerate. Add more seeds pods (or flower buds; see variation, at left) as they become available, repeating step 2 each time. Let marinate in the refrigerator for at least 2 weeks after the last addition before using.

Pickled Milkweed Pods

This is a perfect example of taking advantage of what nature provides. Commonly thought of merely as a weed, the milkweed plant has many culinary uses. The tender, newly formed pods have traditionally been pickled by Native North Americans and have a texture much like a large caper.

Makes about two pint (500 mL) jars

● ● ●

Tips

Look for milkweed plants as they start to grow in early summer. Once the purple flowers finish blooming, the pods form and grow quickly. Pick pods when they are between 1 and 1½ inches (2.5 and 4 cm) in diameter at the largest point. Be sure to get permission to harvest the pods if they're not on your own property and pick only where you know they haven't been sprayed with insecticides or herbicides.

Leave some pods on each plant so the seeds will form and the plant will reproduce. Do not pick any of the leaves, as they are the sole food source for monarch butterfly larvae.

Serving Suggestion

Serve with cured meats and other exotic pickles for an appetizer platter.

4 cups	small milkweed pods (see tips, at left)	1 L
1 tbsp	granulated sugar	15 mL
1½ tsp	pickling or canning salt	7 mL
2 cups	cider vinegar	500 mL
½ cup	water	125 mL

1. Prepare canner, jars and lids (see pages 7 to 8).
2. In a pot of boiling water, blanch milkweed pods for 15 seconds. Drain and immediately plunge into ice-cold water to chill. Repeat blanching, draining and chilling two more times to remove bitter flavor. Taste a small piece of a pod to check for bitterness and repeat again if necessary. Drain well.
3. In a saucepan, combine sugar, salt, vinegar and water. Bring to a boil over medium-high heat, stirring often until sugar and salt are dissolved. Boil for 1 minute. Reduce heat to low and keep liquid hot.
4. Pack milkweed pods into hot jars, leaving 1 inch (2.5 cm) headspace. Pour in hot pickling liquid, leaving ½ inch (1 cm) headspace. Remove air bubbles and adjust headspace as necessary by adding hot pickling liquid. Wipe rim and place hot lid disc on jar. Screw band down until fingertip-tight.
5. Place jars in canner and return to a boil. Process for 10 minutes. Turn off heat, remove canner lid and let jars stand in water for 5 minutes. Transfer jars to a towel-lined surface and let stand for 24 hours. Check lids and refrigerate any jars that are not sealed.

New Orleans Pickled Mirlitons

Crunchy pickles with a little kick are a welcome addition to a meal inspired by the Deep South.

Makes about seven pint (500 mL) jars

● ● ●

Tip

Mirlitons, also known as chayotes, chow-chows, cho-chos, chouchos, vegetable pears or alligator pears, are a member of the gourd family. They're often available at specialty produce markets, Asian, South American or Latin American grocery stores and some well-stocked supermarkets.

6	mirlitons (about 4½ lbs/2.25 kg)	6
1 lb	carrots	500 g
1	onion	1
4 cups	ice cubes	1 L
14	cloves garlic, halved	14
¼ cup	granulated sugar	50 mL
¼ cup	pickling or canning salt	50 mL
½ tsp	cayenne pepper	2 mL
6 cups	white vinegar	1.5 L
7	bay leaves	7
	Mustard seeds and black peppercorns	

1. Cut mirlitons in half lengthwise and trim out seeds. Cut into 4- by ½- by ½-inch (10 by 1 by 1 cm) sticks, or the length that will fit in jars allowing for 1 inch (2.5 cm) headspace. Cut carrots into the same size sticks. Cut onion in half lengthwise and trim out root, then cut each half lengthwise into wedges about ½-inch (1 cm) thick and separate into layers.

2. In a large bowl, layer mirlitons, carrots, onions and ice cubes, using about one-third of the vegetables and ice cubes per layer. Add cold water to cover by about 1 inch (2.5 cm). Place a plate on top to weigh down vegetables. Cover and let stand at a cool room temperature for 3 hours.

3. Meanwhile, prepare canner, jars and lids (see pages 7 to 8).

4. In a colander, working in batches, drain vegetables; set aside.

5. In a large pot, combine garlic, sugar, salt, cayenne, vinegar and 2 cups (500 mL) water. Bring to a boil over medium heat, stirring often until sugar and salt are dissolved. Add vegetables and simmer, stirring gently, for 5 minutes or until vegetables are hot. Remove from heat.

6. Using tongs, pack vegetables into hot jars, leaving 1 inch (2.5 cm) headspace. Add 1 bay leaf and ½ tsp (2 mL) each mustard seeds and peppercorns to each jar. Pour in hot pickling liquid, leaving ½ inch (1 cm) headspace. Remove air bubbles and adjust headspace as necessary by adding hot pickling liquid. Wipe rim and place hot lid disc on jar. Screw band down until fingertip-tight.

7. Place jars in canner and return to a boil. Process for 10 minutes. Turn off heat, remove canner lid and let jars stand in water for 5 minutes. Transfer jars to a towel-lined surface and let stand for 24 hours. Check lids and refrigerate any jars that are not sealed.

Hawaiian Pickled Onions

A luau wouldn't be complete without these pickles. Serve them with roasted pork or chicken or grilled fish and whip up some tropical drinks to complete the party.

Makes about four pint (500 mL) jars

● ● ●

Tips

You'll need about 2 green bell peppers. If the strips are longer than 4 inches (10 cm), you may want to cut them in half so they fit nicely into the jars.

Hawaiian sea salt is available at some specialty stores. If you happen to have some, use it in place of the pickling or canning salt.

Use natural rice vinegar for this recipe. "Seasoned" rice vinegar contains added sugar and salt, which would throw off the balance of ingredients.

2 lbs	2- to 3-inch (5 to 7.5 cm) onions	1 kg
12 oz	green bell peppers	375 g
2 tbsp	pickling or canning salt	25 mL
3½ cups	rice vinegar	875 mL
2¼ cups	water	550 mL
1½ cups	white vinegar	375 mL
	Hot pepper flakes	

1. Prepare canner, jars and lids (see pages 7 to 8).
2. Cut onions in half lengthwise and trim out roots. Cut each half lengthwise into wedges about ¼ inch (0.5 cm) thick and separate into layers. You should have about 10 cups (2 L). Set aside.
3. Trim off stems and cut out seeds from green peppers. Cut lengthwise into ½-inch (1 cm) slices. You should have about 2 cups (500 mL). Set aside.
4. In a pot, combine salt, rice vinegar, water and white vinegar. Bring to a boil over medium heat, stirring often until salt is dissolved. Reduce heat to low and keep liquid hot.
5. Working with one jar at a time, place ¼ tsp (1 mL) hot pepper flakes in hot jar. Pack onions and green peppers into jar, dividing as evenly as possible and leaving 1 inch (2.5 cm) headspace. Pour in hot pickling liquid, leaving ½ inch (1 cm) headspace. Remove air bubbles and adjust headspace as necessary by adding hot pickling liquid. Wipe rim and place hot lid disc on jar. Screw band down until fingertip-tight.
6. Place jars in canner and return to a boil. Process for 10 minutes. Turn off heat, remove canner lid and let jars stand in water for 5 minutes. Transfer jars to a towel-lined surface and let stand for 24 hours. Check lids and refrigerate any jars that are not sealed.

Mexican Pickled Jalapeño Peppers

These pickles are the quintessential topping for tacos, nachos and other Mexican favorites, and are even better when you make them yourself.

Makes about six pint (500 mL) jars

• • •

Tips

To avoid burns, wear disposable rubber gloves when handling hot peppers and be sure to wash all utensils and the cutting board well after preparing the peppers.

It is tricky to remove the seeds while maintaining the ring shape of the jalapeños. You can hollow out the whole pepper with a narrow paring knife before slicing the rings or use the tip of the knife to flick out seeds from each ring. Or simply leave them in and let them fall to the bottom of the jars.

3 lbs	jalapeño peppers	1.5 kg
1 tbsp	pickling or canning salt	15 mL
6 cups	white vinegar	1.5 L
4 cups	water	1 L
6	cloves garlic, halved	6
6	sprigs oregano (4 inches/10 cm long)	6

1. Prepare canner, jars and lids (see pages 7 to 8).
2. Trim off stems and cut jalapeños crosswise into ¼-inch (0.5 cm) slices, discarding seeds if desired (see tip, at left). You should have about 12 cups (3 L). Set aside.
3. In a pot, combine salt, vinegar and water. Bring to a boil over medium-high heat, stirring often until salt is dissolved. Reduce heat to low and keep liquid hot.
4. Working with one jar at a time, place 2 garlic pieces and 1 oregano sprig in hot jar. Pack peppers into jar, leaving room for liquid and leaving 1 inch (2.5 cm) headspace. Pour in hot pickling liquid, leaving ½ inch (1 cm) headspace. Remove air bubbles and adjust headspace as necessary by adding hot pickling liquid. Wipe rim and place hot lid disc on jar. Screw band down until fingertip-tight.
5. Place jars in canner and return to a boil. Process for 10 minutes. Turn off heat, remove canner lid and let jars stand in water for 5 minutes. Transfer jars to a towel-lined surface and let stand for 24 hours. Check lids and refrigerate any jars that are not sealed.

Brandied Scotch Bonnet Peppers

I was first introduced to Scotch bonnet peppers by cookbook author Judith Finlayson. Judith adds these peppers to soups and stews to spike them with Caribbean flair.

Makes about two pint (500 mL) jars

• • •

Tips

Scotch bonnet peppers are extremely hot. They look like tiny, wrinkled bell peppers and come in a variety of colors: red, green, yellow and orange. They are closely related to, and often interchangeably labeled as, habanero chile peppers.

This isn't a very big batch, so you can omit the hot-water processing if you prefer and simply store the peppers in the refrigerator. They'll last for up to 6 months.

Serving Suggestions

Cut stems and seeds from drained peppers and finely mince. Add in place of fresh peppers in recipes such as salsas and curries.

Add a little of the peppered brandy to spike the flavor of soups, especially those with squash, sweet potatoes or seafood.

1½ cups	brandy	375 mL
⅔ cup	water	150 mL
4 cups	Scotch bonnet chile peppers (about 1 lb/500 g), long stems trimmed	1 L

1. Prepare canner, jars and lids (see pages 7 to 8).
2. In a deep saucepan, combine brandy and water. Bring to a simmer over medium heat, being careful that the brandy doesn't get hot enough to ignite. Reduce heat to low and keep liquid hot.
3. Pack chile peppers into hot jars, leaving 1 inch (2.5 cm) headspace. Pour in hot pickling liquid, leaving ½ inch (1 cm) headspace. Remove air bubbles and adjust headspace as necessary by adding hot pickling liquid. Wipe rim and place hot lid disc on jar. Screw band down until fingertip-tight.
4. Place jars in canner and return to a boil. Process for 10 minutes. Turn off heat, remove canner lid and let jars stand in water for 5 minutes. Transfer jars to a towel-lined surface and let stand for 24 hours. Check lids and refrigerate any jars that are not sealed.

Hot Lemon Pickle

There seem to be as many versions of hot lemon pickle as there are Indian cooks. This one is prepared like a cucumber pickle but with the spicy, salty, sour and slightly bitter flavor of more traditional recipes.

Makes about four 8-ounce (250 mL) jars

● ● ●

Tip

Some lemons have very thick rinds with a lot of white pith. If the pith is thicker than $\frac{1}{8}$ inch (3 mm), use a grapefruit spoon or the dull side of a knife to scrape some from the quartered rinds before dicing.

Serving Suggestions

For a more traditional flavor, when you open a jar, drain off the pickling liquid and pour in warmed vegetable oil to cover (about $\frac{1}{2}$ cup/125 mL per 8-ounce/ 250 mL jar). Let cool, cover and refrigerate for at least 1 day and use within 1 month.

A small spoonful of lemon pickle perks up a simple dish of lentils and rice.

Serve with a mild curry to add heat or a hot curry to add more fire and tang.

Day 1

12	lemons	12
$\frac{1}{3}$ cup	pickling or canning salt	75 mL

Day 2

10	curry leaves	10
2 tbsp	mustard seeds	25 mL
$1\frac{1}{2}$ tsp	cayenne pepper	7 mL
1 tsp	fenugreek seeds	5 mL
$\frac{1}{2}$ cup	water	125 mL

Day 1

1. Scrub lemons gently under running water. Cut lemons in half crosswise and squeeze out juice. Strain juice and measure 1 cup (250 mL); transfer to an airtight jar and refrigerate. Reserve any extra juice for another use. Cut rinds lengthwise into quarters and scrape out membranes. Cut into about $\frac{1}{4}$-inch (0.5 cm) dice. You should have about $4\frac{1}{2}$ cups (1.125 L).

2. In a non-reactive bowl, combine lemons and salt. Let stand at room temperature for at least 12 hours or for up to 24 hours.

Day 2

1. Prepare canner, jars and lids (see pages 7 to 8).

2. In a colander, drain lemons and rinse well. Drain again, squeezing out excess liquid. Set aside.

3. In a large pot, combine curry leaves, mustard seeds, cayenne, fenugreek seeds, reserved lemon juice and water. Bring to a boil over medium-high heat. Add lemons and simmer for about 3 minutes or just until heated through. Remove from heat.

4. Using a slotted spoon, pack hot lemons into hot jars, leaving room for liquid and leaving 1 inch (2.5 cm) headspace. Pour in hot pickling liquid, leaving $\frac{1}{2}$ inch (1 cm) headspace and dividing spices as evenly as possible. Remove air bubbles and adjust headspace as necessary by adding hot liquid. Wipe rim and place hot lid disc on jar. Screw band down until fingertip-tight.

5. Place jars in canner and return to a boil. Process for 10 minutes. Turn off heat and remove canner lid. Let jars stand in water for 5 minutes. Transfer jars to a towel-lined surface and let stand for 24 hours. Check lids and refrigerate any jars that are not sealed.

Tangy Green Mango Pickle

Traditional Indian green mango pickle is made with a highly spiced oil rather than vinegar.
This version uses the same fragrant spices but turns the recipe into a tangy North American–style
pickle suitable for hot-water processing.

**Makes about
six 8-ounce
(250 mL) or three
pint (500 mL) jars**

• • •

Tips

Look for green mangos
at Asian grocery
stores or well-stocked
supermarkets. They're
often displayed with
the vegetables rather
than the fruit. In a
pinch, underripe, hard
sweet mangos can be
used in place of true
green mangos.

Use a Y-shaped peeler
to remove skin from
the mangos, then cut
the flesh away from the
pit in slices. Place the
slices flat side down
and dice into evenly
sized pieces. You'll
need about 10 small
green mangos or
7 larger ones to get
7 cups (1.75 L) diced.

Serving
Suggestion

Turn green mango
pickle into a salad by
tossing it with diced
red onion and red bell
peppers and a little
vegetable oil.

7 cups	diced peeled green mangos	1.75 L
3 tbsp	pickling or canning salt	45 mL
1 tbsp	fenugreek seeds	15 mL
1½ tsp	each cumin seeds and fennel seeds	7 mL
18	curry leaves (optional)	18
¾ cup	granulated sugar	175 mL
1 tbsp	mustard seeds	15 mL
1 tsp	hot pepper flakes	5 mL
½ tsp	ground turmeric	2 mL
2¾ cups	white vinegar	675 mL
1½ cups	water	375 mL

1. In a non-reactive bowl, layer mangos and salt, using about
   one-third of each per layer. Place a plate on top to weigh
   down mangos. Cover and let stand at a cool room temperature
   for 1 hour or until liquid is released.
2. Meanwhile, prepare canner, jars and lids (see pages 7 to 8).
3. In a colander, drain mangos, gently squeezing out excess
   liquid. Set aside.
4. In a small dry skillet, over medium heat, toast fenugreek
   seeds, cumin seeds and fennel seeds, stirring constantly,
   for about 30 seconds or until slightly darker and fragrant.
   Immediately transfer to a large pot.
5. Add curry leaves (if using), sugar, mustard seeds, hot pepper
   flakes, turmeric, vinegar and water to the pot. Bring to a boil
   over medium-high heat, stirring often until sugar is dissolved.
   Boil for 1 minute. Add mangos and simmer, stirring gently,
   for about 5 minutes or until mangos are heated through.
   Remove from heat.
6. Using a slotted spoon, pack mangos into hot jars, leaving
   1 inch (2.5 cm) headspace. Pour in hot pickling liquid, leaving
   ½ inch (1 cm) headspace and dividing spices as evenly
   as possible. Remove air bubbles and adjust headspace as
   necessary by adding hot pickling liquid. Wipe rim and place
   hot lid disc on jar. Screw band down until fingertip-tight.
7. Place jars in canner and return to a boil. Process for
   15 minutes. Turn off heat, remove canner lid and let jars
   stand in water for 5 minutes. Transfer jars to a towel-lined
   surface and let stand for 24 hours. Check lids and refrigerate
   any jars that are not sealed.

Japanese-Style Pickled Plums

This version has the sour, salty flavor of traditional umeboshi *but has been developed for home canning. It will be a little different from the original, but will still give the same flavor sensation.*

Makes about four 8-ounce (250 mL) jars

● ● ●

Tip

True *ume*, used to make *umeboshi*, is actually a Japanese apricot rather than a plum. For this recipe, use any small, firm plum, such as prune (blue), damson, greengage or yellow. It's best to avoid soft plums, as they'll get too mushy.

Serving Suggestions

Serve with cooked rice.

Purée plums with pickling liquid and add a little vegetable oil to make a salad dressing.

Day 1

| 2 lbs | small plums (about 40) | 1 kg |
| 2 tbsp | pickling or canning salt | 25 mL |

Day 2

| 1 cup | rice vinegar | 250 mL |
| ¼ cup | water | 50 mL |

Day 1

1. Using a fork, prick plums all over. Using a small paring knife, starting at the stem and the natural indent in the plum, cut in half around the pit. Twist each half in the opposite direction and separate halves. Discard pit.

2. In a non-reactive bowl, sprinkle plums with salt and stir gently to coat plums evenly. Cover and let stand at a cool room temperature for at least 8 hours or for up to 18 hours.

Day 2

1. Prepare canner, jars and lids (see pages 7 to 8).

2. In a pot, combine rice vinegar and water. Bring to a boil over high heat. Add plums and accumulated juices; heat just until mixture returns to a boil and plums are heated through.

3. Using a slotted spoon, pack plums into hot jars, leaving room for liquid and leaving 1 inch (2.5 cm) headspace. Pour in hot pickling liquid, leaving ½ inch (1 cm) headspace. Remove air bubbles and adjust headspace as necessary by adding hot pickling liquid. Wipe rim and place hot lid disc on jar. Screw band down until fingertip-tight.

4. Place jars in canner and return to a boil. Process for 20 minutes. Turn off heat, remove canner lid and let jars stand in water for 5 minutes. Transfer jars to a towel-lined surface and let stand for 24 hours. Check lids and refrigerate any jars that are not sealed.

Indian Spiced Pickled Peaches

Fragrant, sweet peaches combine with zesty spices for an interesting cross between a pickle and a chutney. All of the tastes are incorporated — sweet, sour, hot and bitter — making these pickles lovely to eat on their own or to serve as a condiment.

Makes about six pint (500 mL) jars

● ● ●

Tips

Choose freestone peaches that are firm and heavy for their size. This is a good recipe in which to use peaches that are a little too large to pickle or can as halves.

Whole cardamom pods and fenugreek seeds are commonly used in Indian cuisine. You can find them in the spice section of well-stocked supermarkets, at specialty spice emporiums and at Asian grocery stores. Buy small amounts at a time, as even whole spices lose their flavor when stored for a long time.

8 cups	water	2 L
¼ cup	freshly squeezed lemon juice	50 mL
6 lbs	firm ripe peaches (about 24)	3 kg
3	sticks cinnamon (each about 3 inches/5 cm long), broken in half	3
2 tbsp	mustard seeds	25 mL
1 tsp	cumin seeds	5 mL
1 tsp	fenugreek seeds	5 mL
6	whole green cardamom pods	6
2 tbsp	minced gingerroot	25 mL
2 cups	packed brown sugar	500 mL
2 tsp	pickling or canning salt	10 mL
¼ tsp	hot pepper flakes	1 mL
4 cups	cider vinegar	1 L
1½ cups	Gewurztraminer, Vidal or other off-dry white wine	375 mL
¼ cup	chopped fresh cilantro (optional)	50 mL

1. Prepare canner, jars and lids (see pages 7 to 8).
2. In a large bowl, combine water and lemon juice. Peel peaches (see page 16). Using a small paring knife, starting at the stem and the natural indent in the peach, cut in half around the pit. Insert both thumbs into the dent at the stem and gently pry apart into halves. Cut each half lengthwise into about ¾-inch (2 cm) slices, discarding pit. Add peaches to the lemon water as they are peeled and cut. Set aside.
3. In a small dry skillet, over medium heat, toast cinnamon sticks, mustard seeds, cumin seeds and fenugreek seeds, shaking the pan constantly, for about 1 minute or until seeds are fragrant and just slightly darker. Immediately transfer to a large pot.
4. Add cardamom, ginger, brown sugar, salt, hot pepper flakes, vinegar and wine to the pot. Bring to a boil over medium heat, stirring often until sugar and salt are dissolved. Boil for 1 minute.
5. Drain peaches, discarding soaking water. Increase heat to medium-high, add peaches to pot and simmer for about 3 minutes or until peaches are heated through. Remove from heat and stir in cilantro (if using).

6. Using a slotted spoon, pack peaches into hot jars, leaving 1 inch (2.5 cm) headspace. Pour in pickling liquid, leaving $\frac{1}{2}$ inch (1 cm) headspace and dividing spices as evenly as possible. Remove air bubbles and adjust headspace as necessary by adding hot pickling liquid. Wipe rim and place hot lid disc on jar. Screw band down until fingertip-tight.

7. Place jars in canner and return to a boil. Process for 20 minutes. Turn off heat, remove canner lid and let jars stand in water for 5 minutes. Transfer jars to a towel-lined surface and let stand for 24 hours. Check lids and refrigerate any jars that are not sealed.

Serving Suggestion

Make an interesting *Spiced Peach Raita:* Drain and finely chop pickled peaches and mix with thick or drained plain yogurt and chopped fresh cilantro or mint.

Thai Sweet Chili Sauce

I love to eat cold salad rolls, and though the rolls themselves are incredibly tasty, I think it's really this sauce I'm most fond of. It's classically served with Thai food as a dipping sauce, but you can use it to add zest to many things.

Makes about six 8-ounce (250 mL) jars

• • •

Tips

Thai chile peppers are small, hot chile peppers that are about 1 to 2 inches (2.5 to 5 cm) long and about ¼ inch (0.5 cm) thick. They may also be called bird or bird's eye chile peppers.

To avoid burns, wear disposable rubber gloves when handling hot peppers and be sure to wash all utensils and the cutting board well after preparing them.

Serving Suggestions

Use as a dipping sauce for Thai appetizers.

Brush a little over grilled seafood, fish or poultry for the last couple of minutes of cooking.

Marinate thinly sliced carrots and cucumbers in sauce for a lovely salad.

¼ cup	minced red Thai chile peppers	50 mL
¼ cup	minced garlic	50 mL
4 cups	granulated sugar	1 L
2 tsp	pickling or canning salt	10 mL
2 cups	rice vinegar	500 mL
1 cup	white vinegar	250 mL
2 tbsp	grated lime zest	25 mL
1 cup	freshly squeezed lime juice	250 mL

1. Prepare canner, jars and lids (see pages 7 to 8).
2. In a pot, combine chile peppers, garlic, sugar, salt, rice vinegar and white vinegar. Bring to a boil over medium heat, stirring often until sugar and salt are dissolved. Increase heat to high and boil for 1 minute. Remove from heat. Stir in lime zest and juice.
3. Pour hot sauce into hot jars, leaving ½ inch (1 cm) headspace and dividing spices as evenly as possible. Remove air bubbles and adjust headspace as necessary by adding hot sauce. Wipe rim and place hot lid disc on jar. Screw band down until fingertip-tight.
4. Place jars in canner and return to a boil. Process for 15 minutes. Turn off heat, remove canner lid and let jars stand in water for 5 minutes. Transfer jars to a towel-lined surface and let stand for 24 hours. Check lids and refrigerate any jars that are not sealed.

Latin American Zesty Salsa

Because the tomatoes and onions aren't cooked in this salsa recipe, it has a flavor and texture similar to the fresh salsa served with almost every meal in Latin American cuisine.

Makes about eight 8-ounce (250 mL) or four pint (500 mL) jars

• • •

Tips

For instructions on peeling tomatoes, see page 17. To seed the tomatoes, cut each in half crosswise and use a spoon or the end of a knife to scoop out seeds and pulp. Removing the seeds and pulp gives a firmer texture to the salsa.

Use olives that have been cured and preserved in brine (not oil) to make sure they are high in acid. Drain and rinse well. To chop, place olives narrow end down on a cutting board and, using a sharp paring knife, cut the flesh away from the pit in about 4 slices. Place slices flat side down on board and cut into small pieces. You'll need about 15 large olives.

¼ cup	finely chopped seeded jalapeño peppers	50 mL
¼ cup	minced garlic	50 mL
2	bay leaves	2
2 tbsp	granulated sugar	25 mL
2 tsp	pickling or canning salt	10 mL
2 cups	white vinegar	500 mL
1 cup	water	250 mL
8 cups	chopped seeded peeled plum (Roma) tomatoes	2 L
2 cups	finely chopped onions	500 mL
½ cup	chopped drained rinsed brine-cured black and/or green olives (see tip, at left)	125 mL

1. Prepare canner, jars and lids (see pages 7 to 8).
2. In a large pot, combine jalapeños, garlic, bay leaves, sugar, salt, vinegar and water. Bring to a boil over medium-high heat, stirring often until sugar and salt are dissolved. Reduce heat to low, cover and simmer for 5 minutes or until liquid is flavorful. Discard bay leaves. Stir in tomatoes, onions and olives. Remove from heat.
3. Using a slotted spoon, pack vegetables into hot jars, leaving 1 inch (2.5 cm) headspace. Pour in hot pickling liquid, leaving ½ inch (1 cm) headspace. Remove air bubbles and adjust headspace as necessary by adding hot pickling liquid. Wipe rim and place hot lid disc on jar. Screw band down until fingertip-tight.
4. Place jars in canner and return to a boil. Process for 20 minutes. Turn off heat, remove canner lid and let jars stand in water for 5 minutes. Transfer jars to a towel-lined surface and let stand for 24 hours. Check lids and refrigerate any jars that are not sealed.

South American Red Onion Salsa

This recipe is based on salsa criolla, served with many South American meals, especially grilled meats. Though this version is cooked, rather than the usual fresh style, the flavors remain true.

Makes about six 8-ounce (250 mL) or three pint (500 mL) jars

• • •

Tip

You can vary the heat of this salsa by adding fewer or more jalapeño peppers. Two give it a touch of heat and 4 will make it on the hot side. If you can find aji chile peppers, a South American variety, use them instead of the jalapeños.

3 lbs	red onions	1.5 kg
2 tbsp	pickling or canning salt	25 mL
2 to 4	jalapeño peppers, seeded and minced	2 to 4
1 cup	granulated sugar	250 mL
1 tsp	freshly ground black pepper	5 mL
4 cups	white vinegar	1 L
2 tsp	grated lime zest	10 mL
½ cup	freshly squeezed lime juice	125 mL
½ cup	chopped fresh cilantro	125 mL

1. Cut onions in half lengthwise and trim out roots. Cut lengthwise into thin wedges. You should have about 8 cups (2 L).
2. In a large non-reactive bowl, combine onions and salt. Cover and let stand at room temperature for about 1 hour or until wilted.
3. Meanwhile, prepare canner, jars and lids (see pages 7 to 8).
4. In a colander, working in batches, drain onions and rinse well. Drain again.
5. In a large pot, combine onions, jalapeños, sugar, black pepper and vinegar. Bring to a boil over medium-high heat, stirring often. Reduce heat and boil gently, stirring often, for about 5 minutes or until onions are almost translucent. Stir in lime zest, lime juice and cilantro.
6. Ladle hot salsa into hot jars, leaving ½ inch (1 cm) headspace. Remove air bubbles and adjust headspace as necessary by adding hot salsa. Wipe rim and place hot lid disc on jar. Screw band down until fingertip-tight.
7. Place jars in canner and return to a boil. Process for 10 minutes. Turn off heat and remove canner lid. Let jars stand in water for 5 minutes. Transfer jars to a towel-lined surface and let stand for 24 hours. Check lids and refrigerate any jars that are not sealed.

Coconut and Cilantro Chutney

The fresh taste of cilantro is best suited to a refrigerator chutney rather than one that is processed for room temperature storage. This is so easy to make that it's no trouble to whip up another batch when you've eaten it all.

1 tsp	cumin seeds	5 mL
4	serrano or long hot green chile peppers, seeded and chopped	4
2 cups	packed fresh cilantro leaves	500 mL
½ cup	packed fresh mint leaves	125 mL
2 tbsp	granulated sugar	25 mL
1 tsp	pickling or canning salt	5 mL
½ cup	white vinegar	125 mL
1½ cups	lightly packed grated fresh coconut (see tips, at left)	375 mL

1. Place jars on a rack in a pot. Fill pot and jars with water. Bring to a simmer over medium heat. Simmer gently for at least 10 minutes to sterilize jars. Wash plastic storage lids (see page 11) or two-piece metal lids. Remove jars from water and let cool.

2. In a small dry skillet, over medium heat, toast cumin seeds, stirring constantly, for about 30 seconds or just until fragrant and slightly darker. Immediately transfer to a bowl and let cool.

3. In a food processor or blender, combine cumin seeds, chile peppers, cilantro, mint, sugar and salt. Process until finely chopped, scraping the sides of the bowl or jug as necessary to incorporate ingredients. With the motor running, gradually add vinegar through the feed tube and purée until fairly smooth. Add coconut and pulse just until blended.

4. Serve immediately or pack into sterilized jars, leaving ½ inch (1 cm) headspace. Remove air bubbles and adjust headspace as necessary by adding chutney. Wipe rim and place lid on jar. Screw down until fingertip-tight. Refrigerate for up to 2 months.

Date and Tamarind Chutney

The contrasting sweetness of dates and tang of tamarind marry into a succulent combination in this jammy chutney.

Makes about eight 8-ounce (250 mL) jars

● ● ●

Tips

Tamarind is a sour fruit that grows in a pod and is often sold in pressed blocks, similar to dates, but with seeds and skin that need to be removed. It is available in Asian grocery stores and well-stocked supermarkets.

To avoid burns, wear disposable rubber gloves when handling hot peppers and be sure to wash all utensils and the cutting board well after preparing them.

This chutney thickens quite a bit upon cooling, so stop the cooking when it's thinner than you want the final texture to be.

4 oz	piece tamarind block (see tip, at left), broken into small pieces	125 g
2 cups	boiling water	500 mL
1	long hot green chile pepper, seeded and minced	1
4 cups	finely chopped onions	1 L
4 cups	chopped dried dates	1 L
2 tbsp	minced garlic	25 mL
1 cup	packed brown sugar	250 mL
1 tbsp	mustard seeds	15 mL
1 tsp	pickling or canning salt	5 mL
½ cup	cider vinegar	125 mL

1. In a heatproof bowl, combine tamarind and boiling water. Let stand for about 30 minutes or until soft.
2. Meanwhile, prepare canner, jars and lids (see pages 7 to 8).
3. Press soaked tamarind pulp through a sieve into a large pot, discarding seeds and skin. Add chile pepper, onions, dates, garlic, brown sugar, mustard seeds, salt and vinegar. Bring to a boil over medium heat, stirring often. Reduce heat and boil gently, stirring occasionally, for about 30 minutes or until onions are translucent and mixture is thickened to a thin jammy consistency.
4. Ladle hot chutney into hot jars, leaving ½ inch (1 cm) headspace. Remove air bubbles and adjust headspace as necessary by adding hot chutney. Wipe rim and place hot lid disc on jar. Screw band down until fingertip-tight.
5. Place jars in canner and return to a boil. Process for 15 minutes. Turn off heat and remove canner lid. Let jars stand in water for 5 min. Transfer jars to a towel-lined surface and let stand for 24 hours. Check lids and refrigerate any jars that are not sealed.

Banana, Tamarind and Mint Chutney

Sweet, sour, fruity and a touch of spice — this lively chutney is so delectable you might find yourself eating it straight from the spoon.

Makes about six 8-ounce (250 mL) jars

● ● ●

Tips

Tamarind is a sour fruit that grows in a pod and is often sold in pressed blocks, similar to dates, but with seeds and skin that need to be removed. It is available in Asian grocery stores and well-stocked supermarkets.

Check your package of tamarind to see if there is salt added. If not, increase the salt to 1½ tsp (7 mL).

If fresh mint isn't available, add 2 tsp (10 mL) dried mint with the brown sugar.

Serving Suggestions

This makes a fantastic dip for Indian snacks such as pakoras or samosas.

Serve on grilled fish or with fish or seafood curries.

6 oz	piece tamarind block (see tip, at left), broken into small pieces	175 g
3 cups	boiling water	750 mL
1½ cups	finely chopped onions	375 mL
1 cup	raisins	250 mL
3 tbsp	finely chopped gingerroot	45 mL
1½ cups	packed brown sugar	375 mL
1½ tsp	garam masala	7 mL
1 tsp	salt	5 mL
1 tsp	ground cumin	5 mL
½ tsp	cayenne pepper	2 mL
8	ripe bananas (see tips, page 317)	8
¼ cup	cider vinegar	50 mL
2 tbsp	chopped fresh mint	25 mL

1. In a heatproof bowl, combine tamarind and boiling water. Let stand for about 30 minutes or until soft.
2. Meanwhile, prepare canner, jars and lids (see pages 7 to 8).
3. Press soaked tamarind pulp through a sieve into a large pot, discarding seeds and skin. Add onions, raisins, ginger, brown sugar, garam masala, salt, cumin and cayenne. Bring to a boil over medium heat, stirring often. Reduce heat and boil gently, stirring occasionally, for about 20 minutes or until onions are very soft and liquid is syrupy.
4. Meanwhile, mash bananas and measure 3 cups (750 mL); reserve any extra for another use.
5. Stir bananas and vinegar into pot. Increase heat to medium and boil gently, stirring often, for about 10 minutes or until thickened to a thin jammy consistency. Skim off any foam.
6. Ladle hot chutney into hot jars, leaving ½ inch (1 cm) headspace. Remove air bubbles and adjust headspace as necessary by adding hot chutney. Wipe rim and place hot lid disc on jar. Screw band down until fingertip-tight.
7. Place jars in canner and return to a boil. Process for 15 minutes. Turn off heat and remove canner lid. Let jars stand in water for 5 minutes. Transfer jars to a towel-lined surface and let stand for 24 hours. Check lids and refrigerate any jars that are not sealed.

Moroccan Apricot Lemon Chutney

Toasted spices add depth of flavor to sweet-sour apricots and tart lemon. Serve this chutney with a curry or a meat or vegetable tagine and dazzle your taste buds.

Makes about six 8-ounce (250 mL) jars

● ● ●

Tips

You may need more or fewer lemons, depending on their size. The volume measures of the rind and flesh are important for the balance of the recipe. It's best to buy a couple extra, just in case.

Use a grapefruit knife or spoon to scoop the lemon flesh from the rinds.

This chutney thickens quite a bit upon cooling, so stop the cooking when it's thinner than you want the final texture to be.

4	lemons	4
1 tsp	each ground coriander and cumin	5 mL
½ tsp	ground cinnamon	2 mL
6 cups	chopped apricots	1.5 L
1½ cups	chopped onions	375 mL
1 tbsp	minced gingerroot	15 mL
2¼ cups	granulated sugar	550 mL
1½ tsp	pickling salt	7 mL
½ tsp	cayenne pepper	2 mL
¼ tsp	freshly ground black pepper	1 mL
1 cup	white vinegar	250 mL

1. Prepare canner, jars and lids (see pages 7 to 8).
2. Scrub lemons gently under running water. Cut lemons in half crosswise and scoop out flesh. Cut rinds in half lengthwise, then cut crosswise into thin strips; measure ½ cup (125 mL). Remove any seeds and coarsely chop flesh; measure 1 cup (250 mL) and set aside.
3. In a large pot, combine lemon rinds and 2 cups (500 mL) water. Bring to a simmer over high heat. Reduce heat and simmer for about 10 minutes or until rinds are very soft. Drain off liquid and return rinds to pot.
4. Meanwhile, in a small dry skillet, over medium heat, toast coriander, cumin and cinnamon, stirring constantly, for about 1 minute or until spices are fragrant and slightly darker. Immediately transfer to a bowl.
5. Add spices, lemon flesh, apricots, onions, ginger, sugar, salt, cayenne, black pepper and vinegar to the pot. Bring to a boil over medium heat, stirring often. Reduce heat and boil gently, stirring occasionally, for about 20 minutes or until onions are translucent and mixture is thickened to a thin jammy consistency.
6. Ladle hot chutney into hot jars, leaving ½ inch (1 cm) headspace. Remove air bubbles and adjust headspace as necessary by adding hot chutney. Wipe rim and place hot lid disc on jar. Screw band down until fingertip-tight.
7. Place jars in canner and return to a boil. Process for 10 minutes. Turn off heat and remove canner lid. Let jars stand in water for 5 minutes. Transfer jars to a towel-lined surface and let stand for 24 hours. Check lids and refrigerate any jars that are not sealed.

Jamaican Banana Ginger Chutney

Robust, tropical flavors combine in this easy chutney that will liven up any Caribbean fare.

**Makes about
five 8-ounce
(250 mL) jars**

• • •

Tips

To avoid burns,
wear disposable
rubber gloves when
handling hot peppers
and be sure to wash
all utensils and the
cutting board well after
preparing the peppers.

You may need more
or fewer bananas,
depending on their
size. The volume
measure is important
for the balance of the
recipe. It's best to buy
a couple extra, just
in case.

It's easiest to mash
2 or 3 bananas and
measure 1 cup
(250 mL) at a time.
To prevent browning,
combine the mashed
bananas with
the vinegar after
measuring them.

**Serving
Suggestions**

Spread on a roti
and top with jerked
chicken or mashed
chickpeas.

Spoon on top of grilled
tilapia, other whitefish
or shrimp.

1	Scotch bonnet or habanero chile pepper, seeded and minced	1
1½ cups	chopped sweet onions	375 mL
½ cup	finely chopped gingerroot	125 mL
1⅓ cups	packed brown sugar	325 mL
1 tsp	pickling or canning salt	5 mL
½ tsp	ground allspice	2 mL
1 cup	water	250 mL
12	ripe bananas	12
1¾ cups	cider vinegar	425 mL

1. Prepare canner, jars and lids (see pages 7 to 8).
2. In a large pot, combine chile pepper, onions, ginger, brown sugar, salt, allspice and water. Bring to a boil over medium heat, stirring often until sugar is dissolved. Reduce heat and boil gently, stirring occasionally, for about 20 minutes or until onion and ginger are very soft.
3. Meanwhile, mash bananas and measure 5 cups (1.25 L); reserve any extra for another use.
4. Stir bananas and vinegar into pot. Increase heat to medium and boil gently, stirring often, for about 15 minutes or until thickened to a thin jammy consistency. Skim off any foam.
5. Ladle hot chutney into hot jars, leaving ½ inch (1 cm) headspace. Remove air bubbles and adjust headspace as necessary by adding hot chutney. Wipe rim and place hot lid disc on jar. Screw band down until fingertip-tight.
6. Place jars in canner and return to a boil. Process for 15 minutes. Turn off heat and remove canner lid. Let jars stand in water for 5 minutes. Transfer jars to a towel-lined surface and let stand for 24 hours. Check lids and refrigerate any jars that are not sealed.

Preserved Lemons

Chef Neil Baxter of Rundles Cooking Classes in Stratford, Ontario, first introduced me to the delightful flavor of preserved lemons. They complement Moroccan foods in a way that just can't be matched by any other ingredient.

Makes one quart (1 L) jar

● ● ●

Tip

It is easiest to use a wide-mouth jar. You can use a canning jar or the type with the glass lid and rubber sealer, as long as it has a tight seal when closed.

Serving Suggestions

Add thin slices of preserved lemon rind to Moroccan tagines.

Simmer a slice of preserved lemon when cooking rice. Discard before serving.

Use a twist of preserved lemon to add punch as a cocktail garnish.

Day 1

5	lemons	5
1/3 cup	pickling or canning salt	75 mL
3	whole cloves	3
1	stick cinnamon (about 3 inches/7.5 cm long)	1

After 1 Week

1 cup	freshly squeezed lemon juice (approx.)	250 mL

Day 1

1. Place jar on a rack in a pot. Fill pot and jars with water. Bring to a simmer over medium heat. Simmer gently for at least 10 minutes to sterilize jar. Wash plastic storage lid (see page 11) or two-piece metal lid.

2. Scrub lemons gently under running water. Trim off stem end. Working with one lemon at a time, place stem end down on cutting board and, using a serrated knife, cut lemon lengthwise into sixths, almost, but not all the way through. Repeat with the remaining lemons.

3. Empty water from jar. Holding a lemon over the jar, pack a scant 1 tbsp (15 mL) of the salt inside the cuts of the lemon and place in the jar, cut side up. Repeat with the remaining lemons, packing tightly to fit as necessary. Add cloves and cinnamon stick. Sprinkle the remaining salt over top. Wipe rim and place lid on jar. Shake jar gently.

4. Place jar in a cool, dark place and let stand for 1 week, gently rotating jar daily to swirl juices and salt around the lemons.

After 1 Week

1. Remove lemons from jar and place them back in the jar in reverse order (so the ones from the bottom are now on top). Add enough of the lemon juice to cover the lemons by about 1/2 inch (1 cm). Store in a cool, dark place for 3 weeks. The lemon rind should be translucent and most of the salt should be dissolved. After 3 weeks, transfer the jar to the refrigerator and store lemons for up to 1 year.

To Use

1. Cut the desired size piece of lemon, returning the remaining lemon to the jar. Scrape flesh and membranes, and some of the white pith if it is thicker than 1/8 inch (3 mm), from the lemon rind. Cut rind into thin slices or mince to use in recipes.

Preserved Oranges

The floral flavor of orange rind gets even more intense when it's preserved in salt. This ages-old practice can add new life to your cooking.

Makes one quart (1 L) jar

● ● ●

Tip

It is easiest to use a wide-mouth jar. You can use a canning jar or the type with the glass lid and rubber sealer, as long as it has a tight seal when closed.

Serving Suggestions

Simmer in a beef or pork stew.

Finely minced preserved orange rind adds depth to spicy curries.

Day 1

5	small oranges	5
⅓ cup	pickling or canning salt	75 mL
2	bay leaves	2
½ tsp	black peppercorns	2 mL

After 1 Week

1 cup	freshly squeezed orange juice (approx.)	250 mL

Day 1

1. Place jar on a rack in a pot. Fill pot and jars with water. Bring to a simmer over medium heat. Simmer gently for at least 10 minutes to sterilize jar. Wash plastic storage lid (see page 11) or two-piece metal lid.
2. Scrub oranges gently under running water. Trim off stem end. Working with one orange at a time, place stem end down on cutting board and, using a serrated knife, cut orange lengthwise into sixths, almost, but not all the way through. Repeat with the remaining oranges.
3. Empty water from jar. Holding an orange over the jar, pack a scant 1 tbsp (15 mL) of the salt inside the cuts of the orange and place in the jar, cut side up. Repeat with the remaining oranges, packing tightly to fit as necessary. Add bay leaves and peppercorns. Sprinkle the remaining salt over top. Wipe rim and place lid on jar. Shake jar gently.
4. Place jar in a cool, dark place and let stand for 1 week, gently rotating jar daily to swirl juices and salt around the oranges.

After 1 Week

1. Remove oranges from jar and place them back in the jar in reverse order (so the ones from the bottom are now on top). Add enough of the orange juice to cover the oranges by about ½ inch (1 cm). Store in a cool, dark place for 3 weeks. The orange rind should be translucent and most of the salt should be dissolved. After 3 weeks, transfer the jar to the refrigerator and store oranges for up to 1 year.

To Use

1. Cut the desired size piece of orange, returning the remaining orange to the jar. Scrape flesh and membranes from the orange rind. Cut rind into thin slices or mince to use in recipes.

Preserved Limes

The color of preserved limes is a little dark and dull, but the taste is anything but! The depth of flavor that comes from even the smallest piece will amaze you.

Makes one quart (1 L) jar

● ● ●

Tip

It is easiest to use a wide-mouth jar. You can use a canning jar or the type with the glass lid and rubber sealer, as long as it has a tight seal when closed.

Serving Suggestions

Use a small piece of preserved lime rind instead of wild lime leaves in recipes. Discard rind before serving.

Instead of salting the glass rim for a margarita, serve a sliver of preserved lime for garnish, rubbing it around the rim before adding it on top of the drink or perching it on the edge of the glass.

Day 1

10	limes	10
⅓ cup	pickling or canning salt	75 mL
3	whole green cardamom pods	3
1	bay leaf	1

After 1 Week

1 cup	freshly squeezed lime juice (approx.)	250 mL

Day 1

1. Place jar on a rack in a pot. Fill pot and jars with water. Bring to a simmer over medium heat. Simmer gently for at least 10 minutes to sterilize jar. Wash plastic storage lid (see page 11) or two-piece metal lid.

2. Scrub limes gently under running water. Trim off stem end. Working with one lime at a time, place stem end down on cutting board and, using a serrated knife, cut lime lengthwise into quarters, almost, but not all the way through. Repeat with the remaining limes.

3. Empty water from jar. Holding a lime over the jar, pack a heaping teaspoon (5 mL) of the salt inside the cuts of the lime and place in the jar, cut side up. Repeat with the remaining limes, packing tightly to fit as necessary. Add cardamom pods and bay leaves. Sprinkle the remaining salt over top. Wipe rim and place lid on jar. Shake jar gently.

4. Place jar in a cool, dark place and let stand for 1 week, gently rotating jar daily to swirl juices and salt around the limes.

After 1 Week

1. Remove limes from jar and place them back in the jar in reverse order (so the ones from the bottom are now on top). Add enough of the lime juice to cover the limes by about ½ inch (1 cm). Store in a cool, dark place for 3 weeks. The lime rind should be almost translucent and most of the salt should be dissolved. After 3 weeks, transfer the jar to the refrigerator and store limes for up to 1 year.

To Use

1. Cut the desired size piece of lime, returning the remaining lime to the jar. Scrape flesh and membranes from the lime rind. Cut rind into thin slices or mince to use in recipes.

Altitude

Heat processing times in this book are based on elevations from 0 to 1,000 feet (0 to 305 m). Processing times must be adjusted for altitudes above 1,000 ft (305 m), where water boils at a lower temperature. The processing time is longer at higher altitudes to make sure the food is exposed to adequate heat for long enough to destroy any microorganisms that may be present (see page 6 for more information).

To determine the altitude of your location, check with your local Cooperative Extension, planning commission or zoning office, municipal office or airport. You can also find elevation information on online mapping websites such as Google Earth.

Altitude Adjustment Chart for High-Acid Foods Processed in a Boiling-Water Canner

Feet	Meters	Increase in Processing Time
1,001–3,000	306–915	5 minutes
3,001–6,000	916–1,830	10 minutes
6,001–8,000	1,831–2,440	15 minutes
8,001–10,000	2,441–3,050	20 minutes

Purchase and Preparation Guide

Here are some guidelines to help you determine how much produce you'll need to purchase for your pickling recipes. These amounts are approximate, so it's always best to err on the side of caution and purchase a little more to make sure you've got enough for your recipe.

Fruits

Apples
1 large = 8 oz (250 g) = 1 cup (250 mL) chopped; about ¾ cup (175 mL) finely chopped; about ⅔ cup (150 mL) shredded

Apricots, fresh
3 medium = about 1 cup (250 mL) chopped

Apricots, dried
1 cup (250 mL) chopped = about 7 oz (210 g)

Bananas
1 medium = ⅓ to ½ cup (75 to 125 mL) mashed

Blueberries
1 cup (250 mL) = 5 oz (150 g)

Cherries, sour (tart)
1 lb (500 g) = 2½ cups (625 mL) whole = about 1⅔ cups (400 mL) pitted and chopped

Cherries, sweet
1 lb (500 g) = about 2¼ cups (550 mL) pitted and chopped

Clementines
10 medium = 1 lb (500 g)

Crabapples
1 lb (500 g) = about 18 (each 1½ inch/ 4 cm diameter)

Cranberries
1 bag (12 oz/340 g) = about 3 cups (750 mL)

Currants, black and red
1 cup (250 mL) stemmed = 6 oz (175 g)

Figs
3½ large = 1 cup (250 mL) chopped

Grapes
1 cup (250 mL) = 6 oz (175 g)

Lemons
1 medium = ⅓ cup (75 mL) juice; about 1 tbsp (15 mL) grated zest

Limes
1 medium = 3 tbsp (45 mL) juice; about 1 tsp (5 mL) grated zest

Mangos, sweet
1 medium = 1 cup (250 mL) chopped = 7 oz (210 g)

Mangos, green
1 medium = ¾ cup (175 mL) chopped = 5 oz (150 g)

Oranges
1 medium = about ½ cup (125 mL) juice; about 1 tbsp (15 mL) grated zest; about ⅔ cup (150 mL) chopped peeled flesh

Papaya
1 medium = about 2 cups (500 mL) chopped

Peaches
5 small or 4 medium = 1 lb (500 g); 1 medium = ⅓ to ½ cup (75 to 125 mL) peeled and chopped

Pears
1 medium = 7 oz (210 g) = about ¾ cup (175 mL) peeled and chopped

Pineapple
1 large = about 4 lbs (2 kg) = 5 cups (1.25 L) peeled, cored and chopped

Plums, prune (blue)
1 lb (500 g) = 8 medium = 2 cups (500 mL) chopped

Strawberries
1 quart (1 L) = about 9 oz (270 g) = about 2 cups (500 mL) hulled = about 1 cup (250 mL) crushed

Vegetables

Asparagus
20 spears = about 1 lb (500 g)

Beans, green or yellow (wax)
1 quart (1 L) = about 8 oz (250 g)

Beets
1 lb (500 g) = about 3 medium = about 1½ cups (375 mL) cooked, peeled and shredded

Cabbage, green
1 large = about 5 lbs (2.5 kg) = about 28 cups (7 L) cored and shredded

Cabbage, red
1 medium = about 2 lbs (1 kg) = about 11 cups (2.75 L) cored and shredded

Carrots
5 to 6 medium = 1 lb (500 g); 1 medium= about ½ cup (125 mL) shredded; about ⅔ cup (150 mL) chopped

Cucumbers, pickling
1 lb (500 g) = eleven to fourteen 3- to 4-inch (7.5 to 10 cm) cucumbers; about twenty-two 2½- to 3-inch (6 to 7.5 cm) cucumbers = about 3 cups (750 mL) ¼-inch (0.25 cm) crosswise slices; about 3 cups (750 mL) finely chopped

Corn
1 medium cob = about ½ cup (125 mL) kernels

Daikon radishes
1 medium = about 2 lbs (1 kg) = 6 cups (1.5 L) quartered slices

Eggplant
1 medium = 1¼ lbs (625 g) = 5 cups (1.25 L) peeled and chopped

Fennel bulb
1 small = 1 lb (500 g) trimmed of stalks; 15 oz (450 g) with core removed = 3¾ cups (925 mL) sliced and 3⅓ cups (825 mL) finely chopped

Gingerroot
One 1-inch (2.5 cm) piece = about 1 tbsp (15 mL) finely chopped

Horseradish root
1 lb = about 2 cups (500 mL) peeled and shredded

Onions, regular
1 medium = 4 oz (125 g) = 1 cup (250 mL) chopped; about 1¼ cups (300 mL) sliced

Onions, sweet
1 medium= 7½ oz (225 g) = 1½ cups (375 mL) chopped

Peppers, bell
1 medium = 8 oz (250 g) = 1⅓ cups (325 mL) chopped; 1⅔ cups (400 mL) strips

Peppers, jalapeño
1 medium = about 2 tbsp (25 mL) seeded and minced

Peppers, long hot red or green
1 medium = about 2 tbsp (25 mL) seeded and minced

Rhubarb
1 lb (500 g) = about 11 stalks (each ½ inch/ 1 cm thick) = 3¼ cups (800 mL) chopped

Tomatillos
2 to 3 medium= 5½ oz (160 g) = 1 cup (250 mL) chopped; 1 lb (500 g) = about 3 cups (750 mL chopped

Tomatoes, globe
1 medium = 8 oz (250 g) = about 1 cup (250 mL) peeled and chopped

Tomatoes, green
1 large = 7 oz (210 g) = about 1 cup (250 mL) chopped

Tomatoes, plum (Roma)
5 medium = 1 lb (500 g) = about 2 cups (500 mL) peeled and chopped

Zucchini
1 medium = 6 oz (175 g) = 1⅓ cups (325 mL) finely chopped or thinly sliced

Pickling Resources

There are some excellent online resources for more information about pickling and food safety for home canning. In general, it is best to rely on information from reputable companies, universities and government agencies. Other sites may not include instructions and recipes with optimal, current food safety standards.

National Center for Home Food Preservation
www.uga.edu/nchfp/index.html

The United States Department of Agriculture Complete Guide to Home Canning
foodsafety.cas.psu.edu/canningguide.html

Jarden Home Brands (Ball and Bernardin)
www.freshpreserving.com
www.homecanning.ca

Acknowledgments

Creating a cookbook isn't as simple as jotting some recipes on paper and binding the pages together. It takes the hard work of many talented and supportive people, and my sincere thanks goes to each one of them. Thank you to my publisher, Bob Dees, for thinking of me for this project and for your support; to Marian Jarkovich for your marketing expertise; and to Nina McCreath of Robert Rose, Inc. To my editor, Sue Sumeraj, you deserve extra thanks not only for your superb editing skills, but also for your excellent suggestions for improvement and your diligence, juggling abilities and much-appreciated moral support.

Special thanks to Kevin Cockburn for the beautiful design, as well as to Andrew Smith, Joseph Gisini and Daniella Zanchetta at PageWave Graphics. Thanks to photographer Colin Erricson, food stylist Kathryn Robertson and props stylist Charlene Erricson for taking my jars of pickles and turning them into works of art. Thanks also to proofreader Sheila Wawanash for your keen eye and Gillian Watts for carefully providing the index, an invaluable element in a cookbook.

Thank you to all of the friends and family members who tasted the seemingly endless amounts of pickled foods, gave constructive feedback and diligently returned jars for refills, especially the Barker, Edwards, Johnson, Lacarte, Long, Newton, MacDonald, Kleuskens, Moluchi, Lockhart, Paboudjian and Paton families. (If I've left anyone out, please forgive me; I believe the vinegar fumes may have affected my memory. Thank you, too.)

Thank you to Teresa Makarewicz, fellow professional home economist and my good friend, not only for your friendship, but also for your research skills and for helping me keep other projects afloat while I was knee-deep in pickles. Thank you to my colleague and friend Carol Sherman for your patience with me on other projects while I worked on this one.

To the staff at our store and café, In A Nuttshell and Nuttshell Next Door, Amanda, Barb, Martine, Miguel, Rachel and Victoria: my thanks to you for keeping things going smoothly at work so Jay had time to help me. To Annie and Lucía, thank you for making all those trips to the farmers' market so much fun, for picking up ingredients when I couldn't get to the market and for letting me use the stroller to wheel bushels of produce around when I got overzealous.

I truly appreciate and respect the hard work of the farmers who endure everything nature throws at them to grow wonderful produce for us to nourish ourselves, enjoy and preserve. In particular, thanks to the Etheringtons at Buckhorn Caza Berry Farm, Hayla Evans at Deer Bay Apple Farm, the Jacksons in Lakehurst, the MacLeans in Buckhorn and all of the farmers at the Peterborough Farmers' Market who endured my endless questions, such as "When will the tomatoes be ripe?" and "Do you have any more little cucumbers?" and fulfilled all of my special requests.

Everything I do is possible only because I have a wonderful family who is with me every step of the way (no matter what I get myself into). Jay, thank you isn't nearly enough — I'm sure hauling groceries and testing recipes was the last thing you wanted to do when you got home from work, but you did it anyway. You put up with our home being turned into the Bubba Gump pickle factory and managed to get meals on the table that consisted of more than condiments. And amid the craziness, you support me tirelessly. I love you for all of that and more.

To Alicia, John, Brent, Dale, Rick, Jack, Zoey and Melanie, thank you for reminding me of the importance of family and life beyond work. And special thanks to Melanie for impressively eating many, many versions of pickled beans to make sure I got them just perfect.

Mom, you are always there for me,

and that means so much. Thank you for introducing me to the joy of preserving when I couldn't even reach the counter, for not groaning when I asked you to dig up yet another old recipe and for testing recipes and offering your expertise to improve them. Dad, thank you for never tiring of eating my experiments or telling whoever will listen about my accomplishments. I dearly love having you as my #1 fan.

I dedicate this book to you, Mom and Dad — thank you for teaching me about passion and enduring love.

Library and Archives Canada Cataloguing in Publication

MacKenzie, Jennifer
    The complete book of pickling : 250 recipes from pickles & relishes to chutneys & salsas / Jennifer MacKenzie.

Includes index.
ISBN 978-0-7788-0216-7

1. Pickles. 2. Cookery (Relishes). 3. Chutney. 4. Salsas (Cookery).
I. Title.

TX805.M33 2009   641.4'62   C2008-907506-4

Index

Martini Olives, 85

melon

Classic Sweet Watermelon Rind Pickles, 134

Gingery Cantaloupe Pickles, 112

Savory Pickled Watermelon with Basil, 137

Spicy Watermelon Rind Pickles, 136

Mexican Green Tomato Relish, 270

Mexican Pickled Jalapeño Peppers, 303

Mild Pickled Okra, 82

Mild Tomato and Sweet Pepper Salsa, 153

Milkweed Pods, Pickled, 300

mint (fresh)

Apple Plum Chutney, 189

Banana, Tamarind and Mint Chutney, 315

Coconut and Cilantro Chutney, 313

Herb-Pickled Eggplant, 70

Peach, Jalapeño and Mint Salsa, 162

Pear Mint Chutney, 222

Peppery Strawberry Salsa, 163

Pineapple Mint Chutney, 227

Mirlitons, New Orleans Pickled, 301

Mixed Vegetable Mustard Pickles, 104

molasses

Classic Barbecue Sauce, 174

Coffee-Spiked Barbecue Chili Sauce, 176

Major Grey Mango Chutney, 212

Major Grey Pear Chutney, 220

Mom's Rhubarb Chutney, 230

Moroccan Apricot Lemon Chutney, 316

mushrooms, 16

Dill Pickled Mushrooms, 81

Fennel-Scented Pickled Exotic Mushrooms, 82

Herb and Garlic Pickled Mushrooms, 80

Mushroom and Lemon Tapenade, 280

mustard

Mixed Vegetable Mustard Pickles, 104

Mustard and Relish Combo, 257

Mustard Pickled Green Beans, 51

N

Nasturtium Capers, Pickled, 299

New Mexico Pepper and Tomato Salsa, 156

New Orleans Pickled Mirlitons, 301

9-Day Pickles, Diana's, 42

nuts, 17. *See also* coconut

Apple Walnut Chutney, 193

Pear and Sweet Onion Chutney, 223

O

okra

Dill Pickled Okra, 84

Pickled Okra and Hot Peppers, 83

Old-Fashioned Sweet Pickled Peaches, 121

olives

Latin American Zesty Salsa, 311

Martini Olives, 85

Olive and Herb Tomato Sauce, 170

Tomato and Olive Antipasto, 184

onions, 16, 323

Apple, Onion and Ale Relish, 244

Apple, Onion and Sage Chutney, 191

Apricot, Date and Raisin Chutney, 195

Blueberry, Tart Apple and Onion Chutney, 199

Bread-and-Butter Pickles with Onion and Red Pepper, 36

Caramelized Onion Relish, 276

Carrot and Onion Relish, 262

Clementine and Sweet Onion Relish, 264

Coffee-Spiked Barbecue Chili Sauce, 176

Date and Tamarind Chutney, 314

Dill Pickled Onion Rings, 92

The Family Chili Sauce, 143

Fire and Spice Pearl Onions, 88

Hawaiian Pickled Onions, 302

Juniper and Gin Pickled Onions, 90

Maple Apple Onion Relish, 243

Orange, Date and Onion Chutney, 215

Pear and Sweet Onion Chutney, 223

Pepped-Up Chili Sauce, Jen's, 144

Pickled Beet Slices, Classic (variation), 54

Red Onion and Raisin Chutney, 216

Savory Grape and Cranberry Relish, 266

South American Red Onion Salsa, 312

Spiced Pearl Onions, 86

Sweet Cherry and Onion Chutney, 201

Sweet Pickled Onion Rings, 91

Three-Onion Relish, 275

oranges, 322

Beet and Orange Chutney, 196

Chile Orange Tomato Salsa, 159

Clementine and Sweet Onion Relish, 264

Clementine Pear Chutney, 205

Cranberry Orange Relish, 265

Major Grey Mango Chutney, 212

Major Grey Pear Chutney, 220

Orange, Date and Onion Chutney, 215

Plum Orange Chutney, 229

Preserved Oranges, 319

Sangria Citrus Chutney, 204

oregano (fresh)

Black Bean Tomato Salsa, 157

Double Tomato and Herb Tapenade, 282

Herb-Pickled Eggplant, 70

Mexican Pickled Jalapeño Peppers, 303

Out-of-the-Freezer Chutney, 238

P

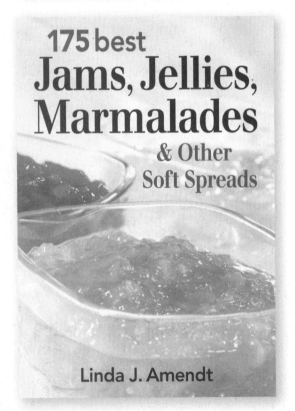